W9-AED-258

BL1810
.B87

RELIGION IN COMMUNIST CHINA

☆

RICHARD C. BUSH, JR.

KANSAS SCHOOL OF RELIGION
UNIVERSITY OF KANSAS
1300 OREAD AVENUE
LAWRENCE, KANSAS 66044

ABINGDON PRESS

NASHVILLE AND NEW YORK

Department of Religious Studies
Moore Reading Room
University of Kansas

RELIGION IN COMMUNIST CHINA

Copyright © 1970 by Abingdon Press

All rights in this book are reserved.
No part of the book may be reproduced in any
manner whatsoever without written permission of
the publishers except brief quotations embodied in
critical articles or reviews. For information address
Abingdon Press, Nashville, Tennessee.

ISBN 0-687-36015-3

Library of Congress Catalog Card Number: 70-109678

SET UP, PRINTED, AND BOUND BY THE
PARTHENON PRESS, AT NASHVILLE,
TENNESSEE, UNITED STATES OF AMERICA

To Mary, without whom . . .

CONTENTS

List of Abbreviations

BSMEP	*Bulletin de la Société des Missions Etrangères de Paris*
CHIBUL	*China Bulletin*
CMBA	Composite abbreviation for publication which began as *China Missionary*, was changed to *China Missionary Bulletin*, then to *Mission Bulletin*, and finally to *Asia*.
CNA	*China News Analysis*
CURBAC	*Current Background*
FLP	Foreign Languages Press
JMJP	*Jen-min Jih-Pao*
KMJP	*Kuang-ming Jih-pao*
NCCCUSA	National Council of the Churches of Christ in the U.S.A.
NCNA	*New China News Agency*
RCDA	*Religion in Communist Dominated Areas*
SCMM	*Survey of China Mainland Magazines*
SCMP	*Survey of China Mainland Press*
URS	*Union Research Service*

PREFACE

Twentieth-century China has provided poor soil for the growth in depth and strength of any religious movement. Seasons of economic chaos, political upheaval, and military holocaust have impeded the development of religious groups time and time again. Intellectuals, like their counterparts in most ages of Chinese history, either ignored or despised religion, or what they understood religion to be, and thus welcomed those currents from the West which were agnostic or positivist, which currents of thought were in turn passed on to several generations of students.

From the middle of the nineteenth century, Roman Catholic and Protestant Christians with great seriousness and increasing numbers sought to build the church and its related institutions, only to be brought to their knees in the most agonizing questioning of the whole enterprise, as missionary relationships were cut off and the church's life drastically undercut. The Buddhist Abbot T'ai Hsü pressed vigorously for reform of clergy and temple life in the 20's and 30's, but his efforts had just begun to make an impact in Buddhist circles when the numbers of monks and nuns were decimated and large numbers of temples were confiscated by the new government. Confucian and Taoist philosophers who were being read with great interest in the West were regarded as relics of a bygone era by most of their latter-day countrymen. Taoist and folk religious practices were more and more dismissed as superstitions for back country rustics when the Communists equated this religious potpourri with the feudalism they were out to destroy. These trends have culminated in the astounding fact of our time:

a nation state, with one fourth the earth's population, in which religion as an effective force seems to be all but nullified.

The story of developments leading to this end—a state with hardly a trace of religion as man has known it—can be seen most graphically in accounts of how particular religious groups or individuals have fared under communism. I know of no major effort to place these respective accounts in some kind of parallel perspective, to see them in relationship to each other. There is no lack of primary and secondary source material, at least for the decade 1949-59, but most of it that I have seen has not had wide circulation, whether in book or article form. In this volume I have tried to bring together what I regard as the most important developments in the story of religion during the first twenty years of the People's Republic of China, and to indicate their meaning with sufficient illustrations and examples. Many times I have wondered whether elements of the story which are so interesting to me will evoke any interest from readers. And still more often I have put aside other materials and (to me) fascinating details for the incidents I have related, hoping that I could later find a place for them. Such were my false hopes.

As one may see from a look at the table of contents, I have pursued my goal with an introduction on matters of Communist policy toward religion, several chapters on Catholic and Protestant Christianity, and a chapter each for Islam, Buddhism, the Confucian tradition, and Taoism-cum-folk religion. The amount of material available to me on Christianity in Communist China has been voluminous. There are people outside mainland China who have devoted major periods of their working time to gathering, translating, and interpreting what has happened to Christianity in China. Other than one scholar who has devoted considerable time to Buddhism and another who has given time to philosophical developments, I know of no one who has made or is making non-Christian religious movements in Communist China an object of significant study. Therefore the materials upon which I have depended for my treatment of Islam, Buddhism, Confucianism, and Taoism are much more limited than those which I have had available for the sections on Christianity. It is for this reason that there is a great imbalance in this work, more than half of which is devoted to Christianity; both branches of Christianity never totaled more than 1 percent of the population. Since this book is published in the West, it is of course likely that readers will have more interest in Christianity and will not object to its receiving a disproportionate amount of attention, but this is not necessarily as it should be and is not my reason for the imbalance. If there should be an opportunity for a revision, I hope to develop the last four chapters much, much further.

The question inevitably arises: "How can you write about Communist China, or any place for that matter, without having been there?" This book would have been much better if I could have spent some time there, talking at length with Bishop Ting or Ma Chien and checking records on Bishop Kung or the monk Pen Huan. I have read dozens of books and articles by people who have been there, however, and have been disappointed both by the limited circle in which they were allowed to move and by the meager information they were able to glean. There are exceptions, of course, and I have noted the observations of a few correspondents and scholars with gratitude. But I frankly confess, if people from Europe and Asia can find out so little, what point is there in an American imperialist trying his hand?

During the summer in which I finally brought this project to a conclusion, the American government announced its willingness to allow various categories of American citizens, including scholars, to travel to Communist China. When the People's Republic will allow such people to enter is another question. Should the day come when some of us who have a scholarly interest in things Chinese may be allowed to do research there, I would hope that this volume might serve as a springboard, a taking-off point for further investigation. There are many gaps in my information; there are many points at which I have assumed, on the basis of evidence available to me, that such-and-such prevailed. I naturally welcome the day when these gaps can be filled and these assumptions corrected or refined.

Most writers about Communist China are biased strongly in favor of it or against it. This is not necessarily bad, except that quite a few of them are not aware of any bias and see themselves as "just presenting the facts." After trying to decipher just what the facts are in such works, I find my gratitude increases immeasurably to the agencies and individuals devoted to collecting

11

and translating documents—agencies such as the Union Research Institute and the American Consulate in Hong Kong, and individuals such as Father Léon Trivière and Dr. Francis Jones. I am also grateful to those who gather and translate but also go on to interpret and analyze carefully and responsibly, as Dr. Jones has done and as Father J. Ladany does in *China News Analysis*.

These men, whether they work in agencies or as individuals, have their biases, too, which may come out in the selection of documents for translation and the way they are translated, as well as in the interpreting; they are human and bring to their work a point of view. I have brought to my work a very human and fallible point of view which is evident throughout this book. Given the fact that all of us have our biases, I have felt a greater measure of confidence in working with documents themselves and with the careful interpretation of men like C. K. Yang, Lefeuvre, Welch, Jones, Ladany, *et al.*, than I have in working with the accounts of visitors.

As indicated in the closing pages of this work, I hope in the near future to carry out further study on Chinese Communism as a religion. Since that topic is so closely related to the present volume, any definitive conclusions concerning religion in Communist China will be set forth in the concluding section of the proposed second volume. And, since some of my material in this first work will be utilized in the second, the general bibliography will be appended at the end of the later work. Anything of value which has been used in this first work is cited in the footnotes.

Father Jean Lefeuvre, whose *Shanghai: Les Enfants dans la Ville* is a sensitive portrayal in depth of the Catholic experience in that city, was kind enough to read the sections in my work on Catholicism. Professor Searle Bates, who has been working for years on the history of Christianity in China in the twentieth century, did the same for the sections on Protestantism. Both made many helpful suggestions, although, as the standard inscription goes, only the author is responsible for errors of fact or interpretation which remain.

Various Catholic libraries in Taiwan have allowed me to look through their materials, as has the Foreign Service Institute here in Taichung. The Missionary Research Library in New York has loaned by mail very valuable documents. My friend and colleague, the Rev. Donald E. MacInnis, has kept me posted on late developments with many a xeroxed copy of some item inaccessible to me. My greatest debt of gratitude in this respect, however, must go to the Memorial Library of the University of Wisconsin, various members of whose staff continually went beyond the call of duty in helping me find my way through that library's magnificent collection. Most of my research was done there and in Hong Kong; most of the writing has been done during summer recess periods here in Taiwan.

I am grateful to the publishers for their patience as I postponed the finished product again and again. Mrs. Beth Meyer Baird, Miss Winnie Chu, and Mrs. Martha Hodge Bush have typed portions of the manuscript. The lion's share of the typing has been done by my wife, who with our children has endured several periods of unanswered questions, vacant stares, and general neglect as I have tried to complete what seemed to be and is an endless job.

Richard C. Bush, Jr.
September 10, 1969

I

The Chinese Communist View of Religion

What is the official Chinese Communist policy toward religion and religious groups? What is the basic understanding of religion upon which this policy is based, and how is the policy implemented in general? These three closely related problems—policy, theory, and implementation—provide an appropriate introduction to a consideration of religion in Communist China and are essential if one is to understand what has happened to specific religious groups, as well as the religious nature of communism in China.

POLICY

Article 88 of the Constitution of the People's Republic of China states: "Citizens . . . of China enjoy freedom of religious belief." [1] Freedom of religious belief stands alone in one article; freedoms of speech, the press, assembly and association, procession and demonstration, are enumerated in the preceding article.

It is significant that belief is mentioned, and that practice, activity, propagation, and the like are not. One might assume that the freedoms of assembly and association, procession and demonstration, which are granted in Article 87, would apply to religion, but such an assumption does not necessarily follow. As will be seen in the following treatments of various religions, activity outside walls of churches and temples is prohibited. A joint

[1] *Constitution of the People's Republic of China*, English ed. (Peking: Foreign Languages Press [hereafter FLP], 1961), p. 39.

15

religious gathering to denounce American imperialism would be an exception.

One should note parenthetically that Article 86 of the People's Republic Constitution states that all citizens over eighteen years of age have the right to vote and stand for election, with the exception of the insane and those who have otherwise been deprived of these rights.[2] Irrespective of what the rights could have meant in the first place, Liu Shao-ch'i, the Chinese Communist Party's outstanding theoretician until he fell from favor in the Cultural Revolution of 1966, wrote in September, 1954, that "circumstances" made it necessary, "in accordance with law, to deprive feudal landlords and bureaucrat-capitalists for a given period of their right to vote and stand for election." [3] As the law may exclude landlords and capitalists, so it may exclude counterrevolutionaries; in which category religious believers have been grouped on many occasions, and thereby deprived of much more than real or nominal voting rights. What constituted counterrevolutionary activity is defined with such ambiguity that almost anything a person does, or does not do, may put him in that classification. The point here is that the constitutional provisions for freedom of religious belief or right to vote can be set aside by stating simply that a citizen has done something contrary to law.

Liu Shao-ch'i continues in this vein with a statement which is basic to the understanding of the Communist interpretation and application of the constitutional provision on freedom of religious belief. In the context of defenses against foreign criticism of the constitution he says:

Other foreign commentators find it strange that while we safeguard freedom of religious belief for our citizens, we punish those imperialist elements and traitors who don the cloak of religion, but in effect engage in counterrevolutionary activities. Of course, anyone who expects us to protect the freedom of imperialist elements and traitors who carry out subversive activities against the Chinese people's democratic power is likewise bound to be disappointed. As provided in the Draft Constitution, our state will, as it has done in the past, effectively safeguard freedom of

[2] *Ibid.*, p. 40.
[3] *Report on the Draft Constitution of the People's Republic of China* (Peking: FLP, 1954), p. 35.

religious belief for its citizens. But safeguarding freedom of religious belief is quite a different matter from safeguarding freedom of counter-revolutionary activities; these two just cannot be mixed up. Nor, similarly, will our constitution and laws ever provide the slightest facility for those elements who engage in counterrevolutionary activities under the cloak of religion. There is nothing difficult to understand in this reasoning.[4]

It is obvious that Liu Shao-ch'i is sensitive to criticism from outside China which has pointed to the incongruity of freedom of religion in a Communist dictatorship. It is also obvious, to Liu as well as his critics, that freedom has different meanings in different societies—a conclusion which hardly needs further discussion. But there is good reason to discuss at this point the reasons for including freedom of religious belief in the Constitution of the People's Republic, whatever freedom may mean to its framers, or however readily the law may be interpreted so as to exclude someone from that freedom.

Americans would say, for example, that comparable freedoms in the American constitution were placed there because its framers believed that these freedoms were "inalienable rights." It is assumed, in spite of occasional evidence to the contrary, that the American government, past and present, wants its citizens to have such freedoms, and expects freedom of the press to lead to the development of the press, freedom of religion to benefit religious groups, etc. There is a subtle contrast, however, in what Chang Chih-i has to say in an article on "A Correct Understanding and Implementation of the Party Policy Concerning Freedom of Religious Belief."

Our Party adopts a policy of freedom in religious belief because only this policy can agree with the laws of religion and their natural characteristics. Religion is a necessary product of a certain stage of development of human society.[5]

He then develops the classic Communist thesis that religion arose in primitive society because man feared the forces of nature, and

[4] *Ibid.*, p. 41.
[5] *Min-tsu T'uan-chieh* [Unity of Nationalities], April, 1962, pp. 2-5. Translated in *Union Research Service* [hereafter URS] XXVIII (August 31, 1962), 295.

was replaced by systematic religion when class divisions occurred and the exploiting classes used religion to oppress the lower classes.

As the root of the genesis and existence of religion is man's oppression by the forces of nature and society, therefore, only when class exploitation has been eliminated from human society and man's power to control nature has been greatly developed, and on this basis man's consciousness and scientific-cultural level have been greatly raised, may religion gradually die out. From this it can be seen that religion has its own laws governing its birth, development, and extinction which are not determined by the subjective will of any man. Therefore, it is radically impossible to use compulsory methods as the solution when dealing with people's religious beliefs; only by adopting a policy of freedom in religious belief can we agree with the law within religion.[6]

Freedom of religion accords with the inherent laws of religious development, which laws call for the *demise* of religion. Such a policy allows, for the moment, the utilization of certain "activist" religious leaders in a common cause aimed at "educating and remodeling" the majority of religious people. As Chang goes on to say, this process of education is intended to destroy the roots of religion, which are class oppression and fear of natural forces. Thus freedom of religious belief, along with education, of course, is expected to bring about not the growth and spread of religion but its opposite, which is the actual reason for the adoption of such a policy.

Further insight into what freedom of religious belief means in a Communist setting is provided by a former official of the Chinese Religious Affairs Bureau. He states that he and similar officials from various parts of China were told by the Central Committee of the Chinese Communist Party that the constitutional provision was to be understood in the following manner:

1. People who believe in a religion have freedom.
2. People who do not believe in a religion have freedom, including the freedom to be against religion.
3. People have freedom to change religious belief.[7]

[6] *Ibid.*
[7] "From the Other Side of the Desk," *China Notes* I (September, 1963), 3-4. The material in the *China Notes* article contains only about half of a

The second point was regarded by the Central Committee as meaning that no religious services might be held outside of specifically religious buildings, such as churches, temples, or monasteries, on the grounds that the freedom of nonbelievers would be impaired. Numerous writers to be considered in our discussion of theory often repeat these three points.

That such is still the understanding of freedom of religious belief, with unexpected and paralyzing implications, was attested by three Japanese pastors who visited China on a peace mission late in 1964. They were told by Chinese Christians that

before Liberation, Christians received undeserved privileges because of the backing of the imperialists. Now, all religions receive equal treatment. Now, religion and government have been totally separated. Moreover, our Communist government does not even think of utilizing religions for achievement of its purposes. There has been mutual agreement that atheists do not come into the churches to propagate their atheistic concepts, and religious people do not go out to public places to propagate their religion.[8]

The statement that the government would not think of utilizing religion for its own purposes is so patently hypocritical in view of the way Buddhist and Muslim groups are used to curry favor with Asian and Middle Eastern countries that no comment is necessary. The last sentence, however, points to the paralysis: the interior of churches and temples is religious and is the only place where religion may be taught. Public places are not religious and may therefore be used for atheist, not religious, teaching. This is indeed separation of church and state into distinct and mutually unassailable spheres—vast expanses for atheism; only the smallest, most restricted area for religion. The freedom to propagate

---

manuscript written by the former official of the Religious Affairs Bureau. The remainder, left in typescript, contains interesting material about various religious groups which shall be referred to later. The official is the man to whom George Patterson refers in *Christianity in Communist China* (Waco, Texas: Word Books, 1969), as Hsiao Feng. Several of Patterson's quotations from Hsiao are from the typescript and from the *China Notes* version, although without documentation.

[8] Article in a Japanese publication *Risoo-sha* [Ideal], (Tokyo, December, 1964). Translated by the Rev. Kyogi Buma for *Religion in Communist Dominated Areas* [hereafter *RCDA*], March 15, 1965, p. 35.

atheism is real; the freedom to propagate religion is limited, to say the least.

To return to the former official: he says the clause "freedom to be against religion" was usually not mentioned in the hearing of believers. He also says that the third point about freedom to change makes it possible not only for one to change his religious allegiance or disavow it, but also to be a member of several religious groups at the same time. It also means that "a man can introduce some different religious ideas in his church, and openly oppose present doctrines, rules, and practices." [9]

Numerous writers interpret the freedom to be against religion as the freedom to propagate atheism. Ya Han-chang, for example, says it is only natural that atheists be allowed to propagate atheism if theists are allowed to propagate theism.

If freedom is given only to the theists to propagate theism and not to the atheists to propagate atheism, it will amount to misinterpreting the policy of freedom of religious belief. Similarly, if freedom is given only to the atheists to propagate atheism and not the theists to propagate theism, it will likewise amount to misinterpreting the policy of freedom of religious belief. It can thus be seen that the conduct of atheist education among the masses of the people is not in the least contradictory to the Party policy of freedom of religious belief but actually implements this policy in an overall manner. [10]

This writer is quoted somewhat at length, in spite of his rather tortuous reasoning, because sufficient context must be given for a strange notion which emerges from this passage and others like it. Although the author or any good Communist would deny it, the whole tenor of such passages strongly suggests that atheist education is cut from the same cloth as religious education, that religion and atheism are two contending religions. A most interesting question is whether belief in no-God, like belief in God, is a religious belief. It would seem to be so for the Communists, despite vociferous protestations to the contrary.

[9] *China Notes* I (September, 1963), 3-4.
[10] "A Discussion on Translated Works on Atheism," *Jen-min Jih-pao* [People's Daily, hereafter *JMJP*], October 30, 1962. Translated in *Survey of China Mainland Press* [hereafter *SCMP*], November 19, 1962.

A sidelight on religion in the Constitution of the People's Republic appears in Article 3 dealing with "nationalities," those minority groups which are not Han Chinese, but who live within the designated borders of China. This article states that these minority groups "have the freedom to use and develop their own spoken and written languages, and to preserve or reform their own customs and ways." [11] According to Liu Shao-ch'i's report, the concluding phrase of this paragraph originally read "customs, ways, or religious beliefs." He states that since freedom of religious belief is provided in Article 88, several people suggested that inclusion of religious beliefs in the article dealing with nationalities was redundant, and therefore the phrase was dropped. It was included in the first place, according to Liu, because many of the minority peoples are Muslim or Buddhist (especially Lamaist), so religion was and is a considerable factor in dealing with them.[12] As we shall see later in the discussion of Islam, the Communist government has campaigned vigorously against, and at times has sought to suppress, Muslim "customs and ways" as well as religious practices, regardless of the number or location of constitutional provisions.

In addition to these observations about the meaning of freedom of religious belief in the Chinese Communist setting, there is a still more important consideration, namely, that it is freedom of religious *belief* which is allowed. If belief can be maintained as an internal affair, if one's belief does not affect conduct or relationships with other people or the state, then there is freedom. The whole range of religious experience and its expression in practice and association can be questioned. Belief is free; but when the belief is stated in a sermon, inspires activity, or leads to an association, an element of risk enters the picture immediately.[13] Such activity may be judged counterrevolutionary on grounds which are determined by the state and never made quite clear.

In an article written for minority nationalities on the subject of

[11] *Constitution of the People's Republic*, p. 9.
[12] *Report on the Draft Constitution*, pp. 50-51.
[13] I made this point in my article "What Has Happened to the Church in Communist China," *World Encounter* II (April, 1965), 12. Tu Mo says that it means freedom of thought, consciousness, and private life, but not of relationships with others. See his *Chung-kuo Ta-lu T'ien-chu-chiao Chen-hsiang* [The Real Situation of the Catholic Church in Mainland China], (Hong Kong: Chiu Shih Hsüeh She, 1966), pp. 7-8.

21

freedom of religious belief, Chang Chih-i acknowledges that "religious belief must necessarily express itself in a definite form of religious activity." But in the following statement he clearly says that such activity shall be proper, permitted, and arranged:

All proper religious activities of the believers, professional men of religion performing proper religious duties in churches or temples which accept people who are willing to become followers or monks, should be permitted. Religious believers permitted to perform proper religious activities must be allowed to have fixed places for such activities. In places where religious believers are numerous and grounds for religious activities are difficult to provide, a suitable solution should be sought in accordance with actual conditions. Contradiction, to a greater or lesser degree, occurs between the religious activities of the believers and production. Suitable solutions should be sought by means of patient education among the believers and full consultation with them to enable them to make reasonable arrangements for production and religious activities.[14]

Religious activity was allowed but circumscribed, at least until August, 1966, when the Cultural Revolution and its Red Guards struck. Had anyone dared to object to the suppression of religious freedom at that time, Communist officialdom could have replied that the constitutional provision guaranteed only freedom to believe, not the freedom to worship, preach, or to perform religious acts of any kind. When Red Guards closed and desecrated churches and temples in 1966, whether or not their action was sanctioned by the government, there was no departure from the constitutional freedom of religious belief.

THEORETICAL FOUNDATIONS FOR THE POLICY

It is now commonplace to note that Karl Marx, having borrowed a choice phrase from Charles Kingsley, called religion an "opiate of the people." It is just as well known, in China at any rate, that

[14] *Min-tsu T'uan-chieh*, April, 1962, pp. 2-5; *URS*, August 31, 1962, p. 299. See also his "Atheists and Theists Can Cooperate Politically and Travel the Road of Socialism," *Che-hsüeh Yen-chiu* [Philosophical Studies], February 15, 1958; *Current Background* [hereafter *CURBAC*] 510, 11-20. Chang Chih-i was deputy head of the United Front Department of the Party Central Committee.

Friedrich Engels defined religion as "the fantastic reflection in men's minds of those external forces which control their daily life." The general view of religion that prevails among the theoreticians of the Chinese Communist Party and that provides the basis for its policy toward religious groups is an unimaginative, tedious footnote to such statements.

Primitive man, so this theory goes, was afraid of the forces of nature. Since he knew nothing of how to control such powers and since he believed them to be in the hands of gods and spirits, he either accepted what happened as the will of the gods or he prayed to the gods in the hope of escape or of some benefit to be received. Chi Yü-chang, a contemporary writer in China, has illustrated this part of the theory with a survey of such practices in early Chinese history. He says that "imploring gods and consulting oracles" and the "exorcism of evil spirits to cure diseases," as described in the *Spring and Autumn Annals,*

were all designed to tell that the life or death of a man or the consequences of a certain thing were all determined by gods and spirits, and that nobody could change them. Accordingly, they tied many people down, delayed the proper execution of many things, put off until it was too late many cases of illness that could have been cured . . . and killed a great many people.[15]

Fortune-telling and physiognomy continued this trend, spreading the fatalistic idea that future events were predetermined by heaven, or various gods or spirits. Geomancy, the determining of sites for buildings or graves, was related to the ancestors by the belief that the position of ancestral graves affected one's present life. Chi regards such activities as superstitious, but he maintains that they are just as powerful among the common people as are religious activities.

As people began to live together in settled communities, so the theory continues, classes developed and with them the class struggle. The upper classes found religion a convenient tool with which to control the workers; thus feudal lords kept their serfs in sub-

[15] "Oppose Superstition," *Chung-kuo Ch'ing-nien Pao* [China Youth], August 20, 1963; *SCMP,* September 18, 1963, p. 11.

mission, and in modern times capitalists were able to exploit the working classes. By focusing attention on a spirit world the exploited are distracted from the problems of their miserable existence, and their desire to revolt against exploiters and oppressors is numbered. The oppressed bear their pain and adversity in the hope of a future paradise rather than revolting against their masters.

This leads to the role of the religious professional in Marxist theory. In primitive societies everyone had to work, so religious ceremonies were carried out by elders of the clan or tribe. But as society develops and there are surplus products for nonproducers, a class of professional religionists appears which is supported by the exploiting classes in order to keep the masses occupied with ritual and gods. Lenin is quoted by Chinese writers as saying that "all oppressing classes need to have two social functions, the function of the executioner and that of the priest." [16] Religious leaders are parasites, for they receive from the exploiters some of the fruits of the masses' labor, in some instances share in the instruments of production and political privilege, and thus actually join in the exploitation of those they ostensibly serve. This last idea, that religious leaders carry out political and economic oppression "under the cloak of religion," recurs again and again in Chinese Communist literature. It is held that imperialists used Protestantism and Catholicism to carry out aggression against China from without, and that feudal interests utilized Buddhism, Taoism, and Islam to exploit and oppress from within.

The present stage in this process is the coming of communism, when the workers rise up in a class struggle to throw off the oppression of the exploiting classes. During the period of transition from capitalism or feudalism to communism, the battle continues, for religious leaders of all types are constantly maneuvering in order to regain their power. They are, in fact, still a force because of their widespread influence among the masses, which influence cannot be wiped out in a short time.

[16] Liu Chün-wang and Yu Hsiang, "Religion and Class Struggle in the Transition Period," *Kuang-ming Jih-pao* [literally Glorious Daily, a newspaper emphasizing cultural affairs, hereafter *KMJP*], March 21, 1964; *SCMP*, April 20, 1964, p. 1.

Imperialist elements and other reactionary elements hiding under the cover of religion often collect intelligence for imperialism, fabricate rumors, and even organize insurrections and carry out other current counterrevolutionary activities. They spread reactionary views which are hostile to new China, oppose the Communist Party, and slander the socialist system. They exploit religion to obtain money under false pretenses, rape women, cause loss and injury of life, and upset the social order and the production order.[17]

Although this statement by a prominent writing team is cited here as an indication of the Communist view of religion, it is noteworthy for another reason. Since it purportedly describes current religious activity, it may be regarded in all of its extravagance as an admission that religion was still something of a force in Communist China in 1964.

Against the background of this monolithic, orthodox view of religion, a most interesting disagreement erupted during the years 1963 to 1965.[18] A certain Ya Han-chang stated in a number of articles that he believes religion, superstition, and theism are not the same. He maintains that theism is only an idea, a belief in souls, spirits, god, or gods. "The essence of the theist idea is the belief that all things in this world are created, arranged, and determined by supernatural spirits and gods (including God, the Creator, Providence)."[19] Religion, on the other hand, includes such beliefs but also has organizations, groups, activities, leaders, initiation rites, collection of money, and punishments for those who have violated a rule. It is this area of organization and activity that accounts

[17] Liu and Yu, "The Correct Recognition and Handling of the Problem of Religion," *Hung Ch'i* [Red Flag], February 26, 1964; translated in *Survey of China Mainland Magazines* [hereafter *SCMM*], March 31, 1964, p. 43.

[18] I discussed some of the questions raised by various writers on this subject in unsigned articles in *China Notes* II (December, 1963), 5-8, and II (October, 1964), 3-5. A later writer in *China Notes* surveyed this material again, III (October, 1965), 1-7, with bibliography. *China News Analysis* [hereafter *CNA*], December 17, 1965, was devoted to this subject. The author, presumably Father J. Ladany, saw in the Liu-Yu position an indication of a shift in Party policy toward intensified struggle with religious believers. This material was surveyed again by Winfried Glüer in "Religion in the People's Republic of China," *Ching Feng* X (Autumn, 1967), 34-57.

[19] "On the Difference between the Theist Idea, Religion, and Feudal Superstition," *Hsin Chien-she* [New Construction], February 20, 1964; *SCMM*, April 20, 1964, p. 4.

primarily for religious differences. He concludes: "Since the theist idea and religion are not the same thing, it follows that theists and religious believers are not the same thing. Generally speaking, all religious believers are theists, but not all theists are religious believers." [20] Evidently Mr. Ya thinks of a theist as one who, like certain deists of the Aufklärung, believes in a god or supreme being on intellectual grounds, but has nothing to do with the church or any religious society and does not engage in any religious practices. By way of contrast he mentions a priest who was nevertheless a "great atheist."

Ya goes on to distinguish between religion and superstition. Here the point seems to be that religion has some form of organization whereas superstition does not. He lists as superstitions such practices as fortune-telling, physiognomy, casting of horoscopes, geomancy, and even the worship of local Chinese deities like the earth god and the dragon king. Ya concludes: Although feudal superstition could not exist without the notion of souls, spirits, and gods, theism and superstition are not the same. And although theism, religion, and superstition are all idealist and unscientific, they are three different phenomena and must be dealt with as such.[21]

Liu Chün-wang and Yu Hsiang take sharp exception to Ya's distinctions, because, no doubt, Ya's distinctions began as criticisms of the Liu-Yu thesis that theism, religion, and superstition are essentially the same. They maintain that organization is not a necessary factor in religion, indeed that organization and practice are only external trappings. The theist idea includes organization and practice because there can be no such thing as pure idea. In fact, when he says that religion derives from theism, Ya ignores the true source of religion in material forces. Ideas arise from matter, not material or social forces from ideas. Liu and Yu claim that Ya's emphasis makes religion an opiate only in a class society where it has taken on organization and activity.[22] They are appalled by the fact that Ya, as they understand him, has dared to differ with Engels' dictum that "religion is nothing but the fantastic reflections in man's mind." To follow Ya would be to

[20] Ibid.
[21] Ibid., pp. 5-7.
[22] "The Problem of Understanding Religion," KMJP, March 7, 1965; SCMP, March 29, 1965, p. 12.

substitute theism for religion in that classical utterance, and thus to say that Engels was wrong. Then they proceed to quote a number of classical Marxist texts to show that religion is only an idea and does not need an organization.[23] The final problem for Liu and Yu is that the struggle against religion is also a struggle against theism and superstition, and if they are distinguished as Ya distinguishes them, theism and superstition would continue unchecked.

Although Liu and Yu would admit a slight difference between superstition and religion, since the former is to be found in primitive societies and the latter in systematized form in a class society, they conclude:

We believe that in a broad sense and as a matter of scientific definition, religion (or a religious idea), the theist idea, and superstition (or religious superstition), all denote man's belief in supernatural, mystic forces. That is to say, they all exist in man's mind as ideas. These ideas are fantastic reflections of the objective world in man's mind. Their characteristic consists in reflecting the objective world in the form of supernatural mystic forces, . . . [or] in regarding certain supernatural mystic forces as determinants of natural and social phenomena. Therefore, they are one and the same thing.[24]

In defense Ya says that the confusion of theism, religion, and superstition is the result of the Western bourgeois science of religion, thus hinting broadly that Liu and Yu are not the thoroughgoing Marxists they pretend to be. Although Ya's knowledge of the science of religion stops with the beginning of the twentieth century (the lack of sources for the last fifty years, or failure to use them, is quite evident in numerous writers on this subject in mainland China), he gives an excellent discussion of the reaction by the outstanding intellectual Liang Ch'i-ch'ao to religious questions, and shows that there is a distinction in the Chinese setting between the theist idea and religion. He maintains further that confusion of the three means freedom for superstition which, in the name of freedom of religious belief, rides in on the coattails of religion.[25]

[23] *Ibid.*, pp. 3, 8, 9.
[24] *Ibid.*, p. 5.
[25] "Drawing a Dividing Line with the Bourgeois Science of Religion," *KM-JP*, June 31, 1965; *SCMP*, July 21, 1965, p. 6.

There are several voices raised along the sidelines in this debate. Chou Chien-jen says that religion is more deeply rooted than superstition and has material support.[26] Tseng Wen-ching says that religion and philosophical idealism are essentially the same; both must be exposed and attacked.[27] The trend in Chinese Communist thinking appears to be toward regarding religion, theism, and superstition as essentially the same thing and equally reprehensible. Ya's effort to seek clarification is commendable, however superficial his arguments may be; but the underlying purpose is still to bring pressure to bear on all three. Those who fall under his category of religion may rejoice that they are to be distinguished from the superstitious ones, but they are not thereby relieved of Party or government pressures. The distinction of theists from religionists can have little value since atheists must struggle with both as well as with superstitious peasants. Even the man who treats his religion as a matter of belief alone is not really free from those who would struggle against him. All of which leads to the method to be employed in dealing with religious believers, those who participate in superstitious practices, and theists, whether conceived as belonging to the same breed or to different orders.

Thus, the Communists view religion as a great hoax which had its origins in a time when men knew no better, and which was seized by the exploiting classes as an instrument of oppression. Religion is a profound hindrance to the progress of any nation; it has been such in the history of the Chinese people, and its adherents must be reformed if they are to contribute to socialist construction. As has been suggested in the foregoing discussion, the exposition of this theory by Chinese Communist writers leaves much to be desired. Not only are they limited in the use of source materials; the treatment of source materials which are available is childish and

[26] "On the Question of Breaking Down Religion and Superstition," *KMJP*, April 2, 1964. Translated in *China Series* 2066 of British Information Service.

[27] "Religion and Idealist Philosophy," *JMJP*, March 23, 1964; *SCMP*, May 12, 1964, pp. 1-7. This may be the same author as one listed simply as Wen Ch'ing who wrote in the mid-50's "A Brief Treatise on the Question of Religion," *Chung-kuo Ch'ing-nien Pao* 3 (1955), and, in the same publication, "Several Problems Concerning Religion" 14 (1955). The last-mentioned article was translated in *Mission Bulletin* [hereafter *CMBA*] VIII (November, 1956), 671-74.

repetitive. A college sophomore in any university East or West could demolish almost any point in the literature under discussion in ten minutes.

The most difficult aspect of dealing with such literature is that of trying to discover what people like Liu and Yu are really trying to say. Once that is discovered, an answer is no problem. Perhaps the most obvious sign that freedom of discussion does not exist in China is the lack of any replies to these writers by the very competent Christian and Buddhist thinkers who still live in that country. It is obvious that it would be dangerous to enter the lists, and, given the danger, there is no point in replying to such inconsequential statements about religion. The Communist statements about religion, in the last analysis, are not made to elucidate the subject, but rather to call attention to its eventual decline and disappearance, and to the methods which may be expected to hasten its decline and fall.

IMPLEMENTATION OF POLICY

Specific programs by which Chinese Communist religious policy has been implemented may best be considered in terms of specific religious groups. There is, however, a basic pattern for dealing with religion as a whole which should be described before the patterns for dealing with individual groups.

The Chinese Communists learned from the Russian experience that efforts to completely stamp out religious groups provoke only ill will abroad and undue resistance, even martyrs, at home. Although the government of People's China has never seemed concerned about the goodwill or ill will of Western nations, they have been most concerned to win and keep the goodwill of Afro-Asian nations, many of which are predominately Buddhist or Muslim. Also leaders of China know well their country's history which has some rather startling examples of revolutions that were organized or stimulated by religious or semireligious groups. These factors, accompanied by the belief that religion will eventually wither away, pointed in the early years of the Communist regime to measures for the control of religious groups, but not to an attempt to wipe out religion overnight or in a decade.

29

Despite popular articles and books on Communist oppression of religion, there is evidence to indicate that the Chinese Communists moved cautiously and carefully. Officials charged with handling religious affairs appeared to know little about religion, or what to do about it; hence, conditions in various parts of the country varied in severity. There are indications that officials became increasingly aware of the complexities involved in dealing with religious leaders and their groups, resulting in an increasing sophistication in methods for handling them.

The early Communist theoreticians, notably Lenin, are quoted often by contemporary writers on religion in China to the effect that religion, if effectively circumscribed in its own sphere while the class struggle moves relentlessly against it, will eventually fade away. It is a "protective" approach, as Mao Tse-tung himself is quoted as saying to a delegation from Tibet in 1952:

The Communist Party adopts a policy of protecting religion: it protects all believers and nonbelievers in religion no matter what that religion is, and respects their religious faith. Today it adopts the policy of protecting religion and in the future it will go on adopting the same policy.[28]

Mao's earlier and more graphic terms are quoted frequently by contemporary writers and have become the chief guideline for implementation of religious policy:

The idols were set up by the peasants, and in time they will pull down the idols with their own hands; there is no need for anybody else to throw away prematurely the idols for them. The agitational line of the Communist Party in such matters should be: "Draw the bow full without letting go the arrow, and be on the alert."[29]

A footnote to the effect that the bow-and-arrow quote is from Mencius goes on to say that "while Communists should develop the

[28] "Talk by Chairman Mao in His Interview with the Homage Delegation from Tibet on October 8, 1952," *JMJP*, March 23, 1964; quoted by Chang Chih-i in the article cited in note 14. Rensselaer W. Lee, III, "General Aspects of Chinese Communist Religious Policy, with Soviet Comparisons," *The China Quarterly* 19 (July-September, 1964), 161-73, finds in this policy of allowing religion to wither the primary distinction between Chinese and Russian policies, the latter emphasizing atheist propaganda.
[29] Mao Tse-tung, *Report of an Investigation into the Peasant Movement in Hunan* [made in 1927] (Peking: FLP, 1953), p. 45.

political consciousness of the peasants to the fullest extent," the actual destruction of superstitious practices should be left to the peasants themselves. The metaphor suggests a controlling power which is alert and ready to act, but only remains in readiness so long as no one steps out of line. Such was hardly the case at various times in the 1950's, nor in August, 1966. It would be difficult to argue that at any of these times religious groups provoked intensive pressures. It seems much more likely that the Red Guards of 1966 may be seen as the peasants who finally rise up and "pull down the idols with their own hands." No Maoist would quibble because Mao originally spoke of peasants tearing down idols they themselves had set up. Any idols will do when the peasants finally act.

On the official level during the early days of the Communist regime, thoroughgoing restraint and control of religious groups was the order of the day. Procedures and machinery for dealing with religious groups were developed with this in view. The former official of the Religious Affairs Bureau, who has previously been quoted, lists the Bureau regulations for his work as follows:

1. To regularly investigate and study religious organizations and the activities of their personnel.
2. To control all types of religious activity.
3. To lead both Catholics and Protestants into the Three-Self Movement, and to organize Buddhists, Taoists, and Muslims for regular patriotic learning sessions.
4. To carry out thoroughly the religious policy of the central government.
5. To unceasingly teach and propagandize religious leaders and all believers concerning policies of the state with respect to current situations in order to raise their political awareness.
6. To bring church leaders closer to the government and push believers of all religions into a positive alliance for the construction of socialism.
7. To strike at politically obstinate reactionaries in churches, and cooperate with public security officers in order to tranquilize hidden counterrevolutionaries in all religions.
8. To entertain foreign religious guests.[30]

[30] "From the Other Side of the Desk," *China Notes* I (September, 1963), 4. In a later statement by the same man who once served as an official in the

Two points in the list require comment. There were numerous and lengthy sessions for religious leaders, both clerical and lay, to carry out number five. These sessions dealt not only with religious questions, but with government programs of every conceivable nature—the war in Korea, a campaign against corruption, or an advance in production emphasis. Religious Affairs officials were also responsible for guiding foreign guests who had some interest in religious matters. The local official involved had to plan, with due instructions from headquarters, an itinerary to certain approved temples or churches and interviews with Chinese religious leaders who could be trusted to give the official view, thus communicating a most favorable image of the religious situation in China.

Drawing the bow to the full without letting the arrow go does not begin to suggest the tremendous program of ideological education, propaganda devices, and subtle pressures used on religious leaders. There were lectures and study groups for everyone, regular visitation of those who were slightly suspect, reform by labor for those who resisted, prison and perhaps death for those who never gave in or who openly criticized. Party officials preferred the first two categories involving discussion, criticism, and persuasion, as they put it, except when dealing with those who were "stubborn" or "obstinate." Imprisonment or death was always made to appear to be the result of the people's will expressed through a popular court acting in righteous indignation against those accused of committing crimes against the state.

Mao's essay *On the Correct Handling of Contradictions Among the People* was written originally in early 1957 to accelerate the Hundred Flowers Campaign, when intellectuals, writers, students, and even the common people were to set forth their views (and later to undergo reform by labor for their criticisms). He says quite categorically:

We cannot abolish religion by administrative orders; nor can we force people not to believe in it. We cannot compel people to give up idealism, any more than we can force them to believe in Marxism. In settling mat-

Religious Affairs Bureau, the importance to the Communists of religious leaders is stressed. Large sums of money were used to conduct study classes for pastors and priests because it was believed that lay people would follow their respective religious leaders. *China Notes* IV (January, 1966), 2.

ters of an ideological nature or controversial issues among the people, we can only use democratic methods, methods of discussion, of criticism, of persuasion and education, not coercive, high-handed methods.[31]

In commenting on the above statement, Ya Han-chang, whose views on religion have already been discussed, makes the following astute observation:

The adoption of the method of administrative orders can at best dissolve religious bodies and prohibit religious activities in the open. But it cannot effectively compel people to give up their concept of theism. What is worse, the use of administrative orders to compel people to discard theism will inevitably drive religion underground, make lawful things unlawful, and turn open activities into clandestine activities. It will only strengthen the faith of the theists and religious disciples, who will then become more unwilling than ever to give up their beliefs and more fanatical than ever to worship their gods and adhere to their religion.[32]

Here again is the notion that by correctly implementing the policy of freedom of religious belief, with emphasis on *correctly*, religion will disappear. As Chang Chieh, Party-sponsored vice-chairman of the Chinese Islamic Association, stated in 1962, "As long as there are still people who believe in religion, [the Party] will resolutely stick to the policy on freedom of religious belief." [33] That policy is expected to bring about the end of religion, as Mr. Chang's oblique statement makes quite clear. If believers do not follow along as expected, as during the Hundred Flowers Period, more extreme and extensive measures may be taken, not as religious measures but as measures of public security.

Those who know anything at all of the way in which the Com-

[31] (Peking: FLP, 1957), p. 16. There are two excellent treatments of the Hundred Flowers Period, Roderick MacFarquhar, *The Hundred Flowers Campaign and the Chinese Intellectuals* (New York: Frederick A. Praeger, 1960), to which I refer later in this volume, and Mu Fu-sheng, *The Wilting of the Hundred Flowers, Free Thought in China Today* (London: William Heinemann, 1962), which will be a major source of my projected study of Chinese communism as a religion.

[32] "A Discussion on Translated Works on Atheism," *JMJP*, October 30, 1962; *SCMP*, November 19, 1962, p. 7.

[33] "The Party's Policy on Freedom of Religion Further Implemented Among Muslims," *Min-tsu T'uan-chieh*, April, 1962; *SCMM*, July 16, 1962, p. 32.

munist government actually dealt with religious groups in China find the irenic statements of Mao and his associates unbelievable. As we shall see in succeeding chapters, implementation of the religious policy meant an intensive involvement of the individual person in a dialectic encounter with his neighbors, aimed at getting each person to confess his "bad thoughts," or to accuse his neighbor of such thoughts. There was no doubt that everyone had bad thoughts. To engage in confession or accusation too politely was to be classed as bourgeois. Every man was in three cell groups— residence, work, and association—in one of which he was sure to be seriously involved.

A most delightful example of the way in which the official policy of religious freedom was adapted by local leaders is Sister Mary Victoria's story of a village official who likened the people of China to the traditional Chinese daughter-in-law who had to obey or be thrown out. The mother-in-law grants freedom to plant and sell opium, to buy and sell playing cards, but anyone caught smoking opium or playing card games must be punished. So with religion: the church is allowed to remain open and the foreign devil to preach, but the government is free to prevent people from going to the church.[34]

In all probability Chairman Mao did not like having his government referred to as a mother-in-law any more than those who practice religion appreciate comparison to gamblers and smokers of opium. Party logic was applied in a wide variety of ways as the government's religious policy was implemented in different parts of the country. One official followed the letter of the law or exceeded it; his successor looked the other way for no obvious reason whatsoever. These variations provide a convenient loophole for defenders of the Communist regime in China who admit that on rare occasions a party cadre in a particular place may have been too severe or enthusiastic in carrying out his assigned task, but shrug it off as do those cheering for a football team noted for the number of fouls it commits. "The boys just get carried away—they want so much to win."

Although people were ostensibly free to choose between religion

[34] Mary Victoria, *Nun in Red China* (New York: McGraw-Hill, 1953), pp. 34-35.

or no-religion, theism or atheism, that choice could not be construed as a decision to be made without guidance. If people were to decide, they had to be confronted with the claims of atheism, since it was assumed that they had already been confronted with the claims of religion. At regular intervals through the years, programs of intensive ideological education have been instituted at all levels, including atheist education to counteract religion. This is the "other side" of the constitutional provision for freedom of religious belief, namely, freedom to teach atheism as well as religion. Turning to Ya Han-chang again, atheist education has two meanings: Broadly conceived it involves any type of scientific education which may be expected to undercut unscientific religious teachings; narrowly conceived it means the use of historical materialism to analyze and criticize religious concepts.[35] Among his practical suggestions for atheist education Ya advises attractive presentations so as to win a voluntary response from people.[36]

Liu Chün-wang and Yu Hsiang assert that the task of a Marxist-Leninist political party with respect to religious groups should be to eliminate religious roots and influences gradually among the masses by the spread of knowledge and education, as well as by the removal of the masses' fear of natural forces.[37] Definite action is necessary; it is impossible for Communists to exist with religion or be neutral to it.[38] Liu and Yu recognize, however, that there are "patriotic religionists" who have a "democratic tinge," and advocate forming a United Front with them in order to counteract the efforts of those who would exploit them both. Such patriotic religious people have been deeply influenced by imperialists so they do not trust the Party. Therefore, the task of the Party is to unite with them in order to struggle with them. Liu and Yu do not see any contradiction in this for they emphasize that it is a purely political alliance and is not based on the world outlook of religion or the outlook of Marxism-Leninism. The world view of religion is ob-

[35] "A Discussion on Translated Works on Atheism," *JMJP*, October 30, 1962; *SCMP*, November 19, 1962, p. 6.
[36] *Ibid.*, p. 7.
[37] "The Correct Recognition," *Hung Ch'i*, February 26, 1964; *SCMM*, March 31, 1964, pp. 46, 48.
[38] *Ibid.*, p. 46.

viously unacceptable to Communists. On the other hand, to make Marxism-Leninism the basis for such an alliance would

imply the demand that the religious adherents accept the Marxist-Leninist world outlook and abandon their religious belief as the condition for cooperation. This is a demand which the United Front itself cannot bring up and has no need to bring up.[39]

The only foundation necessary is a

common political foundation [which] consists of anti-imperialism, anti-feudalism, and antibureaucratic capitalism during the period of the democratic revolution; anti-imperialism, patriotism, abiding by the law, accepting Party leadership, and taking the socialist road during the period of the socialist revolution and socialist reconstruction.[40]

It is not difficult to see what such an approach actually entails. It calls for deliberate association with religious believers who are attracted to the goals of national welfare and growth (and who could afford not to be?) and must discuss how religion has been a hindrance in the past, how imperialists have waged aggression under the cloak of religion, etc. Believers are in no position to decline, and thus must cooperate, as religious people, in a program whose ultimate goal is the elimination of religion.

Such an approach also means that religion as such and religious leaders as such need never be attacked. As we shall see, whenever the Communist government moved against the church or any other religious group, the announced purpose was always to purge the church of imperialistic elements, or to single out those who stood in the way of the people's progress, or to punish the unpatriotic. This was confirmed in a pamphlet, *The Catholic Church and Cuba: Program for Action,* a Spanish publication of the Foreign Languages Press in Peking, which described for Cuban leaders the way in which the Catholic Church in China had been subjugated. The aim was to isolate "antipatriotic, criminal elements," even to put them under such compulsion that "they feel themselves strongly driven to protest and make martyrs of themselves; and, in consequence,

[39] *Ibid.,* p. 44.
[40] *Ibid.,* p. 45.

they compromise themselves in antipatriotic acts." [41] Thus, in contrast to the early years of the Communist regime when officials were to avoid making martyrs, we move to a policy which allows the provoking of martyrs, if, of course, antipatriotic grounds can be established—in which case the condemned is a traitor or criminal, never a martyr.

Therefore, by Communist definition, there has been no religious persecution in China. On the contrary, religious people have been liberated from feudal, imperialistic, unpatriotic, and reactionary forces, and thus are free to unite with all the Chinese people in socialist construction to build the new China.

Such is the nature of Chinese Communist policy toward religion, the general understanding upon which it is based, and the approach made by Chinese officialdom toward religious groups as a whole. In succeeding chapters this policy and its implementation will be examined in terms of what it has meant to the two major branches of Christianity, to Buddhism and Islam, and to the indigenous religious traditions of China.

[41] Originally published in Spanish (Peking: FLP, 1959); it appeared under the title "Comment détruire l'Église" in Église Vivante, XV (1963), 365-75. It was summarized by Professor Searle Bates in "Christianity in the People's Republic—A Time for Study to Understand," China Notes VI (April, 1968), 7-8.

II

Eradicating Christianity's Foreign Connections: Missionaries

Communist attitudes toward religion and policies which incorporated these attitudes, as described in the preceding chapter, were expressed ambiguously in the early days of the Communist regime. Contradictory statements to religious leaders, conflicting press releases, and a wide variety of actions toward religious leaders and religious groups were the order of the day. Numerous observers have suggested that this ambiguity was the result of considerable uncertainty in the minds of the Communist leaders themselves. These leaders certainly had little or no use for religion, but there is little indication that they intended to stamp it out. The theorists repeatedly asserted that religion eventually would wither away, but the question remained: How might good Communists contribute to the withering? How could the roots be destroyed so that the plant would disappear without being cut down?

The first answer to this question which occurred to the Communists, as they considered the tiny Christian minority, was to strike at its foreignness. They saw a considerable number of missionaries, particularly in the Roman Catholic leadership, and a host of Protestant and Catholic institutions which were dependent on foreign subsidies or which had been in the past. Missionaries and institutions often came into focus together because a missionary could usually be found on the staff of an institution. The head of any institution was supposed to be a Chinese, but there were "Western advisors" who did not in all cases twiddle their thumbs. Moreover, the Communists were not blind to the role of missionary contact in order to insure a better flow of funds from the West to institutions in China.

Buddhism and Islam came to China from other lands. Both groups have had and still have foreign connections, but this did not seem to bother the Communists. Indeed, Buddhist and Muslim relationships with Asian or Middle Eastern countries have been exploited by the Communist government for diplomatic purposes.

Christian foreign connections, on the other hand, were regarded by the Chinese Communists as instances of imperialist aggression against China. Relationships of the Chinese Christian community with other Asian Christians, admittedly negligible, were ignored by the Communists, who would undoubtedly regard the presence of the Christian church in any Asian country as an instance of Western imperialist aggression against that country. Christian foreign relations, which in Chinese Communist eyes were entirely with the West, constituted an exposed root which obviously needed cutting. Thus, the first thrust in dealing with Christianity was directed against missionary personnel and the institutions which Communists regarded as grave instances of imperialist aggression.

THE EXODUS OF PROTESTANT MISSIONARIES

There was much speculation in Protestant circles as to whether any form of missionary activity might continue in China. Opinion on this matter was divided as the civil war in China dragged into the latter part of 1948 and into 1949. Dr. E. E. Walline reported to the Thirty-fourth Annual Meeting (1948) of the China Council of the Presbyterian Church, U.S.A., that missionaries "are entering into a period of great opportunity in China."[1] The Methodist Board of Missions, at its annual meeting in January, 1949, "pledged to carry on its missionary work in China despite dangers and obstacles created by the Chinese civil war."[2] Missionaries were still arriving in China in 1948, both "old hands" returning after extended furloughs because of World War II, and fresh recruits eager to serve in such a "challenging situation."

[1] *China Daily Tribune*, September 20, 1948.
[2] Noted in *CMBA* II (January, 1949), 87.

The American Lutheran Church, however, decided late in 1948 to withdraw its missionaries from China, and the Lutheran Theological Seminary at Hankow evacuated to Hong Kong. Most American Protestant mission boards expected to continue work while allowing those missionaries who requested withdrawal to do so.[3]

Several missionaries sent encouraging reports. Richard Bryant, American Presbyterian in Tsinan, traveled in late 1948 to Tsingtao, a distance of 250 miles, with special papers and guard provided by the Communists. A group of Congregational missionaries in Foochow stated in late 1949 that churches and institutions were continuing to operate as before, and noted that posters proclaiming "freedom of worship" and "protection of foreigners" were plastered all over the city within a few hours after the Communist occupation of it in August, 1949.[4]

In spite of what might be called a cautious optimism, various groups were making preparations in case missionaries might not be allowed to continue to work. The Seventh-day Adventist China Division Executive Committee met in Hong Kong for five days in late January, 1950, and turned over all administrative, publication, educational, and institutional leadership in China to Chinese leaders. These leaders did not think their extensive medical work would be interrupted, since a large corps of Chinese doctors and nurses had been trained.[5]

A most significant statement with respect to Protestant missionaries in China appeared to confirm the cautious optimism which led missionaries in China and their board executives in the West to expect to continue, albeit on a more limited scale. Entitled "A Message from Chinese Christians to Mission Boards Abroad,"[6] it expressed appreciation for what the missionary movement had accomplished and received wide publicity. Specifically disavowing any direct relationship between missionary work and government, the document outlined the challenge which faced Chinese Christians in the new regime, as Christians and as Chinese. Two of the

---

[3] Frank Cartwright affirmed this policy in his article, "Protestant Missions in Communist China," *Far Eastern Survey*, December 28, 1949, p. 304.

[4] *CMBA* II (January, 1949), 87; *China Mail*, December 30, 1949.

[5] *CMBA* II (III) (March, 1950), 318.

[6] *Documents of the Three-Self Movement* [hereafter *Documents*], ed. Francis P. Jones (New York: National Council of Churches, 1963), pp. 14-18.

three specific recommendations to mission boards set forth the idea that determination of policy and administration of finance must pass into Chinese hands completely, but the framers added that mission funds were still welcome if no strings were attached and if funds were regarded as temporary. A long statement concerning the future of missionary personnel began: "There is nothing in principle which makes the future position of the missionary untenable, or renders his service unnecessary." He is to serve, not to administer; he must expect difficult physical and mental readjustments in a political-economic environment to which he is unaccustomed. Travel would probably be restricted. Families would experience a more difficult adjustment than single individuals.[7]

Such words of caution to the missionary would have applied in almost any earlier period of missionary history in China, with the possible exception of the ambiguous reference to the new political environment. The fact that China was passing out of the hands of Chiang Kai-shek, a Christian, into the hands of Communists, whose counterparts in Russia and Eastern Europe were known to be unfriendly and even hateful toward religion, would cause one to conclude that the new political environment might involve more than merely being "different to the one he is accustomed to." But the concept of the missionary vocation—"To Be, to Share, and to Live"—was not unfamiliar to young missionary candidates in those days, and missionaries young and old rejoiced that the church in China wanted them.

Several of the Chinese Christians who signed this statement, and who, incidentally, later became active members of the Three-Self Movement, were in the group selected from seven Protestant denominations which met with Chou En-lai in May, 1950, to discuss problems which had arisen relating to church and government. In connection with a discussion on imperialism, Chou stated that no new missionaries could enter China, and no furloughed missionaries might return. Those who were already in China might stay if there was no question of their having engaged in political activity. Both foreign missionaries and Chinese workers should not try to reach areas being affected by land reform, which would be drastic. Chou suggested that the church rid itself of imperialism by an inward

[7] *Ibid.,* p. 17.

cleansing of all imperialist connections, which cleansing would result in government protection.[8]

It was during this May, 1950, meeting with Chou En-lai that the famous Christian Manifesto was worked out with the Premier by a group of Protestant Christians. This Manifesto, which will be discussed in greater detail in a subsequent chapter, said with respect to missionaries that since they came from imperialistic countries, "Christianity consciously or unconsciously, directly or indirectly, became related with imperialism," thus implying that missionaries were bearers of imperialism. Although there was no direct reference as to whether missionaries might continue or be sent home, there were references to "vigilance against imperialism," to the fact that churches should "oppose imperialism, feudalism," etc., and should "purge imperialistic influences from within Christianity."

All Christian churches and organizations in China that are still relying upon foreign personnel and financial aid should work out concrete plans to realize within the shortest possible time their objective of self-reliance and rejuvenation.[9]

Chou En-lai's oral word—no new missionaries and no return of furloughed missionaries—plus the call to churches to end reliance on missionaries as soon as possible left little doubt in the minds of Protestant leaders that the day of the missionary was at an end. The Korean war which followed the above-mentioned meeting by a month and the entry of the Chinese into the war the following November brought any speculation concerning a possible future role of the missionary in China completely to an end.

The Church Missionary Society of London said on September 7, 1950, that all European Anglican bishops in China had resigned and that episcopal vacancies had been filled by elevation of former

[8] *CMBA* II (III) (September, 1950), 787. A report to China Bulletin [hereafter *CHIBUL*] on the May, 1950, meeting with Chou said that he left the door open "for some missionaries to come back later as teachers." The report also states, "All who have reported on the meeting have spoken of the good impression Premier Chou's reasonableness made upon them, especially as contrasted with the desire of some other government representatives for more drastic action." *CHIBUL*, June 19, 1950.

[9] *Documents*, pp. 19-20.

assistant or suffragan bishops, all of whom were Chinese. The first account of the resignation stated that it was in protest against Communist restrictions, but a later statement attributed it to the insistence by the Chinese government on Chinese leadership as a prerequisite to recognition.[10]

In view of the preceding facts it is all the more striking that Bishop Ralph Ward of The Methodist Church, passing through Hong Kong in mid-November, 1950, on his way to attend meetings in the United States, apparently expected to return to China. He stated in an interview that the Communists, at that time, were not trying to suppress the Christian or any other religion. There had been physical violence, but it had not been extensive, and the church in his area (Shanghai and central China) had been able to proceed without interference provided it broke no laws.[11]

When China entered the Korean war, feelings which had been restrained under exteriors of icy politeness broke forth. Miss Helen Ferris, missionary teacher at Ginling College in Nanking, corrected a line in a student's composition which read "The United States sent an army to Korea," to read "The United Nations sent an army to Korea." The students demanded that "she frankly admit her reactionary behavior during her twenty-year stay in China and confess that she [was] an element of imperialism," and demanded further that she place an advertisement in the newspapers apologizing to everybody for the whole business.[12]

The Rev. Olin Stockwell, a Methodist missionary who had previously written statements friendly to the incoming Communists, was picked up by the police at his residence in Chengtu, Szechwan, on November 26, 1950. He was imprisoned for two years, charged first with mishandling furniture belonging to the Joint Committee for Rural Reconstruction and later with espionage and other crimes.

Headlined by *Time* (May 18, 1953) as "The Missionary Who

[10] *Hong Kong Standard*, September 9, 1950; *CMBA* II (III) (October, 1950), 881. *CHIBUL*, June 13, 1950, says this transition in Episcopal leadership was underway by the spring of 1950.

[11] *South China Morning Post*, November 18, 1950. Missionaries about to depart also had to place ads in the newspapers inviting anyone who had business to settle with them to come and do so. *CHIBUL*, November 12, 1951.

[12] *Hong Kong Standard*, December 6, 1950.

Lied," Stockwell has been criticized sharply for confessing that he was a spy, but his interpretation of what this meant to the Communists is most revealing. By charging that he was a spy the Communists meant that he had sent information to America about China, and that his "speaking and writing had made the Chinese friendly to the United States and cool to revolutionary doctrine." [13] Stockwell maintains, however, that the issues were not black and white—that he and the judges both knew they were playing a game; that he took care to put all blame on himself or upon individuals and organizations far out of Communist reach; that the situations he embellished with extensive and apparently convincing detail were beyond the power of the officials to check; and that if he had taken the road to martyrdom he would not have been a martyr to Christ, but would have been depicted throughout China as a martyr to imperialism and capitalism. Most of all, he was convinced of God's guidance in the whole business.[14]

Dr. William Wallace, American Southern Baptist missionary doctor and superintendent of Stout Memorial Hospital at Wuchow, died in prison on February 10, 1951. The U. S. State Department announced that he was in good health when imprisoned on December 19, 1950.[15] At about the same time word was received of the death of Bishop Gene Carleton Lacy of The Methodist Church in Foochow. There were rumors that feelings against American missionaries ran so high in this city famous for Methodist missionary service that only an old servant who had been with the Lacy family through the years dared follow the casket to the place of burial. Bishop Lacy had been under house arrest for a year; his wife had gone on to Boston.[16]

When Chinese Christian leaders were called to Peking in April, 1951, to consult with government leaders on how they might completely break the ties with American imperialism, one of the methods proposed (or ordered), and immediately inaugurated, was that of the accusation meeting. The roll call of those accused on that

[13] F. Olin Stockwell, *With God in Red China* (New York: Harper and Brothers, 1953), p. 228. See also his *Meditations from a Prison Cell* (Nashville: The Upper Room, 1954).

[14] *Ibid.*, especially pp. 228-38.

[15] *Hong Kong Telegraph*, March 2, 1951. See also Jesse C. Fletcher, *Bill Wallace of China* (Nashville: Broadman Press, 1963).

[16] Death only reported in *CMBA* IV (V) (February, 1952).

April 18 was impressive, including Timothy Richards (long since dead and, since he was British, a most outstanding example of American imperialism!) and four distinguished Chinese Christians, who will be considered in a later chapter. Heading the list was Presbyterian missionary Frank Price, and the most prominent of his accusers was his longtime associate in the Church of Christ in China, its General Secretary, H. H. Ts'ui (Ts'ui Hsien-hsiang). Ts'ui accused Price of being anti-Communist and anti-Russian, and charged that he was an adviser to Chiang Kai-shek and took orders from the U. S. State Department. Ts'ui claimed that Frank Price had once arranged for fifty Chinese students going to America to stay in American private homes. It was not, as Price claimed, so that these students could enjoy the American way of life. It was "really to poison the minds of the Chinese young people." Ts'ui concluded by pledging never to speak to Price again, never to write him a letter, and never to allow him to enter the Church of Christ in China again.[17]

Although this was perhaps the most famous accusation of an American Protestant missionary, the accused was never imprisoned as such. Dr. and Mrs. Price finally left in the fall of 1952, after having waited two years for an exit permit.

By the end of 1950, even before the accusation meetings began. incidents intended to embarrass or incriminate missionaries had become so common that the new year 1951 dawned with virtually a complete reversal of policy in the statements of Protestant mission board executives. Whereas two years earlier the attitude was one of cautious optimism and a year earlier had been one of simple determination to continue wherever possible while remaining in the background, early 1951 saw the beginning of wholesale withdrawals. At that time it was estimated that eighteen to nineteen hundred Protestant missionaries were still in China, but that at least five hundred of them already had applied for exit permits.[18]

---

[17] The accusation speech from *T'ien Feng*, May 8, 1951, may be found in Leonard M. Outerbridge, *The Lost Churches of China* (Philadelphia: Westminster Press, 1952), pp. 221-23.

[18] *Hong Kong Standard*, January 22, 1951. The figure of 500 applications for exit permits, attributed to Dr. Roland Cross, Far East Secretary, NCCCUSA Division of Foreign Missions, is probably low. The Rev. Bruce Copland wrote in May, 1951, that only 400-500 Protestant missionaries remained in China. *CHIBUL*, May 21, 1951.

There were long delays in some cases, definite refusals in others. Bishop Z. T. Kuang (Chiang Ch'ang-ch'uan) of The Methodist Church in North China advised all Americans in his area that "unpleasant incidents" might develop if they tried to continue. Congregational and Episcopal missionaries from the United States were requested by their respective organizations to return as quickly as possible.[19] About the middle of the year 1951, the China Inland Mission began to speak not of large-scale withdrawal of missionaries but of complete evacuation.[20]

The exodus of Protestant missionaries which began in earnest in early 1951 was virtually complete by the end of that year. For example, in early 1952, 20 out of 637 China Inland missionaries, 7 out of 571 Lutheran missionaries including European as well as American, and 3 of the 350 American Methodist missionary contingent remained. For the British missionaries the story was almost the same. In early 1952 there was only one woman of 60 Anglican missionaries, two couples of the London Missionary Society, and one British Baptist left in China.[21] The British Missionary Societies' East Asia Committee reported that by January 1, 1953, all of the 1,298 British missionaries who had been in China in 1949 had left the country.[22] This list does not include Mrs. Margaret Kiesow, an English Presbyterian who was married to a Chinese national. Mrs. Kiesow remained on the Cheeloo University campus until September, 1953, and suggests that she was not pressured to depart even then.[23] Dr. Ralph Lapwood, who arrived in Hong

[19] *South China Morning Post*, January 6, 1951.

[20] *International Review of Missions* L (July, 1951), 728.

[21] From summaries in *CMBA* IV (V) (April, 1952), 323-24; and V (November, 1952), 775. *CHIBUL*, September 13, 1951, reported that all Episcopal, Disciples, Reformed Church in America, Church of Brethren, Evangelical and Reformed (from America), plus all Canadian Presbyterians had left.

[22] *CHIBUL*, April 20, 1953.

[23] E. Margaret Kiesow, *China the Challenge* (London: Presbyterian Church of England, 1954), p. 2. Most Protestant missionaries had experiences different from those related by Mrs. Kiesow. In addition to Stockwell's books, cited above, one may consult the following: Roy Belmer, *The Teeth of the Dragon: The Incredible Story of a Woman's Survival* (London: Epworth Press, 1964); Geoffrey Bull, *When Iron Gates Yield* (Chicago: Moody Press, 1955); Lawrence Earl, *She Loved a Wicked City* (New York: E. P. Dutton, 1962) [previously published as *One Foreign Devil* (London: Hodder and Stoughton, 1962)]; *The Hand That Guided*, ed. Anne Hazelton (London: China Inland Mission, 1952); Luella G. Koether and Janet T. Surdam, *Two Hundred Days as Prisoners of the Chinese Communists* (Mason City, Iowa:

Kong in October, 1952, in advance of Mrs. Lapwood who remained in Peking for a peace conference, said that he was invited to teach mathematics for another year in China but decided he could do more for China in England.[24]

Ecumenical Press Service reported that out of 1,027 missionaries from European countries (not including the United Kingdom) who were in China in 1948 only two remained in 1953.[25] One of these was Miss Ellen Nielsen, a Danish missionary in Takushan, Manchuria, who had previously elected Chinese citizenship. A letter received from her in early 1954 when she was eighty-two years of age related that she supported herself by the sale of milk and butter from three cows which she cared for herself, and indicated in radiantly unselfconscious language her modest but significant role in a Christian community which had no pastor or other professional religious leadership.[26] She died in 1960.

A few others managed to stay in one capacity or another. Mr. and Mrs. Harry Gould of the China Inland Mission found employment with the commerical firm of Butterfield and Swire in Shanghai until 1955. In the same city Miss Helen Willis managed to keep a Christian Bookroom going until 1958, when it was closed and she was placed under house arrest. She was tried and expelled from the country in April, 1959. She had occasional contact with pastors and lay Christians during the whole period and had a continual stream of students who came to study Greek with her.[27] Loyal Bartel, a Mennonite Brethren missionary-farmer who elected Chinese citizenship, continued in Shantung. Miss Talitha Gerlach of the YWCA and Miss Margaret Turner continued to stay in China, though not as missionaries in the ordinary sense. And there

---

Arrow Printing Company, 1956); Isobel Kuhn, *Green Leaf in Drought-Time* (Chicago: Moody Press, 1957); Dorothy S. McCammon, *We Tried to Stay* (Scottsdale, Pa.: Herald Press, 1953); Harold M. Martinson, *Red Dragon over China* (Minneapolis: Augsburg Publishing House, 1956); Sara Perkins, *Red China Prisoner* (Westwood, N. J.: Fleming H. Revell, 1963); W. J. Sheridan, *Watching the Chinese Curtain Fall* (Vancouver: Mitchell, n.d.); Victor E. Swenson, *Parents of Many* (Rock Island, Ill.: Augustana Press, 1959).

[24] *CHIBUL*, September 15 and November 3, 1952.
[25] *CHIBUL*, October 12, 1953.
[26] *CHIBUL*, February 15 and April 24, 1954.
[27] Helen Willis, *Through Encouragement of the Scriptures; Recollections of Ten Years in Communist Shanghai* (Hong Kong: Christian Book Room, 1962).

was word in the late 50's of Jehovah's Witnesses and Seventh-day Adventist foreign missionaries encountering difficulties, but there are no details available to me.

By 1952 most missionaries leaving China showed signs of real strain, and a few were in desperate condition. Miss Gertrude Cone arrived in Hong Kong on February 18, 1952, on a stretcher and died two days later of malnutrition which doctors said was one of the worst cases they had ever seen.[28] Felix Paulsen of the Schleswig-Holstein Lutheran Mission arrived in Hong Kong on September 5, 1952, after being imprisoned since November, 1950, one of the few instances of imprisonment of a European Protestant missionary.[29] Four American Baptists who came out on December 28, 1952, and January 2, 1953, had been confined, technically under house arrest, since April, 1950.[30] In the spring of 1953, ten American Protestant missionaries were still in China, eight of them in prison.[31]

As the Protestant missionary exodus drew to a close, a European Lutheran missionary quoted a colleague who said:

It's no use staying. Mission buildings are taken over, some in part, some entirely. We can't go out to meet the people. No Chinese can safely come to the house to talk with us. By staying, we'd make things still worse for the Christians.[32]

This simple observation, far from being an alibi, is actually a remarkable summary of the basic feelings of the Protestant missionaries who were departing. In the first place, it was clear that they could do nothing. At various times and places in the history of the missionary movement such has been the case, but in such times it was usually believed that the presence of the missionary was a source of quiet strength and comfort to the Christian community. It was for this reason that so many stayed as long as they did. At this point, however, the second reason for departure comes to the fore. By staying, these Protestant missionaries

[28] *CHIBUL*, February 25, 1952.
[29] *CHIBUL*, September 29, 1952.
[30] *CHIBUL*, January 15, 1953.
[31] Based on list of twenty-two in CHIBUL, November 17, 1952, and reports that as of April, 1953, twelve on that list had left China.
[32] *CMBA* IV (V) (April, 1952), 323.

believed that they were either a source of embarrassment to Chinese Christians who were already being labeled running dogs of imperialism, or that their safety was one more source of concern for Chinese Christians who had enough to worry about anyway.

One must remember also that for years there had been a steady drive toward the development of a strong, indigenous church in China and a consequent diminution of the missionary role. Although there were missionaries and Chinese Christians who dragged their feet along this path, the basic impetus of the period in missionary strategy was toward devolution of the missionary role and accelerated development of national leadership, control, and support.[33] Although most of the missionaries who withdrew undoubtedly thought it was premature and regretted having to do so, they took the step and did not regard their request for an exit permit as necessarily a sign of failure or defeat.

THE HANDLING OF ROMAN CATHOLIC MISSIONARIES

The story of how Catholic missionaries fared under the Communist regime is considerably different from the story sketched of the Protestants. Catholics shared little of the optimism with which Protestants assessed possibilities under the Communists, largely because of what had happened to Catholic missionaries before and during World War II in areas already under Communist control.

Father Vincent Lebbe, a Belgian priest who was captured and kept under Communist guard in the spring of 1940, was one of the first to encounter Communist techniques.[34] Although he was not physically mistreated, it was believed that his death in June of that year was hastened by the experience. Some of the Brothers of St. John the Baptist, the congregation he founded, met suffering and death at Communist hands.

According to Greta Palmer, whose account suffers from lack of

---

[33] Creighton Lacy, "The Missionary Exodus from China," *Pacific Affairs* XXVIII December, 1955), 301-14. Lacy shows how this trend toward devolution distinguished Protestantism from Catholicism, pp. 307-9.

[34] There is a scholarly biography of Father Lebbe by Levaux and a more popular one by Leclercq, neither of which I have been able to consult. There are references to Father Lebbe in Raymond J. de Jaegher and Irene Corbally Kuhn, *The Enemy Within* (Garden City, N. Y.: Doubleday and Co., 1952).

documentation,[35] the pre-1949 story is one of imprisonment, torture, and execution of Catholic missionaries in Communist-held areas. In many instances a missionary captured and tortured by the Japanese would upon release be seized by Communists and punished as a spy for the Japanese. Father Carlo Suigo tells of experiences under both Chinese Communists and Japanese during the war, although he managed to escape in 1945 just as the war ended.[36]

Father Alberto Galter relates in a most systematic way, and with better documentation than Miss Palmer, the campaign against Catholic missionaries and the church in Communist areas before 1949, particularly the ways in which the people's courts, which were to become so common after the Communist takeover of the whole country, were first employed against missionaries from 1946 to 1949.[37] The people's emotions were stirred to the point of violence. Missionaries were charged with torturing the sick in hospitals, refusing food to children in orphanages, and murdering Chinese to eat their hearts. Acts of cruelty toward the accused were carried out before, during, and after the trial. If the foreign missionary admitted his errors he might be released and sent from the area. Otherwise he was imprisoned or beaten; occasionally one was put to death. Catholic authorities estimate that around a hundred priests, both foreign and Chinese, were put to death in 1946 and 1947, including the burial alive on August 17, 1947, of twelve Cistercian monks after frightful torture.

Comic relief was provided by the arrest of two Polish priests at Shihchiachuang in Communist territory in December, 1947. After several months in prison they were charged with "political activity on behalf of their home government." When the embarrassed police

[35] *God's Underground in Asia* (New York: Appleton-Century-Crofts, 1953), chapter I. Several scholars whom I am inclined to trust confirm that about forty Catholic missionaries and fifteen to twenty Protestant missionaries lost their lives due to actions which can be attributed to Communists in the pre-1949 period.

[36] Carlo Suigo, *In the Land of Mao Tse-tung* (London: George Allen and Unwin, 1953). See also the concluding article in a series by J. L. Van Hecken, "Communistes and Missionaires chez les Mongols de la Mongolie Intérieure," *CMBA* IX (April, 1957), 222-30, which also includes brief accounts of Protestant missions in Inner Mongolia under the Communists.

[37] *The Red Book of the Persecuted Church* (Westminster, Md.: Newman Press, 1957), pp. 165-70.

discovered that Poland was Communist, the priests were released and expelled from Communist territory.[38]

Father Nicholas Maestrini, on the eve of the Communist takeover, evidenced in the following statement a much greater reserve about the future than did a number of Protestant statements of the period. Although the overall policy of toleration adopted by the Peking government did not allow a fierce persecution, Maestrini noted that

a slow and steady movement of strangulation is evident everywhere. . . . There are instances of foreign missionaries being jailed on accusation of offenses against financial regulations or such like laws, but on the whole they remain free at home. On the other hand, more or less severe restrictions on their movements, varying according to locality, are imposed: for example, permission is not granted to leave a certain small territory.[39]

The hope was expressed that if missionaries "identify themselves with the poor" in the spirit of St. Francis of Assisi and demonstrate that they are "working for the rehabilitation of the people, they may be permitted to remain." [40]

There were observations from many parts of China that confirmed the impression that relative peace and quiet prevailed after the arrival of the first Communist troops, in some places for as long as a year. After the chaos of the war and the postwar period, the discipline of the Communist troops was a welcome relief. There is even the winsome account from the archdiocese of Mukden, where Father Albert Caubrière was killed by a robber in June, 1948:

The communist police chief of Haichen personally dressed Fr. Caubrière's body for burial, placing a rosary in his hand and a crucifix on his breast. [The police chief also] arranged for the church and residence to be returned to the Catholic mission by the functionaries who occupied them, and requested that a priest be sent to Haicheng to succeed Fr. Caubrière.[41]

[38] CMBA (September, 1948), 486.
[39] CMBA II (September, 1949), 2.
[40] Ibid., p. 3.
[41] CMBA I (October, 1948), 629.

Thus, by mid-1950, one might still describe the situation of the Catholic community as one of touch-and-go. There were definite instances of standing firm against the authorities and getting away with it. There were numerous other instances of more vigorous controls against which outward resistance proved futile. Ominous indeed were the signs even in early 1950 of letters sent to the Catholic Church in a certain place, only to have the letter returned with the words "Firm Extinct" stamped on the envelope in English, with an additional phrase by hand in Chinese: "This mission has ceased to exist." Letters sent to missionaries or church offices in Manchuria were sometimes returned with "There is no Catholic Church" written across the envelope.[42]

The Korean war, especially the entry of Communist China into it, was the watershed for Catholics as for Protestants. A diocese in Central China reported at the end of 1950 that "missionary endeavor hit an all time low" for that year: nine of its fourteen mission stations had been seized by Communists, absolutely no travel by missionaries was allowed, churches were requisitioned more frequently for lectures and rallies, and harassment and annoyance multiplied.[43]

A new "hard line" was being applied all over the country. A priest who had administered last rites to a dying villager in the Yingkow diocese of Manchuria was arrested because prayer was "not allowed" in that place. He was then paraded with his catechist as a foreign spy through the city streets. Their impression that they were being led to execution was confirmed by a soldier who protested such an execution, which had been ordered by the regional police chief, on grounds that they were good men and did not deserve such a penalty. They were released.[44]

In Hunan, Father Quentin Olwell, Passionist missionary in Yuanling diocese, was deported because he asked his people to pray for the repose of the souls and remission of sins of two Catholics executed as bandits. To pray for such was judged "counterrevolutionary."[45] A bishop in an unspecified place who was assessed an

[42] *CMBA* II (III) (March, 1950), 326.
[43] *CMBA* III (IV) (January, 1951), 75-76.
[44] *CMBA* III (IV) (March, 1951), 358.
[45] *CMBA* III (IV) (June-July, 1951), 531.

amount equivalent to $7,000 managed to get a note through to Hong Kong in a kind of slang code which read:

Yesterday I sent you a telegram asking for HK$40,000 at once. I was entertained as a lord of the earth [thus treated as a landlord] and if I don't pay up in seven days I shall be entertained again. I have a nice shiner and bruises; I feel my age all over. Such is life.[46]

The Benedictine Monastery of Saints Peter and Andrew at Sichan, near Chengtu in West China in 1950 began to suffer harassment intended to divide Chinese from European monks, resulting in the deportation of the prior and other Europeans, as well as the dispersal of sixteen Chinese monks in 1951.[47]

In late 1950 or early 1951, six missionary priests on the Tibetan border were placed under house arrest at Weishi, where they were able to engage in language study, prayer, editing of publications, and manual labor, until they were accused and deported on January 16, 1952.[48]

There are regular reports during this period of priests, both Chinese and foreign, who died in jail or were released when death was imminent so that they might die outside instead of inside the jail, thus avoiding the creation of martyrs. The same timing was used in giving exit permits, so that a missionary whose health had deteriorated in prison or under house arrest because proper food or medicine were unattainable might die in Hong Kong under the imperialists.

Bishop Ford of Maryknoll was put under house arrest December 23, 1950, then was transported with his secretary, Sister Joan Marie, from Kaying to Canton in April, 1951. The story of how they were abused and maltreated at each stop along the way is one of the most revolting tales from those horrible days. Bishop Ford's health deteriorated rapidly in the prison in Canton until he could scarcely walk, and indeed he was carried about toward the end. He died there on February 21, 1952, but Sister Joan Marie was not told of it until August of that year when she was made to sign a statement

[46] *CMBA* IV (V) (January, 1952), 72.

[47] Cary Elwes, *China and the Cross* (New York: P. J. Kenedy and Sons, 1957), pp. 274-75.

[48] Robert Loup, *Martyr in Tibet*, trans. Charles Davenport (New York: David McKay, 1956), pp. 231-32.

saying that he had died of natural causes. The following month she was allowed to visit his grave (in a cemetery reportedly turned into a rice field a few years later), and was then expelled from China.[49] The *China Missionary Bulletin* is replete with brief reports of missionary experience under the Communists and interpretation by missionaries of that experience. There are also a number of books by Roman Catholic missionary priests and nuns, through which one may see in the most intimate detail their lives under pressure. There is a good bit of repetition, which means that the very detail which makes the stories valuable often makes them dull, but there is something rewarding in each. The majority are written by Americans, but there are a few "priestly biographies" by French and Italian priests, as well as the incidents related about priests of other nationalities. All indicate that, in the last analysis, nationality had very little to do with the lightness or the severity of the treatment.

Father Jean de Leffe, a French Jesuit who had served as chaplain at Aurora University in Shanghai since 1940, was able to continue in his role as "spiritual father" to the university for two years after the Communist capture of Shanghai.[50] In February, 1951, his students were called on to sign a declaration of love for their country. Ecclesiastical authorities said the Catholic students could sign all but a statement which pledged support of the Communist Party. At the same time, Father de Leffe let all students know that support of the national church advocated by the Communists would bring excommunication. For this he was accused of not supporting the government and was charged further as a criminal, because leaflets dropped by a Nationalist plane were found on his desk and because he had written a letter of recommendation to a Catholic college in Hong Kong for a student who had re-

---

[49] A most convenient and readable summary of Bishop Ford's life, imprisonment, and death under the Communists is in John F. Donovan, *The Pagoda and the Cross: The Life of Bishop Ford of Maryknoll* (New York: Charles Scribner's Sons, 1967), pp. 175-215. Essential details may be found in the introductory memoir to a collection of Bishop Ford's writings edited by Raymond H. Lane, *Stone in the King's Highway* (New York: McMullen Books, 1953), pp. 38-47.

[50] Jean de Leffe, *Chrétiens dans la Chine de Mao* (Paris: Desclée de Brouwer, 1955), pp. 32-37.

ceived permission from parents and government to leave China. He states that the discussions on Communist theory in prison made him feel like he was in a confirmation class.

Monsignor Gaetan Pollio, Italian Archbishop of the archdiocese of Kaifeng, Honan, was under house arrest from October, 1949, until April 1, 1951, when he was imprisoned for six months. After a people's trial for five hours on September 21, 1951, he was ordered to leave China by "the will of the people," and arrived in Hong Kong on October 8, 1951.[51] He was alleged to have written to bishops and missionaries against the reform church movement, sent circulars to Christians, instituted the Legion of Mary, declared an apostate seminarian named Ly Mao-te a renegade, maintained that the Legion of Mary was not a subversive organization trying to overthrow the popular regime in the interest of imperialists, exhorted the faithful not to follow the Three-Self Movement, prevented young Catholics from entering the popular front, and threatened with excommunication those who would join the national church. In addition to these formal charges he was accused of being an American spy, of collaborating with Chiang Kai-shek, of criticizing Russia for its persecution of religion, and of possessing a radio transmitter used to spread calumnies against China. Pollio says he was "guilty of the eight formal charges; the additional ones were imaginary." [52]

Father Thomas Phillips, who as rector of Christ the King in Shanghai in 1949 was the only foreigner serving as the superior in a Catholic parish, was not arrested until June 15, 1953, quite late for an American, and for reasons not nearly so well defined as for Monsignor Pollio.[53] He was released three years later, on June 15, 1956, in Shanghai with Father John Clifford. Both Jesuits were presented with documents to sign in which they would have acknowledged crimes, but they refused and got away with it. Clifford has also told his story in which he admits that he shouted back at his captors, although without ever answering their questions, and

[51] Gaetan Pollio, *Le Calvaire de L'Église dans la Chine Nouvelle*, translated from the Italian by Marie Clemy (Paris: Libraire P. Tequi, 1962), pp. 42, 55-57, 151-60, 166.

[52] *Ibid.*, pp. 74-76.

[53] Kurt Becker, *I Met a Traveller: The Triumph of Father Phillips* (New York: Farrar, Straus, and Cudahy, 1958).

maintains that the only way to survive attempts at brainwashing was to refuse to give an inch.[54]

In contrast with Clifford one sees the difficulty which Father Robert Greene experienced by trying to go along (for good reasons) and then trying to pull back.[55] He surrendered his ordination picture to an agent and was later confronted with a photostat of it in which a toy medal and a U. S. chaplain's insignia had been imposed, all to indicate that Greene was not a priest but a spy. A guerrilla chieftain who had fought against the Communists was produced with the claim that Greene had induced him to become a guerrilla. Since Greene had given medicines to guerrillas, which he admitted, he was therefore against the Communist troops.

Father Mark Tennien, a Maryknoll missionary in Kwangsi province, was stationed at Shumkai near Wuchow in 1946.[56] His arrest and imprisonment provide an interesting variation since he was under house arrest both before and after a period of imprisonment. During both periods of house arrest he was able to observe quite a bit that was going on around him, but maintains that he was bothered more at all hours of the day and night while under house arrest than he was in his prison cell. He was allowed to keep a fountain pen in jail and managed to write up his experiences. He tried to smuggle one of two copies out with him, but it was confiscated. The other copy, which was mailed to a colleague in Hong Kong, surprisingly reached its destination. Tennien later returned to Hong Kong to serve as chairman of the group which edited and published *Mission Bulletin.*

Another foreign priest who was imprisoned in China relates nothing unusual about his arrest or imprisonment in his flamboyant account, but the circumstances of his being in a position to be arrested are somewhat astounding.[57] Father Harold W. Rigney was a missionary of the Divine Word Society in Africa and was transferred to China on the eve of the Communist takeover to serve as

[54] John Clifford, *In the Presence of My Enemies* (New York: W. W. Norton, 1963).

[55] Robert W. Greene, *Calvary in China* (New York: G. P. Putnam's Sons, 1953).

[56] Mark Tennien, *No Secret is Safe* (New York: Farrar, Straus, and Young, 1952).

[57] Harold W. Rigney, *Four Years in a Red Hell* (Chicago: Henry Regnery, 1965).

rector of Fujen University in Peking. Undoubtedly a distinguished administrator and without question one who functioned ably under the circumstances, he was nevertheless a foreigner in a top administrative post with only a minimal knowledge of the Chinese language and no previous experience in China, precisely at a time when the church was being accused of foreign cultural aggression against China.

The Belgian Father Albert Sohier, whose back was broken by beating and by soldiers jumping up and down on him to get him to confess, after which the priest lay paralyzed for six months, reports that the judge in Peking said to him on his release, "That your back was broken here is a fact. We do not ask you to deny it, but we do ask you not to exaggerate the facts." Another official told him: "If you are objective you will admit that we no longer beat prisoners. We have made mistakes in the past, but our methods have been improved; time was required to get the situation in hand." [58]

Of all these stories, perhaps the most moving is that told by Mary Victoria in *Nun in Red China*. In a simple conversational style, a Maryknoll sister who worked in the village of Wang Ding in South China focuses attention on the people around her rather than herself.[59] Her story of the trial of a village priest at a neighboring place and of two postulants whose training was interrupted makes vivid the struggle of the Chinese Catholic clergy. Sister Mary was confined with a few other sisters in a room above the Communist Youth Hall. Once they were called downstairs, then directed back to their room and told to pick up a bucket upside down on the floor under which there was a package. After a ceremonious opening, opium was found to be inside and the sisters were arrested. Depressing experiences in various prisons followed, in the last of which she was placed with some real dregs of humanity, each of whom was spying on someone else in the hope of finding something which would bring release as a reward for tattling. She was finally sentenced to be deported because her passport had expired (after being confiscated by the police) and because she had used Hong Kong currency. It was Mary Victoria who, before cross-

[58] Father Sohier's own account is in *CMBA* VII (March, 1955), 189-95.
[59] (New York: McGraw-Hill, 1953), pp. 141, 201-7.

ing the bridge at Lo Wu into Hong Kong, was told by the baggage inspector on the Communist side: "Don't worry, Sister. You'll come back."

Father Francis X. Legrand, of the Belgian Scheut order and in charge of the Catholic Central Bureau, was arrested on September 6, 1951. Intense pressure was put on him, including a six-day-and-night session of constant interrogation to get him to admit that he had murdered a man and then that he had engaged in espionage. In the first instance, when he was in an extremely weak condition, his interrogators suggested a compromise, namely, that he at one time had a gun in his pocket which had gone off accidentally and killed a man. He signed, and then a few days later was confronted with a revised confession of the accidental killing of two men, which he says he had a hazy recollection of signing. The charges of espionage were based on the fact that he had started the *China Missionary Bulletin*, which the Communists claimed provided information about China to its enemies. Legrand signed, but without the clause that it involved espionage. When he was called for sentencing on April 28, 1954, one of the three judges read a document listing the crimes with which he was charged. The priest insisted on reading it for himself, whereupon he discovered that several new ones were included. He refused to sign in spite of a barrage of loud argument, and since the prison wagon was waiting at the door to take him to the train, the officials gave in and let him go, ordering him expelled forever from China.[60]

Father Robert Juigner was given an indoctrination course in prison and was handcuffed for three months of the time because he made no progress. Toward the end of this time, a leper was placed in the crowded cell where the priest and eighty other prisoners were packed. The other prisoners huddled even closer together to stay away from the new cellmate, but Juigner helped the leper feed himself and shared a blanket with him. The Communist guards told the other prisoners that the priest's kindness was a result of his indoctrination course in communism. When three months had passed the officials told him he now knew what a sinner he was and would therefore be expelled. Father Juigner, who was in a German prisoner of war camp during World War II for a year and a half,

[60] "Another Mindszenty Ordeal," *CMBA* VI (September, 1954), 602-5.

said, "At least the Germans didn't try to make us believe in Nazism. Here you try to force conversion on us." [61]

As an exception to the general pattern, Father Victorino Garcia, S. J., was able to continue teaching at the seminary in Shanghai until the end of 1954. He said it "was the last place to receive the destructive attention of the Communists," but that no charges were made against him personally. At the time of his departure he reminded officials of Chou En-lai's statement that foreigners who obeyed the laws could remain. The official replied, "This declaration is purely political and does not hold for your case." [62]

There are many more testimonies of what it was like for missionaries to live under Communist oppression.[63] There are two relatively short ones, however, which have that rare quality of being penetrating in what they reveal of the missionary who speaks, shaking in what they do to the one who reads. The first is a sensitive account of prison life as told by Father André Bonnichon in his small pamphlet *Cell 23—Shanghai*.[64] Although it is quite clear how difficult the poor sanitation, miserable food, infrequent, germ-infected baths, and frequent indoctrination sessions were for the fifty-year-old Jesuit, through his eyes the pain and agony of the Chinese with whom he shared his cell are even clearer. Par-

---

[61] *CMBA* IV (V) (May, 1952), 415.

[62] *CMBA* VII (May, 1955), p. 445.

[63] In addition to sources already cited, one may consult the following for the experiences of Catholic missionaries: Alain van Gaver, *J'ai été Condamné à la Liberté* (Paris: Le Centurion, 1953); Ludwig Lenzen, *In China bebt die Erde: Das Schicksal der deutschen Kansu-Mission* (Berlin: Morus Verlag, 1961); James A. McCormick, *Blueprint for Enslavement* (St. Paul, Minn.: Catechetical Guild Educational Society, 1952); Edward McElroy, *Life in Communist China* (Dublin: Browne and Nolan, 1958); Jean Monsterleet, *Martyrs in China*, trans. Antonia Pakenham (London: Longmans, Green and Co., 1956); Raphael Montaigne, *China in Chains* (Chicago: Franciscan Herald Press, 1958); Generoso de Nino, *Il vero volto della Cina* (Sulmona: Tipografia Labor, 1955); Richard Reid and Edward J. Moffett, *Three Days to Eternity* (Westminster, Md.: Newman Press, 1956); Rémy [Gilbert Renault-Rouler], *Pourpre des Martyrs* (Paris: Librairie Arthème Fayard, 1953); Ambrose Rust, *Die Rote Nacht: Schweizer-missionare erleben den Kommunismus in China* (Munich: Rex Verlag, 1956); *But Not Conquered*, ed. Bernard T. Smyth (Dublin: Browne and Nolan, 1958); Efrem Trettel, *Rivers—Rice Fields—Souls*, trans. Else Micallef (Chicago: Franciscan Herald Press, 1965); Florence Wedge, *Franciscan Nun in China: Sister Mary Joseph Hubrich* (Pulaski, Wis.: Franciscan Publishers, 1963).

[64] (Oxford: Catholic Social Guild, 1955), reprint from *Études* and *The Month*.

ticularly staggering is the pressure to say anything, to inform on someone, just to get out to one's family. The hopeless family conditions of that time were made vivid by the pitiful assortment of articles a wife managed to get together to send to her imprisoned husband on the biweekly occasions when sending such things was allowed. Visits were not allowed.

The other testimony is by Alberto-Felix Verwilghen, who writes of his experience as the only foreigner among thousands of Chinese workmen on the Mongolian desert, ordered by Communist officials to build a dike where one had never existed before.[65] As part of this mass of men he submits to what admittedly is tyranny, recognizing that in the process everyone must internalize any independent thoughts or questions. This he hated, of course, but he admits freely that it was exhilarating to work in common with his fellows, and that the new Communist bosses evoked in him a kind of consent to work in a common cause, in spite of the fact that he knew they hated religion and made life for the church increasingly difficult. This incredible combination, of wanting to participate in the life of six hundred million people, but at the same time "to feel in my soul and my body their bitterness and their contradictions, the rape and the mutilation of conscience," [66] is what he calls "the monstrous lie."

The statistics, clothed with flesh and bone and spirit by the personal accounts of these men and women, are quite striking. In 1948 there were 5,496 Catholic foreign missionaries in China: 3,046 priests, 414 brothers, and 2,036 sisters. By January, 1951, the total number had been reduced to 3,222; and by January, 1952, the number had dropped further to 1,848. *Fides,* the Catholic news agency, reported that 1,240 Catholic missionaries left China in 1951. There were about 750 at the beginning of 1953, less than 250 by early 1954, and less than 90 at the beginning of 1955. A terse account in *Mission Bulletin* for January, 1956, states that 16 priests and 11 sisters remained, that 13 of the priests, including one bishop, were in prison. It is quite probable that most if not all of

[65] Albert-Felix Verwilghen, "An Experience" [Part II of "The Church of Silence," a symposium], *Cross Currents* VI (Spring, 1956), 108-18.
[66] *Ibid.,* p. 45.

the sisters were engaged in a school for children of foreign diplomats in Peking, where eight of them taught until 1966.[67]

Two brief comments on these statistics appear to be in order. At the beginning of 1952, when practically all Protestant missionaries had left China, almost two fifths of the pre-Communist Catholic missionary force were still in that country. The second observation is that regardless of the order by the Catholic hierarchy to missionaries to remain at their posts, excepting the aged, infirm, and ill, 2,274, or half of the 1948 Catholic missionary force, were expelled or left of their own accord or met death between 1948 and the end of 1950.

INTERPRETING THE EXODUS

The overriding consideration in the stories of Protestant and Catholic missionaries, and their arrests, trials, and imprisonments, is that the Communist government was seldom content simply to deport them, which has happened in many countries throughout Christian missionary history. It was essential to the Communist strategy to find these missionaries guilty of some crime, presumably to justify their expulsion, whether to the outside world, to the Chinese people, or to themselves. So a worn-out radio receiver is found in a closet and the missionary is accused of possessing a radio transmitter on which he sends messages to the enemy. Or another enthusiastic search group finds a typewriter which they judge to be a telegraphic instrument.

Reports which busy missionaries ground out in order to gain greater support at home, usually at the expense of time which might have been devoted to their assigned jobs, were scanned carefully by Communist agents. If by chance any figures about the economy of the country or social conditions were included, the missionary was accused of espionage. The time-honored missionary stories, which stressed the plight of those who needed the gospel in order to shake loose a few more pennies from sending churches, were evidence to Communist agents of derogatory slurs against China. Espionage and cultural aggression were the recurrent

[67] Figures from *CMBA* VI (February 1954), 180; VI (September 1954), 601; VII (January 1955), 83-85; VIII (January 1956), 85; XII (September 1960), 680. Also from *Fides*, December 15, 1951, NE 357.

themes in trials of missionaries all over the country. For these offenses long prison sentences under grim conditions were meted out, and ostensibly for such offenses missionaries were deported from their land of adoption and field of service.

Although it seems ludicrous to make a case for aggression with such odd evidence, it is well to remember, as the Chinese do, that missionaries have entered China on the coattails of Western political power. Whether the mid-twentieth-century corps of missionaries actually had political connections or not, their forebears profited sufficiently from unequal treaties and various humiliating incidents to place several succeeding generations in a bad light. Leonard Outerbridge is somewhat extreme when he says that each of the five exoduses of missionaries from China "has resulted from the repercussions of political entanglements." [68] In the fifth exodus, at any rate, it seems logical to put more weight on a Communist government which quickly came to the conclusion that missionaries had to go. Friendship with the Nationalist government, citizenship in a Western nation, or mention of political issues could be cited along with countless other reasons for sending them on their way.

All that has been said above might apply to Protestants as well as to Catholics, but the Catholic missionary had to deal with an additional factor—his absolute loyalty to the Vatican. Since the Vatican was heralded as a bulwark against Communism, Catholic missionaries were in a highly vulnerable position in a country which had recently come under the control of a militant Communist government.

Although many missionaries undoubtedly were hurt by the charges and accusations leveled against them in the press and in accusation meetings, they were in time able to accept the fact that old friends and colleagues in the Chinese Christian community who had turned accuser were doing so under pressure. Chou En-lai and others had made it clear that the ties with imperialism had to be cut, and cut decisively, if the church was to continue. In the long run one's own good name did not matter nearly so much as the

[68] *The Lost Churches*, p. 159. A convenient collection of articles which illustrates a wide variety of Chinese attitudes toward Christian missions may be found in Jessie G. Lutz, ed., *Christian Missions in China: Evangelists of What?* (Boston: D. C. Heath, 1965).

future of the church in China, however limited and circumscribed its position might be.

"Barnabas" records the instance of a Chinese pastor who signed an antimissionary statement, but assured his missionary friend that the attack should not be taken personally but simply as a means by which the pastor hoped to survive in the new order. It never occurred to the Chinese pastor, according to "Barnabas," that the Westerner was not concerned about a personal affront, but for the principle of truth which had been violated by statements which were clearly false in the document which the pastor had signed.[69] The fact that an older missionary's thirty- or forty-year record of service might be blackened in the eyes of friends who in their hearts knew better is a negligible matter. On the other hand, that the missionary movement should be depicted as nothing but cultural aggression by imperialist nations to a whole generation "who knew not Moses" was heartbreaking indeed.

It is possible to note with Paul Varg "the paternalistic attitude" of many of the missionaries and especially the sense of racial superiority among a few of them.[70] Or one may accept his thesis that Christian missionaries and the American government did not grasp what China's real needs were, although it is not clear what a foreign religion or a foreign government could have done in terms of the economic and political needs which Varg stresses.[71] The point is that the Communists and their supporters saw the Christian mission as nothing but imperialism. *All* the people connected with it were imperialists.

Practically every time Wu Yao-tsung, leading advocate of the Three-Self Movement, opened his mouth or took pen in hand he

[69] Barnabas [pseud.], *Christian Witness in Communist China* (London: SCM Press, 1951).

[70] Paul A. Varg, *Missionaries, Chinese, and Diplomats* (Princeton: Princeton University Press, 1958), p. 321.

[71] *Ibid.*, pp. 319-26. Varg makes the point that missionaries did suggest the imperialism which the Communists seized on, often in spite of themselves. Missionaries have also realized this. With great soul-searching, a group who returned to America recognized that their higher standard of living, control of the purse strings, tendency to dominate affairs in the church, while not precisely imperialism, did contribute to that image in the minds of people other than Communists. This recognition was expressed in a most important document, *Lessons Learned from the Experience of Christian Missions in China*, published in mimeographed form by the NCCCUSA., 1951.

referred to the consular or governmental relations of Robert Morrison, or to E. C. Bridgman's advocacy of the political value of missionary work.[72] When he needed a more modern example Y. T. Wu would cite the appointment of Presbyterian Leighton Stuart, President of Yenching University, as American Ambassador to the Nationalist government, to show how missionaries were utilized by the imperialist nations. And so it went into the 1960's: with missionaries dead, deported, or in jail, one could read an occasional article in the mainland press on the imperialist aggression of missionaries.[73]

That men under pressure to demonstrate their patriotism should make such blanket judgments is not surprising, nor is it surprising that people around them continually subjected to such barrages should believe and propagate them. It is surprising and even incredible that European observers, both from within and without the church, should accept uncritically the wholesale indictment of missionaries and the missionary movement. Dr. Hewlett Johnson, when Dean of Canterbury, toured China in 1952 and came up with the observation that the Communist government would not countenance persecution of missionaries or Christians. He acknowledged persecutions in "isolated places" if missionaries before liberation had "been actively supporting the bitter persecution of Chiang Kai-shek," or if they had not actively tried "to restrain the brutalities of the landlords, or protested against the shameful poverty of the peasant workers." [74] Although Johnson did not say so explicitly, he implicitly accepts the charges that most of the missionaries were spies or in other ways promoted the interests of American im-

---

[72] E.g., "New Life for the Chinese Christian Church," reprinted in CMBA IV (V) (March, 1952), 237-40.

[73] H. C. Taussig, "Religion and State in China," Eastern World XI (February, 1957), 12-14, even heard from the head of the Religious Affairs Bureau that Catholic missionaries were welcome to visit China, in spite of their previous political acts. But Wu En-p'u, "Concerning the Problems of Foreign Missionaries' Activities in China during the Sixteenth and Seventeenth Centuries," Hsin Chien-she [New Construction], March, 1960, criticizes another writer who maintained that the Jesuits did a few good things in spite of economic motives. (In URS, April 22, 1960, pp. 88-104.) See also attacks on alleged Catholic missionary efforts to control the people of Mongolia in Li-shih Yen-chiu [Historical Research], 5-6, 1964, summarized in China Notes III (July, 1965), 3-4.

[74] Hewlett Johnson, China's New Creative Age (London: Lawrence and Wishart, 1953), p. 110.

perialism. Since he does not distinguish between missionaries of various nationalities, it must be presumed that he included British and European missionaries as promotors of American imperialism.

A Professor Dobretsberger of Graz, Austria, visited China in 1956, then wrote a pamphlet entitled *Catholic Life in Today's China* which was published in East Germany. Blaming the poor situation for Catholics in China on the "mass flight of foreign missioners," he tells of a Pastor Simon Wang, a mailman John Tien, and the Vicar General of Peking, Francis Li, who "with bitterness in their otherwise smiling faces" told him:

"The foreign missioners left their flock in the most difficult period. Although those missioners, who had a good record, could doubtlessly have remained here even after 1949, they clearly didn't have the courage. They were foreigners; China wasn't their homeland. So they fled to their own country in order to ensure their own safety." [75]

Dobretsberger heard an even more astounding interpretation from Ho Chen-hsiang, the head of the Bureau of Religious Affairs:

In 1949 . . . the foreign missioners were already prepared for the coming events. Most of them left the country, and in not a few cases, they took with them every movable piece of church property. Then we expelled all those whom we proved guilty of counterrevolutionary activities. The investigations of these activities were at that time very objective and reliable. Those who were not guilty could remain, yet only ten Catholic missioners chose to remain, as for example, the American Bishop Walsh. [76]

Both the catalog of events related, as well as events which came after 1956, which will be considered in succeeding chapters, reveal how ridiculous these statements are. It is like a host who makes it quite plain to his visitor that he is not welcome, so the visitor takes his leave. Later the host says, "He left of his own accord!" Such twisted logic might make the above remarks applicable to Protestant missionaries who believed they were not welcome and decided to leave, but Ho and company were speaking of Catholic

[75] Quoted in John Fleckner, "The Catholic Church in China," *CMBA* XII (September, 1960), 679-83, quote from p. 679.
[76] *Ibid.*, pp. 679-80.

missionaries, who, except for the ill and aged, were under orders to stay and had to be ejected.

A former Canadian missionary to China, Mary Austin Endicott, and a British journalist, Peter Townsend, also raised no question about the statement both heard in China that missionaries were not deported or otherwise forced to leave, but that they chose to go.[77] Mrs. Endicott, in contrasting Catholics with Protestants, commends those Protestants who "appreciated the situation" and chose to go home, and gives the Catholics a black mark for their land holdings and political intrigue.[78] Townsend quotes a student who condemned the missionary head of a college in China who, as a "guest of China," allowed Kuomintang (Nationalist Party) "thought control." [79] Missionaries were accused on many occasions of supporting the Kuomintang or failing to oppose this or that Nationalist program or activity.

These critics do not suggest what the missionary, as a citizen of a foreign country, and indeed a guest, might have done, other than to work with the Communists, who in turn have maintained consistently that there is no real working together for Marxists and Christians. It would be interesting to ask the student interviewed by Mr. Townsend, and Mr. Townsend himself, if a missionary who remained in China after the Communist takeover should criticize a policy or practice of the Communist government. The reply would probably be that there is nothing to criticize.

Although some critiques of the missionary movement in China have been unjust or on too sweeping a scale, one must not ignore the fact that there was deep-seated resentment of foreigners in general and missionaries in particular among many Christians of China. The deep personal friendships which existed between Chinese Christians and missionaries did not mean that traditional Chinese mistrust of the foreigner had disappeared.

Missionaries gave selflessly of spirit and strength in the life of the church and were instruments of help and comfort to many people, but this only added to the burden in many instances. It is

[77] Mary Austin Endicott, *Five Stars over China* (Toronto: privately printed, 1953), pp. 393-402; Peter Townsend, *China Phoenix: The Revolution in China* (London: Jonathan Cape, 1955), p. 334.
[78] Endicott, *Five Stars*, pp. 402-4.
[79] Townsend, *China Phoenix*, pp. 333-34.

difficult to receive aid and not resent the one who gives it, especially if the one aided has not lost sight of the notion that his land is the middle country, the center of the world. That this resentment was expressed so bitterly and on occasion with violence is difficult to explain, either by those who expressed the bitterness or by those who received it. One may hazard the guess that the Chinese regret it, and those who received it are inclined to ask forgiveness for all men, even themselves.

There were those who looked back upon the exodus of missionaries from China and wrote "First Thoughts on the Debâcle of Christian Missions in China," [80] or with David Paton said, "We were wrong . . . God found us wanting." [81] Words such as debacle, failure, and collapse were on many lips as addresses were made and booklets issued on the "lessons" which were to be learned.[82]

One of the most thoughtful interpretations is to be found in a relatively recent volume by Austin Fulton, entitled *Through Earthquake, Wind, and Fire: Church and Mission in Manchuria, 1867-1950* [83] He aligns himself with those who saw validity in much of the judgments quoted above, but who also noted a fallacy in the conclusion that withdrawal or expulsion of missionaries from any field meant that a mission had failed. He is aware of many mistakes made by missionaries, but he asserts that missionaries did "build a church that could stand on its own feet and was willing to accept responsibility." [84] Missionaries also stimulated in that church the recognition of the need for Bible study, of the responsibility for evangelism, and of the need to recognize the leadership of the Holy Spirit.

With unsensational but determined candor, Fulton goes on to

[80] An article by an anonymous author which appeared in *International Review of Missions* (October, 1951).

[81] *Christian Missions and the Judgment of God* (London: SCM Press, 1953), p. 54.

[82] For example, the document *Lessons Learned from the Experience of Christian Missions in China*, cited in note 71, and Victor E. W. Hayward, *Ears to Hear, Lessons from the China Mission* (London: Edinburgh House Press, 1955).

[83] (Edinburgh: St. Andrews Press, 1967). In the seventh chapter, pp. 295-339, Fulton credits an unpublished manuscript by Dr. John Stewart, entitled "The Lessons of China," as a source for much of his (Fulton's) interpretation.

[84] *Through Earthquake*, pp. 328-29.

acknowledge, however, that missionaries were "tainted with imperialism" and "unconsciously arrogant," that the church established was weak theologically, and that mission and church lacked unity, mobility, and imagination. He quotes from an unpublished paper, "The Lessons of China" by Dr. John Stewart, the following statement:

One of the bad failures was that almost no missionary seems to have realized that China was ripe for revolution. The need for it was acute. It had been brewing since the middle of the last century.[85]

Although there is hardly enough evidence to speak of the failure of the total missionary movement in China, one may point indeed to many failures. One must also make the distinction when speaking positively: although it may not be possible to claim any permanent or lasting contribution for the Christian mission in China, it is possible to recognize individual contributions made by particular and sometimes unique people at quite specific times and places. Thus, with frank recognition of both failures and contributions, one records the end of foreign missionary service in the mainland of China as we have known it in this generation.

[85]*Ibid.*, pp. 330-37. Quotation from p. 337.

III

Eradicating Christianity's Foreign Connections: Institutions

Institutions are a perennial problem for the missionary movement. Many of them have seen long periods of service to church and society, but any one of them may reveal at some time in its history the ease with which an institution gets into a rut of self-satisfaction. Some institutions point with pride to their record in evangelism and are accused from within and without of using education or medical care to win converts. Institutions whose advocates say that the best witness to the gospel is quality teaching or merciful care of orphans are criticized for not being sufficiently evangelistic. Great sums of money have been spent in establishing schools and hospitals, only to discover that their continued maintenance is beyond the capacity of local churches to bear. Bishop Ford, for example, just before the Communist takeover, wrote an article in which he maintained that the Roman Catholic Church had entirely too many buildings for the size of its constituency in China.[1]

In the following survey of how Christian institutions fared in China, first schools, both Catholic and Protestant, will be discussed with emphasis on the universities. The emphasis in the treatment of hospitals and orphanages is on Roman Catholic institutions; the consideration of literature agencies and Bible society work is limited to Protestant programs.

[1] Francis X. Ford, "Mission Buildings in China," *CMBA* I (II) (October, 1949), 104-6.

THE ELIMINATION OF CHRISTIAN HIGHER EDUCATION

From the beginning of Protestant Christian work in China there was an emphasis on education and on the development of schools: primary, middle, and collegiate. The Christian colleges and universities were a striking phenomenon in themselves by the beginning of this century. The most prominent of these institutions proved to be union enterprises in which several mission boards cooperated. Thirteen such colleges and universities had a close working relationship with each other and made joint appeals for funds in America through the United Board for Christian Colleges in China. These schools were Yenching University (Peking), Huachung University (Wuchang), the University of Nanking and Ginling College, both in Nanking, Fukien Christian University and Hwa Nan College, both in Foochow, Soochow University, St. John's University (Shanghai), the University of Shanghai, Cheloo or Shantung University (Tsinan), Hangchow University, Lingnan University (Canton), and West China Union University (Chengtu).[2] Although in need of funds and personnel, all these schools had weathered the war years in such a way that administrators, teachers, and students faced the late 40's with a remarkable *esprit de corps* and had great hopes for the future.

It is, of course, impossible to relate the details of the Communist takeover of all these institutions. There is particularly good source material on two universities in Peking—Yenching, referred to above, and Catholic Fujen University. I shall concentrate on these two and make only brief references to others.

By the middle of 1949, the new Communist government had issued two official statements with respect to the church and higher education that gave some hope to Christians that these institutions might continue. The Shanghai Municipal Education Department

[2] The history of most of these schools has been told in a series of volumes published by the United Board of Christian Colleges in China, now the United Board for Christian Higher Education in Asia, New York. Those volumes consulted in this study are as follows: Charles Hodge Corbett, *Shantung Christian University* (Cheloo), 1955; Clarence Burton Day, *Hangchow University*, 1955; Dwight W. Edwards, et al., *Yenching University*, 1959; Mary Lamberton, *St. John's University*, 1955; W. B. Nance, et al., *Soochow University*, 1956; Roderick Scott, *Fukien Christian University*, 1954; Mrs. Lawrence Thurston and Ruth M. Chester, *Ginling College*, 1955; L. Ethel Wallace, *Hwa Nan College*, 1956.

70

(of the Cultural Control Commission of the Military Control Commission) said with respect to mission schools, apparently in a directive to its cadres:

Toward mission schools, be sure not to look down on them, but these schools must certainly keep the laws of the People's Government, and follow directives with care. Foreigners may teach, but they absolutely cannot, as before, impose an enslaving education. The property of the school cannot be treated as private property; it cannot be moved or sold privately at will. The school affairs are the People's affairs. Any teacher, servant, or student of the school whatever has the right to inquire about school affairs.[3]

The prerogatives thus given to teachers, students, and servants to "inquire" into school affairs, which opened the door to interminable grievance sessions in which the administration was always wrong, became the order of the day in Catholic and Protestant schools throughout the country. Students who felt they had received an unfair grade in the past, teachers who were ambitious, or a janitor who thought he was underpaid could cause serious trouble. Obviously in numerous instances there was just cause for complaint, but as time wore on, the trend was established that the complaint was justifiable automatically and had to be satisfied since it had been made by "the people." Students might accept or reject the confessions of past or present sins, real or imaginary, by teachers and administrators. The administration itself retained no power of decision with respect to any aspect of school life.

The second official statement was made by Chou Yang, Minister of Education of the Provisional Government of Peking, to Father Harold Rigney, listed as ex-rector of Fujen University, in June, 1949. Chou Yang said that no written laws or orders had yet been made, but that the following policy applied: schools which "obey laws and regulations of the People's Government and are not against the . . . New Democratic Principles, will be permitted to exist." [4] One can read between the lines a death knell for Christian institutions. They were already judged to be against the "new

[3] In *Ta Kung Pao*, June 9, 1949, translated in *CMBA* I (II) (November, 1949), 272.
[4] *CMBA* II (III) (March, 1950), 261.

principles" *per se* and thus would not be permitted. Allowance was made in the policy, however, for guidance and supervision by church leaders, plus "necessary and possible assistance according to their history and government." [5] When asked what rights the church had in the administration of Fujen, Chou replied:

I do not understand how "right" here is explained concretely. Generally speaking, it is an infringement upon Chinese educational rights when foreigners establish schools in China. If the foreign friends really want to assist the Chinese people, and not aim to invade the Chinese people, they should give up all demands and feelings for privileges of school adminis-tration. They should give [real, not merely formal] important adminis-trative powers to the Chinese, rely upon the Chinese, and have the same position as the Chinese professors. [6]

Requests might be "drafted" by the university council to reduce expenses and the number of students and sent to the Higher Education Committee of the government for approval. Staff members were to be engaged only by the university council, which with the Staff Members' Association had authority to decide "powers" of staff members. [7]

A university would be required to satisfy "proper democratic claims of the students," who had the right to organize associations and "to appoint representatives to participate in the university ad-ministration under certain conditions." The first matter of concern in finances was whether finances "agreed with the demands of the people." "Demands of the church" was a secondary concern, and had to be harmonized with the first. [8]

The Minister of Education affirmed that "Material Dialectics" and "Historical Materialism" were required courses, and had the following to say about courses in religion:

Education and religion must be separated, because the cultural and educational work under the New Democratic Principles is national, scientific, and for the masses. If religion should be taught as a regular course in the classrooms for religious propagation then it would be

[5] *Ibid.*
[6] *Ibid.*, p. 262.
[7] *Ibid.*
[8] *Ibid.*

contrary to our educational policy. . . . The Communist Party and the People's Government permit the freedom of religion and permit missionary works [in the schools] after classes. If the aforementioned courses are given for scholastic research, they can be given as elective courses, but the University must guarantee that the students really take said courses entirely on their free will and that no coercion is used.[9]

The minister's concluding word was that Fujen in the past had oppressed Chinese staff members and must now cooperate with them. If mistakes were corrected and said cooperation took place on "an equal basis in a democratic spirit, . . . we still welcome you." [10]

Parenthetically one must note that the Nationalist government passed a law in 1929 which also forbade required courses in religion:

Private schools are not permitted to give religion as a required subject nor is any religious propaganda permitted in class instruction. In private schools founded by religious bodies, students shall not be compelled nor induced to participate.[11]

Although on paper both Nationalists and Communists allowed religion as an elective course only, a Catholic editor points out that throughout the whole Nationalist period, courses in religion were "bootlegged" under such headings as philosophy and ethics.[12] On the other hand, the Communists barely allowed electives and these for only a short time.

Following the interview with the Minister of Education, Father Rigney stated in an address on June 19, 1949, that the Deputy Director of the Bureau of Education "has told us that religious courses which the church considers as of moment can be taught in the university." [13] Although there was some cause to rejoice, it soon became clear that any religion courses allowed were far out on the elective fringe, and that courses setting forth Communist theory on various subjects were to be in the main stream. The

[9] *Ibid.*, pp. 262-63.
[10] From Communist-approved English translation of minutes of meeting, published in *CMBA* II (III) (March, 1950), 261-63.
[11] Quoted in *CMBA* I (October, 1948), 211.
[12] *Ibid.*
[13] *CMBA* I (II) (October, 1949), 178.

North China Higher Education Committee (government) announced in the fall of 1949 that

every university, college, academy, and normal school must require all students in all departments to follow courses in historic and dialectic materialism and in the doctrine of the New Democracy. Both courses are to be given three hours a week during one semester.

Colleges of Arts and Law are to have another required course, three hours a week for one school year, in approved political economy.[14]

Obviously the men to teach such courses had to be approved by the government, and they were often assigned to the schools by the government.

A variation was recorded at Tsinku University in Tientsin, where the students demanded, along with the reformation of the school, that "the Fathers permit and favour the teaching of Marxism, communism, and atheism." [15] The priests refused, the students demanded their resignations, and the rector and all priests on the faculty resigned. Since all the major courses were taught by priests (however unfortunate in the mid-twentieth century), all these courses were suspended. The students requested the priests to reconsider their decision. The rector of the university was invited to discuss matters with the mayor of the city, who apologized and asked the priests to continue. The rector replied that he had been asked to resign and that the whole matter was not of his doing. Then the military governor intervened and asked the priests to continue. He gave them signed guarantees they would not be held to teach subjects opposed to Catholicism and that further disturbances and attacks on the Catholic religion would not be permitted. The military governor then issued the following directive:

The liberty of everyone to search out truth and embrace religion will be strictly honored. At the same time, no student will be obliged to attend lectures on religion.

However, the faith of those who have embraced religion will be respected by disbelievers. Insulting language and disturbances will in nowise be tolerated.

Only those controversies in the course of intellectual investigation

[14] In *CMBA* I (II) (November, 1949), 293.
[15] *CMBA* II (III) (April, 1950), 403-4.

which pertain directly to the study of religion will be countenanced in their proper place.[16]

The statement concludes by saying that the students should study and "offer" their help, that the university council should accept at least in part their suggestions, and that financial burdens on the students should be moderate. Once again there is an illustration of the sense of fair play on the part of the military, which was observed in many instances in various parts of China.

In spite of such reassuring statements, the situation in church-related institutions deteriorated rapidly in 1950, culminating on October 12 with the takeover of Fujen by the government.[17] On the other hand, the following statement concerning Ginling College in Nanking is illustrative of a fairly typical, nonextreme, situation:

For about a year and a half after the Communist regime took over Nanking, a large part of college life went on very much as before. The noticable differences were frequent interruptions of work for special lectures, parades, and other political functions usually announced at the last moment, thus involving constant changes in other plans and programs; the large amount of time given regularly by both students and teachers to discussion groups and other meetings which diminished inevitably the time and strength left for regular work; and the formation of the "Labor Union" of servants and faculty and staff, which gradually took over certain aspects of college administration.[18]

Communist strategy in the schools, Catholic and Protestant, utilized every possible device to win the student mind. All schools reported that students and faculty had to listen to interminable lectures and to participate in intensive discussion groups. Communist students quickly gained control of these groups from Christian and other non-Communist students.[19] The Young Communist League, which had been present in cells in every college and university, blossomed forth as a most powerful organization. The leader of a

[16] *CMBA* II (III) (July-August, 1950), 679.
[17] There is an account of the takeover of Fujen University by Helen Ferris, *The Christian Church in Communist China to 1952* (Lackland Air Force Base [Texas]: Air Force Personnel and Training Research Center, 1956), pp. 19-20. Father Rigney gives an extended version in *Four Years in a Red Hell*, chapters I and II.
[18] Thurston and Chester, *Ginling College*, p. 144.
[19] Lamberton, *St. John's*, p. 249.

school's student committee possessed great power, and often claimed to be able to get a job for a student after graduation or to be able to kill his chances for a job, depending on the student's response to "re-education."

"Political courses" or "big courses" were introduced in all schools: Historical Materialism and Social Revolution, Principles of the New Democracy, Political Economy, and the History of Social Development. The first two appear to have been required of all students.[20] Courses in the Russian language were introduced, and in some instances Russian texts were substituted for English texts in the natural and social sciences. Dwight Edwards states, however, that for Yenching the emphasis was on the Chinese language in the classroom and on the use of Chinese textbooks.[21] Teachers for these courses had to be approved by the government authorities.

Although Christian students were steadily encircled and deprived of leadership positions in campus associations, those who were able to write from Christian schools during 1950 referred to a vital Christian life on campus. In the face of Communist anti-Christian propaganda, Fukien Christian University students worked harder in witness to their faith.[22] Even freshmen at Hangchow University showed "real interest in religion," and there were numerous Bible study and inquirers' classes.[23] Both Hwa Nan and Ginling Colleges reported that chapel was well attended, although Ruth Chester says that some Christian students were drawn into the "progressive circle" because it seemed that Communist social goals might be more quickly realized.[24]

As a sidelight to what was going on in Christian institutions there is a description of how Christian students were faring at Peking University, a government institution which was regarded as the top university in China. Maria Yen, who at the time was not a Christian, indicates that she and her fellow students did not have a very high opinion of either Catholic or Protestant students

[20] Edwards, *Yenching*, p. 432.
[21] *Ibid.*, p. 426.
[22] Scott, *Fukien*, p. 122.
[23] Day, *Hangchow*, p. 138.
[24] Wallace, *Hwa Nan College*, p. 125; Thurston and Chester, *Gingling College*, pp. 144-45.

and had little use for Catholic priests and nuns. She says that the turning point came for Christian groups on the campus when they began to hear reports of mobs invading rural churches, while local military and police officers stood aside and refused to oppose what represented the "will of the masses."

In the face of this campaign, even the few religious groups which had once shown some signs of life at Peita (Peking University) withered now into complete silence. The more courageous and the more devout continued to attend services and to practice their faith. But the services were reduced to dim, flickering affairs in candlelight, attended by a handful of the really dedicated. Catholic priests and sisters were compelled to move off the campus. Choirs were disbanded. . . . Some Christian students lashed out in furious denunciations of their former thoughts and actions in an effort to get back into official favor, declared their resolution to learn from the people and their determination to cease serving the imperialists and their cultural aggression. Such people were not greeted with enthusiasm, particularly since some of us knew that behind their own doors they continued to kneel and pray. As far as we were concerned, they were the real "rice Christians," who followed the trail of rice back to the state.[25]

Perhaps it was that "handful of the really dedicated" which ultimately impressed the writer of this paragraph, for she later became a Catholic. It is her attitude as a non-Christian, however, toward those who tried to play both sides that makes her statement so valuable.

In the midst of this muddled situation with its increasing number of difficulties, the Chinese Communists entered the Korean war. About a month afterward, on December 16, 1950, the American government froze Chinese assets in America. Anti-American feelings throughout China came to a climax, for Christian institutions at least, in the Administrative Yuan (Council) action, December 29, 1950, which demanded that "Chinese Christian churches and other organizations should immediately sever all relations with American mission boards." [26] The council, with Chou En-lai in the

---

[25] Maria Yen, *The Umbrella Garden* (New York: The Macmillan Co., 1954), p. 122.

[26] *CHIBUL*, October 31, 1951. A *yuan* is a council of which there are several types, legislative, judicial, etc., in Chinese political organization.

chair, went on to say that organizations "which have been carrying on service projects, such as medical and benevolent organizations," might continue if finances permitted, and if a board of managers suitable to the government was responsible for carrying out government regulations. Should finances in such organizations be insufficient, the organization might ask the government for funds or ask the government to take over the institution.

The December, 1950, resolutions passed by the Administrative Yuan contained the euphemistic statement that mission boards might give institutions unconditionally to Chinese churches, and that these churches might receive part or all of said gift. Thus, even if a mission board were to turn over an institution to the Chinese church, the church would not necessarily receive the gift. An institution might receive balances which were on deposit abroad before December 29, 1950. Every organization which received funds by post had to register such receipts with the government.

A few days later Kuo Mo-jo, vice-chairman of the council, stated that the government was assisting "American-subsidized cultural, educational and relief organizations, and religious bodies [to become] completely self-sufficing [self-sustaining or supporting]." "The American-subsidized relief organizations should be completely taken over and run by the People's Relief Administration of China." He proposed, however, two alternatives for cultural, educational, and medical organizations. One was takeover and transformation into state-owned enterprises; the other was an ambiguously stated plan by which such institutions could be operated by private organizations under control of the government. Finally, "American-subsidized Chinese religious bodies should be brought under complete management of Chinese believers." [27] In this same release Kuo Mo-jo referred to the "great indignation" with which the Chinese people were reacting to the use of cultural, educational, medical, and relief projects by American imperialism.

Teachers, students, medical workers, and employees and workers in the missionary schools, churches, and hospitals in various places have everywhere held patriotic anti-American demonstrations, accused the

[27] "Decision of U.S.-Subsidized Cultural, Educational, Relief Organizations, Religious Bodies," *The Shanghai News*, January 1, 1951. Released by *New China News Agency* [hereafter *NCNA*], Peking, December 30, 1951.

American imperialist elements of reactionary and disruptive activities, and urgently demanded that these organizations be taken over by the government or transformed into bodies completely operated by the Chinese people.[28]

Then Chou En-lai called a conference of Christian leaders in Peking for April 16-21, 1951, to discuss "The Disposal of American-Subsidized Missionary Institutions and Groups," and thus to "work out measures to enable the churches of China to achieve independence in maintenance, administration, and religious teaching." [29] With Ho Chen-hsiang, director of the Religious Affairs Bureau in the chair, Lu Ting-yi, chairman of the Committee on Cultural, Religious, and Educational Affairs of the Administrative Yuan, addressed the group of two hundred delegates, invited guests, and "working comrades" on the ways in which American imperialists had used money and cultural institutions to do all manner of evil things to China. He assumed that all American missionary groups had engaged in cultural aggression, every trace of which should now be uprooted and exposed. This was the same meeting at which the pattern of accusation meetings described in the previous chapter was inaugurated.

In the interim between the State Council meeting of December 29, 1950, and the conference of Christian leaders with Chou En-lai in April, 1951, the two remaining Catholic universities and the first of the Protestant universities came under Communist control. Less than a year after positive assurances (as cited above) were given to Tientsin Catholics by the military governor of that city, Tsinku University was taken over, on January 9, 1951. Aurora of Shanghai followed in March of 1951. Jesuit priests were allowed to live at the latter school until they were finally ordered to evacuate on July 15, four months later. They bade farewell with an open-air Mass attended by a large crowd in spite of heavy rain. Founded in 1903, the school was just shy of its fiftieth anniversary.

The story leading up to the takeover of Yenching University by the government on February 12, 1951, is an absorbing one.[30] Its prestige was such that when its long-time president, Dr. Leighton

[28] *Ibid.*
[29] *Changhai News*, April 19, 1951.
[30] Edwards, *Yenching*, pp. 420-38.

Stuart, was appointed American ambassador to China in 1946, the appointment was welcomed by none other than Chou En-lai, who said that Dr. Stuart would "immediately win the trust of the Chinese people." [31] The university was under an administrative committee until Dr. Lu Chih-wei was made chancellor in February, 1949, after the Communists had taken Peking. It is significant that from November, 1948, the Yenching Board of Managers held no meeting until the time when the school ceased to be a private institution and passed under government control.

In 1949 Yenching was named by the Communist government as one of four universities to continue in Peking. Dr. Lu seemed sure that a *modus vivendi* with the government could be worked out. Dr. T. C. Chao (Chao Tzu-ch'en), dean of the Yenching School of Religion and the most famous Protestant theologian in China, wrote articles hailing the new order. In 1950 and 1951 a number of faculty members volunteered for service in the land reform movement and felt that their ivory tower attitudes had been shattered. But the lectures and discussion groups, the relentless pressures of the new regime and those who backed it, took their toll, so that by 1951 it was clear that the university could not continue as a church-related institution. Dr. Bliss Wiant, a specialist in Chinese church music who was the comptroller during this period, says that Chou En-lai came to Yenching in person to get the keys of the university and its financial records in January, 1951.

Just before the takeover of Yenching, Chancellor Lu's confession of how he was used by the American imperialists in the life of Yenching appeared in the Chinese press.[32] Lu was later denounced by his own daughter as "a Christian who is without political feeling for the Communist Party." [33] He was finally cleared and assigned by the government to do research work.[34] T. C. Chao, accused by

[31] *Ibid.*, pp. 417. On November 24, 1951, however, at an all-day Yenching denunciation meeting, T. C. Chao denounced Stuart, *CHIBUL*, January 15, 1952.

[32] Lu Chih-wei, "U. S. Imperialism as Seen in Yenching University," *Hsin Kuan-ch'a* [New Observer], February 10, 1951; *CURBAC*, August 15, 1951, pp. 2-4. Also translated in the same issue of *CURBAC*, pp. 11-12, is the confession of a Ginling College student, Yin Su-ying, "I have Been Deeply Poisoned by American Cultural Aggression," from *Ta Kung Pao*, April 23, 1951.

[33] *CHIBUL*, August 25, 1952.

[34] Edwards, *Yenching* p. 430.

students of pro-American sympathies, was dismissed from his deanship of the School of Religion and shorn of his clerical privileges and responsibilities in the Sheng Kung Hui.[35]

Roman Catholic observers pointed out that Yenching led Protestant colleges and universities in providing workers for the Communist cause.[36] Communist observers, however, pointed out quite the opposite about Yenching: "As the tuition and boarding fees were rather high, an overwhelming majority of the students came from bureaucrat, landlord, and capitalist families." [37] This "paradise" (Yenching) shut off from the outside world,

had for the past twenty years attracted many professors and students, deepened their utterly erroneous concept of staying above politics and class, made them intoxicated with the luxurious American way of life, and drove some of them to the extent of making themselves the tools of U. S. imperialism for aggression! [38]

It is possible that both judgments represent partial truth. Without question there were students and teachers at Yenching who leaned toward the left along with a host of Chinese intellectuals all over China, but that is hardly to be laid at the door of the school itself. Some of Yenching's most loyal supporters acknowledge, on the other hand, that there was an ivory tower atmosphere, in reaction to which some of Yenching's graduates may have been motivated to join the Communist cause.

Other Protestant universities and colleges were taken over by the government in rapid succession: Huachung University in Wuchang in mid-July of 1951; the University of Nanking and Ginling College were merged and brought under control of the government Ministry of Education on September 19, 1951; West China Union University in Chengtu followed on October 6, 1951. During 1951 almost all the institutions associated with the United Board of Christian Colleges in China were joined by denominational colleges in the new status under the government and designated as "divorced from American missions." [39]

[35] *CHIBUL*, August 25, 1952. Sheng Kung Hui is the designation for the church in China related to the Anglican communion.
[36] *CMBA* I (October, 1948), 197.
[37] *CMBA* VII (February, 1955), 160-67.
[38] *Ibid.*
[39] Summarized from Ferris, *The Christian Church*, pp. 16-22. Cf. *CHIBUL*, November 12, 1951.

Dr. Wu Yi-fang, who had been head of Ginling College for Women, was appointed vice-president of the new institution in Nanking. Dr. Wu tells the story in Mrs. Endicott's book of her new outlook on life as a result of the new order in China.[40] Mrs. Margaret Kiesow, who remained at Cheloo University until September, 1953, testified to a continuing Christian life on the campus and in a nearby church at least until her departure. The Cheloo campus was turned over to the new Shantung Medical College.[41]

Middle schools and primary schools, obviously, were brought under government control and no longer continued as Christian schools. In many instances this was done by direct takeover, but in others the transition was in two distinct steps. Six church middle schools in Canton, for example, were cut off from foreign support in 1951, but were not "officially adopted as government schools" until October, 1953, according to Cora Deng, YWCA secretary.[42]

Catholics estimated at the end of 1951 that nine tenths of their facilities had been either destroyed or confiscated by the government. By the end of 1952 the *China Missionary Bulletin* reported that "of the 13 Catholic universities, 189 secondary schools, 2,011 primary schools, and 2,234 prayer schools providing education for some 320,000 [corrected figure] students, hardly one school remains in Catholic hands today." [43] One of those rare exceptions was the Industrial School in Peking operated by the Salesian fathers. It suffered little interference until January 26, 1954, when the police came and accused the priests of sabotaging the government and refusing to obey the laws. Father Fels asked how one who understood as little Chinese as he did could have talked against the government, but the officers were not impressed and the priests were taken out the back door of the school and deported.[44] Thus, with the exception of a few seminaries which managed to stay open until the late 50's, and the school in which Franciscan Sisters of Mary taught foreign children in Peking by special permission of the government, which school was closed in 1966, Roman Catholic formal education in China ceased.

[40] *Five Stars Over China*, pp. 319-34.
[41] *CHIBUL*, January 18, 1954.
[42] "Christian Life and Activities," *China Reconstructs*, November-December, 1953. Excerpts in *CHIBUL*, January 4, 1954.
[43] *CMBA*, V (VI) (January, 1953), 2.
[44] *CMBA* VI (April, 1954), 389-90.

CONSOLIDATION OF THEOLOGICAL SCHOOLS

Protestant and Catholic seminaries were able to function as relatively independent institutions under a measure of church leadership for a longer period than other schools in both systems were able to do. Nanking Seminary, where all training for the Protestant ministry was eventually consolidated, kept its doors open until 1966. On the other hand, no Roman Catholic seminary as such was still in operation in 1960, and one may assume that this was the case by 1958.

Half the Roman Catholic major seminary at Kaifeng, Honan, was occupied by the authorities in 1949 for use as an indoctrination school; so Christian and Communist studies were going on under the same roof. A reporter commented that the seminarians were getting "a most realistic education." [45] About two years later, in December, 1951, students at the same seminary were sent by the authorities to work with land reform units, which might be more accurately termed thought reform. Ten days after returning to their classrooms the seminarians were ordered by the same authorities to take a forty-day indoctrination course at the Protestant Bible School in Kaifeng with students from all Protestant groups in the Kaifeng area, half of which were young women. Each discussion group was composed of two or three Catholic students, eight Protestant students, and two Communist cadres. They discussed imperialist activity within the church, including Archbishop Riberi, Archbishop Pollio (of Kaifeng), a bishop who had been sentenced to life imprisonment, and the Legion of Mary.

Protestant students acceded to the request to accuse their missionaries as imperialists, but the Catholic students refused to admit any factual basis to the Communist campaign against the Catholic Church or its leaders. The indoctrination course ended with an accusation meeting in which about twenty members of the local Independent Church Committee accused the seminarians

of being running dogs of the imperialists, of insulting the "Reform Committee," of saying that the Communist newspapers printed lies, of being

[45] *CMBA* II (III) (February, 1950), 195.

against the government because they refused to approve the expulsion of Archbishops Riberi and Pollio or the suppression of the Legion of Mary.[46]

A few days after the students were returned to the seminary, Paul Che, a Catholic seminarian who had been one of the chief targets at the accusation meeting, was arrested and imprisoned.

A standard technique for dealing with Catholic seminaries was a compulsory indoctrination course intended to point students toward an autonomous church. Those who proved completely impervious were allowed to return to their homes. This was the case with the Chala Seminary in Peking in 1950, and again with students in Zikawei Seminary in Shanghai in the months after Bishop Kung's arrest in 1955, during which time it was taken over by Patriotic Catholics.[47]

A major portion of the seminary building at Chengtu, Szechwan, was occupied in 1950 and converted into a weaving factory utilizing about 160 workers. The seminarians were permitted to occupy one small section of one wing of the building, in which crowded quarters 78 students continued their studies for a time. Manual labor in the gardens occupied a major portion of the students' time, partially due to the influence of their new neighbors and partially in order to meet some of the financial burdens imposed by heavy taxation of the school and the mission.[48]

At the beginning of the year 1952, there were still 16 Catholic major seminaries in China. One ceased operation during the year, and 2 were occupied, leaving 13. Later reports indicated that 2 of the schools had little difficulty, but 4 others continued in "great misery." News of the others was very limited, but it was estimated that less than 150 seminarians were enrolled in major seminaries and about 180 in the minor seminaries at Christmas, 1952, not including 3 major seminaries from which there had been no information.[49]

The seminary in Peking was closed by the government on Ash Wednesday, 1954. About a year later one finds reference to a minor

[46] *CMBA* IV (V) (October, 1952), 684.
[47] *CMBA* VIII (November, 1956), 692.
[48] *CMBA* II (III) (October, 1950), 874.
[49] *CMBA* V (VI) (February, 1953), 199.

seminary "of the Communists" in Peking, although there were some of the courses usually found in a major seminary. Both the head and the teachers were paid by the government. Of the 50 students, 10 were actually studying theology, 7 were in philosophy, and the remainder were in a minor seminary; but there had been added as required courses "The Love of Country," "The Struggle Against Imperialism," etc., and each Saturday all students were required to participate in a special study group on politics.[50]

When Father Fernand Faucher, the last Canadian Catholic priest in China, was expelled in April, 1955, he reported that there were about 180 students from 10 different dioceses studying in the Zikawei Seminary of Shanghai where he and 7 Chinese priests had been teaching. He stated that the rector, Father Aloysius Chin, had been successful up to that time in preventing Communist indoctrination at Zikawei, one of the most outstanding Catholic seminaries in China.[51] According to a report in mid-1955, it was the only Catholic seminary remaining in China, but this evidently does not include seminaries being run by the Patriotic Catholics. In various periodicals there is mention of seminaries in Tientsin, Fukien, Pu Chi in Shensi, and one for Hupei and Hunan, as well as the one at Zikawei in Shanghai, all apparently in operation in 1957. All were undoubtedly under the control of the Patriotic Catholic movement. In 1957 or 1958, possibly in connection with the Great Leap Forward, all these seminaries closed their doors. The seminary buildings at Zikawei became a center for the indoctrination of youth in 1957, an anti-Catholic museum in 1958, and a center for the Communist People's Committee in 1960.

On his visit to China in 1960, Edgar Snow was told that no Catholic seminary was in existence. He was told that the last Catholic seminary to be closed, probably at Zikawei, had been dissolved in 1958 by the "members" (faculty?) themselves because it was "riddled with past contaminating influences," due to having been "poisoned by the control of Father McCarthy and Bishop Walsh." Snow's informant, a Father Shen, said that he was in a group of Chinese priests who were preparing an appropriate curriculum for a new seminary which could be opened in the old

[50] *CMBA* VII (May, 1955), 463.
[51] *CHIBUL* (August, 1955).

property as soon as they were ready. Mr. Snow himself questioned whether Father Shen spoke sincerely and acknowledged that his remarks may have been colored by the fact that a Party representative was present.[52]

Father Felipe Pardinas, a Mexican Jesuit who managed to visit China in 1965, was told that "the counterrevolutionaries destroyed the preparation of priests," but that "in Peking they [?] are about to build a seminary." [53] Since 1958, visitors to China have been told of plans for this new seminary. Since it was not under way by the fall of 1965, and since even existing schools were closed during the Cultural Revolution which broke the following summer, there is no reason to believe that any Catholic seminary ever was organized or functioned in the 1960's.

During the days when operation of seminaries was becoming increasingly difficult, the story was told of ordained priests who were followed on their rounds by a handful of young candidates for the priesthood. As they walked about, the priests would lecture on theology, church history, and even Latin, and together they would learn the liturgy of the Catholic Church. In 1960 a few young men were said to be receiving a kind of apprentice training under older priests. Father Pardinas was told that preparation of new priests was each local pastor's responsibility, but even this type of informal theological training seems most unlikely today.

Protestant theological education was able to continue on a much steadier note than did training for the Catholic priesthood. During the early years of the Communist regime, first this seminary and then another went through the process of having various faculty members accused of possessing the imperialist taint, to which some confessed and others did not. There were also severe financial problems, since foreign funds had been cut off and the number of students decreased. Courses in politics were added to the curricula of the schools, and care had to be exercised in teaching the standard seminary subjects, but seminary education continued.

The major event in Protestant seminary life was the unification of eleven East China seminaries achieved during a meeting in

---

[52] Edgar Snow, *On the Other Side of the River* (New York: Random House, 1962), p. 557.

[53] "A Visit to Red China," *World Mission* XVII (Fall, 1966), 67.

Shanghai, August 25-29, 1952. The reorganization took place under the sponsorship of the Three-Self Movement whose general secretary, Y. T. Wu, was much involved in the negotiations, was first chairman of the board of directors, and who gave the principal address at the inaugural service on November 1, 1952. The editor of the *China Bulletin*, Dr. Francis P. Jones, who had been a member of the Nanking Theological Seminary faculty in former years and was acquainted with professors from many of the uniting schools, was able even from America to provide penetrating analyses of the curriculum of the new school, the changing composition of its board of directors and faculty, and its policies.[54]

The union institution was called Chinling (or Ginling) Union Theological Seminary, using an older name for the city of Nanking. Its aim was summarized as follows:

To nurture spiritual life, study the Bible, raise the level of understanding of national loyalty, prepare workers for the New Church in China who will serve the people, and press forward the Three-Self Reform Movement.[55]

General principles adopted refer to the Old and New Testaments as the basis of faith, to following the government's Common Program and cooperation with the Three-Self Reform Movement, and to a spirit of cooperation and mutual respect vis-à-vis denominational differences. A significant note is a constitutional provision that the Board of Directors was to be chosen by the Preparatory Committee, later the Executive Committee, of the Three-Self Reform Movement,[56] thus assuring Three-Self control.

The Rev. Ting Kuang-hsun, who had been a secretary of the World's Student Christian Federation, and who was later elected a bishop of the Sheng Kung Hui (Anglican), was chosen the first president of the institution, with a remarkable faculty drawn from the uniting institutions. There were 105 students enrolled in the first year of the new school, with the majority coming from the

---

[54] Beginning with *CHIBUL*, December 29, 1952, and continuing until June, 1962, when *China Bulletin* ceased publication and was succeeded by *China Notes*.

[55] CHIBUL, December 29, 1952.

[56] *Ibid.*

Church of Christ in China, and the Episcopal, Baptist, and Methodist churches. In 1965 several visitors reported 85 students, but it seems quite likely that a major fraction were part-time students. In the early days of the institution two and one-half days a week were devoted to political studies. President Ting said patriotism, not Marxism-Leninism, was taught in the school, and maintained that full academic freedom prevailed; but it was not freedom to "pervert the Scriptures, spread rumors, oppose those fighting for the right, and uphold imperialism." [57] Ting said in 1964 that a half-day each week was devoted to "political discussion," and that each student was required to give twenty days each year to "productive work on the land." [58]

Support for the new seminary came largely from rentals of property owned by the uniting schools, which had been the means of support for individual schools after Western funds were cut off. The union institution also received continuing contributions from the churches. President Ting said in 1953 that no funds were received from the government, and in 1964 that each student was supported by the church from which he came.[59]

A similar unification of institutions in the Peking area took place in the spring of 1953, and again in 1956, resulting in a total of eleven theological schools. The unified institution, called Yenching Union Theological Seminary, had 70 to 80 students in 1956.[60] There were reports in the early 60's that this school had closed, and other reports that it was still open. The most likely conclusion to be drawn is that the Peking seminary became a kind of graduate research center with very few students, whereas the Nanking seminary was the actual center for the training of Protestant clergymen.

The Chungking Theological Seminary led by the Rev. Marcus

[57] *CHIBUL*, May 10, 1953.

[58] "China's Living Church," [Interview with Ralph Lapwood by Cecil Northcott] *Christian Century*, January 13, 1965, p. 40. Lapwood was one of those reporting an enrollment of eighty-five students in the Union Seminary at Nanking.

[59] "Nanking's New Union Theological Seminary," *China Monthly Review* CXXIV (July, 1953, 11-14. Last portion of article in *CHIBUL*, August, 1953. Ting's 1964 statement was reported orally in Hong Kong by a visitor from China.

[60] Edwards, *Yenching*, p. 437.

Cheng (Ch'en Chung-kuei), a conservative evangelist who became an ardent advocate of the new regime and a supporter of the Three-Self Movement, seems to have been the primary training center for ministers in the West China area. Another conservative, the Rev. Chia Yü-ming, was able to continue his Spiritual Cultivation Seminary for several years in Shanghai. The Canton Theological Seminary was still being mentioned in 1956. These schools in Chungking, Shanghai, and Canton probably all closed in the late 50's.

The seminary in Nanking did not reopen for the fall term in 1966, and there has been no report of any classes since that time. There were reports that the faculty, with the exception of Bishop Ting, were still under detention in a camp as of December, 1967, and further reports in late 1968 that Bishop Ting underwent reform by labor in that year but had been released.

HOSPITALS, ORPHANAGES, AND LITERATURE SOCIETIES

Since a large majority of the hospitals in China in 1948 were mission hospitals, and more than half the hospital beds were in these Christian hospitals, the Communists were forced by sheer expediency to move a bit more slowly in taking over these institutions. In many parts of China a priest or nun who knew something of medical care was able to continue a bit longer, even though beset with difficulties. Many church hospitals functioned at full capacity in order to take care of wounded soldiers. In Pakhoi, Kwangtung, a priest changed his school into a "hospital" for wounded soldiers, whereupon the government paid all expenses and allowed him to continue in charge. In West China wounded Communist soldiers were left in a Catholic hospital for a considerable length of time. When their commanding officers finally returned, the soldiers were heard to say to the officers: "You dropped us off here and abandoned us, . . . didn't care how badly we were hurt or . . . if we were dead or alive! . . . Only these foreigners had any sympathy for us." [61]

Since Chinese already held almost all administrative positions, and since Westerners handled hospital funds in only a few cases,

[61] *CMBA* II (III) (June, 1950), 593-94.

the government had only to make the governing boards entirely Chinese in order to have control in the hands of Chinese. Remaining Western doctors and nurses might still be utilized for much needed services. Government doctors and nurses were desperately needed on the Korean front, so Western medical personnel were allowed to continue working longer than their educational and evangelistic colleagues. Those who did remain in such posts were subjected to a series of annoying incidents. Chinese Christian administrators also encountered continuing difficulty with newly organized workers' unions, whose demands for increased wages and more extended vacations escalated quickly with new-found power.

The medical institutions themselves passed under Communist control about the time the colleges and universities did. For example, Union Hospital, a Protestant institution in Hankow, was taken during the summer of 1951, followed gradually by the others. In many cases a hospital would be closed to all but military or Communist Party members or the police, the general public being turned away.

A Catholic hospital in Foochow was turned over to Chinese Catholic clergy to operate in May, 1951, but was taken by the provincial police for their use in October of that year and closed to the public. Government authorities asked the sisters to remain, but they refused to do so if no priest was allowed to enter and administer the sacraments. Members of the hospital staff were pressured by the authorities to accuse the sisters in a meeting, but no one would, so finally the sisters were told they could leave.[62]

By the end of 1951, only 12 of the 216 Catholic hospitals which existed in China in 1948 were still functioning under the aegis of the church. Many of the 800 Catholic dispensaries had also passed from church control, although there were continued reports of Chinese priests and sisters maintaining them wherever possible.[63] In the opinion of one priest, the authorities recognized that a dispensary was for the good of the people and that working in one was useful work.[64]

[62] Ferris, *The Christian Church*, p. 24.
[63] *Ibid.*
[64] *CMBA* II (III) (June, 1950), 601.

Although such may have been the Communist attitude toward small dispensaries and the priests or nuns who worked in them during the transition period, the official position was far different. It is expressed in a relatively recent diatribe against Peking Union Medical College Hospital in which that institution is classified as another instance of American imperialist aggression. The author notes that it was founded by American and British missionaries in 1906, but expresses no particular criticism of them. The main stress is on the fact that "the school was later bought by Rockefeller . . . for the purpose of carrying out cultural aggression against China." There is further emphasis on the fact that only English was spoken in the medical school, that American medical practice was followed in both school and hospital, and that American doctors (all of them) used Chinese people young and old to conduct the most gruesome kind of experiments which were later written up in American medical journals. There is no recognition of any good done or service rendered in all the hospital's previous years; but after liberation and the exposé of imperialist "crimes," the hospital has been able to truly serve the people. Such would be the standard interpretation by the Communists of Christian medical work in China.[65]

The story of Catholic orphanages in China illustrates more than any other the Communist concern to embarrass foreign personnel at any cost. Whereas hospitals were taken over without much fanfare, and the takeover of schools involved charges of espionage and cultural aggression against missionary teachers, the nuns who had worked in orphanages were in numerous cases accused of murdering children, selling their blood for transfusions, plucking out eyes, and eating the food intended for the children. No evidence could be offered to support all these charges unless one should maintain that murder was evidenced by statistics which showed a particularly high rate of deaths in the orphanages. Dr. Leon Volodarsky, Canton WHO director from 1948 to 1951 and onetime chief medical officer of UNRRA, reported extremely high mortality rates of children

[65] *Kung-jen Jih-pao* [Workers' Daily], April 4, 1965; *SCMP*, April 20, 1965, pp. 36-38; summarized in *China Notes* III (July, 1965), 3. The same type of diatribe may be found in *KMJP*, May 26, 1964; *SCMP*, June 2, 1964; pp. 17-18.

brought to the Holy Infant Orphanage in Canton; but he supplemented his figures with additional ones on the high rate of disease, such as tuberculosis and beri-beri, among the children brought to the orphanage. The last mentioned factors were ignored by the Communist authorities when they jailed, on March 11, 1951, five Canadian nuns of the Congregation of the Immaculate Conception, who were alleged to have confessed to "criminal negligence resulting in the deaths of 4,000 infants" in that orphanage.[66] When the Communists first came to Canton they commended the nuns on the cleanliness and efficiency which prevailed. And when the nuns offered to stop taking children, the authorities urged them to continue and "even directed the Red police to bring foundlings picked up on the streets of Canton to the orphanage." [67]

The accusation meeting against the nuns was broadcast and picked up by receivers in Hong Kong. People were aghast at the ferocity of the proceedings, a graphic indication to the outside world of what went on in accusation meetings. Three of the nuns were deported and two were imprisoned; the latter two were allowed to leave China in 1952.

Mrs. Endicott could remember how infants were often received half dead in a Christian orphanage, but she accepted without question the Communist charges against the other orphanages. Basil Davidson, however, in reporting the case accepts without question every detail presented to him by the authorities, or by one who claimed to have carried the babies to the common graves. He does not see how the case could possibly be regarded as an attack upon religion.[68]

Although the Holy Infant Orphanage in Canton became the *cause célèbre* in the drive against orphanages, the story was repeated all over China. An estimate of the 180 orphanages under missionary supervision revealed that in 1952 more than half had been taken over.[69]

An ironic sequel to the Canton orphanage story has it that the

[66] H. Madigan, "Catholic Orphanages in Communist China," *CMBA IV* (V) (June-July, 1952), 447-52.
[67] *Ibid.*
[68] Davidson, *Daybreak in China*, p. 177. Cf. Endicott, *Five Stars.*
[69] *CMBA* IV (V) (June-July, 1952), 447-52. Cf. Raphael Edwards, "The Story of China's Orphanages," *World Mission* III (Summer, 1952), 147-58.

Communists wanted to use a home for the aged in another part of the city. They conducted the smear campaign against the orphanage in order to have reason to close it to children, and therefore have a place to which the aged might be transferred. Thus they would be able to use the former home for the aged for government offices.[70] The story sounds farfetched, but is not entirely contrary to tales of government bureaucracy elsewhere.

Before World War II, agencies producing Christian literature concentrated on the translation of Western religious texts into Chinese. After the war these agencies shifted to a stress on production of indigenous Christian literature. At this point Communist pressures forced a drastic cut in literature production and limited the remaining materials to a steadfast presentation of Communist ideology.

Officials of the Central Publications Bureau in Peking, along with several branch officials, met with seven representatives of Christian publishers, March 16-22, 1951.[71] The conference adopted an "Energetic Plan for the Future of Christian Publications," which included the following principles: (1) to receive no further funds from abroad, (2) to purge their thinking (and that of all Christian publishers) of imperialism and put the Three-Self Movement into effect, (3) to respect and keep the Common Program (of the government), (4) "to immediately proclaim the vitality of the Christian's New Democratic Love of Country," (5) to replace influences of capitalism and imperialism with new thought in keeping with the Chinese church, and (6) to form a united association of Christian publishers as a step in the direction of one publishing body. Several steps were set forth by which the publishers, duly reorganized, should seek first to work together with a division of labor and gradually achieve the one publication body recommended. All their publications were to be carefully scrutinized to see if love of country was sufficiently stressed.[72]

Mary Liu, who was working with the Christian Literature Society in Shanghai, relates through her biographer some of the details which Sun En-san, a representative of the society, told the

---

[70] *Ibid.*
[71] Ferris, *The Christian Church*, p. 75.
[72] *Ibid.*, Appendix E, pp. 71-72.

staff upon his return to Shanghai from the March meeting in Peking. Most of the addresses were made by government officials who promised a subsidy for the united program. There was to be a unified structure for all religious bookshops with the Christian Literature Society Bookshop as central supplier. The YMCA (Association Press), the Sunday School Union, the Baptists, and the Christian Literature Society agreed to the proposed plan and Y. T. Wu was put in charge. Wu left shortly for the Vienna Conference of the World Peace Movement and was too busy spreading its message upon his return to do anything about the literature program. A virtual paralysis of the sale of religious literature resulted.[73]

Miss Liu also says that Sun En-san was rejected by the Communist government as a delegate to the Conference of Christian Leaders which followed in Peking in April, 1951. Sun committed suicide soon afterward, for which he was derided by the Communists. It was the era of accusation meetings and the time when numerous people, including Protestants and Catholics, were being jailed.[74]

By July, 1951, the 136 Christian magazines, newssheets, etc., which were published before 1949 had been reduced to 56, which in turn were reduced to 24 by November of the same year. Only 7 of these were registered with the government. Two of these, *T'ien Feng* (Heavenly Wind), which became the official Three-Self Movement publication, and *Hsieh Chin* (United Progress), the Chinese NCC publication, continued for quite a while before the latter disappeared. From one half to two thirds of the Christian books and tracts examined by a Literature Purging Committee appointed by the Christian literature societies on August 4, 1951, were found to be questionable, some to be suppressed and others to be revised. Miss Liu says only 20 percent remained.[75] Any book that was judged to have an imperialist, capitalistic, or feudalistic point of view, to espouse internationalism at the expense of patriotism, or to support the ecumenical church without "distinguishing friend and

[73] Edward Hunter, *The Story of Mary Liu* (New York: Farrar, Straus, and Cudahy, 1957), pp. 153-57.
[74] *Ibid.*, pp. 161-65.
[75] *Ibid.*

foe," was questionable, as was any book which opposed communism, Russia, the People's Government, Chinese culture, the Oppose America–Aid Korea movement, or the Three-Self Movement. The same tests were applied to materials for religious education, lay training, and home and family life institutes, so very few materials came out unscathed.[76]

The Farmer, successor to the *Christian Farmer* which had stopped publication in 1950, announced in its first issue, November 15, 1951, that the Christian publishers of China had decided to "take a step forward by uniting all of the publishing concerns, as far as staffs and equipment are concerned." [77] Although the details had yet to be worked out, it appeared that the demands of the government had been executed in about seven months, with the result that Christian literature was under its control.

A related area of work, that of the American Bible Society, first felt the blows of the Communists in their attacks on Ralph Mortenson, its secretary in China. He was charged with espionage because he sent a copy of the government's Common Platform to the United States before it had been released locally, and because he sent private reports on Chou En-lai's meeting with T. Y. Wu, but Mortenson was not arrested. His successor, Dr. Li Pei-en (Baen Li), was arrested in 1955 on charges that he was put in the office because he was sympathetic with Mortenson and would "undermine real Bible Society work." After the arrest of Li a new governing committee for the China Bible House announced that in the future, only the Scriptures would be published—without comment—and that they would no more be a tool of imperialist aggression. An exhibit was set up purporting to show how the Bible House had been used by American imperialism, before which an old man was supposed to have said: "To think that they [imperialists] would lay

---

[76] E.g., the August-September, 1951, issue of *Religious Education* had an article examining various materials. Almost all were unacceptable and therefore to be destroyed, or were in need of drastic revision. The only exceptions were a few Bible lessons, a Lay Leadership Training Series, and two volumes on village worship and village play. Summarized in *CHIBUL*, January 4, 1952. Another example of a publication discontinued was the Chinese translation of *The Upper Room*, discontinued April 30, 1952, because it was "spreading much harmful and poisonous thinking." Reported in *CHIBUL*, July 31, 1952.

[77] Ferris, *The Christian Church*, p. 28.

their bloody hands on our precious treasure, the Bible!" [78] In one of those strange twists of irony, the Three-Self Movement publication *T'ien Feng* insisted that Li Pei-en had been proved conclusively to be an imperialist agent, but the government later admitted that the charges against him were groundless and released him.[79]

In this survey of how Christian institutions fared under the Communists any treatment of the Young Men's and Young Women's Christian Associations, which clearly belong in the framework of institutional expressions of Christianity, has been omitted. In many ways, however, the YMCA and YWCA were an exception to the general pattern of Christian institutions in China. They were independent of foreign control, implicit as well as explicit, and they were largely Chinese supported and staffed. Far more important for our treatment is the fact that the YM-YW leaders were among the first Christians to support the Communist cause. As we shall see, YMCA leaders like Y. T. Wu, Liu Liang-mo, and Tu Yü-ching, plus Miss Cora Deng (Teng Yu-chih) of the YWCA, were a powerful force in swinging the Protestant leadership behind the Three-Self Movement.[80]

Although YM-YW activities quickly took on the political coloring of the new regime, and therefore represented an alteration of original purposes, the activities themselves remained essentially the same. Free schools covering a wide range of subjects, including several on the new ideology, vocational schools, sports, recreation and health education, student conferences, musical programs, and various community services, went on as before.[81]

Whereas the YMCA in several other parts of the world was regarded as little more than an athletic club, it was, whether for good or ill, "church-centered" in Communist China. Kiang Wen-

[78] *CHIBUL*, September 26 and October 10, 1955.

[79] Francis Price Jones, *The Church in Communist China: A Protestant Appraisal* (New York: Friendship Press, 1962), p. 108.

[80] Hu Chang-tu *et al.*, *China, Its People, Its Society, Its Culture* (New Haven: Human Relations Area Files Press, 1960), p. 128.

[81] Kiang Wen-han, "Chinese YMCA Enters New Era," *China Monthly Review* CXX (April, 1951), 173-76. YWCA activities, are presented in the YW Executive Committee report of 1955, *CHIBUL* (July, 1955). Tu Yü-ching, "What the YMCA is Doing," *China Reconstructs* IV (July, 1955), 10-12, stresses the church activities of the secretariat.

han says, "After Liberation, the YMCA has come to be looked upon in some ways as a 'bridge' between the churches and the government." [82] He attributes the formulation of the crucial Manifesto and its adoption, which will be considered in chapter 6, to the work of various YMCA secretaries, and thus indicates the most obvious reason why the YMCA and YWCA fared much better than other Christian institutions in Communist China.

Communist attitudes toward Christian institutions in China and the process by which government authorities dealt with these institutions are summarized in the following passage from an article in the review *Research on International Questions,* published in China in late 1959 or early 1960:

American imperialists . . . worked with zeal under cover of educational and "charitable" organizations to oppress and poison the spirit of the People. In 1950, they possessed about half of the cultural, educational, and aid institutions in China: hospitals, orphanages, leprosaria, publishing houses, libraries, museums. . . . Among religious organizations fifty-eight were directly under control of Americans. These represented half of all the organizations that were in the hands of foreigners, and to them must be added six or seven Catholic churches [*sic*] to say nothing of the Chinese religious organizations that received American subsidies.

After liberation, American imperialists constantly made use of these organizations for their reactionary propaganda, to spread rumors and insinuations, to publish and distribute reactionary books, to hide arms and to collaborate in the espionage of secret agents of Chiang Kai-shek.

These activities were increased during the Korean war and the exasperated Chinese people asked their government to take these organizations in hand. It was then that the religious circles of the country set afoot the "Three Autonomies Movement" and decided to break their ties with the imperialists.

On December 29, 1950, in a report to the Council of State on the cultural and religious organizations that were functioning with the aid of American subsidies, Vice Premier Kuo Mo-jo decided that all these organizations must be registered. In 1951, the Chinese Government finally started a mass campaign to put an end to them. It was thus that the Chinese people freed themselves of the American cultural aggression and its influence.[83]

[82] "Chinese YMCA Enters New Era" (see note 81), p. 174.
[83] *CMBA* XII (March, 1960), 317.

A Communist writer in 1966, inveighing against U.S. imperialism and what he regarded as continued aggression through the Peace Corps and various aid programs, reiterated the charges that missionaries past and present are an important part of the "ideological offensive" which the United States carries on in the world. Missionaries have established schools and hospitals in order to carry out espionage and subversion, he said, and in order to blunt the edge of revolutionary movements in the name of "reformism." They preach love and forgiveness in order "to calm the Afro-Asian anti-imperialist temper." [84]

The world Christian community had reason to hope that, with all vestiges of outside influence and control obliterated, regardless of the reasons for that obliteration or the methods by which it was carried out, the church in China might be able to survive as an authentic instrument of the divine purpose. Spokesmen of the Communist Party and the government it established repeatedly declared that their objection to Christianity was due to the use of the church by foreign imperialists to commit aggression against China. It was reasonable to hope, therefore, that with missionaries out of the way, all institutions taken over by, or no longer a problem to, the government, all foreign funds cut off, and all ties with churches or Christian organizations abroad severed, the church which remained would be able to continue its work and witness without serious objection or opposition. The extent to which this has proved or not proved to be the case may be discerned in the story of the church as such, Catholic and Protestant, which follows.

[84] Chen Yao-hang, "Yankee Imperialist Cultural Aggression in Asia and Africa," *Peking Review*, March 10, 1966, pp. 15-18.

IV

Catholic Resistance to Communist Efforts to Control the Church

INITIAL THRUSTS AND RESPONSES: 1946-1951

As various parts of China came under Communist control in the late 40's, the Catholic Church experienced increasing interference with its work, ranging from harassment and intimidation to imprisonment, beatings, and even the death of priests and laymen. Perhaps the most conspicuous example was that of Christians in the village of Siwantze who were imprisoned and beaten until Father Legrand, the missionary pastor who was in jail, agreed to sign away part of the mission property. Facing trial and execution, he was called from this place in the remote Chahar province by his bishop, and the Communist cadres proceeded with the communization of a completely Catholic community.[1]

During the chaotic period before the actual takeover, one could find a comparatively mild situation in one diocese but a terribly severe situation in another; people fled the Communist armies from remote areas to the cities, then from north to south. In the first issue of the *China Missionary Bulletin,* for example, one reads on facing pages that in Jehol province "violent persecution [is] raging," and in the diocese of Chowchih in Shensi province "a most perfect tranquillity reigns. . . . All the different functions are proceeding in . . . good order." The report for Jehol tells of both priests and nuns imprisoned, of priests hung by the thumbs and beaten, of one dragged over roads and fields with a man on his

---

[1] "Another Mindszenty Ordeal," *CMBA* VI (September, 1954), 602-3.

chest, of buildings looted and occupied by Communists, of forced confessions, and of seminarians forced into training to become Communist propagandists.[2]

In a place in Manchuria, for example, the Communist soldiers were even friendly to the local priest; but functionaries came in from outside, accused him of teaching "American religion," imprisoned him, later led him out and shot him, and were reported to be trying to get Christians to apostatize.[3] Shortly afterward there was a report from the San Pien district of Ninghsia, already under Communist control, that missionaries were allowed to visit quite a few Christian communities which they had been forbidden to visit for six years. Numerous Christians gathered for mass, some schools were reopened, a dispensary resumed services, and the winter's missionary activity brought great fruit. In the diocese of Ts'ingtao, Shantung, however, Father Anthony Ma, who had been a refugee in the town of Ts'ingtao, went back to his native village of P'ing-tu for Easter. While hearing confessions he was apprehended, tried in a people's court, judged guilty, and put to death.[4]

Thus in the prelude to the storm, the church discovered in large measure what the storm was to be like. Many reiterated the judgment that the late 40's were more chaotic than the period immediately following the Communist victory. There are numerous testimonies to the effect that after the arrival of the more disciplined Communist troops there was a period of relative peace and quiet, to be followed by the political cadres who systematically tightened the screws.

In this period, as later, the courage of the priests inspired tremendous devotion by the people who were drawn closer together. Offerings for charity often increased under the stimulus of visible need all around, and laymen undertook the duties of the priests wherever possible. Great numbers of priests and missionaries became laborers, and many wrote that they found it a blessing.[5]

As a rule Catholics remained faithful; both the number of conversions and church attendance increased. Contrary to what one usually expects, it was not always the old who were strong and re-

[2] *CMBA* I (September, 1948), 114-15.
[3] *CMBA* I (October, 1948), 220.
[4] *CMBA* I (II) (June, 1949), 696, 698.
[5] *CMBA* I (II) (October, 1949), 41-42.

mained true; it was not always the young who fell by the wayside.[6] Church activities in the larger cities were largely undisturbed, but there was a general air of insecurity.

On the eve of the Communist victory in China, Father Nicholas Maestrini assessed the situation on the mainland from Hong Kong. The overall policy of toleration did not allow a fierce and bloody persecution, but "a slow and steady movement of strangulation is evident everywhere." [7] He also acknowledged that heavy taxation imposed by the new government on churches and religious institutions was not directed against these religious institutions alone, but was a burden felt by all alike. Stating that use of church buildings by soldiers or government cadres was a "common-place of mission life" at that time, he added that the soldiers usually returned the buildings to the church and made repairs in the process. Propaganda courses against the Christian faith often gave splendid opportunities for witness to the faith, and people who had never showed any interest in religion began to inquire about it.[8] A priest in the Wuhu diocese of Anhwei Province even changed his mind about the bother of having Communist soldiers wandering around his chapel. "I discovered by being present in the chapel when these boys passed through I had another chance to preach Catholic doctrine. Explaining objects in the church is a good way of telling pagans about the Faith." [9]

In passing it should be noted that there were Catholics in the army. Some of these young men would seek out a priest, even a missionary, to hear confession, or would wait in a Catholic dispensary until patients had gone in order to contact the priests or nuns in charge who would arrange confession.[10]

Retreats were held for young men and women in many places during the Chinese New Year holidays of early 1950. They discussed the life of Christ, the theology of the incarnation and redemption, and the meaning of the Eucharist.[11] A display of

---

[6] *CMBA* I (II) (November, 1949), 257-58.
[7] *CMBA* I (II) (September, 1949), 2.
[8] *Ibid.*, pp. 141-44.
[9] *CMBA* III (IV) (February, 1951), 177.
[10] *CMBA* II (III) (December, 1950), 1041-42.
[11] "Beau succès d'une sèrie de retraites," *CMBA* II (III) (July-August, 1950), 634-42. See also Eusebe Amaiz, "Retraites pour Prêtres et missionaries," *CMBA* III (IV) (January, 1951), 10-14.

religious books in Anking provoked great interest and led to the conversion of several students and professors.[12] Catholic literature was distributed all over the country, reaching many people who had had no previous contact with religion. Thousands were enrolled in correspondence courses.[13]

In view of all that was happening, and in light of Catholic experience in Eastern Europe, extensive preparations were initiated in order to survive under the Communist control which was sure to come.[14] It was recognized that all priority should be given to instruction in the faith. Questions flung at those who had already endured interrogation by Communist officials were tabulated and answers formulated. Most of the questions had been bandied about for centuries, such as "Why pray for rain?" "If there is a god, where is he?" and questions ridiculing the theory of creation as "spiritualism." Regardless of how banal the questions might be, it had become clear that the circumstances of the questioning made any thought impossible, so precise answers had to be ready. At a slightly more mature level, both teachers and students in Catholic schools were prepared to answer questions they might face in the indoctrination sessions which were being introduced in all the schools. In several places these preparation sessions continued after the Communists were in power.

The Legion of Mary, which was later to be one of the prime objects of Communist attack, played an important role in lay leadership. The most trustworthy Catholic young people were organized to instruct non-Christians and inadequately prepared Christians, distribute literature and devotional articles, counsel with people in trouble, carry a consecrated Host to those in danger of death, and assist priests in all manner of ways, particularly those who had no freedom of movement. They helped women with household chores, allowed their own homes to be used for secret midnight Mass, and were authorized to baptize when no priests were available. From its beginning in China in 1948, about a

[12] *CMBA* II (III) (October, 1950), 873.

[13] Thaddäus Hang, *Die Katholische Kirche im chinesischen Raum* (München: Verlag Anton Pustet, 1963), pp. 116-17.

[14] An excellent survey of the church's preparation for survival may be found in "Face au Problème Communiste," *CMBA*, I (December, 1948), 426-38.

thousand chapters or praesidia had been organized in 94 of the 144 dioceses of China by 1951.[15] The militancy of the organization made it a most valuable element in the life of the church as Communist pressures increased. That same militancy also infuriated Party and government officials, whose almost frantic efforts to stamp it out were a testimony to its success.

The atmosphere of relative freedom which allowed such preparatory activities continued well into 1950, with continual reports of increased faith on the part of Catholics, of increased attendance at Mass, and of new converts asking for baptism. Missionaries with long experience in China testified that religious devotion far exceeded anything in their memory.

One pastor of a village church in central China reported the baptism of 657 adults for the first half of the year 1950, an average of thirty or forty a week. The number of conversions in this village parish had been very few in the previous years. When the missionary was restricted to his own house, the Christians grouped together to organize religious instruction for the non-Catholics. The record number of conversions was a direct result of their apostolate. Friends and neighbours were attracted and fired by the zeal of these lay apostles. Although eminently striking, this instance is not a solitary example of the vitality of lay Catholic action in China today. Another missionary, a bishop of one of the Mongolia dioceses, recently lauded with highest praise the cooperation of laymen in the conversion apostolate of his mission.[16]

A report in mid-1950 from Tatung, Shansi, an area under Communist control for a year at that time, compares the life of eleven Chinese priests with Christian life in the pre-Constantinian Roman empire:

The worldly possessions of these priests embrace little more than the clothes they wear. Dressed as farmers, they travel from one Catholic home to another administering to their "parishioners." Although no one house is their fixed abode, they are at home in every Catholic hamlet. Each priest is assigned to a district, the Christian villages of which he visits over and over again. The children, being advised of his itinerary, follow

---

[15] Palmer, *God's Underground*, pp. 63-67.
[16] *CMBA*, II (III) (September, 1950), 702.

him daily from house to house for religious instruction as long as he is within walking distance of their homes.[17]

The reporter says that this itinerant ministry was necessitated by heavy taxation, which had forced the closure of many buildings, and by pressures against the preaching of religion. At Tatung itself there was no prohibition against attending Mass, for which people often waited for hours.

Several directives which seemed quite fair to the churches were promulgated by the new government in 1950. A decree issued to government agencies and reported in *Jen-min Jih-pao* instructed officials (1) "to permit freedom of religious activity," (2) not to seize religious edifices, (3) to protect the buildings and properties of religious societies," (4) to consult with religious leaders if it was actually necessary to requisition certain buildings, and (5) to "fully restore to their rightful owners" such buildings as were used by the government.[18]

Another *Jen-min Jih-pao* article claimed that the only basis upon which the government might arrest someone involved in a religious group or suppress a religious group was evidence that the individual or the group had engaged in rebellious activity or had been involved in a counterrevolutionary plot. "Certain proof" had to be established after inquiry. Furthermore, the arrest of a member of a group did not imply that the group was guilty, nor should property belonging to the group be confiscated if only one or a few of its members were found guilty of some offense.[19]

Provincial officials interpreted these directives in their own way, however. Although an official here and there continued a quietly sympathetic treatment of Christians, harshness became the order of the day. Disturbances at the local level were ignored by the authorities. Obscenities were shouted at priests and plastered on church walls. People were warned not to take the elements at Mass because of the danger of poison.[20] In one place priests were arrested; from another place there were reports of priests released from prison.

[17] *CMBA* II (III) (June, 1950), 585.
[18] *CMBA* II (III) (April, 1950), 405-6.
[19] *CMBA*, IV (V) (March, 1952), 181.
[20] *CMBA* II (III) (June, 1950), 592.

In the midst of this confusion a most significant step was taken by a few Catholics who advocated, for the first time from within the church, the movement called the "Three Autonomies." This is the same movement, *San Tsz Yun Tung*, which in Protestant sources is translated "Three-Self Movement," a more literal and accurate rendering for the effort to promote a church governed, financed, and propagated by the Chinese themselves.

On November 30, 1950, in Kuangyuan, a town in the northern part of Szechwan Province, a group of 500 Catholics under the leadership of a Chinese priest, Wang Liang-tao, issued a manifesto calling for severance of ties with imperialism and the establishment of a self-governing, self-supporting, self-propagating church. The manifesto deplored the way in which imperialists had used the church as an instrument of aggression and called upon Catholics throughout the country to join in the struggle to cut off ties with imperialism and establish the Three Autonomies.[21] Shortly afterward a Chungking manifesto was published, signed by 14 priests, 7 sisters, 1 brother, and 695 laymen. The ideas and language of the Kwangyuan document were used, but the Chungking document stressed the "unequal treaties which were so galling to the Chinese." [22] The framers and signers of both manifestos regarded their action as participation in the "Oppose America–Aid Korea Family and Country Defense Movement" which then summoned the nation to support the Chinese forces in Korea. Similar manifestos were reported from several other places, practically all of them in West China.

The language of the manifestos and of reports in the Chinese press concerning them was notably ambiguous, both with respect to what cutting the ties with imperialism meant and with respect to what the Three Autonomies actually involved. One exception to this ambiguity was found in a statement from north Szechwan which called for self-support by utilizing the church's properties in production and its priests and nuns in productive work (they must not live at the expense of the church!). In this document, self-government was to be achieved by having an administrative com-

[21] *NCNA*, Peking, December 13, 1950.
[22] Both the Kuangyuan and Chungking Manifestos are in *CMBA* III (IV) (February, 1951), 148-51.

mittee in which three fourths of the members would be laymen or laywomen, which committee would "adopt an attitude of truly democratic cooperation." Propagation of the faith would be done by local priests who had engaged in political study and who would develop patriotism among the people. Foreign missionaries would have no part in either administration or propagation.[23]

There were reports of some Catholics who sincerely wished to express their opposition to imperialism, and who in response to demands from local newspapers submitted signed manifestos which attacked imperialism, but made no reference to the triple autonomies. These never appeared in print. When inquiries were made the signers were told that their statements "had no meaning."[24]

Both Communist agents and those within the church who cooperated with them in promoting the autonomies dissociated religious faith or doctrine from the ecclesiastical structure of the church. They depicted themselves as protectors of religious faith under the policy of freedom of religious belief, and as purifiers of a structure which had been corrupted by the imperialists.[25]

A favorite technique was to divide a meeting into sections of priests and laymen. In the clerical section a speaker would attack the pope as unfriendly toward China; in the lay section attacks would be made against the American church. Chinese and foreign clergy often were separated in such meetings so that the former might be advised of their oppression by the latter.[26]

In an effort to clarify the ambiguities of the government's demands for an independent Catholic Church, Catholic leaders requested a meeting with Premier Chou En-lai, which was granted on January 17, 1951. Nothing of substance was reported in the Chinese press, but Father Lefeuvre has reconstructed from mission publications and archives the substance of the Premier's

[23] Léon Trivière, "Le Mouvement des 'Trois Autonomies,'" *CMBA* V (VI) (January, 1953), 17-29, presents a careful study of the early stages of the three autonomies movement. Jean Lefeuvre, *Shanghai: Les Enfants dans la Ville* (Paris: Casterman, 1962), pp. 4-45, has an excellent treatment of the manifestos and the ambiguities in them.
[24] *CMBA* III (IV) (April, 1951), 357.
[25] Francis Dufay, *The Star Versus the Cross* (Hong Kong: Nazareth Press, n.d. [c. 1953]), p. 116.
[26] *CMBA* III (IV) (February, 1951), 174.

remarks.[27] Premier Chou acknowledged that "the Vatican is the heart of Catholics" and that relations between it and Chinese Catholics should be continued. But continued relations were conditional on whether or not the Vatican supported American imperialism and opposed the political power of the Chinese people. Chou En-lai said relations with the Vatican were to be limited to the "ideological" plane, actually "limited to the domain of 'superstition.'" The whole realm of "practice" was thereby excluded. Father Lefeuvre notes perceptively that this separation of ideology (or superstition) and practice, while not new in history, was given a new meaning in this situation and provided a means by which the church could be brought under control. The Premier called for support of the Three Autonomies as a patriotic movement which had arisen in religious circles. People who loved their country obviously could not have relations with the enemies of their country, and true patriots obviously would weed out any traitors or Judases in their ranks.

On the basis of this conference Catholic bishops sought to draft a document which would distinguish between Catholic patriotic and religious responsibilities, and which would set forth the church's understanding of the Three Autonomies. The result was a pamphlet entitled *The Church in China: Declaration of Principles*,[28] published in February, 1951, and circulated to Catholics in China and, of course, to government officials. The document began with a statement of the traditional Catholic position that Catholics who "willingly separate themselves from the Holy See, also separate themselves from Jesus and from the Catholic Church." Any so-called "national Catholic Church" is schismatic and cannot be regarded as "true, one, and Catholic." There is no alliance between the Catholic Church and imperialism, and, therefore, there are no imperialist connections to sever. Any slander of the pope as an imperialist or as a tool of imperialists cannot be accepted.

Part II of the *Declaration of Principles* presented the reaction of the church to the Three Autonomies. The document claims the church was effecting a "gradual assumption of control of religious

---

[27] *Shanghai: Les Enfants*, pp. 45-48.
[28] *CMBA* III (IV) (May, 1951), 384-88, has Chinese original and English translation in parallel columns.

affairs by native bishops according to the ecclesiastical regulations, and [was establishing] a native hierarchy." Self-support, to the bishops who wrote this document, meant the support of the church by Catholics of any country. If these overall resources "are not allowed to circulate," depriving various churches of mutual aid, then it is not self-support. According to this understanding, only that subsidy which has political implications, whether it comes from abroad or from within China, must not be accepted by the church. Self-propagation, in the terms of this document, meant that "foreign missionaries will propagate the faith in the interests of local churches and not work for the interests of foreigners." The development of a native priesthood is affirmed, but the right to continue using foreign missionaries until the number of Chinese priests is adequate is also affirmed.

As a conclusion to this discussion of the Three Autonomies, the bishops categorically stated that any other interpretation was wrong, a statement which might well have been omitted if rapprochement with the government was really desired. A most trenchant observation on the whole affair follows:

Any movement of self-government, self-support, and self-propagation which is promoted by outside influences is not a voluntary movement, and is of necessity not a real movement for self-government, self-support, and self-propagation.[20]

It appears that this issue—the meaning of selfhood in the Three-Self Movement—was never seriously discussed by the government with Catholics or Protestants.

The declaration concluded with an affirmation that the church itself is interested only in political affairs insofar as they affect faith and morals, that "the church strictly forbids its priests to engage in political activities in their status as priests," but that it "strictly commands Catholics to love their country." There is a final appeal to Chinese Catholics to remain firm in their faith.

Obviously the church's denial of imperialist connections was a joke to the Communists, and the church undoubtedly realized that it would be. What is puzzling is that the church should proffer an understanding of the Three Autonomies which was impossible for the

[20] *Ibid.*, p. 386.

Communists to accept. A Catholic friend says that Chinese priests who participated in the drafting of the document begged not to be designated as superiors because they would be marked immediately as "enemies of the people." If they could continue for two or three years in the lower ranks, they would have that much more time to work effectively. While there is some wisdom in such a delay, the omission of any intention to accelerate the preparation of Chinese clergy for self-government and self-propagation reveals a lack of wisdom, especially when four out of five bishops and about two out of three priests were foreigners. To maintain this "gradualism" in a nationalistic, even xenophobic era, was to ask for trouble.

The Catholic interpretation of self-support may be right in affirming the privilege of a Catholic in any country to give for the support of the church's cause in another, but it ignores the problems in such support as the Communists saw them, as well as the values in support of the Chinese church by Chinese.

The government refused to accept the document as a basis for the continued development of the Catholic Church in China. It was lampooned in the Chinese press with scorn and innuendo. *Kuang-ming Jih-pao* said the "true reactionary nature" of Catholics had been revealed by the document. With characteristic exaggeration, but with telling effectiveness, the editors jabbed:

As we all know, the Catholic Church has been established in China for more than three hundred years. During this time, the administrative and financial powers of the church in China, together with all policies having to do with the propagation of the faith, have always been held in the hands of foreign priests who never had the desire to help us establish our own church.[30]

The barrage about espionage and aggression which followed is no more true than the assertion that no foreign priest worked for an indigenous church; but the shaft was driven home, and the struggle continued.

The spotlight shifted in late spring of 1951 to Archbishop Antonio Riberi, Internuncio of the Vatican to Nationalist China, symbol of the tie between the Vatican and the church in China.[31] In China

---

[30] *Ibid.*, p. 388.
[31] The story of Archbishop Riberi's expulsion was told in *CMBA* III (IV) (June-December, 1951), 526-27, 685, 710-11, 761, 891.

from 1946 to 1951, he warned of the dangers of communism, was instrumental in introducing the Legion of Mary, and opposed the Three Autonomies. In an impassioned appeal he urged (or commanded) all missionaries to stay at their posts in spite of persecution.[32] Any of these actions, in addition to the fact that he was accredited to the Nationalist government, made him *persona non grata* to the Communist leadership.

Criticism of Archbishop Riberi in the press came to a head when he vigorously denied, in a Latin letter to all bishops, having anything to do with a "Nanking declaration" in favor of the Three Autonomies. In May, 1951, he was excoriated in *Jen-min Jih-pao* for having "sabotaged" the independent church movement, and on June 26 he was placed under house arrest. On September 4 he and several associates were taken to Nanking Security Police Headquarters in the afternoon and interrogated until about ten o'clock in the evening. He refused to sign the list of accusations ("Falsehoods!") against him; he and his colleagues were returned to the Internunciature to pack, then escorted to the railroad station at 2:30 the following morning, and put on third-class coaches of a train to Canton. They were searched in Shanghai and Canton, and again at the border before crossing to Hong Kong on September 8. So, without the slightest nod to diplomatic niceties, the "citizen from Monaco," as he was called in the Chinese press, was expelled from China.

CONTINUING RESISTANCE TO MOUNTING PRESSURES: 1951-1954

Actions taken against a representative of the Vatican and against foreign bishops and missionaries, however unjust, are not surprising. The blunt use of power against two Chinese priests, whose stories follow, is almost unbelievable.

When it became apparent in late 1950 or early 1951 that some Catholics in Szechwan were responding favorably to the Three Autonomies, Father John Tung (Tung Shih-chih) volunteered to go from Shanghai to see what was going on. He went as a tradesman,

---

[32] See Palmer, *God's Underground*, pp. 240-41.

since a priest could not get a travel permit, and in his preliminary observation discovered that the accusation of fellow Christians was central to the Three Autonomies. He reported this to his colleagues in Shanghai, expressing his opinion that by joining the accusation movement one could survive a short time, but he said: "You will not be the same man."

Father Tung was back in Chungking when Communist authorities in that city arranged a mass meeting for June 3, 1951, to denounce Archbishop Riberi and demand his expulsion. John Tung agreed to be one of the speakers, along with several priests in the area who had supported the Kuangyuan and Chungking manifestos, in the hope that by his own example he might block or upset the new movement. He began his speech by saying that an attack on Riberi today would be followed by a request to attack the pope the following day, and ultimately by a request to attack Christ himself. As an alternative to this course, he offered himself:

Gentlemen, I have only one soul and I cannot divide it; I have a body which can be divided. It is best, it seems, to offer my whole soul to God and to the Holy Church; and my body to my country. If she is pleased with it, I do not refuse it to her. Good materialists, who deny the existence of the soul, cannot but be satisfied with the offering of my body.[33]

Father Tung said that a triple autonomy movement might be shaped according to Catholic principles if there were a genuine collaboration between church and state, but that the two seemed to be growing further and further apart. He reminded the civil authorities that they had called on him to speak frankly about what he really believed, that there was both freedom of speech and of religion in the new China.

Suppose . . . I go against my conscience, talk contrary to my own opinions, sign what I disapprove of, then I openly (willingly) deceive the authorities; and if I say in secret that I made a mistake because I was forced, I equally deceive the Hierarchy. Would not such conduct sow a ferment of discord between the government and the church? If I strangle the voice of my conscience, deny my God, leave the church and cheat the

[33] *CMBA* III (IV) (October, 1951), 679-81.

government, I am nothing more than an opportunist and a coward. . . .
Who then would want to have me, who would want to help me? I would
only be a miserable outcast deserving of all punishment from the authorities in this world and eternal punishment in the other from divine
justice.[34]

After this personal testimony he went on to say that he admired
the Communists because they were capable of facing death, because
they did not fear being falsely accused, and because they maintained their own faith intact even after they had failed to convince
others. Tung added that he was honored by their "consideration" of
the Catholic Church and their efforts to win its support, which encouraged him to redouble his efforts in the hope of being found a
good Christian by the government.

I do not content myself with admiring the unshakable courage of the
Communists, and [with] thanking them for their noble intention in
trying to win the Christians. I still have a great desire. It is to offer them
. . . the Catholic Church which is so dear to me, in order to bring them to
God and make them our brethren in the faith. Do not say I am a fool who
prattles crazy things, and do not believe that I lack sincerity. I dare say
that Communists who have such an ideal, when the day dawns that they
will really know the Catholic Church, would make Catholics completely
devoted to their faith and would surpass a thousand times a Catholic such
as I am. I also ask God that in the Communist Party there may be found
many Sauls to become Pauls, who will surpass by a hundred yards the
poor priest I am. It is my most fervent prayer. It is now very near to
being heard. To this aim, I spare myself no sacrifice, praying with the
hope that the earthly life that I offer today might be the token of the conversion of the future generation.[35]

He concluded by saying that his "poor speech" had the approval
neither of civil nor church authorities, and that he still hoped for a
reconciliation between them.

One month later, on July 2, John Tung was put in prison.
Newspapers reported the crimes with which he was charged, but
neither the speech nor his fate. Although he was long assumed to
have died in prison, reliable reports in 1965 said that he was work-

[34] *Ibid.*, p. 680.
[35] *Ibid.*, p. 681.

ing in a labor camp in a remote province of China and in good spirits.

There were renewed efforts to force acceptance of the Three Autonomies, but with only slight success. Inspired by Tung's example, priests who had leaned toward the new movement renewed their loyalties to Rome. Whether in reprisal or not, in some parts of the Chungking diocese "Catholics are forbidden to possess rosaries, holy medals, or crucifixes. Homes are searched and prayer books, catechisms, and holy pictures are destroyed if found. In other sections, however, Catholics can attend Mass." [36]

In the summer of 1951 a tremendous campaign was launched against the Catholic Church in Shanghai, perhaps the main center of opposition to the independent church movement. There was an "Oppose America—Aid Korea" indoctrination course particularly pointed at the Catholic community. Accusation meetings were held at which former workmen at various Catholic institutions spoke of ways in which they had been mistreated. Some 500 students in the city were trained by the Communists and sent daily to Catholic homes in an effort to convince Catholics that political, not religious, issues were at stake. Three pamphlets, which denounced the Legion of Mary, pointed out the Christian duty against imperialists and counterrevolutionaries, and accused priests and Catholic organizations, were widely circulated.

During the first week of August, 1951, Father Beda Chang, Father Yao, and Brother Alexander were imprisoned. The key figure among the three was Father Chang, educated at the Sorbonne, rector of St. Ignatius College, dean of the Arts Faculty, and director of the Bureau of Chinese studies. All three were school men (Yao of Gonzaga and Alexander of St. Francis) and all were charged by the government with trying to block student control of their respective schools, as well as supporting the Kuomintang and engaging in counterrevolutionary activities. Additional attention had been given to Beda Chang in the hope of gaining the support of an illustrious priest for the Three Autonomies, although he had consistently opposed the movement. He died in prison on November 11, 1951. His colleagues who were called to collect the body were told that he had been in a coma for several days and that he died of

[36] *CMBA* IV (V) (January, 1952), 68.

a brain tumor. Accounts in the *China Missionary Bulletin* speak of his "emaciated body," so "black with bruises that even his brother could not recognize him"; but a pamphlet relating the whole affair, published under Catholic auspices in Hong Kong, says only that "the constant lack of sleep poisoned his nervous system, and Father Beda fell into a coma." [37] Government authorities forbade a funeral procession; only his immediate family and two priests were allowed to take the body to the graveyard after dark on the evening of November 13.

The churches of Shanghai were packed for requiem Masses, but two hundred priests wearing red vestments also celebrated in private the Martyr's Mass for the repose of his soul. When requiem Masses continued, the police issued an order forbidding them and demanded that this order be announced in the churches. One priest celebrated a low Mass in complete silence except for the announcement that "the police have forbidden us to sing a Requiem Mass for Father Beda Chang this morning, in the name of the Father and of the Son and of the Holy Ghost." Another added to his announcement that Beda Chang had never been tried and condemned. Shanghai priests, including Bishop Kung Pin-mei, were called to police headquarters to "clarify their attitudes." The Shanghai *Liberation Daily* denounced Father Wang Jen-sheng, pastor of St. Peter's Church, for "celebrating a solemn high Mass for the criminal Chang and preaching on martydom during the Mass." Renewed pressure was put on Legion of Mary members to register at the police station, but only a handful did so.

The grave was located in a country district outside Shanghai with a plain stone, for the Communists insisted that his name, if used, be followed by "criminal." In all news items concerning the affair Father Chang was referred to as a criminal, a reactionary traitor who had used the church as a cloak to hide activities aiding

[37] Various aspects of the story of Father Beda Chang are told in *CMBA* III (October, 1951), 722-23, and (December, 1951), 822; also *CMBA* IV (V) (February, 1952), 140-41, and (June-July, 1952), 586. A pamphlet *Father Beda Chang, Witness for Unity* (Hong Kong: Catholic Truth Society, 1953), gives the best overall picture of Chang's background and the crucial incident related. Lefeuvre, *Shanghai: Les Enfants*, pp. 88-90, 94-97, gives the important details, including reference to the way in which the apologia of Father Tung in Szechwan inspired the Catholic community in Shanghai, particularly the students.

the Kuomintang and the American imperialists. The Patriotic Catholic newspaper later mentioned that "otherwise honest people . . . are being deceived," and that "many younger people visit the grave." The editors warned people against believing in the "absurd deception" that Beda Chang was a saint.

Although Beda Chang wrote a very clear statement on the Catholic position toward the Three Autonomies, he did not have the opportunity to leave the kind of testimony which we have from John Tung. Both men remind the church in China and everywhere that "to witness" is derived from the Greek *martureo*, and therefore that witness may ultimately involve martyrdom. John Tung's address belongs with those priceless treasures of the second and third centuries, for those few short pages convey the same spirit which emerges from the *Apologia* of Justin Martyr or Tertullian of Carthage.

On October 8, 1951, shortly after Beda Chang's imprisonment and Archbishop Riberi's expulsion, an official order was issued in Shanghai requiring all members of the Legion of Mary to register at a special office called "the Shanghai Municipal Registration Office for Members of the 'Legion of Mary.'" Attacks had appeared in major newspapers since the early summer of 1951, notably in *Jen-min Jih-pao*, whose editors called the Legion reactionary and fascist and accused it of harboring landlords, spies, and imperialists.[38] Similar charges had been made earlier in Tientsin, where the drive against the Legion began.

The order to Legion members in Shanghai to register could be disregarded easily because there was no Legion there. It was called the "Sodality of Mary" and antedated the organization of the Legion in China. Therefore Sodality members ignored the order and proceeded to accomplish what they could, especially in parishes where priests were circumscribed in their activity, or where for other reasons clerical duties could not be carried out. Although Communist officials apparently did not know the distinction in no-

---

[38] *JMJP*, July 5, 1951. The story of the campaign against the Legion is related by Lefeuvre, *Shanghai: Les Enfants*, pp. 91-102, including a remarkable testimony of faith in a joint letter composed by two Legionaires. See also Leo Roberts, *Mary in Their Midst: The Legion of Mary in Action in China, 1948-1951* (Dublin: Clonmore and Reynolds, 1960), for the story of the early stages of the movement.

menclature, they harangued gatherings of Catholic students thinking that their audience included Legionaires. Sodality members listened, took note of the charges, and went on with their work.

In 1951 there was a concentrated effort to establish the Patriotic Church in Peking. After a mass arrest of missionaries and Chinese priests on July 25, 1951, reform committees were set up by the civil authorities to govern the parishes, both Chinese and foreign priests were denounced in public meetings, and the inevitable manifestos appeared in the press. One of the manifestos, after a recital of "acts of aggression" committed by the imperialists, demanded that the church be cleansed. The committee which prepared the document stoutly denied that any schism would be involved—they were merely carrying out their patriotic duty.[39] Some priests obviously went along with the movement, for there were priests saying Mass in churches controlled by the reform group, but attendance was very poor in these "patriotic" churches.

There is an impressive description of St. Michael's Church in Peking, regarded as a "model of the reformed church." Red flags draped the main altar, communion rail, vestibule, and the path to the gate. The church columns were hung with streamers proclaiming "Long Live Mao Tse-tung," "Long Live Communism," and "Christians Unite—Chase out the Imperialists." Pictures of the Sacred Heart, the Virgin Mary, and various saints were replaced inside and out by pictures of Mao and other leading Communists. An indication of Catholic response to this is found in reports that practically all weddings and baptisms at the church had ceased, and that the number of people at Mass had dropped from four or five hundred to about one hundred, only about a dozen of whom received Communion.[40]

The most repressive measures, however, were reported from the southern province of Kwangtung, where the Ministry of Information announced a new set of rules for both Chinese and foreign missionary workers: (1) churches were to be abandoned as places of worship and used only for public trials; (2) Chinese priests and

[39] Document quoted in *CMBA* III (IV) (March, 1951), 782-85; general survey in IV (V) (August-September, 1952), 554-55.
[40] *CMBA* IV (V) (November, 1952), 765-66.

ministers were to confess their crimes; (3) all foreign priests were to be ordered out; (4) all mission schools were to be closed; (5) church members and friends of priests and ministers were to sign pledges of anti-imperialism; and (6) the regional government was to take over all mission school property.[41] The *China Missionary Bulletin,* in reporting this decree, said the first three had not been fully enforced, but that the last-mentioned three rules had been prevailing practice for months. It was later discovered that not all churches were taken over, that during Land Reform practically all rural churches were closed to their priests, pastors, and congregations for varying periods, and in numerous cases never returned.

Both Catholic priests and Protestant pastors in South China were pressured for membership lists and for lists of those who had studied in mission schools. Times of meetings and services had to be reported in advance to local authorities so that a representative might be appointed to attend and report back to the authorities.[42] Bishop van Melckebeke recalled that the last Mass he celebrated in China, at Christmas of 1951 in the diocese of Ninghsia in Northwest China, came during land reform. The churches had been closed since October, 1951, for land reform, but a low mass without a server was allowed at Christmas. Communist agents were at the doors of the church, but

like waves ever renewing themselves the groups of Christians entered the Church, several of them after two or three days' walk, because there were no priests in their parish to celebrate the feast with them. . . . In the midst of persecution, the Mass remained the light, the joy, and the strength of the Christian people, when all else had been lost.[43]

Equally significant in the annals of Christian devotion was the letter written by Catholic students of Aurora University, by then completely under Communist control, to Bishop Kung Pin-mei at the New Year, 1952. It was in part an answer to statements unfavorable to the church issued by Aurora officials. The students said the diocese was "stirring to noble life" in spite of adversity, and ad-

[41] *Hong Kong Standard,* October 19, 1951.
[42] Ferris, *The Christian Church,* p. 12.
[43] Carlo van Melckebeke, "Liturgical Renewal for China," *CMBA XI* (November, 1959), 905.

dressed the bishop as "our light shining on the darkened road," one who had "protected the integrity of our faith and the traditional spirit of the church." One paragraph expresses well the tenor of the whole statement:

The cross is a crushing load. Only through the cross, however, can man safeguard his faith and strengthen his faltering steps. It is only by the cross that one is able to see the bloom of the flower of victory. In that thought of the unity of the Roman Church, of the future that lies ahead for our Chinese Church, in the prospect of innumerable conversions of the future, of the propagation of our religion in China, of the coming of Mary's Era, we smile and are glad. With laughter we shall carry our cross and make our stations. We are happy because we have the opportunity to live in this happy age. If God should deign to use us as his instruments, how very happy we shall be![44]

This caliber of Catholic witness continued to blunt government efforts to establish the Patriotic Church. It was even reported that Communist officials had criticized the Patriotic Church leaders because their churches were empty for the celebration of Pentecost in 1953, whereas the "uncooperative, nonprogressive churches" were filled to overflowing.[45] One heard occasionally that Catholics whose church had been closed would

put together enough money to rent a hall or room and obtain a priest who has been forced to live at home or with a family for the Sunday Mass. They have devised ingenious ways of receiving the sacraments from imprisoned priests or those in hiding. Wherever the Catholic lay people have shown any weakness or wavering it is not a choice of open apostasy but rather of temporarily submitting until they can find a way out.[46]

The devotion of Catholic laity, plus the fact that no outstanding bishop or priest could be found to head the patriotic movement, resulted in a relaxation of efforts to establish it in early 1953. A Chinese Catholic businessman, who arrived in Hong Kong in the spring of that year, said that he was given permission to leave China only after he had promised to contact Cardinal T'ien to be

[44] *CMBA* IV (V) (March, 1952), 228-29.
[45] *CMBA* V (VI) (September, 1953), p. 688.
[46] *CMBA* V (VI) (January, 1953), 3.

the head of the Patriotic Church.[47] The report sounds pre-posterous, since Cardinal T'ien was then living in America, but there is little question that the Communists felt keenly the lack of a prominent personality to head the movement. Bourassa claims that by mid-1953 only about a dozen out of three thousand Chinese Catholic priests had been won over to the movement, although he acknowledges that about a hundred others were "hesitant." [48]

Then in June, 1953, the Communist government made another move against the church, concentrating again in Shanghai, where about fifty priests were jailed and another forty were placed under house arrest. All were interrogated daily in order to induce confession of crimes. Similar arrests, imprisonments, and inter-rogations were reported from Tientsin, Hankow, and Canton.

Those arrested were charged with counterrevolutionary activity, which by Communist definition consisted of saying that it was a sin to belong to the Young Communist League (and excommunicating those who did belong), that Communists were demons, that the pro-posed reform of the Catholic Church was a "negation of our religion," that patriotic Catholics were apostates, that there was no liberty and no happiness in the new China. They were also accused of sending Catholics into the rural regions to make trouble and in-cite peasants to counterrevolutionary activities. If the charge re-ferred obliquely to evangelistic activity, it provides an interesting insight into religious life of the time.[49]

Catholic resistance received another backhanded compliment when Lu Jui-ching, Minister of Public Security, told the Second Session of the People's Congress in July, 1955, that between May, 1953, and April, 1954, authorities had discovered almost two hun-dred dugouts in the Hsienhsien and Yungnien regions of Hopei province. He said these dugouts, some large enough to hold a hun-dred people, "had been used by secret organizations under the name of the Catholic Church," and were evidence of "counterrevolution-ary elements still working under the cloak of religion." [50]

[47] *CMBA* V (VI) (June-July, 1953), 611.

[48] Leo-Paul Bourassa, *Tactiques Communistes contre L'Église: L'expérience chinoise* (Montreal: Editions de l'Heure, 1962), pp. 51-52.

[49] Léon Trivière, "L'Église catholique en Chine continentale," *Bulletin de la Société des Missions Etrangeres de Paris* [hereafter *BSMEP*] (July, 1957), 579-82.

[50] *JMJP*, July 29, 1955; *CNA*, June 28, 1957, p. 4.

In the cities and towns, churches and residences were searched minutely again and again. Students and other Communist workers visited Catholic homes constantly, trying to get laymen to denounce priests and support the reformed church movement. There were constant attacks in the newspapers and over the radio for weeks.

Father Lefeuvre provides moving examples of courageous Catholic students who stood their ground against the oppressive police, as well as against a priest who cooperated with the police. Young people gathered outside the residences where priests were under house arrest to sing hymns, including "The Great Pope." There were tremendous manifestations of sentiment and emotion if one of the priests happened to appear, especially for the one priest who remained at Christ the King Church after all the others had been arrested. A nine-day period of devotions to the Sacred Heart of Jesus was announced for June 20-29,

to atone for all the vicious words and abuses directed at the Sacred Heart, to ask God to forgive the ignorance of the persecutors, to ask the Holy Ghost to guide the Shanghai diocese, and to ask our Holy Mother to protect priests and Catholics who are suffering for their faith.[51]

Catholics practiced their traditional acts of devotion, especially the Stations of the Cross, with great fervor and intensity.

Just before this wave of arrests began, a new title for the government's campaign among Catholics appeared in the press, replacing the old Three Autonomies. The new designation was "Anti-imperialist Movement for the Love of Country and Church." [52] Priests came under intensive pressure to join and give leadership to the movement. A special representative of the government even approached Bishop Kung and invited him to head the movement, but he refused.

An ecclesiastical congress was called in Nanking for ten days in August of 1953, ostensibly by Father Li Wei-kuang but with obvious government backing, to try to win support for the independent church movement operating under a new name.[53] "Ten

[51] Lefeuvre, *Shanghai: Les Enfants*, pp. 142-56. Also *CMBA* V (VI) (September, 1953), 698.
[52] Lefeuvre, *Shanghai: Les Enfants*, p. 140.
[53] *Ibid.*, pp. 195-99.

Articles," which followed the usual line of denouncing imperialists and counterrevolutionaries but which allowed loyalty to the pope in matters of faith, was presented to the priests to sign. Finally, all those who attended did sign, affirming orally their loyalty to the pope and claiming that they were trying "to save the church." The text of the "Ten Articles" was never published.

The wave of attacks in 1953 against the church spread from Shanghai to other centers, with anti-Catholic exhibits in Foochow and Amoy, and a general roundup in December of Roman Catholic missionaries still at liberty in Peking. In some places, such as Canton, Protestant church leaders were called on to take part in the condemnation of so-called "imperialistic elements" in the Catholic Church. Statements were issued from Bishops Robin Chen, Mao K'e-chung, and Z. T. Kaung, and the Rev. H. H. Ts'ui, which were usually given a positive title such as "Upholding the Patriotic Catholics Who Are Trying to Cleanse Their Church of Imperialism." [54]

In 1954 there was word of a milder line on the part of the government. The progressives stressed the patriotic element in their movement and said nothing about independence or reform.[55] But the process of "strangulation" continued, according to a report at the end of the year. By that time forty or fifty priests were following actively the Communist line, including one vicar general, and another two hundred were following passively the new movement. Word had been received from 133 of the 143 Catholic dioceses in China: 115 dioceses were still faithful in spite of a rebel priest here and there; 14 were progressive, and 4 dioceses were without any priest.[56] Four priests were among twelve people executed on January 16, 1954, at Hankow, so the hard line had not completely disappeared.[57]

As 1954 came to an end Pope Pius XII issued his famous encyclical *Ad Sinarum Gentes* ("To the People of China"), to the bishops, priests, and laity of China.[58] The pope defended the missionary enterprise, distinctly rejected "autonomy of govern-

[54] *CHIBUL*, June 7, 1954.
[55] Bourassa, *Tactiques Communistes*, p. 52.
[56] *CMBA* VII (January, 1955), 85-86.
[57] *CMBA* VII (June, 1955), 539-40.
[58] *CMBA* VII (February, 1955), 87-90.

ment" and any governing role for the laity in the church, affirmed the necessity on the basis of Christian charity to allow mutual support in the church throughout the world, and referred to the "highest degree of cunning" by which leaders of the progressive movement were trying to set up a national church. It would deny the universality of the church, he said, and therefore would not be Catholic. Calling upon those who had erred to repent, he encouraged the faithful to remain firm. The position of the church remained the same, just as the Communists prepared to confront the church with a still greater test.

THE TURNING POINT: 1955

Father Li Wei-kwang, vicar general of Nanking, had been more vigorous in promoting the patriotic church than had Bishop Alfonse Chang of Peking, who had also cooperated with the movement. Evidently with government approval Father Li assumed the title of Bishop of Nanking, which gave him a measure of prestige in certain circles. His excommunication from Rome was first promulgated in late 1954, but was kept secret for a time in the hope that he might repent and retract. The excommunication was made public March 7, 1955. A bit later some daring Catholics of Nanking placed notices on the walls of the cathedral proclaiming that he had been excommunicated. But Father Li continued to campaign for the progressives, claiming that the "anti-imperialist, love-country movement" was in perfect harmony with Catholic doctrine.[59]

By 1955 the situation in Peking had changed considerably from that which prevailed in 1953. About fifty priests in the diocese remained loyal to Rome, but since the vicar general took a "progressive stand" the cathedral parish was therefore progressive.[60] There were four large parish churches and three chapels open for worship in Peking at the end of March, 1955, all reformed except one chapel. There were thirty parish churches and thirty-three chapels before 1949. Only those priests who were reformed or showed reformist tendencies were allowed a degree of liberty and the privilege of contact with the people. The number of

[59] *CMBA* VII (April, 1955), 354; (October, 1955), 717.
[60] *CMBA* VII (September, 1955), 624.

laymen and laywomen who "refused absolutely and heroically to have any contact with the 'reformed churches or priests'" had fallen to 30 percent. People in this group were not allowed at the Mass and were not able to receive Communion, even in secret. It was estimated that 10 percent followed the Communist line, leaving more than half who neither accepted nor opposed it and were thus able to go to church and receive the sacraments.[61]

This rather obvious classification into three groups could have been made all over the country, and was the same as that presented a year earlier in an analysis of the situation, but in 1954 the group which would not compromise with the Communists was considered to be in the majority.[62] By 1955 the majority were taking the middle position, characterized as "nonresistance" in the hope of eventual agreement or conciliation.

Thus, by the middle of 1955 the patriotic church movement could count two vicar generals in its fold, and had increased its strength in several of the major cities. More and more priests were cooperating with it openly, and at least one ordination under its auspices had been conducted.[63] Any Catholic activity apart from the patriotic group was either marginal or had to be conducted in secret. Except for a few strange cases like Bishop Walsh, who still had a limited degree of freedom, there were no foreign priests or bishops to remind Chinese Catholics of the worldwide nature of their church. In spite of the devotion to which attention has been drawn at each juncture of this story, the Catholic community of China by mid-1955 was an encircled community which had no visible means to resist any longer the power of a totalitarian state.

The telling blow against a weakened church was struck in September, 1955, when Bishop Kung Pin-mei of Shanghai was arrested. Priests and laymen in Shanghai and across the country also were put in prison, and an intensive campaign against the whole church was launched. This series of events marked the end of any

[61] *CMBA* VII (May, 1955), 463.
[62] *CMBA* VI (January, 1954), 93-98.
[63] Reported in a Peking dispatch dated June 10, 1955, which stated that "the four-hour ceremony at any rate was marked by faith which, if not Roman, was nonetheless typically and ritualistically Catholic, and poignant in its mystic fervor." *CMBA* VII (September, 1955), 624.

effective resistance by the church and the beginning of a new era in its life in China.

On April 21, the State Council, chaired by Chou En-lai, decided "to intensify the struggle for suppression of counterrevolutionaries and other criminal elements," which decision was soon echoed in the Justice and Public Security departments of the government. In August the Shanghai *Liberation Daily* began publishing a continuous stream of letters from readers attacking "the criminal activities of the antirevolutionary group of Kung Pin-mei," accusing him of

gathering information, organizing acts of violence, encouraging the resistance movement, spreading rumors, poisoning the minds of youth, cruelly killing babies [a reference to the orphanages], . . . listening to Voice of America broadcasts, etc.[64]

It was obvious that another storm was brewing in Shanghai, and it soon struck.

Bishop Kung, along with 21 to 23 priests, 2 Carmelite nuns, and from 200 to 300 lay Catholics, were rounded up on the night of September 7, 1955, and taken to jail. From 15 to 20 additional priests, plus 600 to 700 laymen, were seized on the night of September 26. By the end of November a total of 1,500 were arrested, including about 50 priests and several seminarians.

Two days after the first night of arrests, the government called a meeting of the remaining 54 priests in Shanghai and announced the reasons for the arrests: Bishop Kung had not participated in various patriotic movements and had not allowed others to do so, had denied the sacraments to patriotic Catholics, would not allow children to join Communist groups, had close relations with imperialists, and had opposed the campaign against the Legion of Mary. Not mentioned at the meeting were previous criticisms that he had refused to make repairs on buildings which the Communists planned to take over, and that he did not permit priests to take part in indoctrination courses.

[64] Summary in *CMBA* VIII (February, 1956), 144. An excellent collection of statements by various government agencies which mounted the attack on Bishop Kung and other alleged counterrevolutionaries may be found in Léon Trivière, "Catholiques et Contre-Révolutionnaires," *BSMEP*, Series II, (January, 1956), 26-40.

Peking radio announced these and other arrests on September 14 and 15, and reported further arrests in Fukien, Chekiang, and Shantung of members of the "China Democratic Party," which was operating "under the cloak of religion." The Legion of Mary was mentioned, as well as people who distributed antirevolutionary books and magazines.[65]

Then a mass meeting was called in the Shanghai Canidrome for September 25, the day before the second wave of arrests. An estimated 15,000 Catholics, including about 40 priests, were present, directed by the authorities to approve the bishop's arrest. A group of progressive Catholics were designated as leaders of the Shanghai Catholic community.

Patriotic Catholics in Shanghai issued a statement which 74 priests and lay representatives of 37 churches had signed, repeating the government's charges and expressing great sorrow that they had allowed the Kung clique to gain such power in the church and thus subvert it to imperialist aggression. The statement includes an unusual expression of thanks:

We thank God for His wise guidance in that the People's Government has taken proper measures to save our church in Shanghai from the road of death on which Kung Pin-mei was leading it.[66]

Father Lefeuvre has detailed in personal conversation the background to this statement. About a year before Bishop Kung's arrest, when all previous efforts to break Catholic resistance in Shanghai had failed, a highly respected missionary superior was put in jail. He was notably nervous and in poor health. The Communists discovered that he was sick and taking medicine, whereupon they took away his medicine with the result that his health deteriorated. In such condition he was told that, if he would confess, all the others would be all right. Each time he wrote a confession, officials pointed out contradictions, so he would revise. He was told to accuse Bishop Kung in the process, which he did. Somewhere along the line the missionary superior was induced to tape his confession, including the accusation against Bishop Kung. After the bishop's arrest the priests were called together and were

[65] *CMBA* VII (November, 1955), 806; (December, 1955), 886.
[66] *CMBA* VIII (March, 1956), 222.

told by officials: "We do not accuse Bishop Kung; it is your own leader who has accused." The tape, with the superior's accusation of Bishop Kung, was played for the priests, who followed suit with the statement quoted above. Father Lefeuvre maintains that no priest had accused anyone up to that time. When the missionary superior was finally expelled and arrived in Hong Kong, his mind was like that of a child. Only after several years did he finally recover.

Attacks on the bishop were to be found in newspaper editorials, cartoons, and articles, although they were not as vicious as in previous barrages against the church. Headlines proclaimed that police had "Smashed the Kung Pin-mei Counterrevolutionary clique," and called on people to "Annihilate . . . all counterrevolutionary elements hidden behind Catholicism." Government charges were amplified to make Bishop Kung the most fearsome spy and saboteur Shanghai had seen in years.[67]

There were, of course, numerous corollary events. Immediately following the first night of arrests the Catholic Patriotic Association of Shanghai, claiming about a thousand members, initiated a series of study and discussion groups throughout the city. Progressives were placed with loyal Catholics in an effort to wear them down; those reluctant to follow the new way were not left alone until they capitulated. Robert Guillain, who visited Shanghai toward the end of the year, heard the story of an elderly lady who was unable to leave her bedroom, so the discussion group in which she was expected to participate came to her room and met with her there.[68] Pressure was put on Catholics to go to church in order to show that there were still Catholics in the churches, that only the counterrevolutionaries had been arrested.[69]

[67] See *Union Research Service Bulletin*, October 4, 1955, and October 11, 1955, for translations of attacks on Bishop Kung and the Catholic Church in the Communist press. A comprehensive survey of the way in which Catholicism was ridiculed by the Chinese press, including an outstanding collection of newspaper cartoons which lampooned the missionaries, may be found in Johannes Schütte, *Die katholische China-mission im Spiegel der Rotchineschen Presse* (Münster i. W.: Ashendorffsche Verlagsbuchhandlung, 1957). A careful study of this volume makes clear the kind of pressure to which Catholics were subjected at various times during the first years under communism in China.

[68] Robert Guillain, *600 Million Chinese* (New York: Criterion Books, 1957), pp. 226-27.

[69] *CMBA* VII (December, 1955), 806.

The September, 1955, arrests in Shanghai were felt all over the country. Bishop Joseph Hu, Lazarist of the diocese of Taichow, Chekiang, and one of the first six Chinese bishops consecrated in 1926, was arrested. His all-Chinese diocese had essentially fulfilled the Three Autonomies, except that it still professed loyalty to the pope. When pressed to have his priests take the indoctrination course, Bishop Hu had replied that instruction and leadership of his priests and his faithful was his own proper responsibility which he would not turn over to the government.[70]

In Hankow on September 15, 1955, Father Odoric Liu and Father Peter Chang, administrators of Hankow and Hanyang dioceses respectively, along with ten other Chinese priests were jailed. The remaining priests and forty seminarians were held under house arrest. All priests, in and out of jail, were subjected to daily indoctrination but appeared to remain firm. Some of the laity were arrested. The standard treatment for the laity, however, consisted of visits by teams of Communists in relays both day and night. The effort was intended to produce accusations or denunciations of their leaders by Catholics themselves.[71]

In Canton three priests, two brothers, and one laywoman were arrested, but Bishop Dominic Tang, S.J., apostolic administrator of the diocese, was not.[72] As of January 5, 1956, there were six priests and twenty lay people of the Canton archdiocese in jail—the lay people presumably for refusing to sign a paper condemning the Legion of Mary.[73] A report from the neighboring diocese of Kaying (formerly led by Bishop Ford) at the beginning of 1956 revealed that eight of the Chinese priests in the diocese were in jail, five of them already for two years. The twelve Chinese sisters in the diocese had been dispersed and were living as laywomen; some were reported to be in jail. The report sums up:

The 25,000 Catholics of this Hakka-speaking district, formerly staffed by the Maryknoll Fathers, are now practically without Mass or the Sacraments. All churches have long since been forcibly closed. The Chinese priests managed, in some places, to offer Mass in their own homes, and the

[70] *CMBA* VII (December, 1955), 909.
[71] *CMBA* VIII (January, 1956), 66.
[72] *Ibid.*, p. 69.
[73] *CMBA* VIII (March, 1956), 230.

Catholics attended when possible. With the latest surge of persecution this is no longer allowed.[74]

Word reached Hong Kong in January, 1956, of the arrest of three Chinese priests in Chengtu, Szechwan, in September of the preceding year, giving further indication that the campaign was nation-wide. There was no further news of the remaining fifty-one priests in the Chengtu diocese.[75]

Although the imprisonment of Bishop Alphonse Ferroni of Laohokow occurred long before these events took place, his arrival in Hong Kong on September 7, 1955, dramatized for the outside world the extreme measures characterizing these events. The picture of the aged bishop—eyes staring from their sockets, his weight down from 180 to 70 pounds, his wrists marred by handcuffs—gave vivid testimony that reports of persecution were true, and raised greater fears for those enduring it.

In retrospect, some of the incidents reported by a visiting French journalist are as graphic as any of those reported by the church. Mr. Robert Guillain had a visit with Mr. Hu Wen-yao, a leader of the progressive Catholics, who at the time was deputy for Shanghai in the National Assembly and had cooperated with the Communists in the takeover of Aurora University. He became a progressive in 1951 after saying that he had never really believed in the Catholic faith and would now follow the example of his son who had become a Communist. Mr. Hu told Guillian that

the foreign missionaries had "voluntarily" left China; that they had all been imperialists and spies, and that rifles and hidden arms had been found in their churches; that Rome did not disapprove of the patriotic Catholic movement; and he ended with these unexpected words: "The missionaries wanted a world war." [76]

Hu Wen-yao also repeated to Guillain the government's charges against Bishop Kung, adding that the Shanghai authorities had sought the bishop's friendship but had been repulsed by him. Mr. Guillain heard a different story from others in Shanghai who said

[74] *Ibid.*, p. 232.
[75] *CMBA* VIII (April, 1956), 299.
[76] Guillain, *600 Million Chinese*, pp. 228-29.

that the bishop did not refuse coexistence, that he had tried to find a way whereby the church could cooperate in good conscience with the government.

On his advice, the Catholics were obedient citizens. They never said a word against military service or even against the Korean War, in which they fought like everybody else. But the Bishop, supported by his faithful, clearly defined the limits of the purely religious field and, in this respect, he defended himself heroically. The conflict grew more bitter when the Communist party demanded that communion should be given to the Pioneers—those Boy Scouts with the red scarves. Monseignor Kiong [Kung] replied that the Bishop and his priests were the sole judges as to who should receive the sacrament. He could not entertain giving communion to boys who had sworn to fight for Communism, an atheistic and materialist doctrine. This refusal is today one of the major counter-revolutionary crimes, which will earn him death or "thought reform" in some prison or concentration camp.[77]

Guillain was also told of the Jewish rabbi in Shanghai who found some Chinese praying in his synagogue. When he asked them why, they said they were Catholics and apologized for using the synagogue without asking, but said that, although their religion was different, "God is here, too, and here we can pray to him. Here, the Temple is clean and the house is devoid of lies." They said their own church had been reformed with a strange priest not loyal to Rome in place of their own priest who was in jail.[78]

When Bishop Kung was arrested, the Chinese priests of the diocese elected an elderly priest, Father Chang Shih-lang, as provisional head of the church, but he was not active and served for only a short time. In March of 1956, "progressive elements" elected Father Chang Chia-shu vicar capitular of the Shanghai diocese. In a public address a month earlier Father Chang Chia-shu had tacitly affirmed the charges against Bishop Kung and was therefore acceptable to the government. Father Trivière, in his account of these events based on Communist sources, points out that only those with "advanced thoughts" or "reformed thoughts" were permitted to take part in the election of Father Chang, that the election was sup-

[77] *Ibid.*, p. 230.
[78] *Ibid.*, p. 231.

ported and aided by the government, and that a reception and banquet held afterward was organized and paid for by the government.[79] The Vatican, upon being informed of Chang's election, refused to recognize it and insisted upon the line of succession which Bishop Kung had indicated if he should not be able to continue. Obviously the Communists and the Patriotic Association paid no attention.

During the months after Bishop Kung's arrest the Patriotic Association increased its hold over the Shanghai diocese and other areas. It controlled and adminishered all the parishes, administered the goods of the church, and distributed subsidies to those parishes in its favor. It censored the mail and confiscated the monthly intention folders of the Apostleship of Prayer because it was considered antirevolutionary. The vice-mayor of Shanghai, a non-Christian, served as president of the association, and a Miss Li Wen-tse, a Catholic who decided to cooperate with the regime after a long imprisonment, was vice-president.

A letter from a Catholic girl in Shanghai, written evidently in late spring of 1956, gives a highly personal description of what youth had to endure after Bishop Kung's arrest:

We, the Catholic youth, were especially sought out. We were locked up in a branch of the police bureau for interrogation and to make a confession. We were forbidden to return to our homes. We spent a week in prison and it was very hard. After that we had to participate in the indoctrination meetings of the district. . . . This was very tiring. Sometimes we had to attend four important meetings of the day, and listen to reports and discussions of small and large committees. This indoctrination went on for three months. Then suddenly the government ordered us to bring the Catholic Youth of District X . . . together for indoctrination. We had to go out in the morning and didn't return until night. We thought that we were at school again: but the discipline was very severe and the atmosphere cold because the supervisors were either Comrades of the Security Bureau or Commissars of the People or in the government employ.

The moral hardships we underwent are indescribable. Sometimes the meetings lasted until early morning. During the period of indoctrination

[79] Trivière, "L'Église catholique," *BSMEP*, Series II (August-September, 1957), 709-13.

we were not permitted to relax, not even on Sunday, and this continued for more than a month. Finally we had to make out a written confession. That was the last thing we had to do, but it was terrifying. Now that the group indoctrination is over we must continue to attend individually. The difference is that we only have to go to the police bureau two or three times a week. We are well convinced that we will not be left in peace.

Now our church is entirely directed by the government. A Patriotic Association has been organized and in the affairs of the church, no matter what they may be, the Patriotic Association takes the initiative and does the directing. A Vicar Capitular has been set up. On the occasion of the establishment of the Vicar Capitular solemn Masses were sung in different churches. All possible means were used to force us to go and sing but we did not go. On May 13, Sunday, we were urged to go and sing at Zo-Se [Shrine of the Blessed Mother, on a hill near Shanghai]. We made all kinds of excuses to get out of it. The annoyances we have to go through are innumerable, especially when we encounter the Commissar of the People whom we have to obey under pain of being declared antirevolutionary and sent to prison. . . . How to live? All my family is scattered. . . . Pray for us, that the Lord will bless us and grant us the necessary strength to bear our afflictions and hardships.[80]

Many Catholics refrained from Mass and from receiving the sacraments at the hands of priests they considered unworthy. There were numerous reports of families praying together at home. This did not mean defeat, but it did mean that open resistance to government efforts to bring the church under control had been weakened drastically within a few months. Open resistance was already a thing of the past in the country districts and in practically all the other cities of China. Catholic resistance in Shanghai had been a last ditch struggle, inspiring to Christians throughout the country, galling to the Communists. With the September arrests, the indoctrination sessions which followed, and the renewed efforts to establish the Patriotic Church which were to come, outward resistance by the Catholics of China gave way to outward control by the Communist government of China.

---

[80] *CMBA* VIII (December, 1956), 761. Lefeuvre includes a number of similar letters in *Shanghai: Les Enfants*, pp. 222-31.

V

The Catholic Church Under Communist Control

ACTUAL ESTABLISHMENT OF THE PATRIOTIC ASSOCIATION

From 1953 to 1955 the term "Patriotic Association" gradually replaced "Three Autonomies" as a designation for government efforts to control the Catholic Church. "Patriotic" was a part of the official name from the beginning; and both those who supported the movement and those who opposed it often spoke of the "patriotic church." It was obvious to most observers that promotion of the Patriotic Association was the same old game played under a new name, but the new name was much more difficult to resist. One could object to Three Autonomies on grounds that the nature and structure of the church were affected, but who could object to being patriotic? Furthermore, effective resistance had been crushed; any name would do.

The Patriotic Association of Chinese Catholics already existed in some cities in 1956 when government efforts to establish the association on a national scale began in earnest. Ten priests and laymen met for this purpose in Peking in January of 1956, but little is known of what transpired. Thirty-eight Catholics, including four bishops, were invited to another meeting in Peking July 19 to 25. The thirty-six who actually attended were joined by Ho Cheng-hsiang, director of the Bureau of Religious Affairs of the State Council, and other government officials. In an atmosphere of "love of country and love of religion," a preparatory committee charged with drafting a constitution was established and a proclamation

132

issued. Chou En-lai received the delegates on July 26, inquired in detail about religious life in various dioceses and about the progress of the patriotic movement, and encouraged them to lift high their national pride, to love their country, and to lead well the Catholic Church.[1]

This friendly attitude toward the church may have been due to the launching only two months earlier of the Hundred Flowers Campaign by the government. Mao Tse-tung made an address, the text of which was never published, in which he was said to have quoted a striking phrase from the ancient Warring States period (sixth to third century B.C.)—"Let a hundred flowers blossom, a hundred schools of thought contend!"—and thus to have inaugurated the Hundred Flowers Campaign. People were encouraged to express themselves and a wave of criticism of the regime followed, including rather sharp comments from several Catholic bishops. The government freed several previously arrested bishops, priests, and laymen. Priests, authorized to wear religious dress again, were allowed to visit their parishes and to receive official Catholic documents. Monasteries and nunneries were to be respected, and the restoration of churches was guaranteed.[2] Although this more relaxed atmosphere continued for about a year, so many criticisms of the government burst forth from all ranks of society that the blooming and contending as such was halted in June, 1957.

Government efforts were stepped up again when Religious Affairs Director Ho called a meeting for February 12, 1957, at which time it was decided to organize the National Patriotic Catholic Association in March. The date was again postponed to July. At the February meeting the government claimed that there were more than two hundred local Patriotic Catholic Associations in existence.[3]

Finally 241 Catholics and government representatives gathered

[1] Trivière, "L'Église catholique," BSMEP, Series II (October, 1957), 814-17, based on extracts from the Chinese press.

[2] Ibid., II (March, 1958), p. 229. For a collection of statements during this period from all types of people, see Roderick MacFarquhar, The Hundred Flowers Campaign and the Chinese Intellectuals (New York: Frederick A. Praeger, 1960), pp. 250-53. The Hundred Flowers episode in 1957 will be dealt with in greater detail when we come to Confucianism and the intellectuals.

[3] Free China Review X (May, 1960), 18.

in Peking from June 17 to July 13, 1957, under the supervision of Ho Cheng-hsiang, organized the National Patriotic Catholic Association, and elected Archbishop P'i Shu-shih of Shengyang as chairman. Certain speakers thanked the government for arresting people like Bishop Kung, for such arrests made possible a strict distinction between legitimate religious activities and counterrevolutionary activities, and between priests and honest Christians and criminals. The conference denounced the Vatican for failing to recognize the vicar capitular elected in Shanghai to replace Bishop Kung, and denied any validity to excommunications pronounced by Rome. The delegates passed a most interesting resolution in which they recognized the religious authority of the pope, but not his right to give orders which had a counterrevolutionary purpose. As Father Lefeuvre points out in his summary of these actions, since only "patriotic Catholics" and the Bureau of Religious Affairs were competent to decide what was religious and what was counterrevolutionary, the pope was stripped of power as far as China was concerned.[4]

It is not clear what jurisdiction the national organization had over local associations. The Heilungkiang (provincial) Patriotic Catholic Association's constitution said that the "highest organ of this association is the Catholic Congress of Heilungkiang"; but it is hard to imagine the absence of some central authority.[5] In actual practice all authority rested with the Religious Affairs Bureau. Local, provincial, and national associations merely carried out the policies and programs of the central bureau and kept its officials informed of developments.

On the surface, therefore, it would appear that this first meeting of the National Patriotic Catholic Association went through the usual motions, denounced those who were to be denounced, and set up the type of organization necessary for the period. Other interpretations of this meeting, which appeared five years later and received wider circulation almost ten years later, provide new insights of great value.

One whom we know only as "Mr. Thomas," a witness to the 1957

---

[4] *Shanghai: Les Enfants*, p. 239.

[5] *Heilungkiang Jih-pao*, July 25, 1959; *CURBAC*, January 15, 1960, p. 11.

meeting, relates a three-step process by which the government sought to win support of a national organization.[6] The first was to designate a number of bishops and priests as national or regional political officers in order "to break the tension between church and state." The second was to employ these deputies to promote interest in a general assembly, with the result that eighty out of more than a hundred dioceses polled replied in favor of such an assembly. The third was to offer concessions to the church, such as restoration of church properties, establishment of a national seminary, and permission to publish Catholic journals and newspapers. In offering these concessions Communist leaders even went so far as to acknowledge that they did not understand the church, and therefore had made "mistakes." "Mr. Thomas" claims that a somewhat capricious type of dialogue was initiated, perhaps forced, in which the Communists stressed patriotism, material progress of the nation, and the people's well-being.

"Mr. Thomas" also maintains that the idea of electing and consecrating bishops was proposed and advocated strongly by the Communists at this conference, but that it was rejected. Archbishop P'i was asked specifically if he would consecrate locally chosen bishops and he refused, seconded by other bishops present.

The offer of concessions, which were never granted as far as available records indicate, was only one of many devices used to gain Catholic support for the Patriotic Association. According to *Fides*, some delegates were summoned to a place near their residence and then taken by guards to Peking.[7] Both before leaving their homes and again after arrival in Peking, various delegates received threats that all lines of personal support would be cut off if they did not vote properly. After the conference, word was received in Hong Kong from priests and nuns that support of the Patriotic Association was obtained under duress or had been misrepresented. And the usual devices, such as providing a delegate with a speech to read or reporting speeches in the press which were not delivered,

---

[6] The material related by "Mr. Thomas" is summarized by Fang Che-yong (Mark), "The Catholic Church in China: The Present Situation and Future Prospects," *Concilium* III (March, 1966), 31-42, especially pp. 34-35. The original articles, eleven in all, were published about 1961 in *Free Pacific Magazine*, copies of which I have been unable to secure.

[7] *CMBA* IX (December, 1957), 704.

were again employed. Priests who opposed the formation of the association were arrested after returning to their homes.[8]

That several Catholic laymen courageously criticized the government's action against the church is known through criticisms of these laymen in the Chinese press.[9] Nieh Kuo-p'ing, who had supported the Patriotic Catholic movement in Tientsin, objected to the imprisonment of Catholics for political crimes, defended the Legion of Mary, and demanded the release of Bishop Kung. Kao Ching-sheng, also of Tientsin, "defended the church's teaching on private property and criticized the Communist system for its lack of mercy and justice." Among Shanghai Catholic lay people who witnessed in a similar vein was a laywoman, Mrs. Tung Kuei-min, who demanded rehabilitation for counterrevolutionaries, and advocated especially a review of the cases in which Catholic nuns in charge of orphanages had been judged guilty of infanticide. Shortly after criticisms of these Catholic lay people appeared in the Shanghai *Wen Hui Pao*, there were reports in Hong Kong that forty such outspoken Catholic laymen had been put in jail. Father A. Sohier has pointed out that people who replaced loyal Catholics as leaders in the church, through their control of the Patriotic Associations, were people who previously had been seen only rarely in the churches and were unknown to the clergy.[10]

In order to bring Catholics into line and answer criticisms voiced during the Hundred Flowers Period and after, the government set in motion a new program of indoctrination meetings. Delegates studied Mao's *On the Correct Handling of Contradictions Among the People*, condemned the "unreasonable attitude of the Vatican," and otherwise tried to promote the Patriotic Association. A fifty-day meeting, for example, was held in Chengtu, Szechwan, at which delegates condemned "rightist Catholics" and discussed "the socialist, independent, and autonomous path of Catholicism in China

[8] Reference both to treatment of priests before and after the conference, and to lay criticisms of the conference, may be found in *CMBA* IX (November, 1957), 628; X (January, 1958), 4-5, 72-77; and X (February, 1958), 171.

[9] A. Sohier, "La Religion en Chine Populaire," *Le Régime et les Institutions de la republique populaire Chinoise* (Brussels: Institute de Sociologie Solvay, 1960), p. 144.

[10] *Ibid.*

and the election of bishops." [11] A priest asserted that China would not perish without the Communist Party. Acting Bishop Liu Chien even expressed preference for the old society, threatened clergymen with excommunication if they should sever relations with the Vatican, and said the Patriotic Association "was not a legitimate organization." Nevertheless, Szechwan Catholics were said to have united against such elements, "patriotically ostracized" them, and pressed on with patriotism and socialism in order to safeguard world peace.

Reports in the Chinese Communist press on all of these follow-up meetings present a standard picture: a majority of the delegates favored separation from the Vatican and local election of bishops, but a small minority "frantically opposed the leadership of the Communist Party and the socialist system and were hostile to the new society." At the Harbin meeting one priest defended Bishop Kung, another advocated "loving our enemies," even "counter-revolutionaries, special agents, and spies," since "not to love them was not Catholic." [12] This small minority of "obstructionists" were ridiculed in the press accounts, as they undoubtedly were in the meetings reported, but the fact that their words were reported in the Communist press is clear indication that there was still considerable resistance to the approved line.

This stubborn resistance called forth intensive indoctrination and study sessions from the fall of 1957 through 1958. These sessions were undoubtedly related to similar sessions on political grounds which followed the disastrous Hundred Flowers Period. The indoctrination sessions followed a standard pattern: effusive eulogies of Communist accomplishments in contrast to what Chiang Kai-skek had done or not done, diatribes against Bishop Kung accompanied by exhibits of weapons allegedly used by the bishop in his counterrevolutionary activities (and to kill children!), attacks on the papacy, and, most important, denunciation of "a small remnant group of reactionary forces among the Catholics in Shang-

[11] CMBA X (March, 1958), 283-85. For the general picture see CMBA X (April, 1958), 390-91. The JMJP, December 24, 1957, report on the Szechwan conference is translated in URS, January 21, 1958, pp. 83-85.

[12] These comments from the Chinese press, e.g., Harbin Jih-pao, November 22, 1957, may be seen in the same URS, pp. 84-86.

hai," who "resented this road to patriotism [indoctrination meetings] and tried [by] every means to sabotage the effort." [13]

The study sessions, part of the general tightening which accompanied the Great Leap Forward in 1958, are described vividly by one who says he tormented or brought anguish of mind to young Catholics of Shanghai.[14] There were five distinct sessions from August, 1957, to February, 1959, ranging in duration from three weeks to five months, during which time the participants were involved from 6:30 A.M. to 10:00 P.M. every day except Sunday.

In the first stage participants were encouraged to speak their minds about the regime, during which time all the criticisms of the government by Catholics, such as reported on preceding pages, came out again. These criticisms were noted down and were then attacked by "activists" during the second stage of the sessions. Defense by Catholics was allowed, but what they said was simply added to previously recorded charges against them. In the third stage, those who were making progress turned on those who wavered in the middle and then on those who resisted.

In the fourth phase the participants signed statements of confession and expressions of "irrevocable confidence" in the Party, then joined in a ceremony of "giving one's heart to the Party." The fifth stage was an assembly of celebration to which parents and friends were invited. In a happy atmosphere further statements were signed, photos were taken, and skits were presented which ridiculed the pope, Bishop Kung, missionaries, and reactionary priests.

The cadre who describes this process says those who gave in thought that by doing so they would be allowed to return to normal life. They discovered, however, that they still had to undergo reform by labor, often in frontier places. Those who did not give in faced prison or deportation. Even the Communist cadres and those who cooperated with them recognized that those who gave in were not won to communism, but were victims of fear and fatigue.

[13] *CMBA* XI (April, 1959), 396. For further details and for the arrest of Bishop Dominic Tang of Canton who refused to cooperate, see *CMBA* X (February, 1958), 173 and (April, 1958), 389.

[14] "Le Persécution des Catholiques Chinoise," *Études* XXX (February, 1965), 265-73.

"Their faith remains intact and their profound love for the church is unimpaired, but their conscience is dull." [15]

LOCAL ELECTION OF BISHOPS

With the organization of a Patriotic Association of Chinese Catholics on a national level and a Patriotic Association in existence in most provinces, the stage was set for the local election of bishops. The Shanghai Patriotic Association in the February 27, 1958, issue of its newspaper called for such elections.

The Vatican, in order to sabotage our church in China, has struck at patriotic priests and it continues in its desire to control the nominations of personnel. We can now no longer have any illusion about the Vatican and we ourselves must assume responsibility with regard to the problem of the bishops: we ourselves must elect them and consecrate them.[16]

To justify this action, the editors pointed out that many bishops had been expelled from China as imperialist agents and would not be allowed to return. Chinese bishops such as Kung of Shanghai and Tang of Canton were in jail because, "by betraying the fatherland and wronging the people, they [revealed they] had nothing Chinese in them." Since so many episcopal vacancies have been left, new bishops must be chosen from among the "patriotic priests," the only ones capable of leading the faithful "in love of religion and of the fatherland."

Less than two months later, on April 13, in Wuhan, Bishop Li Tao-nan of Puchi consecrated Father Tung Kuang-ching of Hankow and Father Yuan Wen-hua of Wuchang. They were followed by thirteen more patriotic bishops consecrated in six different places between April 20 and July 20, 1958. Estimates of the number of illegal consecrations by mid-1958 ranged from twenty-three, reported by *Mission Bulletin,* to thirty-two, reported by the Communist press.[17] Consecrators at various times and places were Archbishop P'i Shu-shih of Mukden, and Bishops Li Tao-nan

---

[15] *Ibid.,* p. 273.
[16] *CMBA* X (June, 1958), 595-96.
[17] *CMBA* XI (January, 1959), 74; XI (March, 1959), 296; XI (June, 1959), 601.

of Puchi, Chao Cheng-sheng of Sienhsien, Yi Hsuan-hua of Siang-yang, and Wang Wen-cheng of Shunking. It must be emphasized that the consecrating bishops listed above had been consecrated earlier according to correct Catholic polity and were loyal to Rome.

We have noted that Archbishop P'i, shortly after his election as chairman of the Patriotic Association in the summer of 1957, declined to consecrate bishops who might be elected locally without Vatican approval. Approximately a year later he is mentioned as one of the consecrators of such bishops. It is not known what specific pressures may have induced the change, but Catholic observers state that he spent considerable time in Communist prisons, possibly for as long as six years, before the 1957 conference. It is possible that the memory of those years, along with the prospect of renewed pressure, led him to join the consecrators. Various travelers who interviewed him in succeeding years saw him as a weary, broken man.

Names of the first two bishops to be consecrated, Fathers Tung and Yuan, were sent by cable to the Vatican. The Holy See replied that the election was invalid and warned the consecrating bishop and the two priests that all three faced excommunication.[18] When Father Francis Xavier Chang was elected illegally in Shanghai in place of Bishop Kung, the Vatican responded by granting unusual powers to all priests in three Chinese dioceses. Thus, priests remaining in communion with Rome in the dioceses of Shanghai and Soochow and in the archdiocese of Nanking were authorized to exercise the pastoral office throughout their own dioceses, and in other dioceses where no other legitimate priest was appointed pastor. That decree, issued on March 1, 1957, also authorized legitimate priests to make dispensations in the care of the faithful which would otherwise be reserved for the bishop. Incidentally, the document was denounced by the Bureau of Religious Affairs as a "scheme concocted by the Vatican . . . that interferes with our country's internal affairs, violates its sovereignty, and damages our patriotic movement against imperialism." [19]

In the summer of 1958, when it was obvious that Vatican warnings against illicit consecrations were being ignored, Pope Pius XII

---

[18] Fang, "The Catholic Church," *Concilium* III (March, 1966), 206.
[19] *CMBA* IX (October, 1957), 553.

issued the encyclical *Ad Apostolorum Principis,* "To the Leaders of the Apostles," dated June 29, 1958. He urged bishops, clergy, and the faithful of China to resist Communist efforts to create the patriotic church. It was the third such encyclical in six years (*Cupimus Imprimis,* "We desire in the first place," 1952, and *Ad Sinarum Gentes,* "To the People of China," 1954), and in part summarized what the Communists in China had done to bring the church under its power during that time. Pointing out that bishoprics were indeed vacant, because of the expulsion, imprisonment, or death of the legitimate incumbents, the pope warned against the election of bishops in the manner they were being elected, specifically the election of and consecration of ten Chinese bishops without authority from Rome.[20]

No announcement was made of the 1958 encyclical until the Vatican knew that copies of it had actually reached a number of priests and laymen in China. At first there was no mention of it in the Chinese press, and no mention of it in any meeting, for no Catholic, patriotic or otherwise, would want to acknowledge having it or knowing about it. It was reported later that a poster plastered to the wall of the bishop's house in Canton read: "Father————is a traitor. He has received the imperialist encyclical from the Vatican." [21]

There was, however, an "Assembly of Protest" against the new encyclical at the cathedral in Changsha, Hunan, October 22-26, 1958, which was reported in the local Chinese press. New bishops were consecrated at the meeting, continuing the trend of the previous summer. There was a similar meeting in Nanchang, Kiangsi, in October, 1958, in which three bishops were consecrated by Bishop Wang Chi-kuei, who was himself consecrated without approval from Rome the previous July. The Nanchang meeting was announced as a "Joint Conference of Catholics and Protestants," although there is no indication that Protestants actually participated in the selection and/or consecration of the Catholic bishops. Government representatives were usually present at these affairs, so there is nothing unusual about Protestants being present. There was a discussion at the Nanchang conference on in-

[20] *CMBA* X (November, 1958), 932-34.
[21] *CMBA* X (December, 1958), 1046-47; XI (January, 1959), 77.

dependence and self-administration, in the course of which the delegates "rejected reactionary documents from the Vatican," an obvious reference to *Ad Apostolorum Principis*.[22]

So, while the encyclical may have given the bishops who consecrated and those who were consecrated guilty consciences, the process continued into the mid-60's. In 1958 and 1959, the illegal consecrations were conducted in an atmosphere of defiance against "imperialist Vatican" interference and domination, with many calls for independence and appeals to national pride. Fairly typical, at least of press reports, is the strident account of the May 18-20, 1959, meeting of the Patriotic Association of Kirin in the city of Changchun. According to the newspaper account, the delegates were discussing a report by Premier Chou En-lai to the National People's Congress.

When they reached the paragraph concerning the struggle against imperialism, they called to mind the controls which the Vatican imposed on Chinese Catholics and they expressed great indignation at the imperialist schemes of aggression under the cloak of religion. After exposing and criticizing the reactionary character of the Vatican, the conference studied ways and means to rid the Chinese Catholic religion of imperialist controls and to realize independence, self-determination, and self-administration for the church. Members of the clergy and other representatives at the conference said with one voice that the history of the Vatican was one of extreme reaction, corruption, and ugliness, and that the Vatican consistently advanced the interests of reactionaries and aggressors under the mask of religion. Dioceses in Kirin province, for example, had been, since establishment, under the control of the reactionary Vatican and imperialism, and this state of affairs, which is repugnant to the inviolable independence of the motherland, must be fundamentally changed. The Chinese Catholic Association, the conference decided, must be independent and on its own, electing its own Chinese bishops.[23]

The step-by-step process is summed up in a rather lengthy report from the *Heilungkiang Jih-pao* of a meeting of the Catholic Congress of Heilungkiang Province, held at Harbin, July 4-14. First there is the stereotyped introduction:

[22] *CMBA* XI (June, 1959), 601.
[23] *Changchun Kirin Jih-pao*, June 5, 1959; *CURBAC*, January 15, 1960, p. 4.

In the course of discussions, the delegates cited numerous facts based on their personal experiences to expose the reactionary nature of the Vatican, and unanimously indicated that the Chinese Catholic Church must necessarily break away from all domination of the Vatican, implement the principle of independence, self-determination and self-administration, and continue to launch penetratingly the anti-imperialist, patriotic campaign in Heilungkiang.[24]

Then follows the report of the election of Father Wang Jui-huan as the "first full bishop of the Harbin diocese," and of Wang's consecration by Archbishop P'i Shu-shih of Mukden. At a "celebration meeting" following the consecration the archbishop made a congratulatory speech which the newspaper summarized as follows:

He [the archbishop] said that for several centuries the Chinese Catholic Church had always been under the control of the imperialists. Not only had no Chinese ever been elected bishop, but the Chinese were deprived of the right to elect. The imperialist elements did what they wished, and under the cover of religion, served the imperialists, acting as vanguards for the colonialists. Now, he said, we have waked up, and in order to safeguard our national dignity, exercise the divine rights of independence, self-determination and self-administration, we must free ourselves from all domination by the Vatican.[25]

The reply of the newly elected bishop, in part quoted, in part summarized, reads as follows:

"I have been elected by the Chinese clergymen and laymen, that is, by the Chinese people. I have been 'consecrated' by the Chinese bishops, that is, by the Chinese people. And of this fact I can be justifiably proud." He finally determinedly pledged that he would, abiding by his oath, firmly support the leadership of the Communist Party, strengthen study, continue to reform his thinking, and resolutely embark on the socialist road. He would contribute all his strength to socialist construction and struggle to the end for the elimination of all control of the Vatican and the implementation of the task of independence, self-determination and self-administration of our church.[26]

[24] *Heilungkiang Jih-pao*, July 25, 1959; *CURBAC*, January 15, 1960, p. 8.
[25] *Ibid.*
[26] *Ibid.*

At several points in the story there are references to speeches by priests, nuns, laymen, bishops, the secretary of the Provincial Committee of the Chinese Communist Party, the director of the United Front Department, and the deputy governor of the province. In reading all such reports one must always bear in mind that the speaker's remarks may have been exaggerated or revised or completely rewritten by the reporter.

The consecration ceremony involved certain striking changes. Hutten reports, but unfortunately does not document, that when Archbishop P'i consecrated four bishops in Nanking in November, 1959, the four priests were presented to the archbishop by Bishop Francis Xavier Chao. Archbishop P'i asked: "Have they been elected by the people?" Bishop Chao replied in the affimative, to which the archbishop responded, "Thanks be to God." According to Hutten, the following were among the sixteen questions which Archbishop P'i asked the candidates:

P'i: Will you love your fatherland in imitation of the example of Christ? And under the leadership of the Communist Party and the People's Government will you direct all priests and believers to be participants in the socialist construction of our country?

Candidates: Yes, we promise.

P'i: In accordance with the principle of the unity of love to fatherland and to religion, and to the greater honor of God and to the salvation of your souls, will you lead the church of China on the road of autonomy and independence?

Candidates: Yes, we promise.

P'i: Will you use your natural talents and your education to do what the Holy Scriptures tell you?

Candidates: Yes, we promise.[27]

In similar manner the consecration of bishops without official approval from the Holy See continued. By November of 1959, the

---

[27] Kurt Hutten, *Iron Curtain Christians: The Church in Communist Countries Today* (Minneapolis: Augsburg Publishing House, 1967), p. 436. Translated from the German, *Christen hinter dem Eisernen Vorhang* (Stuttgart: Quell-Verlag, 1962), by Walter G. Tillmans. Similar questions were asked at consecration services, according to *L'Osservatore Romano;* see *CMBA* XII (February, 1960), 199-200.

number had climbed to at least thirty, although there were others elected but not consecrated. In virtually every report of such consecrations in the Chinese press there was the proud assertion that the Chinese of a certain diocese "have themselves elected their own bishop"; and the action was usually referred to as a blow struck against Vatican and U. S. Imperialism. When those loyal to Rome appealed to canon law, those supporting the new bishops attacked canon law as an "instrument of aggression utilized by imperialism to enslave and oppress the church in China." Excommunications based on canon law of those who participated in the irregular election of bishops were "without effect and without validity." [28]

The Catholic press usually referred to these consecrations as "illicit," and to the bishops thus elected as "schismatic." Such terms have been used only rarely if at all because they are loaded terms and miss a most important point made in retrospect by Bishop Carlo van Melckebecke in 1964. Formerly head of the Ningsia diocese, Bishop van Melckebecke asserted that the election and consecration of bishops without reference to Rome could be termed "illegitimate, but not necessarily schismatic, for this requires that they separate themselves from the head of the church knowlingly, willingly, and obstinately." [29] Although Chinese press reports might lead one to believe that this was the manner or spirit with which Chinese Catholics elected their own bishops,

as far as we know, no definite facts warrant such an admission. We know they are desperately trying to maintain the faith, to keep the church alive, to give their Catholic people the sacraments they need. . . . Even if some of their actions are materially wrong, we are not in a position to judge their persons and even less to condemn them.[30]

[28] Trivière collected numerous statements from *Kuang Yang* and other Patriotic Catholic publications in which Patriotic Catholics proudly defend their right to elect and consecrate their own bishops. They denounce the pope and call for a limitation of his powers. See *BSMEP* 132 (February, 1960), 126-247, and, for statements attacking Canon Law, *BSMEP* 140 (November, 1960), 868-75.

[29] *Fides*, September 5, 1964, p. 525.

[30] *Ibid.*

Several similar reactions should be noted. A Canadian Jesuit heard indirectly from a bishop, consecrated without approval by the Vatican, that upon election he had first declined. Then the bishop heard that another Chinese priest who was a real tool of the government would probably be chosen if he declined. He decided to accept consecration, feeling the diocese would be better off under a bishop loyal to Rome than under a bishop who was more likely to do the bidding of the Communist Party. Father Lefeuvre says it is possible that these new bishops accepted consecration under such circumstances with the thought that by doing so they could hold up momentarily the total extinction of the church, and with the hope that at a later time everything might be regularized.[31]

Father Wei Tsing-sing, after being in Europe for thirty years and therefore away from the actual situation in China, may still be said to contribute a Chinese point of view when he says: "The new prelates act in good faith solely with the pastoral intention of preserving the church and protecting their flocks." [32] A Chinese bishop in exile, Monsignor Vitus Chang, also says that the church in China is not schismatic, "even if some of its members have been victims of their humanity." [33] One may hope that the spirit of understanding and forgiveness expressed by these Catholic churchmen may prevail in any attempt to interpret the local election and consecration of Catholic bishops in China.

As a parenthesis to the replacement of bishops loyal to Rome by bishops apparently acceptable to the Communist government, the *coup de grâce* delivered to two bishops who were symbols of loyalty to Rome must be considered. As Bishop Kung's arrest in 1955 marked the essential end of resistance to efforts to establish the Patriotic Association, so the sentencing of Bishop Kung and Bishop Walsh in March, 1960, demonstrated with finality that only those bishops elected by the people or unquestionably cooperative with the Patriotic Association were acceptable.

The fact that Bishop James E. Walsh was not arrested until Oc-

[31] *Shanghai: Les Enfants*, p. 242.

[32] "Open Letter to the West," *Commonweal*, November 25, 1966, pp. 222-25; also in *Information Catholiques Internationales*, September 15, 1966, pp. 20-24.

[33] *Information Catholiques Internationales*, June 1, 1964, p. 10.

tober, 1958, is one of the real puzzles in the whole period considered. During most of this time he was not allowed to do any work, but was allowed a relative amount of free movement near his residence. From three to four hundred Catholics were allowed to visit him in his home on Christmas Eve, 1956. A few days later he communicated with United Press by telephone without difficulty. He was arrested, however, in October, 1958, although the arrest was not made known until December 15, 1958, when it was announced that he had violated unspecified Chinese laws. Word was received in February, 1959, that he was ill and had been moved from a Shanghai prison to a hospital.[34] He was reported to be in good condition but still in the hospital in mid-1959.

A mass trial was held in the Shanghai Intermediate People's Court, March 16-17, 1960, at which Bishop Kung and thirteen other Chinese, as well as Bishop Walsh, were indicted. After five years' imprisonment without trial, Bishop Kung was first accused of "sabotaging the anti-imperialist and patriotic movement of Catholics . . . and persecuting patriotic Catholics." He was also charged with having

invented and circulated rumors, advocated aggressive war by U. S. imperialism, undermined the peace movement, colluded with and offered shelter to imperialist spies and collected restricted State information, harbored special agents and counterrevolutionaries, and worked to undermine the land reform movement and the movement to suppress counterrevolutionaries, set up secret counterrevolutionary organizations and trained special agents, incited young people to flee the country, secretly stored arms and ammunition, and maintained clandestine radio communications, coordinating [these] actions with U. S. imperialist aggression and the efforts by the Chiang Kai-shek gang to make a comeback.[35]

How or why Communist police and counterespionage agents allowed such activity to be carried out by a Catholic bishop is not discussed.

Bishop Walsh was primarily indicted for having used the facilities of the Catholic Central Bureau in Shanghai to instigate Bishop

[34] *CMBA* XI (April, 1959), 393; (May, 1959), 491.
[35] *NCNA*, Shanghai, March 17, 1960; *SCMP*, March 24, 1960, p. 2.

Kung to commit all the crimes detailed above. Through the bureau and the Legion of Mary, Walsh allegedly directed a network of spies all over the country who cooperated with Chiang Kai-shek,

It is not clear whether Bishops Kung and Walsh admitted the charges against them, maintained silence which was interpreted as assent, or tried to deny the charges, but their response was probably silence.[36] At any rate, Bishop Kung was sentenced to life imprisonment on March 17, 1960, and Bishop Walsh to twenty years on the following day.

Catholics and Protestants, Buddhists and Muslims, held mass meetings across the country applauding what was done. Archbishop P'i, seconded by Wu Yao-tsung of the Protestant Three-Self Movement, voiced approval of the sentencing when they spoke to the National People's Congress in Peking.[37] Constant reference was made to the claim that the two bishops were sentenced for political, not religious crimes, as in a statement by Auxiliary Bishop Le Te-p'ei, leader of patriotic Catholics in Tientsin:

All of our patriotic Catholics understand clearly that the . . . Court of Shanghai has severely punished them [Kung, Walsh, *et al*] not because they are Catholics, but because they are counterrevolutionaries and international spies. This is a problem of eliminating our enemies. Our government has consistently protected the freedom of religious beliefs.[38]

A protest to the effect that Bishop Walsh was engaged in religious work, entered by American Secretary of State Christian Herter, was dismissed as nonsense and as further proof that Walsh had connections with U. S. imperialism and practiced espionage.[39]

At a meeting in early May, 1960, less than two months after the

[36] *Ibid.*, pp. 1, 3. It was reported in early 1968 that Bishop Walsh was in fair health and had received small parcels at Christmas, 1967. Bishop Kung was reported to have recovered from a period of serious illness.

[37] *NCNA* from Shanghai, March 19, and from Peking and Tientsin, March 20, 1960, collected in *SCMP*, March 25, 1960, pp. 1-5; *NCNA* from Peking, March 23, from Chengtu, March 25, and Canton, March 27, 1960, in *SCMP*, April 1, 1960, pp. 3-5.

[38] *SCMP*, March 25, 1960, p. 2.

[39] See *NCNA* reports from Peking, March 22, 23, April 5, 1960; *SCMP*, March 29, 1960, pp. 48-51 and April 11, 1960. *SCMP* translations, referred to in this and the preceeding note, mention many names of Catholic leaders and give some indication of what such men were doing at this period.

sentencing of the two bishops, the Shanghai Patriotic Catholic Association was finally established.[40] This group proceeded quickly to elect Father Chang Chia-shu bishop of the Shanghai diocese; Archbishop P'i consecrated him immediately. Father Chang had served as vicar capitular of the Shanghai diocese since early 1956. Hu Wen-yao, the Catholic layman who had proved himself so cooperative with the government during and after the takeover of Aurora University, was elected chairman of the Shanghai Patriotic Association.[41] The long struggle to bring Shanghai Catholics under Communist control came to an end.

CATHOLIC LIFE IN THE LATE 50's AND EARLY 60's

While the spotlight focused on organization of the Patriotic Association and local election of bishops, Christians as individuals and in small groups, in the background so to speak, demonstrated a remarkable tenacity. Priests loyal to Rome had a slight edge over patriotic priests in the city of Tientsin in 1956, whereas progressives controlled all churches in Peking. In both these northern cities as well as in other places throughout the country, priests living as workmen continued to minister to people as opportunity permitted. The Chinese priests of St. Theresa and Our Lady of Peace churches in Shanghai, however, refused to offer Mass publicly; when ordered by Communist officials to do so they said they could only under Bishop Kung's order, *after* he was released from jail. Similar spunk was demonstrated by the Franciscan Missionaries of Mary who still lived in the sisters' quarters of the General Hospital in Shanghai. They were ordered to attend discussion meetings wearing their religious habits, but they always managed to think of some excuse for wearing lay attire.[42]

The Sisters of Charity continued to work in the Tientsin Hospital, which was, of course, operated by the government. The sisters turned over their pay (from the government) to the mother

---

[40] *NCNA*, Shanghai, May 6, 1960; *SCMP*, May 12, 1960, pp. 14-15.

[41] Hong Kong *Ta Kung Pao*, May 13, 1959; *CURBAC*, January 15, 1960, p. 25.

[42] *CMBA* VIII (June, 1956), 463-64, which also contains information cited in following paragraphs.

superior and thus were able to live in community and to have Mass each morning. When a progressive priest was sent to say Mass, the lay people who formerly came stopped coming although the sisters still attended.[43]

Loyal priests found it increasingly difficult to send young men in secret with the sacrament to Catholic homes. Chinese Jesuits in Hopei province were ordered by police to return to their parents' homes, as were seminary students in another place. Back home they were under police surveillance and not allowed to become workers; they could only do odd jobs.

Several articles which appeared in provincial newspapers in mid-1957 provide a candid assessment of the church's situation.[44] The first, written by two priests, one an acting bishop and the other a vice-chairman of the Patriotic Association, hailed the inauguration of the national organization soon to take place, but went on to say that cadres in rural areas "do not have a full appreciation of the religious policy of the government." The two priests cited an instance when a local cadre ordered people to come to local government offices for a meeting at the same time as Sunday Mass. They did so, only to find that he had not gotten out of bed.

When the two priests tried to tell people about the government's policy of freedom of religious belief, they were asked by people: "Can we still believe in religion? Can we still carry out religious activities?" Fears were widespread, they said, that people would be discriminated against when applying for jobs or in academic examinations if it were known that they were Catholics. There is an almost sarcastic reference to the fact that people in the cities have holidays at Christmas and Easter: "Such a thing we have never seen nor heard of in Hunan. What we only hope for is that our church members will be accorded facilities and opportunities to enable them to lead a religious life."

[43] *CMBA* VIII (September, 1956), 534.

[44] Yang Kao-chien and Li Chen-lin, "On the Four Problems of the Catholic Church," Changsha *Hsin Hunan Pao*, June 3, 1957; Hsu Chen-kiang, "To Implement the Religious Policy Is the Business of All," *Shenyang Jih-Pao*, June 4, 1957; Lan Ting-yü, "Contradictions Between Religion and the Communist Party," Paoting *Hopei Jih-pao*, June 12, 1957; "The Government Protects the Freedom of Religious Belief," Hangchow *Chekiang Jih-pao*, May 9, 1957; all translated in *URS*, August 27, 1957, pp. 317-30. Quotations in these paragraphs are from this *URS* collection.

The priests wrote that two church periodicals published in Hunan had been suspended, several study groups had petered out, and some cadres had lost interest in the patriotic movement, so they concluded that "patriotic associations in various places have been lethargic in their work."

A Catholic layman wrote about this time that there was continued discrimination against Catholics. He maintained that Catholics are "good" fellow countrymen, not counterrevolutionaries, and that they recognize their obligation to participate in socialist reconstruction. He implies clearly that they are not allowed to participate. His and other articles refer to church properties occupied and only after much difficulty returned. And there is reference to the awkward situation faced by Catholics in the campaign to get married couples to use birth-control devices. The plea is made that Catholics have their own method of controlling the number of children and that they be excused from those meetings in which birth-control devices are encouraged.

The final article in this series, a news report, quotes a director of the Provincial Religious Affairs Bureau of Hangchow as saying that the religious policy was not understood, the usual way of admitting that it had not been followed. "As a consequence," the official said, "in a small number of areas temples were torn down, clergymen were blackmailed, and other serious violations of religious policy [occurred]." The main point of his remarks seemed to indicate a lack of overall policy and the need for better communication between government and religious people.

In contrast to these bewildered and plaintive accounts, Bishop Li Po-yu, who was consecrated in 1951 before the Patriotic Association came into power but who supported it after 1957, said in the latter year that all was well.[45] He reported crowded churches, an average of nine hundred infants a year baptized, and over five thousand confirmed from 1951 to 1957. There are no other statistical reports against which to check these figures; they are almost unbelievable in view of what was happening. He maintained that church members were in a better economic position, and that

---

[45] "A Catholic Bishop," *China Reconstructs* VI (July, 1957), 20. The article was published to coincide with the July, 1957, meeting at which the National Patriotic Catholic Association was organized.

their increased offerings had made it possible to repair and enlarge several churches and to build three new ones.

Another encouraging sign was a significant Catholic delegation at the Third National Congress of the Youth of China in Peking, April 9-14, 1958.[46] Out of eighty-two delegates from "circles of believers," there were twenty-seven Catholics: twelve priests, a seminarian, and a nun, plus thirteen lay people. Eleven members of the Catholic delegation were elected to the continuing national committee of the Federation of Democratic Youth.

In view of the government's emphasis on colloquial Mandarin, Bishop Chao of Hsien-hsien published in 1957 a revised edition of a prayer book, *Daily Exercises of the Holy Religion,* in which classical and colloquial versions of prayers appeared in parallel columns.[47] A more radical change in the church's liturgy was the suppression by the Patriotic Association in 1958 of certain prayers offered after Mass for peace, for the pope, and to the Immaculate Heart of Mary.[48] The Patriotic Catholics maintained that the prayers were reactionary, that they had been instituted in 1885 "to combat the workers' movement throughout the world," and that mention of Satan was reference to Stalin. Father Chin Yü-p'eng, of the regional seminary of philosophy and theology for Hupei and Hunan, said that the prayers had not been used since 1957.[49]

The 1958 edition of "Apostolate of Prayer," an international calendar indicating objects for prayer, provoked voilent protests in Shanghai because Catholics were asked to pray "that the religious nature of the Chinese would not be corrupted by atheistic materialism," "that all humanity would understand and abhor the danger and the perversity of Marxist doctrine," and "for the Catholic Church in Formosa." The last two intentions clearly indicated to Father Chang Chi-chung of the seminary in Tientsin that the Holy See supported the imperialist policy of aggression against China and the creation of two Chinas, and that the Vatican represented the capitalist classes.[50] Such prayers, as well as those

[46] Trivière, "L'Église catholique," *BSMEP* 136 (June, 1960), 518-24.
[47] Paul Brunner, "The Prayerbook of China," *CMBA* XII (June, 1960), 589-90.
[48] *CMBA* XI (January, 1959), 74-75.
[49] Trivière, "L'Église catholique," *BSMEP* 131 (January, 1960), 46.
[50] *Ibid., BSMEP* 142 (January, 1961), 51-54, quoting from *Kuang Yang,* March 1, 1958, pp. 31-34.

for Bishop Kung—"How can we pray for him?"—were not to be uttered.

By 1958 and 1959 pressures on the church had again mounted. Many churches were closed. The Peking Cathedral and related buildings were annexed by the government. St. Michael's Church in Peking was also closed, but Mass was still being celebrated in Immaculate Conception Church in that city. Only one church remained open in Swatow, and only the cathedral, badly in need of repairs, remained open in Tientsin.[51]

A young man who arrived in Macao in mid-1959 reported:

Few can go to Mass, . . . but most of the Catholics get to confession and receive the Last Sacraments when death is near. Father . . . says Mass secretly . . . [and] at a different hour each day. . . . I went with Father on a sick call late in the night. The soldiers almost caught us.[52]

Visitors to China also reported strange incidents. One asked his guide if there was freedom of religion and received the angry reply: "In the new China there is no religion." One who wanted to go to Mass in Shanghai was told he had to have a visa to go to church. These incidents probably are exceptional, but it seemed to be a fairly common practice for Chinese tourist agencies, which had urged travelers to visit churches in 1956 and 1957, to send visitors in 1959 on routes by which churches would be avoided.[53]

By 1959 practically all priests and nuns were engaged in various forms of manual labor. All along the clergy had raised bees and chickens, grown vegetables and fruits, and done simple handicraft work. Some had peddled simple articles, and had thus been able to maintain contact with people and to utter an occasional word of spiritual counsel. One Catholic layman later wrote that he and a priest worked in a vineyard and that they were therefore able "to receive our Lord."

One may sense both the joy and pain of labor in Sister Suen Tsong-yi's story which was published in a Tientsin Catholic paper:

[51] *CMBA* XI (September, 1959), 715; (October, 1959), 834.
[52] *CMBA* XII (February, 1960), 221.
[53] *CMBA* XI (October, 1959), 835.

All the sisters as well as the bishop and priests are taking part in work in the fields. This lasts from six in the morning until nine at night. At midday we take our meals in turns so that work is not interrupted. Those who did the ground change teams every twenty minutes and those who are breaking stones every ten minutes. When wells are being dug supper is passed over and work continues on an empty stomach until nine-thirty in the evening.

At harvest time we naturally cleared our own fields, but, in the spirit of charity, we also helped to harvest the fields of the cooperative. We rose at three in the morning and then after Mass set out to work.

During the dry season we irrigated the fields. As we turned the handles of pumps we sang songs such as "The New Way" and "The Lighthouse." During rest periods we studied the accounts of Liu Shao-ch'i. Of course we no longer had our religious habits. On our heads we had white coifs shaped like bowls and just big enough to cover our short hair. We no longer feared the sun.[54]

Word was received by *Fides* that about three hundred nuns in the Shanghai area had been grouped together in a former convent at Zikawei, from which they were led every morning to a small steel mill which was a former Jesuit residence. There they were put to work with a number of Jesuit fathers.[55]

There is a report that Jen Tsong (Sister Nan-tai of Hopeh) was so zealous in her work that she was named a "model woman worker" and awarded the "Flower of Glory." She was praised for hard work in the fields, and for doing propaganda work among Catholics on rainy days.[56]

In a report dated September, 1959, Archbishop P'i Shu-shih spoke of Catholics who had been cited as model workers in socialist reconstruction. One had invented a device with which 320 looms could be operated at once, and another had invented a medical device for extracting fluid from the human body. The archbishop gave the following statistics to demonstrate Catholic participation in the life of the nation:

According to incomplete statistics of 1957, more than 400 of our bishops, priests, sisters, and lay members of the church have become deputies to

[54] *CMBA* XI (January, 1959), 80, quoting *Kuang Yang.*
[55] *Fides*, February 28, 1959, p. 68.
[56] *CMBA* VI (January, 1959), 80.

People's Congresses at the national, provincial, municipal, *hsien,* and *ch'ü* levels and members of the Chinese People's Political Consultative Conference. In April this year, six Catholic bishops, one Catholic priest, and two Catholic laymen attended the first session of the Second National People's Congress and a conference of the Third National Committee of the CPPCC. . . . There is also a large number of the Catholic clergy, sisters, and Catholic laity who have been elected members of the Federation of Democratic Youth and Federation of Women at the national, provincial, municipal, and *hsien* levels. In addition, . . . T'ung Shao-sheng, vice-governor of Szechwan, is a Catholic.[57]

In spite of ambiguity and possible exaggeration, this is a sharp contrast to the early days of Communist rule in China when Protestants, Buddhists, and Muslims participated in meetings of various official bodies, and Catholics were conspicuous for their absence. Such a statement in this context undoubtedly indicates that Catholics, at least those who are called "Patriotic Catholics," had met the conditions necessary for survival at that time and had achieved a type of contained existence similar to that which Protestants had achieved some years earlier through the Three-Self Movement.

The pride with which Archbishop P'i undoubtedly gave his report must not obscure the more troublesome factors in the situation as summarized by the editors of *Asia* at the beginning of 1960. They point out that churches in many places were closed or used for such profane purposes as political meetings, showing of films, and Communist stage plays. Even if a church was open, the majority of people would have no time because their days were consumed by work and their evenings by political meetings. The number of active, loyal priests had been drastically reduced by death, imprisonment, deportation, and forced labor, leaving in most instances only the patriotic priests from whom many Catholics did not wish to receive the sacraments. *Asia* editors say the following testimony is heard again and again: "We offer the Holy Sacrifice spiritually. . . . We make spiritual communions. . . . We have family prayers. . . . We recite the Rosary together. . . . Our home

[57] *NCNA,* Peking, September 9, 1959; *CURBAC,* January 15, 1960, p. 1.

is now our church.[58] Such is the general pattern which continued into the 60's.

The Chinese Patriotic Catholic Association held its second conference in Peking, January 5-19, 1962, with a stance firmly in favor of the government. Archbishop P'i gave a report on the association and several government representatives spoke on the national and international situations. The 256 delegates to the conference affirmed that the situation at home and abroad was favorable, saw great progress under the leadership of Chairman Mao and the Party, rejoiced in the success of the Catholic patriotic anti-imperialist movement "thanks to the leadership of the Party and the government and the efforts of clergy and laity." Only in the last clause of the following summary statement of the conference's final resolution was there a religious note. The Chinese Patriotic Catholic Association

must wholeheartedly accept the leadership of the Chinese Communist Party, follow the socialist road, energetically serve socialist construction, hold aloft the anti-imperialist banner, take an active part in the anti-imperialist struggle and the defense of world peace, oppose the U. S. imperialist occupation of our territory of Taiwan and its plot of creating "two Chinas," support the national liberation movements, continue to be vigilant and expose the plot of U. S. imperialism and the Vatican to harm the new China by utilizing Catholics, resolutely shake off the control of the Vatican, and attain thoroughly the goal of independence and self-government for Chinese Catholics in the administration of the church.[59]

The New China News Agency report says that "regulations" of the association were revised but does not indicate in what way. Archbishop P'i was reelected national chairman. Two days after the conference closed, seven new bishops were consecrated in the Nant'ang Cathedral in Peking by Archbishop P'i. The dioceses for which the new bishops were consecrated were widely scattered. There is no indication whether they were elected in their respective dioceses, which is presumed to be the case, or whether they were elected at the national conference. The *Fides* report of the election,

---

[58] *CMBA* XII (February, 1960), 204-5.
[59] *NCNA*, Peking, January 19, 1962; *SCMP*, January 26, 1962, pp. 15-16.

which also does not answer this question, says that as of January, 1962, forty-two bishops had been consecrated without the approval of the Holy See.[60]

Reversing a three-year trend of relative silence about the Vatican, a "Letter to Clergymen, Ecclesiastical Workers, and All Believers in God in the Province (Kwangtung)" demanded that Chinese Catholics "must free themselves completely from the Vatican's control, and expose its imperialist nature and its plot to enslave people the world over." [61] Then in December of 1963, *Kuang-ming Jih-pao* attacked the Vatican's "strategy of peace" as an effort "to chloroform and deceive the whole world." The last three popes, Pius XII, John XXIII, and Paul VI were accused of supporting American imperialism and neo-colonialism through special agents (missionaries) sent throughout the world. *Fides,* in reporting the attacks, saw them as "an indirect reproach to Moscow, which shared responsibility for having the Balzan Peace Prize awarded to John XXIII and allowed Orthodox observers to attend the Council." [62]

In spite of rumors of paper shortages, in 1963 a Chinese Communist publishing company reprinted a seventeenth-century Portuguese Jesuit's commentary on Aristotle's logic.[63] In 1965, however, there was an extensive article in the Canton *Nan-fang Jih-pao* calling on everyone to oppose scholasticism because it divorced thinking from practice. The fact that it prevailed in the church in the Middle Ages, when it was the "handmaid of theology," is noted. Scholasticism, as the servant of ecclesiastical ethics and the feudal system, still "seeks to take people away from realistic struggle, making them submit to the will of God and subjecting them to enslavement by oppressors." [64]

To get a complete picture of the early 60's, again the contrast

---

[60] *Fides,* February 3, 1962, p. 65. This accords with Hang's estimate of thirty-five such bishops consecrated by the end of 1961. See *Die katholische Kirche,* p. 128. For further comments on the conference, on the effects of brainwashing, and on evidence for government control of the conference, see *Fides* February 17, 1962, pp. 90-91.

[61] *KMJP,* December 6, 1963; *Fides,* February 1, 1964, p. 70.

[62] *Fides,* May 4, 1963, p. 283.

[63] *Ibid.*

[64] Canton *Nan-fang Jih-pao,* April 6, 1965, also in *KMJP,* April 16, 1965; *SCMP,* May 5, 1965, pp. 15-19.

between the reports of travelers who entered China and the refugees who left it is necessary. Felix Greene, in his visit to China in the early 60's, attended a service in a Catholic church in Peking which was about half full. He counted 540, more women than men, with quite a few children. He noticed two confessional boxes in operation, and that the priest who officiated at Mass was assisted by a young man in work clothes. About one half the congregation was under forty, about one tenth were in their teens or early twenties. The spirit seemed good as people sang "This Church Is Alive," and as they stood around chatting after church. He saw no national flag as in Protestant churches.[65]

On the other hand, two Catholic Canadians in 1960 tried in three different places to attend Mass on successive Sundays, but found the church empty in Changchung, only one hundred in the large cathedral in Shanghai, and about forty present in Canton.[66]

Another traveler, Edgar Snow, found that in Shanghai priests could maintain shops for making and selling religious articles.[67] They could receive contributions from the laity and payments for Masses and other services, the sum total of course being quite small. In addition to the sources of income mentioned by Snow, a later traveler to China, the German journalist Hugo Portisch, was told that the state still paid "rental interest" to the church for properties it had occupied.[68] He was also told that priests did not receive salaries as such from the government, but could, like other citizens, request financial aid. One of the functions of the Bureau of Religious Affairs, he was told, was to be concerned with the financial needs of priests and to determine which churches were to be renovated and maintained.

Snow was told that worship was permitted, but not proselytization or missionary activity, Sunday schools, or catechetical

---

[65] Felix Greene, *The Wall Has Two Sides* (London: Jonathan Cape, 1962), pp. 109-10. Most observers would say that an appearance of normal church life was maintained in Peking and Shanghai to impress foreign visitors.

[66] Hutten, *Iron Curtain Christians*, p. 440.

[67] Snow, *On the Other Side*, p. 556.

[68] *Red China Today*, rev. ed., trans. Heinz von Koschembahr (Greenwich, Conn.: Fawcett Publications, 1967), pp. 278-79. Original published by Verlag Kremayr and Scherlau in Vienna, 1965; the first American edition published by Quadrangle Books in Chicago, 1966.

instruction. Mr. Snow asked about the possibility of young people continuing in the faith or new people coming into the church when there was so little opportunity for religious instruction to counteract the continual stream of atheist teaching in the schools. A certain Father Chen replied that as long as there was freedom of conscience there was no problem. Instead, the priest was hopeful of attracting "men of high moral and spiritual convictions" to replace the "rice Christians" of former years. Snow does not report that they were or were not getting people of this higher caliber. In reply to Snow's question about an apparently greater interest in applied ethics than in propagation of the faith, the pastor replied that they should be the same and that "under new conditions we can make them so." [69]

Refugees from Shanghai in the summer of 1962 brought a somewhat different attitude. They boasted that they had not set foot in church since the arrest of Bishop Kung in 1955 because the churches were run by patriotic priests. They reported that large numbers of Chinese priests, and all the Jesuit fathers save one, were either in prison or undergoing reform by labor. They added that almost every Christian family in Shanghai had one of its members in the same category.[70]

A refugee metal worker from Canton reported in late 1962 that a few Catholic churches were open in that city, but only about 10 percent of those who used to go to Mass continued because church doors were watched. He added that six priests did say Mass in the cathedral before going to factories where they earned enough to keep themselves from starvation. This particular worker felt that he had been discriminated against because he was a Catholic, and that Christians in general felt this way because they were punished severely for some breach of regulations whereas non-Christians might receive only a few days ideological education.[71]

An extended summary of such reports and their implications may be found in a *Fides* report of midsummer, 1963. Some Catholics saw no fault in receiving the sacraments from patriotic

[69] Snow, *On the Other Side*, pp. 557-58.
[70] *Fides*, September 1, 1962, pp. 497-98.
[71] *Fides*, December 16, 1962, pp. 723-24.

priests; others, like the ones reported above, carried on private religious observances. Cadres were present at most services to take down the names of those who attended, as well as what the preacher might say. Those in work camps were "treated like the lowest coolies obliged to perform the hardest and most menial tasks 'and it is still necessary to be insulted unto death' wrote one of them." [72]

Restrictions on baptism and on religious education, reported by Religious News Service on June 19, 1964, are confirmed in substance by the French journalist Robert Guillain. In spite of rather trenchant criticisms of Chinese pressures on the Catholic Church after his 1955 visit, Guillain was allowed to visit China again in 1964 after France recognized the People's Republic. Guillain says that Catholic parents could no longer present infants for baptism and that only one who had reached the age of eighteen, and who specifically requested baptism, might be baptized. [73]

Guillain says that catechetical instruction was not forbidden, but that any child known to be receiving it was subjected to intense atheist propaganda in his school and excluded from the important Young Pioneers and Youth League. Even religious instruction in the home had to be without the knowledge of outsiders, a feat almost impossible to achieve. [74]

Thus, with restrictions on baptism and religious education, plus a third factor, already mentioned—that Catholic seminaries were closed and no priests being prepared—by 1965 one could foresee nothing but the gradual demise of the church. Even though a few churches were open in the major cities, with their Christmas and Easter services reported in the mainland press, the normal ways by which Christian nurture and continuing life are sustained had all but disappeared. In some fashion the Christian family remained, but even its efforts could provide only the slightest resistance to constant pressures from the other side, certainly not against the tidal wave which was soon to break.

[72] *Fides*, July 27, 1963, pp. 457-59.

[73] Robert Guillain, *When China Wakes* (New York: Walker and Company, 1966), p. 201. Translation of *Dans 30 Ans la Chine* (Paris: Editions du Seuil, 1965).

[74] *Ibid.*, p. 202.

THE MID-60's AND THE CULTURAL REVOLUTION

The picture of the Catholic Church in China on the eve of the Cultural Revolution is best seen in the report of a Mexican priest, Felipe Pardinas, S.J., who was able to accompany some English anthropologists to China in the fall of 1965 at the expense of the Latin American–China Friendship Association. He heard from Archbishop P'i at a banquet that the Chinese Catholic Patriotic Association was a political, not a religious association, and therefore that the archbishop did not consider himself the religious head of the church in China. In reply to the question as to who was the head, P'i replied that "as in the rest of the world, in every diocese, the bishop [is] the spiritual ruler." [75]

The archbishop told Father Pardinas that there were twenty ecclesiastical provinces, seventy bishops, two thousand priests, and three million Catholics, but did not distinguish how many bishops and priests were actually carrying out their duties. He made some vague remarks about baptisms, and made the strange assertion that parents were "not willing to baptize their children. They prefer to wait until the children are old enough to decide for themselves." [76] Marriages were still being held in the churches and a few priests had been ordained.

Father Wang, a priest in Peking, said that his work was "to activate religious life as well as to provide patriotic and anti-imperialist education for a community of approximately four thousand Catholics." Father Pardinas received similar round figures in Nanking, Shanghai, Hangchow, and Canton which are practically devoid of meaning, but Father Wang in Peking told him that there had been only ten baptisms the preceding Easter.

A priest in Canton bemoaned the "failure to recruit and appoint native clergy to high positions" in former years. He claimed, however, that "priests are trying to keep both liturgy and usage intact." He said that priests were supported by rents from houses owned by the cathedral, as well as by government help and salaries from the Patriotic Association.[77]

[75] "A Visit to Red China," *World Mission,* XVII (Fall, 1966), 62-70. Quote from p. 63.
[76] *Ibid.,* p. 64.
[77] *Ibid.,* pp. 66-70 for Peking and Canton visits.

The Mexican priest's conclusion after his visit is rather striking. He predicted that at the present rate the Catholic Church could last for two generations before dying out or becoming a "strange sect." [78]

One must bear in mind that very few churches remained in the hands of the Catholic Church in 1965. All rural churches were closed during Land Reform in the early 50's and many were never allowed to reopen. They were used as meeting halls, schools, hospitals, or granaries—or left unusued or demolished. After 1958, the majority of city churches met the same fate. Church school and hospital buildings, of course, were taken over by the government in 1951 and 1952. The Catholic Church had long been criticized as a "landlord" because of its extensive properties. Cause for this type of criticism disappeared long before 1965; by that time the church's physical position was inconspicuous indeed.

During the last week of Lent, 1966, a Shanghai correspondent found the Zikawei Cathedral open all day, with two early Masses every day and two additional services on Sunday. Fresh flowers were on the altar and the premises were neat and clean, but only two people were present. "Even at Christmas only Low Mass is being celebrated, no children can or are willing to serve as altar boys, and there is no choir." [79]

Catholic refugees who arrived in Hong Kong in 1965 seemed to have kept the faith, but most of them had not served at Mass for five to seven years and were completely ignorant of the Second Vatican Council or of the fact that Pope Paul VI had succeeded Pope John XXIII. They did not know who among their fellow workers in office or shop back in Canton or Shanghai were Christian. They had not dared to arrange baptism for their children, nor to give them any Christian education. [80] Catholics in China, espe-

---

[78] *Ibid.*, p. 70. Father Richardson quotes priests from Southeast Asia who visited China in 1965-66 and reported that "the religious situation 'worsens day by day.'" *China and Christian Responsibility* (New York: Maryknoll Publications and Friendship Press, 1968), p. 98.

[79] "Shanghai Newsletter," *South China Morning Post*, April 15, 1966.

[80] *Informations Catholiques Internationales*, November 15, 1965, pp. 16-17. A French priest, Abbé R. Baron, who interviewed a Chinese priest in 1964, confirms the fact that Vatican II had "absolutely no influence on the Church in China," that liturgical changes authorized by the Council had not been made in China, and that the Church, understandably, "seems to be frightened of any

cially in Nanking and Hangchow, confirmed these features in their own religious life to an editor of *Informations Catholiques Internationales* in August of 1966. A priest at the only Catholic church in Nanking said there were about one thousand faithful, counting those who came from surrounding villages. He himself observed, "As you can see, there are very few youth." In Hangchow it was more dismal: ten people present in the church and only two hundred faithful in the community, according to a priest who had received no information on the Vatican Council.[81]

In its survey of the missionary world for 1965, *Église Vivante* observed a certain calm in maintaining Catholic worship. Bishops managed to make the rounds for confirmation of a few candidates, priests were managing to celebrate Mass, and some of the religious who worked in field or factory during the day maintained a semblance of community. The most significant thing was the fact that bishops in China were able to send occasional orders for religious books to Hong Kong, "a means of manifesting, in indirect fashion, their attachment to Rome." [82] All such bishops and priests at least outwardly supported the Patriotic Catholic Association.

There were miscellaneous indications in late 1965 that the attitude toward Catholicism by Communist authorities had not changed. A review of the play *The Deputy* hailed it for showing "the Vatican's responsibility for Hitler's massacre of the Jews," but added that the play still "reflects a capitalist mentality" and criticized the hero because he did not engage in class struggle.[83] The *China Youth* magazine for November 23, 1965, carried two photographs, one of which showed five foreigners in military uniform and the other, the same five foreigners in religious garb. The caption said:

Look at these North American wolves. Giving up the military uniform they put on a Catholic cassock. These Christian missionaries are really

sort of change." See Father Fang's article, already cited, in *Concilium* III (March, 1966), 33. Baron's article was published in *Église Vivante* XVII (January, 1965), 54-64.

[81] *Information Catholiques Internationales*, September 15, 1966, p. 18.
[82] *Église Vivante* XVIII (May-August, 1966), 194.
[83] *Fides*, December 15, 1965, p. 725.

American soldiers whose hands are stained by the fresh blood of the Chinese people.[84]

As the storm of the Cultural Revolution began to break in the summer of 1966, Catholic observers said it had no specifically religious character. Religion could be classified under any one of the "four olds"—old culture, old thinking, old habits, old customs—and was therefore to be destroyed. Christians and followers of other religions were not attacked as such, but like all people were expected to examine their consciences to see if they had "perverse intentions." It seemed that the government had more to worry about than the small minority religious groups.[85]

In August, Reuters reported that in Peking "red flags are flying on the Catholic church (Nant'ang, or South Church), and the church's walls and entrance are covered with placards denouncing superannuated traditions and customs." [86] Biblical pictures were still hanging but had been crossed out with black lines and by Chinese characters saying that such things were no longer permitted. Foreign newsmen were not able to enter, but they saw a bust of Mao Tse-tung "enthroned" inside, pictures of Communist leaders, red flags and banners, and posters extolling the revolution.

The Catholic church at the center of the city of Canton was stripped of all Christian symbolism, the red flag placed above it, and a propaganda platform with loudspeakers in front of it.[87] A Chinese woman who was visiting Canton in late summer, 1966, said she went through "three days of hell" because she was seen wearing a crucifix by Red Guards, who seized her and subjected her to three days of questioning. She was released at last, but without the crucifix.[88]

The Shanghai correspondent of the *South China Morning Post* announced that "the final page of the history of Christian religion

[84] *Fides*, January 8, 1966, p. 14.
[85] *Fides*, June 22, 1966, p. 365.
[86] *Fides*, August 31, 1966, pp. 451-52.
[87] Based on report of Canadian correspondent David Oancia, cited in *China Notes* V (January, 1967), 3.
[88] *China Notes* IV (October, 1966), 4.

in Shanghai was written on August 24 [1966]." Whether the announcement was premature or not, on that day all churches

were stripped of the crosses, statues, icons, decorations, and all church paraphernalia by the revolutionary students, wearing "Red Guard" armbands and determined to eradicate all traces of imperialist, colonial, and feudal regimes.[89]

The Catholic churches so affected were the Zikawei Cathedral, the Church of the Sacred Heart, associated with the former Francis Xavier College, St. Joseph's Church on Szechwan Road, St. Peter's Church near the former Aurora University, as well as other Catholic churches which had managed to remain open until that time.

Although refugee reports are not to be taken at face value, a merchant from Shanghai told of a Catholic in that city who was found to have a crucifix in his possession when arrested by Red Guards. A "people's court" was set up immediately, the man was found guilty, and was condemned for following the "religion of the running dogs." It was decided on the spot that he be crucified, so he was tied to a wooden cross erected for that purpose on the school playground. Red Guards then stoned him and tortured him with a red-hot bar until his cries brought troops to his rescue.[90]

On the morning of August 25, 1966, Red Guards broke into the compound of the Academy of the Sacred Heart, a school operated for the education of children of diplomatic personnel by Franciscan Sisters of Mary. These French nuns, eight in number, had been allowed to continue this ministry, many years after other foreign missionaries were expelled or interned, because of representation with Chou En-lai by diplomatic personnel who found Chinese schools inadequate for their children. The Red Guards did not enter classrooms on the first day, but planted a red flag on the school tower and a bust of Mao Tse-tung in the campus. They plastered the walls of the school with posters reading "Get out, foreign devil!" and "Chase out running dogs of imperialism." [91]

[89] Hong Kong *South China Morning Post*, August 30, 1966.
[90] Hong Kong *Tin Yin Yat Po*, September 28, 1966; in *China News Items from the Press*, October 5, 1967, p. 6.
[91] *South China Morning Post*, August 27, 1966.

According to the Communist press the school was taken over the following day by the Peking Municipal People's Council "at the demand of Peking's Red Guards and revolutionary masses and to safeguard China's security and the interests of the people." [92] The press report also referred to two mass rallies on August 26 and August 28. At the first the order to ban the Franciscan Missionaries of Mary and take over the school was announced; at the second the immediate deportation of the nuns was announced. Red Guards "indignantly exposed the crimes committed by the Mission," and "revolutionary people and victims trampled underfoot and oppressed by the reactionary missionaries spoke at the [second] rally." The news account refers several times to "counterrevolutionary activities" carried out by the nuns and says that they

secretly colluded with a number of counterrevolutionaries in the Catholic churches in Peking, Hopei, Shansi, Inner Mongolia, and Harbin, undertook espionage of information about China, printed reactionary documents, fabricated and spread rumors, instigated counterrevolutionaries to engage in plots to create riots, and committed acts of sabotage seriously detrimental to China's sovereignty. [93]

The eight nuns crossed the border at Lowu on August 31 after traveling by rail from Peking with an armed guard. About one hundred Red Guards gathered at the railway station on the Chinese side of the border, jeered the nuns as they crossed, shouted slogans and sang "The East is Red." Sister Eamon (Mary O'Sullivan), eighty-five, collapsed as she crossed the bridge and was taken immediately to the hospital; she died the following day, evidently because of exhaustion after an ordeal of eight days in which she and the others had very little sleep. The British Foreign Office protested this treatment of a British subject, as well as the desecration of graves in the foreign cemetery in Peking by Red Guards, but there is no known response. Upon their arrival in Paris on September 30, a French nun, Sister Marie de Saint Sigisbert, said they were very afraid but did not suffer real hardship. She said the boys who en-

[92] *NCNA*, Peking, August 31, 1966; *SCMP*, September 6, 1966, pp. 21-22.
[93] *Ibid.*

tered their convent had "wrecked everything in the building and locked us up in rooms without really ill-treating us, but [were] threatening us with the worst of punishments." [94]

There is some idea of what the Cultural Revolution meant to individual Catholics in two stories, one in a New China News Agency report and the other from an American publication in Hong Kong. The first story comes from Tientsin and is cited as evidence of the "striking change in mental outlook" under "influence of the proletarian cultural revolution."

Typical in this way is Li Yu-chieh, a woman in her sixties. She was known for her devotion to the Catholic religion and had never taken part in any political activities. The Red Guards' exposure of the counterrevolutionary crimes of a handful of reactionary priests, which took place in the course of the proletarian cultural revolution, opened her eyes to her own folly over so many years, in placing blind faith in the Catholic church.

She recollected her past sufferings. A worker's daughter, whose parents died while she was still very young, she worked as a child labourer in a hospital affiliated to a Catholic church. There she underwent every kind of physical and mental maltreatment. She pinned her hopes on God, but God was not much help to her. Her condition remained as wretched as ever. After Tientsin's liberation, the people became emancipated. But Li Yu-chieh remained caught in the spiritual fetters of the Catholic Church. Her earnings from hard and diligent work went to fatten the purses of the Catholic priests.

Now she recalls how each of those reactionary Catholic Fathers, who started out with next to nothing, had become wealthy by squeezing the hard-won earnings out of innumerable poor people like herself. Awakened, she threw aside the God to whom she had prayed so piously all these years. She has become an activist in the proletarian cultural revolution and helped to enlighten other people with her own stories of past sufferings.[95]

The second is the story of Li Han, a Catholic who had spent five years in prison and labor reform from 1958 to 1963. Before 1958 she had lived in Hong Kong, but had traveled back to visit relatives in Kwangtung province a number of times. In early 1958 she had

[94] Reuters dispatch in *South China Morning Post*, October 1, 1966.
[95] *NCNA*, Tientsin, October 2, 1966.

167

occasion to tell several old friends in Canton about the Catholic priests she knew in Hong Kong. One of these friends presumably reported to the authorities, and Li Han was arrested. Six months later she was tried without defense counsel and sentenced to five years of reform by labor. Assuming that her mind had been remolded, the authorities told her to resume her practice of the Catholic religion and to report on the activities of her Catholic friends to the Canton Municipal Religious Affairs Bureau. She could not find anything worth reporting, however, for which she was regarded as noncooperative and called a "bad element." Li Han was a marked target for the Red Guards when they came to Canton in August, 1966. When she went out she was forced to wear a sign on her chest giving her name, sex, address, and counter-revolutionary classification. She reported that the first time she wore it she was so terrified by the jeering, spitting children who surrounded her that she ran back home and refused to go out again. While she was at home the sign had to be hung on the door, in effect inviting the Red Guards to enter and search the house. She reported that there was really no point in going out with such a sign since people with her classification were not allowed to ride buses, go to restaurants or movies, or even to walk in public parks. She finally escaped to Hong Kong.[96]

With the onslaught of terror in late 1966, even the simplest kind of correspondence between the mainland and the outside world ceased. As confusion and chaos continued into 1967, however, letters from a few Catholic priests and laymen began to appear in Hong Kong post boxes. Knowing there was so much confusion in official circles that little time could be devoted to censorship of the mails, people again dared to write. There was little hard news, certainly not about the church, but there was at least some word of survival. Word was received of an old Catholic bishop, a leader in the Patriotic Association, who was reduced to cleaning the house

[96] Stanley Karnow, "Why They Fled: Refugee Interviews," *Current Scene*, October 7, 1966, pp. 7-9. Mr. Karnow acknowledges that refugee interviewees are likely to embellish their accounts, and are certainly not "unbiased," but he reports that the person he calls Li Han had apparently undergone the "most rigorous treatment" of any of the refugees interviewed in the autumn of 1966.

while another occupant earned a little money outside. The bishop himself received less than $4.00 per month "from the people."

There is a consensus of observers that all churches in China were closed and remained closed, but a German visitor to Shanghai in late 1966 reported going to Mass at an out-of-the-way church in that city.[97] As far as is known, there were still no churches open in China at the end of 1967, which means that there has been no public expression of Catholic devotion since August or September, 1966.

In spite of this rather gloomy picture, it would be too hasty to conclude that "Christianity in China is finished." Although it would be too optimistic to expect a return to the pre-1966 pattern, poor as that was, it would be too pessimistic to expect church doors to remain closed permanently. For approximately two years, roughly 1951-1953, all rural churches in China were closed by government order because of Land Reform. No public assemblies of a religious nature were allowed. After Land Reform, however, a small percentage of these churches were allowed to reopen. It seems reasonable under present circumstances to predict that a few selected churches will be allowed to reopen after the Cultural Revolution has run its course. Again, the number will be smaller than before. Their limited activities will be in the hands of priests and laymen unquestionably loyal to the government and under the Party's careful control. Until that time, and even afterward according to some, the true flame of the Catholic religion will burn in the lives of individual Catholics, and in those Catholic homes where all can be trusted to keep a secret while keeping the faith.

[97] Reported in mimeographed paper by Professor Searle Bates, "Churches and Christians in China 1950-1967: Fragments of Understanding."

VI

The Rapid Rise of the Three-Self Movement in Protestantism

INITIAL ASSESSMENTS OF THE NEW SITUATION

The process by which the Protestant movement in China came under Communist direction and control moved at a much faster pace than did the parallel process in the Catholic Church. The most obvious reason for the acceleration in Protestant circles is that there were Protestant leaders who faced the change in government with a measure of guarded hope.[1] Such men saw little hope for the Nationalist cause, in fact were disgusted with the corruption, inflation, and incompetence which had dogged the Nationalists. Furthermore, there were at least a few Protestants who were excited by the possibilities of the new situation and who actively sought to cooperate with the Communists.

There is, for example, the report of a visit made by several Protestant leaders to Nanking on July 12, 1947, for a conference with Generalissimo and Madame Chiang Kai-shek. First Madame Chiang and then the Generalissimo appealed for Protestant support of the government's total mobilization program. The church leaders suggested that the government should first make reforms and give more freedom to the people, then support by the people would fol-

---

[1] For example, a letter written by fifteen Chinese Christians to "Fellow Christians of North America," pled that the cause of the church not be associated with the fate of a particular political group, that Christians in America should pray for Christians, for Communists, and for all of China's people. The letter may be found in Katharine Hockin, *Servants of God in People's China* (New York: Friendship Press, 1962), pp. 50-52.

170

low. These churchmen sensed an increasing lack of confidence in the government and a lack of enthusiasm for the mobilization program.[2]

Bishop Z. T. Kaung wrote on November 17, 1948, that the Christian religion, which he said was nonpolitical, would have something to give, even under the Communists. The people's hunger for the very best could only be satisfied by God's love and God's life. He said that if Christians could not preach, they could "certainly witness by deeds and life. . . . We will be free in the truth and in the life of God. . . . I believe a better and stronger church with a smaller number is emerging." [3]

Dr. T. C. Chao saw hope in the new situation only if the church could repent and reform. When the Communists entered Peking in early 1949, he emphasized the weakness of the church and the power of God's judgment upon it, the need for repentance and reform, a new theology, new methods of evangelism, and relevant social service. The Christian response to the new day ("O time! O day!") is "to bear Christian witness to the Communists." "Communism is man's challenge to Christianity, but it is also God's judgment upon flabby churches." Chao foresaw a time when Communist self-confidence and passion would have to face

the hard facts of human sin and selfishness along with the human need of a spiritual redemption and the human yearning for God in Christ. . . . Then, not a few of the Communists will knock at the door of the church for admission and salvation.[4]

He did not think that the church would be able to meet such a challenge if it continued in its present state, but he called on Christians to "hear the call of God, to have a change of heart, to take courage, and to work together with the Communists for the coming of a new heaven and a new earth." [5]

One is tempted to ask whether such statements represented what Bishop Kaung and Dr. Chao actually hoped, or whether they were

[2] Reported to the Foreign Missions Conference of North America, Far East Joint Office, recorded in *CHIBUL* I (August 7, 1947).

[3] *CHIBUL*, December, 1948.

[4] *CMBA* II (III) (February, 1950), 157-60.

[5] *Ibid.*

reassuring themselves while trying to give a measure of hope to the Christian community in a time of great confusion. Communist officials in the liberated areas held widely varying attitudes toward the church, resulting in fairly decent treatment in some places but crude and brutal in others. Bishop Kaung, when visiting the United States in 1948, told the writer that many Methodist pastors in North China had been beaten severely and that all kinds of restrictions had been placed on their work. In this context, both he and Dr. Chao must be seen as men who were fully aware of the grim realities of the situation, but who were determined in faith that the Christian community should and could see it through.

A most significant meeting of the Ad-Interim Committee of the National Christian Council was held in Shanghai on June 28, 1949, with Bishop Ward of The Methodist Church in the chair. Wu Yao-tsung, still only a YMCA secretary, reported on his consultation with Communist leaders in Peking.[6] These authorities, who had invited him to participate in United Front activities, were cordial toward the Christian movement, but had told Wu that they lacked information and therefore had asked him and others for help. Wu was certain that religious freedom would prevail because the new government recognized that Christianity was a social force and wanted its cooperation in the new United Front. Government leaders also believed that oppression of religion would be a mistake.

Wu stated that difficulties experienced by churches, even cases of persecution, were real but were not in accordance with official policy. The Rev. P. H. Wang in Peking was collecting information concerning such difficulties for submission to the authorities. Wu spoke of liaison work which he, Mr. T. L. Shen, and Miss Cora Deng were doing in preparation for the People's Consultative Congress.

Wu also asserted that although the "dead branches" of the church would have to be cut off, a church based on Three-Self principles would advance with increasingly less difficulty under the new regime. He stressed the necessity of two-way interpretation, of the church to the government and of the government's policy and program to Christians. In the future there would be serious testing in

[6] *CHIBUL*, August 24, 1949.

which actions would count heavily. Wu recommended immediate reorganization of the NCC, since "no legal recognition can be secured of anybody having non-Chinese members on its governing council, and even if recognition is not sought, there may be a noticeable sentiment against such bodies." He also spoke of the need for literature with a new orientation.

Shortly after this meeting of the NCC Ad-Interim Committee, five Protestants and two Buddhists attended the Chinese People's Political Consultative Conference which began on September 21, 1949, in Peking. Y. T. Wu, considered the head of this delegation of "democratic personages from the religious field," made a speech expressing their "complete concurrence and absolute support" of the Common Program of the CPPCC, which maintained, among other things, that the Communist Party had come into leadership in the country and that there would be freedom of religious belief. Wu pledged that there would be no abuse of that freedom, and that religious believers would exert themselves to the utmost to eradicate the corrupt and evil tradition within the religions and their link with feudal power and imperialism in the past.[7]

There was word from Shanghai a few months later that the five Protestant representatives to the CPPCC were chosen by the government, not by Christian bodies, but that the government regarded them as representative. To an observer this indicated "the way in which under the new regime the ruling party retains full control." [8]

Dr. T. C. Chao seconded Y. T. Wu's suggestion that the NCC be composed only of Chinese, and proposed to the NCC Executive Committee when it met in Shanghai, October 25-27, 1949, a total

reorganization of the NCC, so as to make it completely Chinese in administration; the setting up of a national Christian organization with executive powers to act in the interests of the whole Christian movement in China; discontinuance of the present Forward Movement as such; and promotion of revolutionary reform within the Chinese church, deepening of its faith, etc.[9]

[7] These remarks were reported in the Chinese press for late September, 1949, and transmitted by a colleague to the author, unfortunately without designation of the name of the newspaper.
[8] *CHIBUL*, February 24, 1950.
[9] *CHIBUL*, December 8, 1949.

Resolutions calling for self-support and indigenous leadership were passed, but the committee also passed another resolution recognizing the difficulties involved and therefore stating that the Chinese church "earnestly desires the continued help of mission boards." [10] Such statements indicate that leaders of the Protestant Christian community had not given up hope, but were prepared to work out in an admittedly dangerous situation those patterns of organization and activity which would lead to vital witness.

The NCC had issued two messages to the Christians of China in 1948. The first, on March 1, spoke of two special tasks confronting Christians: "to maintain man's liberty to worship" and to practice economic and political justice. The second message affirmed that man "is never able to effect his own salvation," and that "every man is a brother for whom Christ died." In the light of these affirmations, "men and women must always be treated as persons, never as political instruments." [11]

Then came the "Third Message to Christians in China," in which the NCC, meeting on December 10, 1949, recognized that "our country has already entered upon a new era in its history." [12] Attention was called to the contributions made by the church to science, to democracy through education, toward the emancipation of women and children and the working man, and to activities for the benefit of farmers. The framers of the document then pledged continued service to the government according to the government's policies, through schools, hospitals, and social service. They acknowledged the need for self-examination and repentance, training leaders of high caliber, "real implementation of independence and self-support," "determined struggle against the inequities of the economic order and social evils," and the careful use of available property. The concluding appeal reads as follows:

The church should stimulate every individual believer, irrespective of [the] class to which he belongs, to welcome as a citizen, along with his fellow countrymen throughout the country, the advent of these great times, and to assist, each in his own place and to the limit of his strength, in bringing to fulfillment the tasks of reconstruction of this new era. . . .

[10] *Ibid.*
[11] *CHIBUL,* November 10, 1948.
[12] *Documents,* pp. 9-11.

The Christian church in China must serve the people—individuals, small groups, and the masses—with Christian faith, in Christian love. While it is in the world, and while the world lasts, the church must not for a moment cease its effort, by strenuous struggle, self-denying sacrifice and devout prayer, to bring society as well as individuals nearer to God, for this is the hope which God sets upon mankind.[13]

The double-barreled direction of the statement—assurance to the new government of cooperation on the basis of what the writers understood government policy to be, and careful advice to churches and churchmen concerning possible lines of action—expressed adroitly the survival hopes of Protestant leaders two months after the establishment of the new government.

Early in 1950 the NCC was invited by the new government to send delegates to a national conference called to discuss ways and means of combating the famine in central and east China. Delegates were sent and they participated.[14]

The Jesus Family, an indigenous Chinese religious society which practiced communal living according to quite simple standards and which emphasized physical labor, expected to get along well under the Communists. They were already "self-reliant, self-supporting, self-propagating" and had demonstrated a workable manner of cooperation with the new regime.[15] Within a very short time such optimism proved to be quite naïve, but it is a vivid illustration of high hopes on the part of such a Christian group.

Also in early 1950, an article by Rose Yardumian, a staff member of the *China Weekly Review*, said that "rural churches have suffered considerable losses in terms of the number of churches which have closed," but asserted that work in the cities was going ahead, and that in the northwest regions and in south China conditions were normal. A team of five Christian leaders found officials friendly and the situation favorable in central and east China in December, 1949. The fact that two members of the team had just participated in the Chinese People's Political Consultative Conference and were therefore spreading the government's new policy,

[13] *Ibid.*, p. 11.
[14] *CMBA* II (III) (June, 1950), 555.
[15] *Hong Kong Standard*, November 27, 1950; *CMBA* III (IV) (January, 1951), 36-37.

and also that the magazine reporting leaned far to the left, may explain a good bit of the optimistic tone. There was a frank admission, however, that many church buildings were "borrowed" by the government or the army for public meetings, for billeting soldiers, or for storage; this "borrowing" was one of the earlier forms of irritation and a continual source of tension between church leaders and the government. Miss Yardumian concludes by quoting Protestant church leaders to the effect that Protestantism, though the smallest of China's organized religions, would be able to adjust to the new environment successfully.[16]

The report of a missionary, the Rev. Henry D. Jones, expressed this sense of confidence a few months later. Speaking of the Christian community centers with which he was working, Mr. Jones claimed that "with the change of government has come a new spirit in the life of communities in China." He noted a greater sense of self-reliance, for people were saying, "We must do it ourselves." Observing a degree of progress as people tackled their own problems, he said, "I can see that we will have happy and smooth cooperation later." [17]

The Rev. Marcus Cheng (Ch'en Tzung-kuei), a conservative leader and president of the Chungking Seminary, went even further than Henry Jones. Although he affirmed that he was a Christian believer in Jesus Christ and in "Jesus' program for saving the world," after seeing the methods of the new government and the changes wrought in people he was "convinced that the New China has a better way." [18]

Y. T. Wu, of course, was hailing the new era as the only hope for a Christianity which had lost its reforming spirit and had become a slave to capitalism and imperialism. Christianity's only hope, as Wu saw it, was to cast off capitalist and imperialist ties, to become self-governing, self-supporting, and self-propagating, and to

[16] *China Weekly Review*, January 21, 1950, pp. 120-23. Reference to the fact that "rural churches have suffered confirms a report to *CHIBUL*, October 20, 1949, that many rural stations had been closed, although the latter report does not indicate whether mission stations or rural churches or a combination of the two are closing.

[17] "Report to a Conference on East China Christian Community Centers," dated April 25, 1950; *CHIBUL*, June 21, 1950.

[18] *T'ien Feng*, September 30, 1950; translated in *Missionary News Letter*, October 23, 1950; and quoted in Ferris, *The Christian Church*, p. 32.

recognize and repent for the superstitious, reactionary organization it had become. Communism, in the form of the new government of China, would be the instrumentality of the needed reform:

Christianity must learn that the present period is one of liberation for the people, the collapse of the old system, a time when the old, dead Christianity must doff its shroud and come forth arrayed in new garments. It must learn that it is no longer the sole distributor of the panacea for the pains of the world. On the contrary, God has taken the key to the salvation of mankind from its hand and given it to another.[19]

Numerous foreign observers believed that the church in China was in a good position to survive, in spite of real difficulties. It seemed that the pledge to allow religious freedom would be taken seriously, Chinese clergy and laymen were capable, and churchmen as a whole had learned how to adapt to difficult situations during the Japanese war.[20] One of the more hopeful of these foreign observers, John Rose of the British Methodist Mission, stressed nonetheless that the destiny of the church in China was uncertain: "[The] present Government is deeply suspicious of the past association of the Church in China with 'imperialist' countries and makes it clear that the Church will only be tolerated provided it is useful within the new Society." [21]

THE MANIFESTO

This era of cautious optimism and of hope for a genuine *modus vivendi* between church and state came to an end with the Christian Manifesto. Dr. Jones has given a brief résumé of the history of the Manifesto and the text of the document, so there is no need to go into detail here.[22] Y. T. Wu (YMCA), Cora Deng (YWCA), H. H.

[19] Shanghai *Ta Kung Pao*, series of articles appearing July 16-18, 1950; *Documents*, pp. 12-13.

[20] H. A. Wittenbach, "The Church in China," *The East and West Review* XVI (July, 1950), 80-85; also H. A. Maxwell, "Grounds for Optimism in the Chinese Church," *ibid*. XVII (January, 1951), 16-20.

[21] *A Church Born to Suffer, Being an Account of the First Hundred Years of the Methodist Church in South China, 1851-1951* (London: Cargate Press, 1951), pp. 144-45.

[22] Jones, *The Church*, pp. 52-58; *Documents*, pp. 19-20.

Ts'ui (Church of Christ in China), Ai Nien-san (Lutheran), all from Shanghai, were joined by Bishop Z. T. Kaung (Methodist), T. C. Chao (Anglican), and about fifteen others in Peking, where they had conferences with Premier Chou En-lai on May 2, 6, and 13, 1950, on the subject of how the church might best express its loyalty to the new government.[23] The result of these meetings was a draft of the Manifesto, written by Y. T. Wu and approved by the Premier.

The pervading theme of the Manifesto was imperialism, how Christianity has been related to it, how imperialism would continue to threaten China, and how Christians in China should purge themselves of imperialist connections and counter the imperialist attacks of the future. Fundamental aims to be adopted by Christian churches and organizations were (1) to recognize through self-criticism the inroads of imperialism and be vigilant against it, oppose war and uphold peace, understand and support the government's policy of agrarian reform; and (2) to promote a patriotic, democratic, self-respectful and self-reliant spirit by the Three-Self Movement. Concrete methods to attain these aims were (a) to cease relying on foreign personnel and financial aid, and (b) to emphasize "a deeper understanding of the nature of Christianity itself, closer fellowship and unity . . . , better leadership . . . , and reform . . . of church organization," as well as to emphasize "anti-imperialistic, antifeudalistic, and antibureaucratic-capitalistic education," along with various forms of social service.[24]

On June 3 in Shanghai, Wu presented a draft of the Manifesto to church leaders, some of whom proposed revisions, some of whom opposed the whole idea. Wu resisted revisions on grounds that the Premier had already approved the draft, but the group insisted on some changes; so Wu went back to Peking and managed to win Chou's approval. When the Shanghai group met again with Wu on July 6, people who had not been present on June 3 raised further objections. One bishop made the point that Christians in other

[23] Several members of the group which met with Chou En-lai had served as a team which had visited several places in North China in an effort to establish better relations between the churches and the new authorities. The Manifesto presumably reflected the experience of the visiting team in the months preceding the meeting with Premier Chou. *CHIBUL*, August 18, 1950.

[24] *Documents*, pp. 19-20.

parts of the country should be consulted, but this was turned down because several more months would be required.[25] In such manner Y. T. Wu managed to win approval for the Manifesto, which was published in July, over the signatures of 40 prominent Christians, some of whom issued additional statements defending the manifesto and interpreting its significance. Over 1,500 signed it by September of that year, and a reputed 400,000 by 1952.

In April, 1951, when referring to the fact that 180,000 had signed the Manifesto, Wu spoke of its July, 1950, publication date as the beginning of the Three-Self Movement. Although the "Preparatory Committee for the Oppose America–Aid Korea Three-Self Reform Movement of the Chinese Christian Church" was not officially constituted until April, 1951, there are numerous references to the Three-Self Movement in the latter half of 1950. It is possible to say, therefore, that publication of the Manifesto marked the beginning of the new movement, at least as Wu conceived it.

The bishops of the Anglican Church in China (Sheng Kung Hui), all of whom were Chinese by the spring of 1950, did not accept the Manifesto when it was first published, although they later found it advisable to do so. They issued instead a pastoral letter on July 5, 1950, in which they pointedly did not identify the church with imperialism.[26] They stated rather that "the church not only cannot compromise with imperialism, feudalism, or bureaucratic capitalism, but that these are fundamentally against the faith of the church" and must be opposed. Christianity's historic identity with the common people was cited as a basis for support of the new government, and the need for repentance and attainment of holiness was affirmed. Continued efforts to achieve self-government, self-support, and self-propagation were to be followed, and the church as a whole was to promote peace and the spiritual life. The bishops tried to balance "spiritual life and religious education" with "productive labor and social service." When compared to the Manifesto, the Anglican pastoral letter has a far more authentic Christian tone, is much less ambiguous, and avoids a good bit

[25] *CHIBUL*, August 18 and December 5, 1950, provides invaluable information about behind-the-scenes maneuvering, both in respect to the Manifesto and the NCC biennial conference in October, 1950, when the Manifesto was adopted.
[26] *Documents*, pp. 21-22.

of the Communist verbiage of the Manifesto. These are probably among the reasons why the Communist government ultimately found the Anglican pastoral letter unacceptable.

The biennial meeting of the National Christian Council in Shanghai, October 18-25, 1950, during which time the Manifesto was adopted, was a watershed in the life of the Chinese church. It marked the end of an effective NCC as such, for by the following April it was obvious that leadership had passed to the Three-Self Movement. That Christian leaders were nervous about the biennial meeting is indicated by the NCC Ad-Interim Committee action of April 25, 1950, which postponed it from August to November in view of "the need for more thorough preparations and also because of developments in the objective situation." [27]

An outstanding example of "thorough preparation" was a questionnaire on church reform, a thousand copies of which were circulated from March until autumn. The questionnaire was eighteen pages long and included numerous questions concerning the life of the church, attitudes of Christians toward the new government, and ways to bring about Three-Self reform.[28]

The planning committee for the biennial meeting also "tried to ensure that the ecumenical principle be upheld" by allowing a few missionaries eligible to attend to do so. A government official let the committee know that attendance by missionaries would be frowned on and it was agreed that only Chinese should attend.

This was certainly not a government order, but it was just as certainly a subtle method of control. After the meeting had started, a similar informal conference was called at which it was made clear that the now famous Manifesto . . . which the NCC had given assurances would not be brought forward officially at the biennial meeting) must certainly be endorsed by the conference. It was accordingly put on the agenda for that same afternoon, and naturally enough gained "unanimous" support.[29]

An account of the meeting in the *China Monthly Review* by Y. C. Tu of the YMCA acclaims the fact that it was really Chinese for

[27] *CHIBUL*, May 29, 1950.
[28] *CHIBUL*, August 18, 1950
[29] Newsletter sent by China NCC staff member to Far East Joint Office of NCCCUSA, May 3, 1951; *CHIBUL*, May 10, 1951.

the first time, that there was wider representation than before, that there was a spirit of "democratic consultation," and that "the conference was filled with an atmosphere of humility and self-criticism." In commenting on the first point—that it was really Chinese—Mr. Tu says:

It is not because of any deliberate disregard of the ecumenical nature of the Christian faith and fellowship, certainly not because of any feeling of antiforeignism, but rather to give articulate and no uncertain expression to the conviction that the Chinese church must be indigenous in character, that only Chinese delegates attended the conference.[30]

The official minutes of the meeting, written by George K. T. Wu, in the context of a comment on the "wide representation" contain only the simple sentence: "The most regrettable and noticeable part was the absence of missionary friends at the meeting." To support the claim for wide representation, Wu reported "a very genuine desire on the part of non-NCC members to join, [so much so that they] paid their own expenses to the meeting." [31]

The "atmosphere of humility and self-criticism," mentioned by Y. C. Tu in a quotation above, had reference to a discussion of changes to be made in the structure and life of the church so that it might make a contribution to the new society, and was a way of saying that rather heated arguments took place. This is confirmed by the later confession of the Rev. Chester Miao (Miao Chou-sheng) which appeared in the Chinese press in 1951. Dr. Miao admitted that he worked with a committee of delegates who were opposed to the Manifesto and the Three-Self program being presented to the conference. He says that he worked from a conviction that religion should be kept clear of politics, which is a stereotyped confession employed as a prelude to announcing that one will now follow the opposite approach, meaning that he will cooperate with the government.

According to Miao's confession, Y. T. Wu was not even appointed to a subcommittee to work out the wording of the Manifesto until pressure was exerted to have him included. Although his confession appeared in the Communist press, Miao was able to state that a

[30] *China Monthly Review,* December, 1950, p. 133.
[31] *CHIBUL,* December 6, 1950.

"majority of the delegates . . . opposed the acceptance of the 'independence manifesto.' " When those in control realized this, he adds, they rejected the list of delegates on grounds of "misprocedure," and brought in a new list of delegates. The preparatory committee apparently tried to avoid all discussion of the Three-Self program, but were defeated.[32]

Therefore it appears that what Y. C. Tu hailed as a harmonious meeting ushering in a new era was in reality a struggle for power within the NCC between those who would act specifically as an instrument of Christian cooperation and those who would have the council serve as a subsidiary of the government. In addition to the Manifesto, which was heavily weighted on the political side, other resolutions of the council were about equally divided between calls to support vaious government programs—relief for flood refugees, Land Reform, understanding the new era, austerity, productive labor—and calls for revival of the Student Volunteer Movement, to deepen faith, and to depend on the rank and file of Christian believers, which although "religious" in character have a definite political ring in the context in which they appear. One of the secretary's concluding statements seems to make the best of what must have been a shattering experience: "Although human elements did manifest themselves at times, thank God these became nothing when we put God's will above everything else." [33]

The minutes of the Executive Committee of the NCC, which met on October 26, following the NCC meetings as a whole, record the resignations of Miao and Hayward. The Staff Administrative Committee, of which Miao was chairman, was asked to continue until a new general secretary could be appointed and Miao was "asked to continue to head up the committee, in spite of all admitted difficulties." Hayward's resignation was accepted with thanks.

The adoption of the Manifesto by the National Christian Council of China, probably more than the signing of it by however many hundreds of thousands of Chinese Christians, marks the turning point of the Chinese church—a turning away from old alignments

[32] Miao's confession and its implications are summarized in *CMBA* III (IV) (August-September, 1951), 644-45.

[33] All items reported from the minutes of the conference, as well as later comments by an NCC staff member, are from *CHIBUL*, December 5 and 6, 1950.

with the churches of the West, a turning toward a new alignment with the Communist government of China. It was criticized by many Chinese Christians from the beginning, even by some within the group which framed the original draft and the forty over whose signatures it was first issued. Some in this group believed, or were led to believe, that something had to be said which would assure the government of the church's loyalty. That the resulting document failed to express accurately their real sentiments was a factor in the situation which had to be accepted.

In addition to the Manifesto, Christians also joined in signing "patriotic pacts" which were being promoted.[34] The usual citizen's pact started with pledges of support to Chairman Mao, the Communist Party, the Central People's Government, and the People's Liberation Army, in that order, whereas a special pact for Christians, reportedly due to Roman Catholic influence, began with a pledge to support the Common Platform. An observer reported that at a mass meeting in Shanghai in the first part of 1951, the Manifesto, the Citizens' Pact, the Christians' Pact, and a resolution supporting the Second World Peace Congress were all on the same sheet of paper. One could sign one's name once and indicate support for all; presumably there was no natural way to pick and choose.[35]

The interpreter quoted above states clearly the predicament of Christians in Communist China as they sought to fulfill their roles as Christians and as patriotic citizens:

The government has been very clever in making a very clear-cut distinction between what it regards as religious issues and political issues. Since everything capable of any political interpretation whatsoever is included in this latter category, it is easy to suggest that this or that matter has nothing to do with religious freedom, but that Christians have yet to prove themselves adequately progressive and patriotic in their thinking and behavior. Thus while the government on the one hand reiterates its promise of religious liberty, on the other hand by indicating doubts of the patriotism of Chinese Christians, on account of their past imperialistic connections, it makes them peculiarly susceptible to various very real

[34] An example is the Methodist Patriotic Covenant, which may be found in *Documents*, p. 26.
[35] Newsletter of May 3, 1951; *CHIBUL*, May 10, 1951.

forms of political pressure. Seeing that evidence of patriotism has manifestly been made the condition upon which religious freedom is granted, Christians have been tempted to go too far in establishing their patriotic "bona fides." The government has demanded that Christians as such produce evidence of their political standing; they have not been permitted to claim that in political matters they should be treated simply as so many individuals among others who possess a common citizenship.[36]

Undoubtedly there were many who looked upon the Manifesto and subsequent statements and actions as genuine, positive steps to save the church as an institution, and who believed that such statements and actions represented the will of God for the church at that time. It may be that there were those who consciously and deliberately were trying by these measures to bring the church under the control of the Communists. There are indications that Y. T. Wu in his own thinking swayed back and forth between these last two alternatives. One does not want to be unfair to Wu, but one cannot help asking the question, even though there are no "ifs" in history, what the story might have been if he had not pushed as wholeheartedly and aggressively as he did. The probable answer to an impossible question is that the Communist government would have found someone else to espouse their cause, with greater or lesser intensity than Wu advocated and promoted it.

Francis Jones, who detects a certain disappointment in Wu's later speeches, reminds us nonetheless that China had been the recipient of colonialist and imperialist pressures for a century and a half, and Wu is only one of many Chinese who did not forget.[37] Jones does point out, with respect to the Manifesto, that it is a bit unfair for the United States to be the only offender singled out by name. He further acknowledges that the actions of some

[36] *Ibid.*

[37] Jones, *The Church*, pp. 55-56. Included in the material on which "From the Other Side of the Desk" was based, *China Notes* I (September, 1963), but not summarized or quoted in that article, are statements by the former official of the Bureau of Religious Affairs to the effect that Y. T. Wu was thought to be a secret member of the Communist Party, and that he had a directive from the Director of the Propaganda Department of the Central Committee of the Party, to approach Christian leaders in several cities for signatures to the Manifesto. That Wu was a Communist Party member seems highly unlikely, but it is quite possible that there were such pressures on him from the government that he was not precisely a free agent in his promotion of the Three-Self Movement.

missionaries might well support the charge that their work had been aligned with that of Western governments. Still there is a much milder tone to the Manifesto (*viz.*, "Protestant Christianity . . . has made a not unworthy contribution to Chinese society") than one finds in statements made a few months later when vicious attacks and stringent measures made the Manifesto a thing of the past.

"Barnabas" asserts that genuine patriotic motives were present in some people who signed, and that others had resentment against missionary leadership of the church even though they had worked side by side with missionaries for years.[38] He further suggests that adaptation to local political power and their relationship to their fellows seemed more important to Chinese than did international affairs.

Leslie Lyall interprets what he calls the "Manifesto of Betrayal" primarily in terms of what it meant to the missionary movement. It was the "writing on the wall" which signaled the departure of missionaries from China, and thus prompts Lyall to defend his brother missionaries.[39] Although it did indeed play a part in hastening the exodus, the Manifesto is far more important as the first decisive step in the direction taken by the church to abrogate its relationships with the total Christian movement in order to maintain its existence under the supervision and control of the new government. Although succeeding events, especially during and after the Cultural Revolution which began in 1966, make such efforts appear futile, by taking such a direction the church bought an additional sixteen years of continued existence. It was a limited existence and it was bought with a price, but to some Christian leaders in 1950 that existence seemed worth the price.

There was undoubtedly an element of fear in the signing of the Manifesto. The "borrowing" of church buildings, which was referred to above, increased during 1950. When church leaders requested the return of church buildings to the congregation or in other ways were brought into contact with local Communist officials, they confronted

[38] *Christian Witness*, p. 40.
[39] Leslie Lyall, *Come Wind, Come Weather* (London: Hodder and Stoughton, 1961), pp. 22-26.

the jealousy of the official against other influences in the community, his previous prejudice, or the unfortunate relations of Christian work in the past with the wrong people. . . . In general the authorities are suspicious of every case brought to them, and the burden of proof is on the churches.[40]

Members could use the church only on Sunday mornings for one service and were not allowed to take down portraits of Mao and Stalin during the service. Churches in rural areas were used frequently as granaries, which meant that even Sunday services were impossible as long as the interior was filled with grain.[41] Such practices inevitably produced uneasiness and then fear for Christians who already composed only the tiniest of minorities in small towns and villages.

One must not ignore the fact that on October 25, 1950, Communist China entered the war in Korea, which meant that by the time of the NCC meeting a month later, there were demonstrations of Christians in major cities opposing the "American invasion of Korea," Warren Austin's "slanderous speech against China" in the UN Security Council, and American rearming of Japan.[42] It was unquestionably patriotic for Chinese Christians to participate, which only increased the necessity to talk about American imperialists and for Chinese Christians to dissociate themselves from such imperialists.

As already noted, the American government's sanction of December 16, 1950, cut off funds to Christian organizations in China, and the Chinese responded with the edict of December 29, 1950, which called for the registration within three months of all bodies which received funds from abroad, and for subsequent reports of funds received every six months. The effect of these two actions on institutions has been considered, but not the corresponding effect on churches which received subsidies. Although several denominations in China were moving toward self-support with respect to local church expenses, the denominational overhead and inter-denominational activities were usually subsidized from abroad.

[40] "Barnabas," *Christian Witness*, p. 58.
[41] Ferris, *The Christian Church*, pp. 15-16.
[42] New reports of these and later rallies may be found in *CURBAC*, June 4, 1951, pp. 4-5.

There were, of course, indigenous churches which were independent of foreign support and were not affected directly by the December actions, but they could not avoid the general opprobrium which spread to all churches.

One clause of the Chinese edict specified:

8. All Cultural, Educational, Relief, and Religious Organizations registered according to the stipulations of the present regulations, who have truly severed all connections with foreign countries and shall have reported that to the Special Committee of the Local, Municipal or Provincial Committee, shall be released from the regulations governing the Special registration.[43]

This prompted religious organizations to forgo any financial aid which might still be available. The Church of Christ in China, for example, had announced plans in October, 1950, to be financially self-supporting in five years, but on February 21, 1951, the CCC Standing Committee wrote to its cooperating mission boards and societies that these plans had been accelerated.

The present situation does not permit us to hesitate any longer. We have decided, from the beginning of 1951, to receive no further financial aid of any kind from abroad. We call upon all grades of church organization within our church immediately, of their own accord, to plan to maintain with their own strength, the various forms of work in the Church of Christ in China.[44]

ACCUSATION OF FELLOW CHRISTIANS AND INAUGURATION OF THE THREE-SELF MOVEMENT

The year 1951 marked the acceleration of the missionary exodus and the closing, or passing into government hands, of most Christian institutions. It was also a period of great turmoil in the church. Attention focused on an April meeting in Peking of government officials and churchmen during which the accusation movement among Christians was initiated and the Three-Self Movement officially inaugurated. In a sense this meeting brought order out of

[43] *Documents*, pp. 22-24.
[44] *Ibid.*, pp. 24-25.

chaos, for Christians now knew where they stood, but the accusations and denunciations precipitated a new chaos and increased the turmoil.

"The Conference for the Handling of Christian Organizations Receiving Subsidies from the United States of America" was called by the Bureau of Religious Affairs for April 16-21, 1951, in Peking. The effect on institutions of that meeting and the accusations made against missionaries during the meeting have been discussed above, but, for all practical purposes, institutional funds from abroad had been cut off and missionaries were already on the way out. This conference in Peking marked the shifting of attention to the churches themselves, the churches which *had received* funds and missionaries. It became quite clear that Chinese were now to suffer as well as missionaries, and that much would be required of the Christian church in China after missionaries were gone and foreign funds denied.

The conference was attended by about 150 delegates who listened to speeches by government officials and Three-Self advocates. It was clear in the speech made by Lu Ting-yi, vice-chairman of the Cultural Educational Committee of the government's Administrative Council, that the Bureau of Religious Affairs (a subdivision of his committee) was encouraging the Three-Self Movement as an effort to cut off the relations between Chinese and American Christian organizations. This, according to an editorial in *Jen-min Jih-pao*, was the purpose of the conference; the "way for the Chinese Christian church to cut off its relationship with imperialists is to carry out seriously the Three-Self Movement."

Wu Yao-tsung, of course, led the speechmaking of the church leaders, who in this instance were already recognized Three-Self promoters. In commenting on the collection of signatures for the manifesto, he said that 180,000 had been collected but acknowledged:

Although some of them signed their names, they did not learn the reform manifesto, they have no deep understanding of the fundamental spirit of the manifesto; some of them signed the manifesto only in order to muddle along. . . . Some of the church leaders hesitate to sign, others lack sincerity and confidence toward "Three-Self," still others are sitting on the fence, approving the movement in outward appearance, but opposing it in their hearts.[45]

He spoke of the patriotic covenants signed by Christians, of their patriotic activities supporting the "Oppose America–Aid Korea" campaign and of their determination to break ties with imperialism.

The account from the Chinese press states that a speech by Vice-Premier Kuo Mo-jo on April 19 was followed by violent accusations for two days against "imperialist and reactionary elements within the Christian church." Since comment has already been made on the accusations against Dr. Frank Price and other missionaries, the accusations and denunciations of Chinese Christian leaders will now be discussed.

Bishop Kaung's denunciation of his fellow Methodist Bishop W. Y. Ch'en (Ch'en Wen-yuan) is one of the most troubling features of the whole denunciation movement. According to Jones's summary, Kaung accused Ch'en because he was "a speaker much in demand at meetings of the Nationalist Party's Youth Corps," because "he cooperated with Madame Chiang in pushing the New Life Movement" with its rehabilitation of Confucian virtues, and because he spoke in America on behalf of the Nationalists.[46] According to Liu Liang-mo of the YMCA, in the *China Monthly Review,* Kaung also criticized Ch'en for having "urged America to send troops to China to help Chiang." [47] The same article adds a criticism of Ch'en by a Lutheran pastor, namely that Ch'en fed ten dogs for Madame Chiang with food which would have fed four families, while at the same time The Methodist Church was underpaying its workers.

Bishop Robin Chen (Ch'en Chien-chen) denounced his fellow Anglican Bishop Y. Y. Tsü as a "tool of American imperialism," since he "joined the fascistic San Min Chu I Youth Corps with W. Y. Ch'en in 1938," and because he traveled to America with a Na-

---

[45] Both the remarks by Wu and the quote from *JMJP* in the preceding paragraph were from the Chinese press and supplied to the author by a colleague.
[46] Jones, *The Church,* p. 67.
[47] *China Monthly Review* CXX (June, 1951), 282.

tionalist passport. With no observable documentation Bishop Chen maintained that Bishop Tsü "does not love China, . . . is unfaithful to his religion and his motherland." Kiang Wen-han of the YMCA denounced his former chief, S. C. Leung, who had escaped to Hong Kong, primarily on grounds that he had spread lies about China and its YMCA.[48]

An independent evangelist, Ku Jen-en, was also denounced. *Jen-min Jih-pao* in April of 1951 reported a confession in which he admitted to having a U. S. naval chaplain as patron, and to having urged Christian unity against infiltration by "outside forces," by which he had meant the Communists, and to having spread rumors and anti-Communist propaganda. He was also cited for the following "heresies": (1) he had said, "Christ was the liberator of mankind who advocated peace and opposed bloodshed and war," which role "belonged to Mao and the Communist party." (2) He had urged people to listen to both sides, thus America as well as Russia and the Communist Party, "which was in direct opposition to the peaceful policy of 'leaning to one side' advocated by the People's Government." (3) He had quoted scripture—"The ox knoweth his owner and the ass his master's crib"—and thus "compared Chairman Mao to the master and the labouring masses to the oxen and asses." [49]

The meeting of April 16-21 closed with the appointment of twenty-five men as a "Preparatory Committee for the Oppose America–Aid Korea, Three-Self, and the Land Reform Movements of the Church of Christ in China," with Wu Yao-tsung as chairman. Six proposals which were adopted and signed by fifteen delegates may be summarized as follows: (1) The Oppose America–Aid Korea movement now becomes the church's most important work. (2) All imperialistic influence in the church must be cleaned out and destroyed. (3) All those who are friendly to the imperialists must be searched out. (4) All should support the Land Reform program and increased production. (5) Christians should increase their knowledge of politics. A sixth point is a reiteration

[48] *Ibid.* Bishop Tsü had already left China. His full name is romanized Tsü (or Chu) Yu-yü or Westernized as Andrew Yu-yue Tsu.
[49] *CMBA* III (IV) (June-July, 1951), 538-40.

of the first, along with a summons to the church to be a leading force in all these movements.[50]

The accusations continued and spread throughout the country. The 1951 summer issues of *T'ien Feng,* the Three-Self magazine, were full of accounts of accusation meetings. Most of the people who had been accused at the April meeting in Peking came up for denunciation again along with several others at a mass rally of twelve thousand people in Shanghai in June. Y. T. Wu, in commenting on the rally, said, "The common crime of those named, foreign as well as Chinese, was that they used Christianity as a tool to promote the interests of American imperialism." [51] He went on to tell how "the Shanghai rally touched off a series of similar meetings throughout the country." He recognized that it was not easy for Christians to accuse their fellow Christians, but like those in Peking and Shanghai, they must follow Jesus who criticized the scribes and Pharisees.

Awakened Christians now realize that accusation is merely a condemnation of evil in harmony with Christian teaching. They are fully conscious of the need for a housecleaning in the churches and Christian organizations of China.[52]

As an example of the accusations being held across the country, Lu Sao-tuan, a layman employed by the China Bible House in Hankow, was arrested in May, 1951, and in early June was brought with his wife and his associate, An Tung-hsun, before an assembly of seven hundred Christians. Fourteen people accused him

of destroying the Three-Self Movement, of secretly maintaining relationship with the imperialists, of coveting the people's goods and flaying the poor, and of committing adultery. Lu was also accused of being a spy for the Japanese, of having become wealthy through usury, of having traveled to Hong Kong to see "reactionary missionaries" there, and of having expressed joy at the recapture of Seoul [by the UN forces].[53]

[50] From *T'ien Feng,* translated in *Missionary Newsletter,* May 18, 1951, p. 4.
[51] "New Life for the Chinese Church," *People's China,* December 1, 1951; *CMBA* IV (V) (March, 1952), 239.
[52] *Ibid.*
[53] From Hankow *Ta Kung Pao,* June 3, 1951; translated in *Missionary News Letter,* June 9, 1951, pp. 3-4; quoted in Ferris, *The Christian Church,* pp. 3-4.

He was returned to prison, to be punished by the government "according to the will of the people." There were later, unverified reports that Lu was executed.

Two stimuli for holding accusation meetings became apparent. The first was a decree issued by Premier Chou En-lai on July 24, 1951, which made official the actions of the April conference. It was entitled "Regulations of the Administrative Yuan on the Method of Controlling Christian Organizations That Have Received Financial Help from America." In addition to the directives about missionaries and institutions considered earlier, the decree stated:

Self-supporting churches and Young Men's and Young Women's Christian Associations might have taxes remitted on their churches and offices directly used for their work. Every church and organization which had received financial help from abroad should register with the government. Any church which was self-governing, self-supporting, and self-propagating might apply to the government for permission to bring into this country balances which were on deposit abroad on or before December 29, 1950; but the application must show the intended use of such funds.[54]

When a number of churches tried to register in order to have taxes remitted and to qualify for balances, they discovered that a successful accusation meeting against at least four of their own members was a prerequisite for such registration.[55]

The second stimulus appeared when churches in various localities tried to organize local branches of the Three-Self Movement. *T'ien Feng* carried a warning under the lengthy heading, "The Church in every place and its organizations [should] go slowly in setting up a branch" of the "Chinese Christian Oppose America–Aid Korea and the Three-Self Reform Movement Preparatory Committee." Accusation must come first, as the following directive makes clear:

[You must first] *Continue and Intensify the Accusation Movement,* and make a success of your accusation movement. When this has succeeded and you have exposed every kind of crime of the American imperialists in

---

[54] *CHIBUL,* October 31, 1951.
[55] Ferris, *The Christian Church,* p. 11.

controlling and using the church in the invasion of China, and through your accusation movement you have exposed all the past and present imperialist elements and rotters within the church, and distinguished between friends and enemies, and have taken your stand firmly with the people, only then, on the foundation of this thinking, and when you have found out and cultivated in your movement many more active elements, will you be able to take steps to start a branch.[56]

So, in order to either register with the government or organize a local branch of the Three-Self Movement, it was necessary to accuse fellow Christians. It seems that Father John Tung was right when he realized in early 1951 that "Three Autonomies" meant accusing one's fellows. Accusation was certainly well coordinated with the Three-Self Movement for Protestants in that year.

Whether they recognized that Three-Self and accusation movements went together or not, many Protestant Christians rebelled at accusations. The editor of *T'ien Feng* during this time was worried because the accusation movement was lagging. He suggests several reasons for hesitating:

(1) Some did not want to get too much involved for fear of reprisals if the Nationalists should ever return. (2) Others said that because their church had been self-supporting for years, they were already independent and did not need to hold such a meeting. As an independent church they had no material for denunciations. (3) Some said that since their children were studying in America they feared such an act might bring harm to them. (4) Others said they still had funds available for their work so did not need to make any special effort along the line of the Three-Self Movement. (5) Still others opposed the meetings on principle, saying that the meetings were not in accord with the Christian teaching of love and brotherhood. (6) Some drew a distinction between the Christian and the political points of view, saying that what was suitable in politics was not suitable in the church. (7) Others said they would lose face if they had such a meeting. (8) And, most interesting of all, some preachers said that if they held such a meeting their church members would no longer come to church.[57]

Liu Liang-mo attempted to overcome this hesitancy and give

[56] Stress as indicated by italics was in the original statement in *T'ien Feng*, August 11, 1951; *CHIBUL*, September 13, 1951.
[57] *CHIBUL*, October 21, 1951, pp. 1-2.

instruction to the uninitiated in an article entitled "How to Hold a Successful Accusation Meeting Against the Church." He maintained that the primary work of every Christian church and group was to hold successful accusation meetings. In order to help those who have been under the influence of imperialism speedily recognize its evils, leaders "must remove the thought barriers of many Christians who suppose that they ought to 'hide the evil and display the good.' " [58]

As to practical methods, preparation should be made carefully, especially by holding small accusation meetings so people may understand why, what, and how they should accuse, and so they may discover "a few people who accuse with the greatest power." Accusations should be sincere and based on fact, from the heart but not sentimental, and accusers should hold firmly to the Party line. The atmosphere must be dignified; tension should be built up from moderate to higher and higher levels. To follow up, Christians should expend greater effort on the study of current affairs, push the Three-Self Movement, clean imperialists and "bad elements" from the church, join in the suppression of antirevolutionaries, and take part in the Oppose America–Aid Korea Movement.

At about the same time there were reports of "a well-known evangelist, asking why it was that the church was not more vigilant, so as to expose people like Bishop Ch'en and Mr. Ku before the government had itself detected and arrested them." The reporter says that it is impossible to condone such activity: "Terrorism in the church cannot be avoided, but Christians need not call for it." [59] It seems fairly clear that a witch-hunt atmosphere prevailed, which, though resisted by great numbers of Christians, managed to infect enough of them to make the movement a success.

That Chinese Christians should denounce missionaries who had labored among them for so many years seems very strange, but under the circumstances it can be understood and has been forgiven by the vast majority of those accused. That Chinese Christians would agree to denounce their own people is another matter and is far more difficult to understand, and far more difficult to forgive. Dr. Jones has reminded us that "it was a time when nationalistic

[58] *T'ien Feng*, May 2, 1951; *Documents*, pp. 49-50.
[59] *CHIBUL*, May 10, 1951.

feeling was running high, and the demand was put on a patriotic basis. You must not, they were told, allow private sentiment to stand in the way of your patriotic duty." [60] He cites statements by H. H. Ts'ui and Luther Shao (Shao Ching-san) who denounced Frank Price, later agonized over the conflict between private feeling and public duty, and then confessed that "the fulfilling of their public duty brought them peace and satisfaction." [61] Jones also refers to "long suppressed resentments against the semiforeign aspects of church life and a desire to show that Christians were not alienated from the main stream of Chinese culture," as reasons for the denunciations. He adds that the text of what people planned to say was often changed by government editors and one did not dare alter these "official" versions. Further changes were often made by other government editors before the denunciation appeared in the press, and it is the press version upon which we largely depend.[62] All these points are well made, and from many sources one hears that those who have not been involved in such a situation can never appreciate the enormity of the pressures that were brought against people like the bishops who denounced their fellow bishops. Those who have not experienced these pressures have little prerogative to comment, and no prerogative to judge.[63]

What happened to the people who were accused or denounced is seldom clear. Some were imprisoned for a time and then released, after which very limited information about them reached the outside world. Others, after undergoing extended thought reform, returned to a form of life which bore little resemblance to what they had known. Of many others the only thing which can be said

[60] Jones, *The Church*, p. 65.

[61] *Ibid.* Miss Hockin quotes from an article "The Church in China, Failure and Future," *British Weekly*, July 17, 1952, a statement telling of a Chinese Christian leader who wrestled for a whole night with the problem of whether to accuse a fellow Christian, and who later experienced a "great awakening." Although the accusation brought pain to him, joy followed, along with a sense of "new birth." *Servants of God*, p. 99.

[62] Jones, *The Church*, pp. 65-66.

[63] It is easy to quote from England or America, "Judge not, lest ye be not judged," and to point out to the lapsed: "Wherever Christians are faced by a common spiritual foe they cannot afford to criticize one another, much less make a public example of them." Lyall, *Come Wind*, p. 47. It is good advice, but highly obnoxious under the circumstances.

is—no news. Bishop W. Y. Ch'en after being imprisoned for several years was released because of serious illness. Although under house arrest, he was able to translate English and German books into Chinese until his death on November 8, 1968.[64] Anglican Bishop Quentin K. Y. Huang, who was invited to head a proposed government-sponsored church because he was so bright in the study sessions in prison, was able to get out of China.[65]

Dr. T. C. Chao, who was brought before a mass trial in the spring of 1952, had a series of his confessions rejected as insincere, inadequate, or consisting of untruths. He finally refused to deny his Christian faith, though admitting political and intellectual sins, for which he was released from the deanship of the Yenching School of Religion and deprived of clerical privileges in the Anglican Church.[66] Nevertheless, two years later he participated in the 1954 Peking Christian Conference and published several articles in later years attacking American imperialism and defending the new China. A remark Dr. Chao made in defense of the Communist Party when it was attacked by Professor Ko Pei-chi of Peking People's University during the Hundred Flowers Period reveals that 1952 was a bitter time: "In the Three-Anti campaign I ate a great deal of bitterness, more than I can say. [It was] the best and most effective education for an old man set in his ways." [67] One suspects that not many of those who "ate bitterness" in the early 50's were able to look back on it in the way that Chao Tzu-ch'en was able to do.

What was the nature of the Three-Self Movement which by mid-1951 had moved to center stage among the Protestant churches of China? Searle Bates speaks of it as "the one overarching structure, ecclesiastically loose and formless, yet powerful with arbitrary interventions of the force of the state." [68] This structure was the

[64] *CHIBUL*, July, 1961. Bishop Ch'en's death was reported by Religious News Service in early 1969.

[65] *Now I Can Tell: The Story of a Christian Bishop under Communist Persecution* (New York: Morehouse-Gorham, 1954). The book is not nearly so sensational as the title would indicate.

[66] Andrew Yu-yue Tsu, "Christianity in a Political Setting" [one of a series on this subject], *Religion in Life* XXIV (Winter, 1954-55), 30. See also the brief reference in *CHIBUL*, October 1, 1956.

[67] "Some Observations from the Heart," *JMJP*, June 2, 1957, reprinted in *T'ien Feng*, July 8, 1957; *CHIBUL*, September 16, 1957.

[68] Mimeographed paper entitled "Churches and Christians in China, 1950-1967: Fragments of Understanding," p. 17.

means whereby the government let churchmen know what was expected of them, and it was the channel through which the government designated individuals, groups, and institutions for accusation. On the other hand, church leaders who desired the return of "borrowed" churches or who wished to protest some official's behavior had to work through the Three-Self structure in order to get any redress.

One may say that the Three-Self Movement provided a framework for communication and united action in the churches. Since, however, it was established under and was always subject to government pressure, and since it quickly nullified the existing ecumenical structure of the National Christian Council, the ecumenical character of the Three-Self Movement was largely superficial. In fact, with the rise of the Three-Self Movement, ecumenical relations in the sense of the relation of Chinese Christians to "the whole inhabited earth" took a quick and decisive downward swing. Dr. T. C. Chao resigned as one of the presidents of the World Council of Churches, the Church of Christ in China asked the WCC not to send them any more messages, and Anglican Bishop Robin Chen announced at a denunciation meeting that his church had "permanently withdrawn from the World Council of Churches"—all in 1951.[69] There was talk of relations with the Orthodox or the Baptist churches in Russia, and later there were exchange visits with Hungarian Protestants, but nothing concrete emerged.[70] It was even noted that a lengthy Chinese account of the 1961 General Assembly of the World Council of Churches failed to mention admission of the Russian Orthodox Church to that body.[71]

Of the three elements of this movement which assumed leadership and control in Chinese Protestantism, self-administration and self-support are not difficult to grasp. Positions of leadership, the policy-making organs of church government, and the administration of the church should be in the hands of Chinese, and the

[69] Dr. Chao's resignation was widely reported. Reference to the other two actions may be found in *CHIBUL*, May 10 and September 13, 1951.

[70] *China Consultation* (New York: Far Eastern Office, NCCCUSA, 1960), p. 2.

[71] *China Consultation* (New York: Far Eastern Office, NCCCUSA, 1962), p. 7.

total Christian enterprise should be financed by Chinese.[72] Self-propagation may be understood to mean that the preaching and teaching of the gospel, as well as the communication of it through literature and other means, should be handled by Chinese. There was more to it than this, according to the Rev. Victor Hayward, who wrote that the term "self-propagation"

emphasizes not so much the missionary responsibilities of the Chinese Church, as the desire for a new theology, free from the influence of Western imperialistic culture, and more consonant with the thinking of New Democracy. The Chinese church is in general so innocent of any theological thinking of its own that any stimulus to deep study of the content of faith is to be welcomed, even though one cannot be very optimistic as to its probable results, from the standpoint of the universal church. On the negative side, this new emphasis may serve a useful purpose in challenging various traditional interpretations and assumptions of Western theology. The Bible is probably being better studied by Chinese Christians today than ever before (and it has been a joy to witness the quality and quantity of Bible study materials now being prepared and issued by the National YMCA). Marxism is driving Christians to seek a sounder understanding of their own faith. The natural desire to find bridges between Christianity and materialism will lead many to discover the true incompatibilities of the former with any purely materialistic philosophy. Meanwhile the Chinese church embarks on its own search after the realities of the gospel. We may well trust them to the Bible—and to God: though they would do better had they made more truly their own the treasures of the church's heritage.[73]

[72] An interesting example of self-administration and self-finance is the so-called "Nanking plan," according to which the Three-Self Committee in a particular city administered all income-producing church property and distributed the income according to the needs of various churches in the city, not necessarily assigning income from a piece of property to the church which owned the property. CHIBUL, May 4, 1953. Churches were also aided in financial matters by remission of taxes and by direct financial assistance from the government, although there is little to indicate that the latter amounted to a great deal.

[73] CHIBUL, May 10, 1951. "T. T.," in "The Situation of the Christian Church in China: an Attempt at Understanding," Ecumenical Review III (October, 1951), 57, also refers to this weakness in theology. An example of trying to develop self-propagation may be seen in a sermon contest conducted in 1952 by the Christian Literature Society in which sermons that were not based on the scriptures or which were too other-worldly were rejected, and those which "helped and inspired Christians to Love of Country and Love of the Church" were judged satisfactory. Shen Yueh-han, "On Self-Propagation," T'ien Feng, March, 1953; British China Bulletin, New Series XIII (August, 1953), 11.

Whether distinctively Chinese theological thinking resulted from such an understanding of self-propogation receives a very partial answer in the following chapter. A full answer may never be possible.

The Three-Self idea had a much longer history than Y. T. Wu or his colleagues were prepared to acknowledge. Both missionaries and Chinese Christians had worked toward the goal of a church led, supported, and propagated by Chinese, although the results, as Bates has spelled out,[74] left much to be desired. The post-1949 Three-Self Movement had such an anti-imperialistic turn that its leaders could not acknowledge any heritage to the movement, for that would have been to acknowledge that imperialists and the Chinese influenced by them had made a constructive, though inadequate, contribution. On the other hand, by taking terms with which Christians were familiar and investing them with new meaning, through the vehicle of a group of Christians won to support of the new government, Communist strategists had adopted the role of those who come not to destroy but to fulfill. Give the peasants time, and they will tear down their idols by themselves!

The goal of indigenization movements, such as the Three-Self Movement, has usually been genuine independence and freedom of the church, coupled with the self-respect which naturally accompanies such an achievement. Self-respect can be found in some post-1949 Chinese Christian statements, particularly those of Bishop K. H. Ting, which is reason to rejoice. The ironic thing about the Three-Self Movement in Communist China is that it has proved to be the instrument by which the church has come under state control —it receives a measure of financial support from the state and propagates an ideology acceptable to the state. Freed from the imperialists, the church is now captive to the state.

SETTLING INTO NEW PATTERNS

Circulation of the Manifesto, the accusation movement, and study or indoctrination groups within the church, plus a stream of

[74] M. Searle Bates, "The Church in China in the Twentieth Century," *China and Christian Responsibility*, ed. William J. Richardson (New York: Maryknoll Publications and Friendship Press, 1968), pp. 69-70.

public movements throughout the country, such as "Three Anti-" and "Five Anti-," Land Reform, and support for the war in Korea, left the church in a state of almost overpowering confusion.

There need be no further comment on the Manifesto, to which signatures were added by the thousands, but there are numerous examples of accusations or denunciations to which reference must be made.[75] Leaders of the NCC accused the NCC. Members of the Little Flock, an indigenous Chinese sectarian group, denounced their organization and its leaders, particularly Watchman Ni T'o-sheng. Issac Wei, son of Paul Wei who founded the True Jesus Church which was also indigenous and sectarian, accused his own individualism and denounced the church because it had been infected with bourgeois attitudes and had depended on contributions from reactionary Christians. An entire issue of *T'ien Feng* was devoted to a Seventh-day Adventist denunciation and reorganization meeting in Shanghai, October 27-28, 1951.

The Jesus Family, an indigenous Christian group which followed a strict communal discipline, seemed a likely prospect to win Communist favor, but in late 1952 it was torn apart by accusations of the leader, Ching Tien-ying, by his nephew Ching Chen-tung, who accused his uncle of setting up the Jesus Family for purposes of self-aggrandizement. The older man was further criticized for requiring members to fast every fourth day, for insisting that every man below seventy and every woman below sixty be married, and for arranging the marriages with a woman alleged by the nephew to be a paramour. Filial piety had been instituted in the community merely as a means to secure absolute obedience. In reporting the accusations, the editor of *T'ien Feng* adds that the Jesus Family was reorganized as a church, and that details of this process may be found in a book entitled, *The Reconstruction of the Jesus Family at Machuang.*[76]

Chang I-fan, vice-chairman of the Hunan Three-Self Reform Committee, wrote in late 1952 that denunciations were intensified,

[75] *CHIBUL*, July 17, November 27, and December 11, 1951, and April 2, 1952, all reporting material from *T'ien Feng*.

[76] From *T'ien Feng*, February 28, 1953; *CHIBUL*, May 18, 1953. For a brief, but interesting treatment of the Jesus Family, including the way in which it was subverted to Communist aims, see D. Vaughan Rees, *The "Jesus Family" in Communist China* (London: Paternoster Press, 1959).

which evidently indicates an increase over the thirty accusation meetings reported in Changsha, the capital of Hunan, for the first six months of 1951 when the movement was just getting started. In his conclusion, after noting the good results of accusation meetings, he makes two most revealing points:

(1) Nothing will be accomplished in the Reform Movement without close dependence on the government. (2) Only by stirring up the people to real accusation meetings can the Reform Movement be carried through.[77]

The "Three Anti-" and "Five Anti-" movements added fuel to the accusation fire, within and without the church. The first was *anti* corruption, waste, and bureaucracy. The second was *anti* bribery, smuggling, stealing national resources, skimping on work and material, and stealing national economic reports (thus spying). These two movements were directed against businessmen in general; in the process accusations were brought against a number of Christian businessmen and the directors of two Christian hospitals.

The announced purpose of the Land Reform program was to distribute the land more equitably among small farmers, which purpose was more or less nullified a few years later when the farmers "voluntarily" turned the land back to the state in the commune program. Regardless of the main purpose, the most terrifying feature was the series of mass trials of offending landlords, many of whom were executed on the spot. The Catholic Church, which owned a good deal of property, suffered more than did the Protestants during this program. All churches in rural districts were closed, since all public gatherings other than those connected with Land Reform were forbidden.

Kiang Wen-han, a national YMCA secretary who participated in a Land Reform team in the summer of 1951, said that there were too many people to distribute the land effectively, that the main point of the program was to release the people from feudalism. During the three months he was engaged in the program—explaining Land Reform, classifying recipients, detailing the sins of the landlords, and letting peasants cast lots for land—he did not go

[77] *CHIBUL*, February 23, 1953.

to church, read the Bible, or pray, yet he felt he was doing the will of God. He gives a most revealing glimpse of his changing attitudes when he says that peasants were more resolute than he in dealing with the landlords, "partly because they had suffered more deeply and more intimately and partly because my religion made me see only the misery of the landlord in front of me, thus overlooking that in his inner nature he was utterly detestable." [78] To show anything but hatred for a landlord was sinful. On the other hand, *T'ien Feng* praised a Pastor Liu in Canton Shin Ma Baptist Church because "he does not allow landlords and other reactionary elements to attend church." [79]

China's involvement in the Korean war became more of a reality for Christians as money was raised in all churches for guns, ammunition, and airplanes. Several prominent pastors went on "comfort missions" to Chinese troops at the front. Communist China charged the United Nations' forces with using germ warfare; along with purported evidence these charges were prominently displayed all over China. Three-Self leaders testified that they were thoroughly convinced by the evidence and aided government publicity organs in spreading the charges.[80]

At several points in consideration of the Catholic experience in China the nature and the importance of study groups and indoctrination sessions have been pointed out. Through such affairs Christians, like all other people in China, were saturated with new ideology, and were called upon to make confessions and accusations, with the result that reactionaries and counterrevolutionaries were isolated and pressured. In the process, of course, reams of information about individuals and organizations were filed for present and future use.

Although presented as a guide to individual examination in order to "Sweep the House Clean of All Poisonous Thoughts Left by Imperialists" as well as any "possible new poisonous elements," the following questions are typical of what absorbed the attention of Christian study groups during the period:

[78] *T'ien Feng*, September 30, 1951; *CHIBUL*, November 27, 1951.
[79] *CHIBUL*, October 13, 1952.
[80] Dean Hewlett Johnson heard pastors vigorously support these charges. *China's New Creative Age* (London: Lawrence and Wishart, 1953), pp. 112-13.

Does all our thinking lean toward loving America and worshiping America? Do we think religion transcends politics? Have we doubts and fears that we might lose religious freedom under the leadership of the Communist Party? Do we have keen concern to resist America and aid Korea? Do you admit that we Christians should contribute cannon and airplanes? Does the custom of leaning on America for subsidy make us lose our will to independence? Do we freely receive the good from the government and not mutually try to support the public welfare? Do we distort our Bible teachings? Do we have narrow prejudices about the unity of the church? Such poisonous thoughts are too many. If you have only one it is enough to prevent your development in the new life.[81]

Not much reading between the lines is required in order to be aware of the tensions and stresses of 1951.

In the summer of 1951, while such a Three-Self Movement-sponsored study session was held in the mornings at Asbury Church in Peking, the members held what was supposed to be a session of the North China Annual Conference of The Methodist Church during the afternoons. A lay participant states that it was a mockery of an official church conference, and in his report of what transpired gives a remarkable picture of the confusion that prevailed in at least some church circles as adjustments were made to the new regime.[82]

The second-floor hall of Asbury Church, where the meeting was held, was decorated with signs such as "Down with the American Imperialist Lackeys." The first proposal to the conference, which was quickly passed, was to abolish the Methodist *Discipline* as something left by the Americans. Then, one by one, older ministerial members of the conference were purged on various charges: cooperation with American imperialists, unfair treatment of younger pastors, corrupt distribution of relief, unsatisfactory administration of schools, and dishonest handling of funds.

There were, it seems, three groups: the older people who were being booted out, the younger "activitists," and an intermediate or

[81] *NCC Religious Education Fellowship Bulletin*, August 9, 1951; *CHIBUL*, October 2, 1951.
[82] "How the Chinese Church Has Changed in an Urban Setting," Part II. This portion of the article was not published in *China Notes* as was the first part [I (September, 1962)]. The story told here is from a typescript supplied me by the author, a layman who formerly lived in Peking.

moderate group who were older than the activists and "cooperated with the younger group in the purge of older pastors whom they knew better and resented more." One of the younger men, not necessarily a leader of the activist group, was criticized for a quotation in his church bulletin which distinguished between believers and nonbelievers; this distinction was labeled "a hindrance to cooperation and unity between Christians and Communists." Even Bishop Kaung, at the time of the meeting still in Shanghai, where he had just accused Bishop Ch'en of being an agent of American imperialism, was attacked by the Peking group for essentially the same "crimes" for which he had accused Bishop Ch'en. Old correspondence with Americans on church matters was produced as evidence of spying.

The layman whose account is followed here insists that "the Communists adopted an observer's position in this meeting," but it is quite possible that someone was getting direction on the side. It is interesting to note, however, that one of the first to be purged in the meeting was a man who had carried on a liaison with the government through the Religious Affairs Bureau and the United Front Department. The Three-Self Reform Committee, which was elected after much maneuvering, was not even accepted by the Religious Affairs Bureau because those elected were not yet sufficiently "reformed." Thus, those who had sought power lost face; numerous lay people were quite disgusted with them because of the tactics they had employed. The conclusion of our lay observer is heartrending:

This purge meeting, conducted by pastors, made a very bad impression on the church members. Everybody could see clearly that they only wanted to give vent to personal hatred and to attack several senior pastors of the church in order to take over their positions. The most pitiful part was that the meeting place was filled with hatred and shouts of "strike" and "kill." If those sounds had come from other people, they might be excused, but they were from the mouths of preachers whose words in the pulpit were so different. Therefore, after the purge meeting, all Methodist congregations in Peking decreased greatly. Many loyal members would rather stay at home to read the Bible than come to the church to listen to those people any more.[83]

[83] *Ibid.*

Many of those who worshiped in other churches went to Wang Ming-tao's Christian Assembly, where Pastor Wang resisted the government and the Three-Self Movement. This was the case even for the Rev. Li Pu-ch'ing, the principal of the Methodist Theological Seminary in Peking, and several members of the faculty.

A year and a half later Bishop Kaung experienced frustrating delays in trying to arrange for a meeting of the East China Annual Conference. Committees met in Shanghai in December, 1952, and again in January, 1953, with Liu Liang-mo of the Three-Self Movement and various officials of the Religious Affairs Bureau trying to work out satisfactory arrangements. The Methodists were told in the first committee meeting that they could hold the conference only if it were preceded by a study session and only if they adopted the following as a conference theme: "Oppose the enemy, love one's country, and further Three-Self Reform." The conference finally met May 21-24, 1953, with about half the normal attendance, preceded by a study session which lasted from April 27 to May 20 on "Patriotism and American Imperialist Poison." Liu Liang-mo and three representatives from the Bureau of Religious Affairs directed the study and conference plans.[84]

Control of all church meetings received further confirmation with word from Foochow, where representatives of various religious groups were told they could elect delegates to the People's Council of the city. The head of the local Religious Affairs Bureau said those elected should have "(1) a firm political attitude, with a record of accomplishment in opposing imperialism, (2) sympathy with the people, and (3) a real desire to serve." In the election of the three Protestant representatives (two Buddhists and one Catholic also were to be elected by their respective bodies), these requirements were followed closely, and each person nominated had to make a short speech on what he had done since liberation, especially in opposition to imperialism and in support of the Three-Self Movement.[85]

Thus, by 1952 the Three-Self Movement was established and most churches were related to it. The resulting situation evoked high praise from observers friendly to the new regime, but even

[84] CHIBUL, March 9, May 18, and July, 1953.
[85] CHIBUL, March 9, 1953.

their judgments contained elements which belied the overall rosy glow. Dean Hewlett Johnson of Canterbury traveled in China in 1952 and was impressed with the "new morality." [86] In noting that rural churches had been hit hardest because they were more dependent on foreign aid, he confirms that they were at best not faring well. Both Johnson and Dr. Ralph Lapwood asserted that mistreatment of missionaries or Chinese Christians were exceptions and due to mistakes by prejudiced or inexperienced officials in the early years of the new regime.[87]

Lapwood speaks frankly in this connection of seizure of church property, of "pastors forbidden to preach," of "Christians frightened away from church," or of their being submitted to "a massive barrage of argument" and criticized as "backward and muddleheaded, despised and subjected to ridicule." In spite of such pressures, which contributed to a general decline of attendance at churches, Lapwood maintains that "the quality of the life of the churches, judged by the earnestness of Bible study, prayer, and mutual care, greatly improved." [88]

A report to the Church of Scotland at about the same time refers to financial difficulties, takeover of institutions, impossibility of youth work or social work, and checking of sermons and insertion of propaganda into same, and the constant reporting, even by one's closest friends, of one's thoughts and sayings. People in China lived in a continual atmosphere of fear:

Fear is widespread—fear of saying something that will reveal the wrong kind of thoughts, fear of associating oneself by thought, word, or deed with any section of society already considered hostile or reactionary to the new regime; fear of being considered less enthusiastic than others in acclaiming the new liberators of the people; fear of being out of step in any way with what is the done thing; fear of the informer and fear of being placed in such a position that one must inform on others or be regarded as an enemy of the people. Fear is kept acute by dispossession of property, by bringing suspects before "the People's Courts," where

[86] *China's New Creative Age*, pp. 175-88.
[87] Ralph and Nancy Lapwood, *Through the Chinese Revolution* (London: People's Books Cooperative Society, 1954), p. 197.
[88] *Ibid.*, p. 200.

no proper process of law is observed, or by holding accusation meetings where individuals are denounced for real or invented offences.[89]

A collection of articles by Scandinavian observers confirms for the most part what is noted above.[90] In commenting on the situation in Manchuria, Nils Kjøl said that churches and a few institutions in the cities were doing fairly well, but that most congregations in smaller places had lost all property and existed illegally. These congregations assembled in private homes under great danger, since all private meetings were prohibited.[91]

Stories in *China Monthly Review, China Reconstructs, T'ien Feng*, all intended to impress the world with how well things were going, do not prove to be so reassuring. A Baptist pastor said he could visit and hold services in city homes (Ipin, Szechwan), but not in rural districts, and he was unable to preach in tea shops or public parks as he had formerly done. The fact that people were busy was the reason often given, as in this case, for a decrease in membership:

In the new society, idleness and laziness are becoming things of the past. Everyone has work to do. For many, their work occupies them fully and a number of our old members have moved away to be nearer their work.

Then, too, the campaign to suppress the reactionary pseudoreligious society, I Kuan Tao, temporarily confused some people, who mistakenly identified this society with Christianity.[92]

This pastor's conjecture has been supported from many sides: people had no time to go to church after work and meetings, and there was an ever-present fear of associating with religious organizations after what had happened to the church and other religions. This latter factor is usually expressed as a "misunderstanding of the government's religious policy."

In this period, at any rate, such activities as Sunday schools, youth fellowships, choirs, etc., continued, but one writer says

[89] *The Church under Communism* (New York: Philosophical Library, 1953), p. 40.
[90] *Norsk Tidsskrift for Misjon,* No. 1 for 1953, pp. 34-64.
[91] "Communism og Kristendom I Nord-China," *ibid.,* pp. 44-48.
[92] Chang Jen-kai, "A Country Church since Liberation," *China Monthly Review* CXXII (February, 1952), 204-7.

church weddings had become a sign of extravagance. All of the churches had financial problems, which led in some instances to government help, and in most places to pastors taking part-time work or odd jobs to supplement their income.

Miss Cora Deng of the YWCA in late 1953 painted an encouraging picture of conditions in the YW-YM and in the church. She was particularly pleased with instances of Christian cooperation in community and national enterprises, and with the new morality and spirit of brotherhood pervading the nation. She, like Johnson, Lapwood, and numerous other writers, insisted that freedom of religion prevailed, that any imprisonment or other pressures which Christians might have suffered was due to political offenses.

No Christian has ever been subjected to penalities for practicing or propagating religion—though religious status, of course, cannot be invoked to shield those who break the laws by which all citizens are bound.[93]

With the constant repetition of this chorus by its Three-Self leaders, Protestantism emerged from its basic encounter with communism in a most precarious position. Protestant Christians might meet with Buddhists and Catholics to protest American use of germ warfare in Korea, or they might organize Sino-Soviet Friendship Leagues in their churches. They continued with deep dedication their worship, Sunday schools, and some youth activity such as choir singing. There were even reports of evangelistic missions and student Christian conferences. The church was alive, but no one of its members could ever be sure but what some expression of that life would be judged a political offense. By 1953 the situation in Protestantism was not as bleak as it appeared to critics of the Communist regime, but it was not nearly so bright as the Three-Self apologists in China and abroad proclaimed it to be.

---

[93] "Christian Life and Activities," *China Reconstructs* IV (November-December, 1955), 13-18.

VII

The Decline of the Protestant Churches

HAZY PROGRESS AND CLEAR-CUT PERSECUTION

Although the picture is not completely clear, Protestantism in Communist China moved into the mid-50's in fairly good shape. Some of the churches which had been closed during Land Reform were reopened, sometimes as if permission to reopen was a favor from the government. To cite contrasting examples, the Liangt'ien, Hunan, congregation of the Church of Christ in China did not miss a service during Land Reform, but in the Hweian District of the CCC in Fukien Province, only eight of the thirty-seven churches closed during Land Reform were allowed to reopen. Although many rural churches did not reopen, a few new buildings were erected and repairs were made to older churches, which means that one may hardly speak of total decline.[1]

There were reports of the ordination of pastors, the consecration of bishops (Anglican), and the baptism of new members. During the Chinese New Year in early 1954, evangelistic meetings were held in several churches in Shanghai, with over 300 conversions reported in one church and 500 in another. On the other hand, there was the consolidation of churches belonging to the same denomination, which the *China Bulletin* editor said may be "a euphemistic way of saying that the weaker of the two had died." [2] Denominational meetings continued, as did very successful Christian student conferences. The students, incidentally, were quite

---

[1] *CHIBUL*, June 7, 1954, and in various other issues of this journal in 1954.
[2] *CHIBUL*, April 26, 1954.

suspicious of efforts by Three-Self committees to take over the movement, but finally had to accept such controls.[3]

Study sessions continued under the direction of the Three-Self committee in every place. Inevitably a study group involved representatives of several denominations; the topics were primarily political, and each individual had to express himself and give his own opinions or reactions to what was going on.[4] There are references to Christian participation in government, as Christians were elected as people's deputies to provincial congresses all over the country as well as to the National People's Congress. Pressures were exerted to stop the work of various types of faith healers who "were sternly warned that it was not only unscriptural to oppose the use of medicine, but also against the policy of the government." [5]

That the Three-Self Movement and its government sponsors were continuing to meet resistance is seen in an address by Chairman Lu Chu-feng of the Bureau of Religious Affairs.[6] Lu acknowledged that rumors about suppression of religious organizations were floating around, such as: "First it was the I Kuan Tao, next it was the Catholic Church, and next it will be us Protestants." Lu replied by saying that I Kuan Tao, which he identified as Taoist, had to be suppressed because it was a political organization, that it was only the reactionaries among Catholics which were being purged (at the request of patriotic Catholics, of course), and that Protestants had nothing to fear if they had no reactionary elements. Although Protestant patriotism could be attested by their studies, denunciation meetings, and participation in social activities, Lu went on to warn:

[3] *CHIBUL*, May 10, 1954. For example, the Reform (or Three-Self) Committee in Peking sponsored a student conference in February, 1954, which featured addresses by the Rev. Huang P'ei-yung, former YMCA secretary and at that time assistant pastor of Moore Memorial Church in Shanghai. According to the *T'ien Feng* report, the students, who were rather conservative, were impressed with Huang and not so inclined to think that Three-Self leaders did not believe the Bible.

[4] *CHIBUL*, March 1 and April 12, 1954.

[5] *T'ien Feng*, November, 1953; *CHIBUL*, February 7, 1955.

[6] *T'ien Feng*, August, 1954; summarized in *CHIBUL*, June 21, 1954. The editor of *CHIBUL* inserts the explanation that millenarian doctrines were judged political because they implied dissatisfaction with the present regime.

There are, however, several mistakes which the Protestant churches need to correct. 1. Some preachers are unwilling to enroll in study classes, and always find some excuse for avoiding it. 2. Some preachers will interpret the Scriptures incorrectly and emphasize millenarian doctrines. Some had even said that Christ was to come again on Hsiang Shan, Peking, on April 16, 1953. But all such preaching is really political in slant . . . and must be corrected. 3. Faith healing is harmful to the church and to society generally. 4. Some preachers are intolerant of other denominations. 5. The rapid growth of meetings in the home is suspicious. We don't object to meetings in the home in general . . . , but such meetings should be supplementary to the church program. Are these meetings held in secret so that people can say what they please? It is a significant fact that these home meetings are held precisely by the religious leaders who refuse to enroll in study groups. 6. Some churches bring too much pressure on their members to subscribe to the budget of the church. Any giving should be purely voluntary, the church should not put the member under pressure.[7]

Thus, through the eyes of a government official who presumes to tell preachers when they interpret scriptures incorrectly, we receive not only an indication of the government's view of the church, but also an indication of what the centers of religious life really were. Even at this relatively early date we can note the trend toward house meetings which became more and more the avenue through which Christians expressed their devotion. And if these meetings were held in secret "so that people can say what they please," does it not suggest an admission by a government official that Christians could not say what they pleased in their churches?

Three-Self leaders quickly overcame resistance in the True Jesus Church, in which they "assisted" leaders of this indigenous movement to organize a reform committee. A report stated that the True Jesus Church had resisted reform because, being indigenous, they

---

[7] *Ibid.* A typical example of attacks on traveling evangelists was the letter sent by the Shansi province Three-Self Committee to all churches in the province claiming that evangelist Chiang Ch'eng-en was not really progressive, was travelling with a woman not his wife, and that all such evangelists were getting too much money from the churches. In the same vein as Chairman Lu's speech, the people were reminded to "not abuse the freedom of religious belief that the government has guaranteed them." *CHIBUL* April 26, 1954.

did not think they had any "imperialistic poison," but "after appropriate study they realized their mistake." [8]

Protestantism's first five years under communism in China came to a climax in the summer of 1954 with the first National Christian Conference held in the Congregational Church in Peking. It was called on rather short notice, for the Three-Self Committee decided only in mid-May that the conference would meet from July 22 to August 6. The New China News Agency report says 232 members from all over the country met in an atmosphere of close unity, hailed by Bishop Kaung as the first all-China Christian conference since the church had been freed from foreign control. [9]

Y. T. Wu, reporting on the work of his Three-Self Committee during the previous four-year period, claimed "the Chinese Christian churches had in the main rid themselves of undesirable imperialist influences" and now included 400,000 members, referring evidently to the number of signatures to the Manifesto. He reported that Christians had made donations to the Chinese People's Volunteers in Korea, that many had become model workers as they participated in the reconstruction of the country, and that many had signed their names to the Stockholm Peace Appeal. He stressed freedom of religious belief and the unity which had replaced the old denominational divisiveness.

Resolving to support the Three-Self Movement, the delegates set up the "Committee of the China Christian Three-Self Patriotic Movement," consisting of 138 members and headed by Y. T. Wu as chairman and six vice-chairmen: Bishop Chen (Anglican), Marcus Cheng of Chungking Theological Seminary (Independent), the Rev. H. H. Ts'ui (CCC), Dr. Wu Yi-fang (educator), Bishop Kaung (Methodist), and the Rev. Ting Yu-chang (Anglican, not to be confused with Bishop Ting of Nanking Seminary). The conference sent a message of respect to Chairman Mao and passed several resolutions in favor of unity and patriotism and opposing imperialism. [10]

[8] *CHIBUL*, May 10, 1954. See *CHIBUL*, July, 1954 and February 7, 1955, for further details of trouble in the True Jesus Church, including action taken against "renegade" leaders and warnings to faith healers.
[9] *CHIBUL*, August, 1954.
[10] Based on *NCNA* reports from Peking, dated August 6 and 13, 1954, summarized in *CHIBUL*, September 20 and October 18, 1954.

In passing, attention should be called to the fact that "patriotic" has been substituted for "reformed" in the official name of the Three-Self Movement.[11] It has already been noted that a similar change in terminology occurred in Catholic circles at about the same time, when those promoting government control of the churches shifted strategy. The continuing importance of the Three-Self Movement in Protestantism is confirmed by an ominous remark in an address made by H. H. Ts'ui, executive secretary of the CCC, at a unity conference in Shanghai, April 25-29, 1955. In appealing for support of the Three-Self Movement he said: "The government has told us that only the churches which support the Three-Self Movement are assured of a brilliant future." That all did not support and cooperate is indicated by his reference to "illegal activities" in the church, by which he apparently meant those who opposed church unity, specifically those independent evangelists who stated they "belong to the Kingdom of Heaven [and] obey Jesus, not Mao Tse-tung." Such activity, Ts'ui maintained, would "lead to the closing of church doors."[12]

A further indication of the church's state in the mid-50's may be gleaned from the publication of literature. Although the number of publications plummeted in the early 50's, as all Christian Literature Society titles on politics and economics were dropped and books dealing with Jesus, education, and the devotional life were cut severely, books of sermons continued to appear and Bible commentaries and dictionaries were still listed in the society's 1953 catalog.[13] Surprisingly enough, the Three-Self Movement began publication in 1955 of an intended twelve-to-fifteen volume commentary by Chia Yü-ming, leading conservative preacher and head of the Spiritual Cultivation Seminary in Shanghai, probably in return for Chia's joining the movement.[14]

[11] The term "patriotic" was used in a constitution adopted at the conference, and in the revised form adopted in 1961. See *Documents*, pp. 97, 198-99.

[12] *T'ien Feng*, May 23, 1955; *CHIBUL*, October 10, 1955.

[13] *CHIBUL*, April 26, 1954. Miss Brown's article, "The Christian Literature Society, Shanghai," appeared in the *China Bulletin* (British), New Series XV, January, 1954, pp. 1-4.

[14] *CHIBUL*, January 9, 1956. I have seen no report of how many volumes of this commentary were actually published. Another aid to the study of scripture was brought forth under somewhat unusual circumstances. Students who

The outstanding fundamentalist, Wang Ming-tao, vigorous, independent pastor of the Christian Assembly in Peking, did not join the Three-Self Movement. However he may have felt about the new government of China, he opposed collusion with it primarily on theological grounds. Pastor Wang was a classic fundamentalist who was not only opposed to all doctrines which he did not find in the Scriptures, which to him were inspired and inerrant, but also to any fellowship with those who did not hold such doctrines as the virgin birth, physical resurrection, and other traditional beliefs. Wang saw in Y. T. Wu the classic liberal-modernist, who could write that such doctrines were not important and who could even say that all could unite in the Three-Self Movement regardless of belief. So Wang Ming-tao opposed the Three-Self Movement and its leaders from its beginning until those leaders, with the help of the government, silenced him. His silencing, says Francis Jones, "is one of the most clear-cut cases of religious persecution that has come out of China." [15]

Pastor Wang had opposed the idea of a united church from the early days of his ministry in the 20's as well as during the Japanese occupation. Although critical of the missionary movement, he challenged the use of such phrases as "imperialist poison" to characterize everything that had come from the West. He saw Three-Self submission to the government as consorting with atheists, and thus a betrayal of the church.

During the Peking Christian Conference referred to earlier, the Three-Self leaders sent a small committee to confer with Pastor Wang to try to get him to mend his ways and join them, but he refused (some say that he even refused to see them). So in September of that year all churches and Christian organizations were ordered to send delegates to an "Accuse Wang Ming-tao" meeting in the capital. The charges brought against him were

1. He has not shown sympathy with the government, and his words and actions have not been in accordance with government policy. 2. He has not

---

wanted to study Greek mimeographed Leighton Stuart's *Grammar for New Testament Greek, CHIBUL,* January 18, 1954.

[15] *The Church,* p. 105; for Jones's story of Wang Ming-Tao, see pp. 103-7. Cf. Lyall, *Come Wind,* pp. 49-65.

taken part in the Three-Self Reform Movement. . . . 3. His preaching is very individualistic, its purpose is not clear, and he is a danger to the whole Christian movement.[16]

The reporter stated that Pastor Wang looked at the ceiling and never said a word, that many women were secretly weeping, that some spectators tried to leave but were prevented by police. When the demand, customary in such accusation meetings, was raised that he be put to death or at least be imprisoned, only a fourth of those present approved. The rest remained silent.

The reporter went on to say that a few days after the meeting the Student Christian Union of Peking started an "Oppose the Persecution of Wang Ming-tao Movement" which spread throughout the country. The result, our reporter adds wryly, was that "Wang Ming-tao's name became known all over China, and many who had never heard of him before now learned what he had been experiencing." Students comprised a large portion of Pastor Wang's congregation; he had spoken every summer to their popular conferences.

Pastor Wang did not preach for several weeks after the examination, but when he did resume preaching the crowds were larger than ever before. The same was true for his evangelistic meetings during the New Year's vacation; even during the dead of winter people who could not find seats inside the church stood outside and listened to his voice over the loudspeakers. It was known that Communists attended his meetings; whether they came in sincere interest, curiosity, or to gather information against him is debatable.

Pastor Wang's books were still being sold and articles attacking him were appearing in *T'ien Feng* as spring passed into summer. In an article, "We, Because of Faith," published as a pamphlet in June, 1955, Wang quoted extensively from Y. T. Wu and from Bishop K. H. Ting, literally ripping into their ambiguities and tearing them apart.[17] The discussion is largely reminiscent of fundamentalist-modernist debates of the early part of this century in

[16] Based on accounts by Christian women who went to Hong Kong, and reported in *CHIBUL*, June 13, 1955.

[7] *Documents*, pp. 99-114. Wang's speech translated by Frank W. Price.

America, but could not be dismissed as such in China in 1955. The fact that Pastor Wang associated the leaders of the Three-Self Movement with unbelievers, and continued to maintain that believers could not associate with them, was damning evidence against him in the eyes of Three-Self leaders and their government sponsors. It is significant that H. H. Ts'ui's reply to Wang (Wang had also referred to Ts'ui) did not deal with the substance of Wang's article, but tried to make the case that Wang opposed the Three-Self Movement *not* on theological grounds, but because "he opposes the New China," and thus on political grounds was a danger and should be contained.[18]

On August 8, 1955, Wang Ming-tao and his wife and about eighteen students were arrested. Wang was placed in a prison cell where two enthusiastic Communists took turns or worked together on him day and night. About the middle of November, 1955, the Religious Affairs Bureau of Shanghai summoned all Shanghai pastors to a meeting where the arrest of Wang was defended. He had been arrested because he organized independent Bible study groups, because he had favored the Japanese, because he had made treasonable (meaning contrary to government ideology) statements such as "Love your enemies," "Our citizenship is in heaven," "Love not the world," etc. A government representative expressed regrets that Wang's arrest had caused smaller attendance in churches but added that there was "nothing to fear as long as they did what they were told to do by the Three-Self Movement." There were reports that during this period the police were making special investigations of Christian homes and were interested particularly in the Christian literature to be found in these homes.[19] It is likely that discovery of literature published by Wang Ming-tao brought particular difficulty to those possessing it.

About a year later Wang was released after signing a "confession," which probably followed the lines of a message he gave to a Peking Christian audience on September 30, 1956.[20] The

---

[18] *Ibid.*, 114-16.

[19] *CHIBUL*, January 9, 1956. Miss Willis says that a book shop, "a true little shop," which was not under the Three-Self Movement, was closed and its manager imprisoned. It had sold Wang Ming-tao's books. *Through Encouragement*, p. 46.

[20] *Documents*, pp. 117-21.

confession begins in the accepted manner, acknowledging "generous treatment by the government," and confessing that he was a "counterrevolutionary offender." He states that his crimes were: (1) sabotaging the war in Korea by telling Christians it was wrong to join the army, (2) opposing the government "Three Anti" program, (3) stirring up believers against unbelievers and believers against the government by emphasizing theological differences, (4) causing difficulties for socialist construction by disparaging government projects and advising Christians how to be uncooperative, (5) opposing the Three-Self Movement due to failure to recognize it as a genuine anti-imperialist movement on the pretext of theological disagreement, (6) failing to dispel the rumors in 1954 that he had been executed, and (7) for having a hostile view toward the Communist Party. For all these things Wang Ming-tao repented, thanked the government for its magnanimous treatment, promised to take the line opposite to the various evil things he had done, apologized to the leaders of the Three-Self Movement, asked everyone's forgiveness, and promised "to become a truly patriotic and society-loving preacher."

There were various reports that Pastor Wang went about with a very depressed manner, that he was heard to compare himself to Peter or to Judas, and that finally he announced to the government that the confession did not represent his true convictions and was forthwith returned to jail. There were later reports that he was released on house arrest and lived with his wife, who had suffered a nervous breakdown, in her mother's home.[21]

As Jones has pointed out, it was obvious that Wang was arrested because of his opposition to the Three-Self Movement.[22] The fact that his opposition was based on his fundamentalist disagreement with Three-Self liberals, Marcus Cheng to the contrary and notwithstanding, was largely ignored. That the whole affair was given

---

[21] *CHIBUL*, April 7, 1958. In a feature story from Hong Kong which appeared in the Taipei *China Post*, December 28, 1968, Michael Browne, editor of *Asia News Reports*, stated that Wong Ming-to (Cantonese transliteration) "has been in prison, with the exception of one break, continuously since 1955. He is believed still alive, although nothing reliable has been heard of him since the spring of 1967." No documentation is offered to verify the report.

[22] Jones, *The Church*, p. 105.

a political connotation is clear from Y. T. Wu's statement in March, 1956:

During the national campaign to root out counterrevolutionaries, which took place in the latter part of 1955 and the early months of 1956, some counterrevolutionaries hidden within the church were uncovered. These men under the cloak of religion had formed a reactionary imperialistic clique which acted as spies, spread rumors and disrupted all the central campaigns of the Chinese people. Within the church they used the pretext of "faith" to oppose the Three-Self Patriotic Movement, trying in this way to use a religious slogan to cover up their counterrevolutionary activities, confuse their fellow Christians, corrupt youth, and destroy Christian unity in the Three-Self Patriotic Movement.[23]

One of the most ironic points in the whole business was that the Three-Self leaders, who had started the accusation of Christians in 1951, emphasized Wang's criticism of his Christian brethren as a reason for condemning him. There is no question that Wang's remarks against the unity of Christians were unfortunate and based on rather uncharitable attitudes toward anyone who believed differently, but this is (1) hardly cause for imprisonment (2) by a government which specified that the freedom of religious belief involves the freedom to attack religion.

A further point is that Wang Ming-tao was arrested in Peking on August 8, 1955, one month before Bishop Kung Pin-mei was arrested in Shanghai (September 7). One obvious conclusion is that this period was one of severe pressure which the Communist authorities alternated with periods of relatively little restraint, such as the Hundred Flowers Period which followed. More important perhaps is the fact that Wang Ming-tao was a symbol in Protestant circles of resistance to the government just as Bishop Kung was a symbol of resistance in the Catholic Church. After these two men were incarcerated, the remaining "noncooperative" personalities were relatively weak and were nullified in short order.

The case of Wang Ming-tao was the *cause célèbre* among Protestants during the mid-50's, but his was not the only case of op-

[23] *Documents*, p. 123.

pression of a Christian leader by any means. Watchman Ni of the Little Flock was sentenced to fifteen years' imprisonment on June 21, 1956. He appealed, but the sentence was confirmed by a higher court on January 28, 1957. He was charged with having made derogatory statements against the Communist Fourth Route Army in 1944-45, for having told spies in Hong Kong about conditions in Shanghai in 1950, and for having pornographic pictures and literature in his possession. Two leaders of the Little Flock in Chekiang, Lu Hsin-lin and Tung Chin-ching, were arrested on April 20, 1957. Lu was charged with preaching that the Lord would come soon, bringing a return of the Nationalists, and for saying that those who wore red scarves would be put to death, thus causing parents to prevent their children from joining the Young Pioneers (who wear red scarves). Amoy leaders of the Little Flock were arrested in April, 1958, for not having cooperated with the Three-Self Movement and for preaching on the Second Coming during the Korean war.[24]

One may say, therefore, that whereas the churches which cooperated with the Three-Self Movement seemed to be in a fairly good situation during the mid-50's, the ax was still falling on those churches and their leaders which did not follow the approved pattern. No one could remain outside the circle of Three-Self and government control for long.

A BREATH OF AIR QUICKLY SNUFFED OUT

With the exception of the arrests of Wang Ming-tao and Watchman Ni and related incidents, the period from 1955 to 1957 seems to have been the time of greatest freedom for Protestant churches in China. The period corresponds roughly to that of the Hundred Flowers Campaign, which was inaugurated in 1956 and was officially shut off in mid-1957, for one may detect a certain openness for a few months before and after the "blooming and contending."

Considerable background for understanding the effect of the Hundred Flowers and the antirightist aftermath on Protestantism

---

[24] Based on reports in *T'ien Feng*, summarized in *CHIBUL*, August, and September 16, 1957; also November 3, 1958.

in China can be gained from the reports of church-related visitors who were able to gain permission to enter China. Although one must bear in mind that Chinese Christians likely to be engaged in conversation by such visitors were called to briefing sessions where sample questions were posed and possible answers criticized and revised, there is no question but what such visits were extremely valuable.[25] Both those who entered China from the outside as well as the few Chinese Christian leaders who visited Europe and Australia made it possible for Christians in China and in other countries to renew briefly those contacts which had been held in abeyance since the early years of the Communist regime. Beginning in 1955 and continuing for several years afterward, there are records of visits to China by European, Indian, and Japanese Christians which renewed a feeling of fellowship within the world Christian community, even if organizational ties remained severed.

Extremely important are reports made by several of these groups or individuals allowed to enter China: British Quakers in 1955, Australian Anglicans in 1956, and Professor Walter Freytag of Germany in 1957. From what they saw of the church in China, these visitors all affirmed that church life was vigorous, that worship was vital, that evangelism or "extension" was going on, that Sunday schools, YMCA, and YWCA were active. They were assured that the church was free, that it was really Chinese, and that Christians had great respect for and supported the Communist government, especially because of its moral stress and its capacity to get things done.

Mr. Gerald Bailey reported for the Quakers that, contrary to expectation, they had plenty of opportunity to meet and talk frankly with Christians in China, in officially arranged situations as well as

[25] *CHIBUL*, November 3, 1958. One of the earliest visits was made by the Rev. G. Nystrom who accompanied UN Secretary-General Dag Hammerskjold to Peking in 1955. Nystrom, a former missionary to China, served as Hammerskjold's interpreter, was favorably impressed by conditions of religious freedom, and even was invited by Chou En-lai to return as a missionary. Nystrom's account of the visit appeared in the Swedish publication, *Svensk Veckotidning*, which I have not been able to consult. Professor Josef L. Hromadka, several other East European Christian leaders, and Bishop Rajah B. Manikam of India visited China in 1956. The same year a Chinese YMCA delegation visited India and representatives of the YMCA World Alliance visited China. I refer to Bishop Ting's travels in note 30.

in informal groups. He did not seem to realize that even in an informal group it is possible for one member, at a later time and under pressure, to report on another member. Nonetheless, the Quakers felt their contacts were free and relaxed, that they were received with friendliness and hospitality. Bailey does note that Chinese Christians had to accept not only the benefits brought about by the Communist revolution, but also the

"dark side of the moon," . . . the ruthless suppression of dissident opinion, . . . the persecution (—my word, not theirs—) of Christians who will not "accept," and . . . (again my words, not theirs) the slow strangulation of the spirit of man.[26]

The report of the Australian Anglican delegation that visited China in 1956 is a most valuable document.[27] A newsman, Alfred Francis James of the Anglican News Service in Sydney, apparently raised questions which went beneath the surface, even though the answers he received did not necessarily depart from an established stance. Mr. James noticed that practically every discussion members of the delegation had with their hosts was based on politics, which leads him to make some very perceptive and sympathetic remarks about the absorption of the church in an atmosphere charged with politics.

The Chinese Anglicans affirmed their freedom to publish books and literature, to evangelize "within the limits imposed by the state and to receive religious books and literature from outside." They also maintained that the Sheng Kung Hui had not been absorbed by the Three-Self Movement, that it was actually more Anglican than before. James saw that the Three-Self Movement provided machinery for liaison between government and church, that it was actually "an extension of the central government," which was clearly totalitarian, but this did not mean to him that the churches or the movement were thereby "stooges for communism." [28]

[26] "Quakers Visit China," *The Christian Century*, November 30, 1955, pp. 1393-95. A booklet about the same visit was published at about the same time, but I have not been able to secure a copy. Note that the words in parentheses in the direct quotation are Bailey's words.
[27] Alfred Francis James, *Reports on Deputation of Australian Churchmen* (New York: Far Eastern Office, NCCCUSA, 1957). A reprint of articles from the Anglican press in Australia and America.
[28] *Ibid.*, p. 8.

Ho Chen-hsiang, director of the Bureau of Religious Affairs, granted a lengthy interview to James in order to make clear the stand of the government. James inquired about the imprisonments of Wang Ming-tao and Anglican Bishop Kimber Den, the latter having just been released. Mr. Ho insisted that these were imprisonments for political offenses, even in the case of Bishop Den, who, as James pointed out, had been imprisoned for five years without a trial and then suddenly released. Ho replied that the government welcomed criticism, that those responsible for the delays in Den's case "have been severely punished" (adding that the delays were "one of the most unfortunate aspects of this case"), and that the government was only trying to root out espionage.

James obviously did not accept what many observers also have not been able to accept, that which is expressed in the last line of Ho's statement concerning the "unfortunate" things which happened to both Protestants and Roman Catholics:

If you look at it objectively, you must admit that it was a *natural reaction by many Chinese people* after the things that had been done against China under the guise of missionary work. *It was never the policy of the government.*[29]

As evidence of his sincerity Ho said, "We encourage the Anglicans to have contacts abroad, and of course we hope that in that way the truth about China will become known abroad." The fact that Chinese Anglicans who did travel abroad gave a consistently favorable picture of the situation in China underscores the thrust of Ho's statement.[30] Within the country he insisted that pastors and people could criticize but not attack the government, adding that pastors in China had no cause to attack the government as pastors might feel called to do in the West.

[29] *Ibid.*, p. 11. Italics added.
[30] *Ibid.* With reference to Chinese Anglicans traveling abroad, Bishop Ting in the summer of 1956 attended a preparatory meeting for the Lambeth Conference, although he did not get to the Conference itself in 1958. *China Consultation, 1958* (New York: Far Eastern Office, NCCCUSA), p. 19. On the same 1956 trip, Bishop Ting participated in a meeting of the World Council of Churches Central Committee at Galyateto and spoke favorably of the situation in China. "China at Galyateto," editorial correspondence by Theodore H. Gill in *The Christian Century*, September 5, 1956, pp. 1015-16. Dr. Chao Fu-san visited Australia in the late 50's and left favorable impressions there.

The Australian report as a whole communicates a basic and un-qualified sympathy with the Chinese church and the Chinese people, an ungrudging respect for the progress made by China under Communist rule, and great satisfaction at having made contact with the church in China after seven years of separation; but it does not ignore the evasions, the strange logic, and in some instances the sheer nonsense of what the Australians were told. The impression of a degree of stability in the church, which had passed through tremendous pressures and which continued to exist under difficulty, is accurate for this period in the life of the church in China.

Professor Walter Freytag was also impressed with the progress China was making, with the moral vigor of the Communist government, and with the highly political tone of every conversation.[31] He understood this political atmosphere to mean that confidence in the present government was the only course possible for Christians, but he acknowledged in another connection that "the possibility of the freedom of speech . . . can disappear overnight." Freytag sensed a defensive tone in all that was said, as Chinese Christians sought "to destroy the picture of the church in China which has been formed abroad." Positively put, Freytag thought they were insisting that, whatever people from outside might think of them, such people could not say that they had betrayed their Lord. There was no doubt in his mind that Christians knew they were called to witness in that situation and accepted the obligation of witness as their service to Christ.

In spite of the many lacunae in the accounts by these visitors to China, these reports suggest that Chinese Christians had a fair degree of confidence and were therefore willing to say something.

[31] "Meeting Christians in China," *International Review of Missions* XLVI (October, 1957), 410-16. Most of these visitors noted the political character of the conversations they had with their Chinese hosts and the pervading influence of politics in every area of life. Most revealing in this connection is the discernment of a Bristish jurist, F. Elwyn Jones, Q.C., M.P., who visited China in the mid 50's. He sensed "a real concern for justice among the lawyers [he] met, and a desire to create an effective independent court system." But he observed quite frankly that "the Communist doctrine does not accept that the independence of judges from political control is essential to the safe-guarding of the liberty of the citizen." He also noted the lack of habeas corpus machinery, the rarity of lawyers to defend the accused, that social obligations transcended individual rights, and that two thirds of the 1800 prisoners in one Peking prison were there for political crimes as counter-revolutionaries. Cited in Williamson, *British Baptists*, p. 353.

It is essential to recognize this limited sense of confidence in order to understand its expression during this period, not only to visitors from outside but to officials and groups within.

When the call was issued to "Let a hundred flowers blossom, a hundred schools of thought contend," some Protestants did not hesitate to respond. They said that religious leaders and believers were not treated with respect, that they were actually discriminated against. In schools, for example, children of believers would be called for interviews, during which they would be told not to go to Sunday school or they would be expelled. A teen-aged son of a pastor had his application to join the Young Communist League repeatedly turned down.[32]

Kiang Meng-kuang in a *T'ien Feng* article complained about the type and large number of antireligious books circulating. He objected to the fact that they were primarily translations from earlier Russian works that contained dogmatic judgments perhaps relevant to the Orthodox Church in Tsarist days but not to modern China. He also objected to the lack of thoughtful, logical arguments against religion—there was nothing but abuse. Since such literature reviled and abused Christians, it actually worked against the policy of the government and Mao Tse-tung instead of encouraging mutual respect.[33]

It was even more striking when someone who held political office under the Communist regime spoke out. The Rev. Ma Hsing-ke, pastor of the Congregational Church in Paoting, Hopei, and chairman of the Three-Self Movement in that city, was also chief of the General Affairs Department of the Municipal People's Hospital, a people's deputy in Paoting, and a member of the provincial and municipal Chinese People's Political Consultative Conference. When he later came under fire in the antirightist campaign it was alleged that he opposed the control of religious affairs by Party and government, and that he had said the Religious Affairs Bureau was bureaucratic, had "restricted religious activities," and that its cadres were ignorant of religious matters. Because of these attitudes

---

[32] Quoted from *KMJP*, May 29, 1958 (?), by Roderick MacFarquhar, *The Hundred Flowers Campaign and the Chinese Intellectuals* (New York: Frederick A. Praeger, 1960), p. 249.

[33] *T'ien Feng*, May 27, 1957; *CHIBUL* September 16, 1957.

and statements and his proposal that religious leaders should have charge of religious activities, he was later charged with "attempting to usurp Party and government leadership over religious circles." [34]

Marcus Cheng's address to the Chinese People's Political Consultative Conference in Peking on March 19, 1957, climaxed the Protestant "blossoming and contending." [35] A Buddhist delegate and Y. T. Wu had already spoken. Wu had referred to the fact that some churches had not been allowed to reopen, that church buildings and furniture had been appropriated by government offices, that there had been interference with Christian life, and that some cadres had expressed hostile attitudes. Cheng then took the floor, observed that no one had disagreed with Wu, but added that "some friends thought that Mr. Wu ought not to have raised these 'vague questions about the carrying out of the religious policy.'" Then he launched into a forcefully and adroitly phrased "protest" against what had been happening, all in the name of a devoted citizen of the People's Republic opposed to the imperialists who had used missionaries to commit aggression against China.

Marcus Cheng, in much the same vein as Kiang Meng-kuang, pointed to the inappropriateness of the Russian anti-Christian literature, since Christians in Russia had supported that country's war effort in World War II and Christians in China were supporters of the government and cooperated with the Communist Party. He pointed to the fact that Sun Yat-sen, as well as a large number of the Seventy-two Martyrs of the Chinese Revolution, was Christian. But his classic statement, in which he distinguished between the criticism of religion which Christians welcomed and the abuse, which was unfair and to which he objected, came in the early part of the speech.

Therefore believers have freedom to preach their faith, and unbelievers have freedom to criticize religion, and the attempt in this controversy to discover the truth should be carried out calmly, without abuse or name-

[34] *Hopei Jih-pao*, April 9, 1958; *CHIBUL*, July, 1958.
[35] Marcus Cheng's speech first appeared in *JMJP*, March 25, 1957, was reprinted in *T'ien Feng* on May 13, was translated by Dr. Jones for *CHIBUL*, August and September 2, 1957, which translation was included in *Documents*, pp. 151-56.

calling. You speak out your atheism and I will preach my theism, and in this controversy you must not take to abusing my mother, defiling my ancestral graves, or reviling my ancestors. In the eyes of us Christians, God is the Supreme Being, and the churches are His temples, the place where Christians worship Him. In the argument over theism and atheism you must not revile God, or blaspheme His name; you must not take our churches by force. For example, a letter from a minority tribesman just the other day says, "Our church is still occupied and is in terrible condition, as it is being used as a stable." This defiling of our churches is like defiling our ancestral graves, and impresses us very painfully. At the opening of a new steel bridge, an official of high rank gave an address, in which he emphasized that this bridge had been made by human effort, and was not the work of any so-called God. Then he said, "You Christians should throw your God into the dungheap." Such blasphemy of God is, in the eyes of Christians, worse than reviling one's mother. This is not criticism, but abuse of religion. Chairman Mao on November 22, 1952, in a speech in Tibet said, "The Communist Party protects religion. Believers and unbelievers, believers in this or that religion, all are protected and respected." We believers appreciated very much this word from Chairman Mao, and what especially impressed and comforted us was his statement that the government would not only protect, but would also "respect." Now this means that you must not blaspheme the God whom we worship, nor defile the churches in which we worship Him.[36]

The blooming and contending came to an official end in mid-1957; an antirightist campaign was inaugurated, and those who had expressed or were suspected of having rightist or reactionary views were attacked. The Rev. Marcus Cheng was one of the first to be attacked when the Standing Committee of the Three-Self Movement met in Peking late in 1957.[37] He was accused of attacking the Communist Party and of being antisocialist, for asserting that there was any conflict between believers and nonbelievers, and for having compared the Party and the Communist government to the imperialists. The alleged comparison was based on his remark that both Marx and modernist Christians had criticized the Bible,

[36] *Documents*, p. 152.
[37] Reported in *T'ien Feng*, January 6 and 27, 1958. Summarized in *CHIBUL*, January 20 and October 6, 1958. See *China Notes* I (June, 1963), 2-4, where it is reported that Marcus Cheng, along with Mr. Ch'en Hsin-kwei who had written critical articles in *The Farmer*, were no longer classified as rightists.

although he tactfully added, "Even we fundamentalist Christians are glad to accept his criticism." Special reference was made to the comparison and to the fact that such strong language had stirred up other Christians to oppose the Party and the people.

At the same meeting the Rev. Chou Fu-ch'ing, of the independent church in Shanghai called the Ling Liang T'ang, was castigated for appearing to support the Three-Self Movement while actually trying to undercut it with reactionary activities such as support of Wang Ming-tao. Also under attack was the Rev. Chia Yü-ming, president of the Spiritual Cultivation Theological Seminary in Shanghai and an outstanding conservative. Chia proceeded to criticize himself and his progress, or lack of progress, in following socialist education.

Chou Ch'ing-tse of the CCC was accused of "keeping house for the imperialists" while actually serving as a people's deputy, and was charged with all kinds of conniving to undermine the Three-Self Movement. Fang Ai-shih, a Methodist leader in Ningpo and chairman of the Three-Self Movement in that place, had called on the Communist Party to "step down from the throne," had admitted that his work was "opposed to the Communist enterprise," and that his own attitudes were opposed to socialism. Liu Ling-chiu, editor of *The Farmer,* and independent pastors in Shanghai were also criticized.[38]

A political study institute for 240 church workers of Kiangsu province and 96 seminary students, held in Nanking from February 2 to May 13, 1958, saw a number of people condemned as rightists, the most prominent name being that of Luther Shao, a Disciples leader. Intense pressures continued on Shao for about a year, ending in his suicide by drowning in April, 1959.[39]

Dr. Francis Wei (Wei Cho-min), former president of Huachung College, and two other former officers of the same institution were attacked for having been the "brains of an anti-

[38] These accusations were also reported in the January 6 and 27, 1958, issues of *T'ien Feng.* Similar "purge meetings" in the Wuhan area are described in *CHIBUL,* October 20 and December 1, 1958.

[39] Report of the denunciation meeting is from *CHIBUL,* January 19, 1959. Shao, who had agonized so painfully over his accusation of a fellow worker in 1951, was himself denounced along with fellow workers in Kiangsu. Final confirmation of Shao's suicide by drowning, following counter-reports denying the fact, appeared in *CHIBUL,* February 13, 1961.

Communist organization" in the Central China Normal College where the three were teaching.[40] There may have been some connection, at least in the minds of the Communist leadership, between this alleged organization and a student uprising during the Hundred Flowers Period. The attacks on Wei for secret organizational activity were among the first in the whole rightist campaign; they did not focus on his Christian activity as such, but took the line of attacks on intellectuals throughout the country.

Thus, conservatives and "liberals" (there were very few liberals in China), those who avoided Three-Self and those who cooperated with it, along with a host of writers, professors, and intellectuals, were brought to earth in the antirightist campaign. There are those who think that the Hundred Flowers Period was initiated with the precise intent of uncovering those who did not follow the accepted line. It is further suggested that key people loyal to the Party were instructed to make criticisms of the government or conditions in general, in order to encourage genuine critics to speak out. There is some reason to draw this conclusion—that criticism was invited and encouraged in order to flush out hidden opponents—but it is also probable that the amount and intensity of the criticism far exceeded what the leaders expected. The halt suddenly called and the weight of countermeasures in this light are not quite so startling.

At some point in 1958, the stress shifted from denunciation of antirightists to the rooting out of "illegal activities" in the church, such as faith healing (including exorcism of demons in the True Jesus Church), inviting independent preachers, preaching on eschatological themes, and church meetings in homes.[41] This shift in emphasis, as well as much more, can be seen in the use of "Patriotic Resolutions" or "guarantees" (*pao cheng shu*) ; a sample from the Yuling district of Shanghai [42] shows that those who signed agreed to :

1. Observe the five don'ts (don't break laws, preach reactionary doctrine, use healing promises to get converts, invite free-lance evangelists, attend or preach in home services), five musts

---

[40] *CHIBUL*, September 30, 1957.

[41] *CHIBUL*, January 19, 1959.

[42] *T'ien Feng*, May 31, 1958; *CHIBUL*, November 3, 1958. Reprinted in Hocking, *Servants of God*, pp. 102-3.

(cooperate with the government's religious policy, expose free-lance evangelists and home services, be economical, discipline one's body, and take part in every socialist campaign), the five loves (love country, Party, socialism, the Three-Self Movement, and labor), and the five excellences (to improve the openness of one's thinking through the criticism of others and self-criticism, to go further in self-reform by destroying capitalism, to increase mutual respect among believers and between believers and nonbelievers, to improve street activities and relations with neighbors, and improve political study).

2. Build up political study for pastors and organize study classes for laymen.

3. Support government efforts in public hygiene.

4. Heed the call of the government for birth control, in one's own family and by commending it to others.

5. Plant trees in every available spot.

6. Wipe out illiteracy among people fourteen to forty years old during 1958.

7. Send rural people who have come to Shanghai back to the farm for production.

8. (Pastors should) learn six patriotic songs before May 1.

9. Guarantee participation of 85 percent of church members in every social campaign.

10. (Pastors) guarantee to take part in savings programs.

11. Have a criticism meeting once a quarter to check progress on all these points.

If one's reaction is, "what a conglomeration!" it is probably fairly close to the reaction of Christians in China at that time, when this sort of thing characterized their life.

In 1958, China headed into the Great Leap Forward, which called for a complete collectivization of the whole country. First rural and then urban areas were structured into vast communes. In most cases several existing cooperatives were grouped together to form a commune whose geographical boundaries usually corresponded with a township. A cooperative usually became a brigade, which was subdivided into production teams. Families ate together in giant mess halls, service teams were assigned to such tasks as making and mending of garments, small children were placed in nurseries to free their mothers for work in fields or factories. In some places food was provided free, but with lower wages; in other places commune members paid for their board and received slightly higher wages.

The communes were in no sense an antireligious measure and there is no evidence to indicate that Christians suffered more or less than anyone else. Commune regimentation, however, plus the drive to increase production, meant that laymen had neither the time nor the strength for any unrequired activities such as those which had been a part of church life.[43] Both the need for additional income and the need to avoid the opprobrium of giving full time to something like church work led many pastors, sometimes in cooperation with laymen, sometimes with Catholic priests, to organize their own work programs. Two of the most famous were in Kweilin: the Red Light Shoe Factory and the Red Light Pickle Factory. Salt refining was done on this basis in Nanning, iron smelting in the Peking Tengshihk'ou Church, and a factory for making organs was set up by churchmen in Foochow.[44] Earle H. Ballou summarizes clearly the effect of the total commune program on the church:

This complete regimentation of life must make the position of the Christian pastor more and more precarious. There is simply no place for him as a separate, nonproducing unit. He must become a member of the commune, and then his time is no longer his own. How many former pastors are now working full time in communes and trying to hold a church together in what spare time they have there is no way of knowing. We also do not know how the church members' ability to contribute to the church has been affected by the commune organization, but it would seem obvious that the tendency to pay the worker more and more with food and services rather than a cash wage would leave him less and less able to contribute to a church program.[45]

[43] Francis P. Jones, "Church Life in China Today," *Social Action XXVI* (March, 1960), 21-26.

[44] *CHIBUL*, May 11, March 2, and February 16, 1959; January 18, 1960.

[45] "How Has the Church Come through This Period?" Earle H. Ballou, ed., *China Consultation, 1960* (New York: Far Eastern Office, NCCCUSA, 1960), p. 5.

The year 1958 also saw the large-scale unification or consolidation of churches in every Chinese city. This unification was hailed by Three-Self leaders as evidence of Christian unity and of the desire to better utilize personnel and buildings, but suspected by people outside to be a further sign of control of religious affairs. Sixty-five Protestant churches in Peking were consolidated to four. Two hundred churches in Shanghai were reduced to twenty-three. Four churches remained open in Canton, two in Swatow, one each in Hankow and Wuchang. Churches ranging across the denominational spectrum from Anglican and Methodist to the Salvation Army, Seventh-day Adventists, and Little Flock, had to cooperate with each other and usually to worship together on Sunday.

Many pastors and Bible women were thereby released for "productive labor," and hundreds of church buildings were made available for other uses.[46] At various times after 1949, Christian groups were able to rent out church buildings and receive much-needed income. It is possible that the same practice was employed for unused buildings after the consolidation, but such was not always the case. For example, the churches in Chungshan County, Kwangtung, representing seven denominations, united and "freely" donated all surplus property to the commune.[47]

The articles of union for the churches of Taiyuan, capital of Shansi province, stated that governing boards and committees of individual churches were to be abolished in favor of the Three-Self Committee, which would be in complete control. A common ritual with hymns to be chosen by a joint committee was to be used in the unified worship program. Books interpreting the Bible were to be examined for poisonous thoughts—"Only teachings favoring union and socialism shall be used." "Negative and pessimistic teaching" about the evils of this world or the coming day of the Lord was forbidden. Emphasis had to be placed instead on "the need for the union of faith and practice, the dignity of labor, the control of nature, and the dividing line between ourselves and our enemies, between right and wrong." All distinctive features of individual groups, such as personal interviews before breaking of bread in the

[46] *Ibid.*, p. 6.
[47] *CHIBUL*, May 11, 1959.

Little Flock, military appurtenances of the Salvation Army, Saturday sabbath of the Adventists, had to be surrendered.[48]

The Taiyuan articles of union may be extreme. There are continued references to denominational structures, and they probably existed on the eve of the 1966 Cultural Revolution.[49] An unidentified "Correspondent," writing in *The East and West Review*, acknowledged that unions and "amalgamations" all over the country had been effected without conviction, but says the leaders "are clearer and profounder today in their Christian discipleship than they were, say, fifteen years ago." [50]

There were vigorous denials by Chinese leaders that the unification in any way smacked of government interference. Dr. Chao Fu-san, visiting in Australia, said that there had been no pressure from the government, that he as an Anglican clergyman (and dean of Yenching Union Theological Seminary, Peking) had voluntarily taken part in union services which were held at a Congregational church because the Anglican cathedral was "awkwardly sited." [51]

In defending the merger in Peking, a writer by the name of Lu Wen pointed out in *T'ien Feng* that 10 of the 65 churches had no members at all, that 20 other churches had less than 20 members each, and 20 others were controlled by rightists and other "evil elements." [52] The total attendance in all Protestant churches in Peking on a single Sunday, he maintained, was under 500. The fact that 1,000 gathered each Sunday in Wang Ming-tao's Christian Assembly before he was arrested indicates either that Lu Wen's statistics are faulty or that the antirightist campaign and life in

[48] Jones, *The Church*, pp. 156-57. Australian Free Church visitors to China in 1959 were told that Seventh-day Adventists were allowed to hold their services on Saturday, and that denominational structures still functioned. *CHIBUL*, December 7, 1959. See article by E. Lyall Williams, "China's Churches are Still Serving," *World Call*, December, 1959.

[49] Church leaders were introduced under denominational labels to Australian visitors in 1959; these visitors described the process of union as one of "dissolving denominational differences without loss of emphasis," *CHIBUL* November 23, 1949. The reference to 1966 is from Bates's article in Richardson, *China and Christian Responsibility*, p. 76.

[50] "Understanding the Position of the Church in China," *The East and West Review* XXVI (January, 1960), 20-27.

[51] *Ecumenical Press Service*, March 25, 1960, p. 3.

[52] *CHIBUL*, January 19, 1959.

the communes had exacted a greater toll than Three-Self apologists previously would have admitted.

Speaking to the Third Chinese People's Political Consultative Conference, Y. T. Wu explained that the great number of churches in China and their faulty distribution (so many on one street) was due to divisions and competition among churches introduced by the imperialists. After consultation, the number and siting of the churches had been readjusted to meet the needs of the people, with the result that church work was unified, the people were now able to enjoy a normal religious life, and were "contented and happy." [53]

NOTES ON THEOLOGY AND THE ORTHODOX CHURCH

Information on the character of Protestant theology and on developments in the Orthodox Church in Communist China is extremely limited in both cases. Since such information as is available comes largely from the pre-1958 period, this seems to be the most appropriate point to consider briefly these two topics. Theology and the Orthodox Church are not related as far as treatment is concerned and represent what might be called a two-part excursus.

In the opinion of some observers the Chinese church was weak in theology. Dr. Chao Tzu-ch'en, the most creative theological mind in China, soon found it advisable under the Communists to soft-pedal his trenchant, probing, responsible theologizing which had already attracted the world's attention. Indian visitors in the mid-60's said that the Chinese "carefully keep all theological questions out of their discussions." [54] The controversy between Wang Ming-tao and Three-Self Movement leaders was, among other things, a fundamentalist-modernist debate in which Pastor Wang accused Three-Self leaders of ignoring, if not failing to believe, the eternal truths of the gospel.

Although Y. T. Wu revealed a measure of theological insight in a sermon he preached at Yenching University in 1952,[55] he did not

[53] Wu Yao-tsung, "Strip Imperialism of Its Cloak of Religion," *JMJP*, May 1, 1959; *CURBAC*, June 3, 1959, pp. 33-37.
[54] *CHIBUL*, November 25, 1957.
[55] Ralph and Nancy Lapwood, *Through the Chinese Revolution*, pp. 203-7.

deal with theological questions in most of his addresses and articles and devoted himself primarily to the promotion and administration of the Three-Self Movement. Dr. Jones quotes him as saying:

As to how much innate evil there is in man's nature, what percentage of man's total nature it amounts to, and whether it can ever be eradicated —such metaphysical questions as these we have no time for, let the anti-Communist Western theologians impale themselves on the horns of their own dilemma.[56]

There is a series of articles from Wu, however, in which he pities those who so easily forget the creator God, "the Christ whose life was full of mercy and truth." He exclaims: "Do we believe that the Holy Spirit who has hitherto enlightened and guided our hearts, will suddenly stop working? Not so. The eternal triune God does not change with the times." [57]

In Dr. Jones's previously quoted article, "Theological Thinking under Communism," which is practically the only treatment of the subject available,[58] he quotes from an address made by Methodist Bishop Kaung in 1957, in which the bishop said Christians in China were getting new light on such questions as "the Christian and the world, church and state, belief and unbelief, faith and works." Jones found in a study of the more thoughtful *T'ien Feng* articles during the 50's that such theological discussion as one might discover in the Chinese church focused on such problems, rather than the more classical ones of the Trinity, Christology, sin and salvation, and eschatology. He discerned a trend away from a world-denying theology to a world-affirming one, making the point rather well that missionaries had contributed to the former often

[56] Francis P. Jones, "Theological Thinking in the Chinese Protestant Church under Communism," *Religion in Life* XXXII (Autumn, 1963), 534-46, quotation from 540-41.

[57] Three articles entitled "Freedom through Truth" in *T'ien Feng* for January 11, February 1 and 22, 1954, translated in *Documents*, pp. 73-84, quotation from p. 78.

[58] Jones, "Theological Thinking," 538-45. "The Voice of the Chinese Church" [by a former missionary], *East and West Review* XVII (October, 1951), 100-104, is a survey of valuable religious books, some theological, which were circulating in Communist China in early 1951. Unfortunately I have no information concerning Catholic theologizing during the Communist period in China, so there is no parallel discussion of this topic in Chapters IV and V.

without realizing it. The world-affirming stand could be seen in post-1949 opposition to Mrs. Charles E. Cowman's devotional book *Streams in the Desert*, which was condemned finally because it calls on Christians to accept pain, suffering, and sorrow as the will of God.[59]

The way in which Bishop Kaung's other questions were handled may be treated even more briefly. Although various writers allude to certain problems involved, their conclusions are that the church can and should cooperate with the state, the believer and unbeliever may agree to differ, and faith may be known and valued only if it is expressed in works.

Bishop Robin Chen maintained, in 1955, that the Anglican Church in China would remain true to its heritage and hold the mean "between reverence for tradition and freedom for creative innovation." The coming of communism has actually been a help in this process with respect to the doctrine of the church, he asserted in the following statement:

The church of our Lord Jesus Christ was established on earth by the apostles at the command of the Lord. From the time of the apostles until now the church should be one holy and catholic church, and although from the weakness of man we now see it divided, still the pure Body of Christ which is not limited by outward form believes that every people has the right within the unity of this tradition to organize its own church body, and that all such national churches are equal each to each and members one of another, since they are all united to Christ the Head, and one is not below another in rank. The Chung Hua Sheng Kung Hui [Anglican] should have had such a position from the time of its organization, but unfortunately it was seriously bound by imperialism, and was given only a subsidiary and colonial position within the body of the apostolic church. Our church was organized in 1912, with its own General Assembly, but until the Three-Self Movement came, after liberation, our church was dismembered and divided into spheres of influence by the various missionary societies. We did not even have one unified Book of Common Prayer, in spite of the efforts of the General Assembly and the National Committee. At that time the Chung Hua Sheng Kung Hui was not Chinese, for it had not become independent; it was not Holy, for it was

[59] Jones, "Theological Thinking," p. 539. The fact that *Streams in the Desert* was a great favorite of President Chiang Kai-shek undoubtedly contributed to its loss of popularity in Communist China.

still contaminated with imperialism and colonialism; and it was not Catholic, for it was not yet recognized as an equal member in the body catholic.[60]

Bishop Ting Kuang-hsun, president of Nanking Theological Seminary, was the major theological mind in the Chinese church in the late 50's. He exhibited little in the way of theological stature when he commented on a creed adopted by the seminary in July, 1954; the statement of faith is itself about as minimal as one could find.[61] He passes over the use of *Shen* as a name for God in one paragraph and *Shangti* in another as being in accordance with mutual toleration. He brushes off objections that much was left out (only four affirmations concerning Scripture, God, Christ and Holy Spirit), by saying, in so many words,"What of it?" The statement that " 'all Scripture is inspired by God' . . . covers a great deal of territory," including, evidently, all other areas of belief. After "extended and lively discussion by the Board of Managers" the creed was adopted unanimously, which was noteworthy to Ting after the "division and quarreling" of two thousand years.

There is considerable theological depth, however, in two later addresses by Bishop Ting—to the Frontier Luncheon group in Britain in 1956 and to the graduates of Nanking Seminary in 1957. In the first he says that a vague Christianity, whether the liberalism, moralism, and rationalism of the social gospel or the pietism that gives little guidance for ethical living in society, could not give satisfaction in modern China. Therefore,

Chinese Christians by their own path have come to know in greater fullness the Christ who is the Prophet, who is the Priest, who is the King. He is the center of history. His resurrection was victory over sin, over

[60] From the first issues of *Sheng Kung* [Sacred Work], an Anglican publication, February, 1955; *CHIBUL*, August, 1955.

[61] *CHIBUL*, January 19, 1955. The tendency at Nanking Seminary to gloss over theological issues was illustrated when Professor Walter Freytag lectured there in 1957. Drawing upon the German experience under the Nazis, he stated that the good which men seem to do, whether in Nazism or the church, may keep man from God, and spoke of the church as living in an interim before the final judgment. A writer in the *Nanking Theological Review* retorted, with great distortion even of that which he quoted Freytag as saying, that Freytag was trying to "smear" the achievements of the new China, and that Freytag opposed progress and the peace movement. Fulton, *Through Earthquake*, pp. 319-22.

death, and over Satan, and he sits at the right hand of God as the Head of the church and as the Lord of the world. We are now to see the world in a new light—in the light of His victory. And the task of the Church is to proclaim His victory and to manifest His kingship. It is faith in this Christ which gives Christians the hope in its ultimate sense and also the strength for their pilgrimage and responsibilities in daily living.[62]

He then goes on to say that Chinese Christians have learned "how to enter into the mystery of the weakness of the church," that they have discovered that it is in this state of weakness that the power of the grace of God is manifest. The church's "task is just to be itself, to abandon its will to power in the world in a worldly manner, in order to be itself, to gain strength in its weakness." [63] He then went on to talk about the Three-Self Movement, relations with an atheistic regime, and ecumenical contacts in the light of this understanding.

The second of Bishop Ting's addresses, delivered to theological students on June 12, 1957, just as the Hundred Flowers Movement was being phased out, begins with a courageous challenge to Communist dialecticians: "We Christians do not think that it is a satisfactory classification to call all shades of thought either materialistic or idealistic." [64] He also said that Christians rejected the conclusion that all materialists were progressive and all idealists backward. Finally, Christianity does not fit either category:

It is still more impossible to classify Christianity as either idealist or materialist, because although it is in form the product of history, it is in essence not an ideology, not a structure built upon an economic base. Its true substance is revelation, the Incarnation, and thus it transcends all human lines of division.

. . . In itself it [Christianity] is not the fruit of history and the Gospel is not an ideology. The Gospel comes from the free revelation of God. This

[62] "Christian Frontiers in China," *Christian News-Letter IV* (October, 1956), 23-29.

[63] *Ibid.*, p. 25. Toward the end of these remarks (p. 28) Bishop Ting stated that the Three-Self Movement was not against missions and recognized that "the three objects of the Three-Self Movement were in fact the goal of many of the missionaries who went to China with the sole object of serving the Chinese people, the sole object of giving to the Chinese people the best thing they had—that is the Christian Gospel, and their good work is not forgotten." Even though spoken in London, it is a most amazing statement.

[64] *Documents*, p. 157.

Gospel is Christ Himself, through whom all things were made. [When we understand this] we will have a clear understanding from which to perceive that all talk of a comparison of Christianity with communism, of likeness or differences, is beside the point and superfluous.[65]

Ting attacks the idea that Christianity is an opiate, first on the basis of Biblical evidence (Jesus rejected the "opiate" on the cross), and then by pointing out that such phrases are not based on the concrete study of religion but proceed from *a priori* definitions. He expresses his doubt that man by reason can know God and affirms his faith that the knowledge of God comes by revelation alone.

Perhaps the most courageous statements in this address to seminary students were made with respect to sin and salvation. Ting observed that in an atheistic society one is tempted to blame all evils on a bad social system. Although this might be a corrective for Christians who have ignored social problems, it misses the point that sin is real, that it is present in human life, a load which man continues to bear even in a good environment like China.

In today's society the level of moral action has been raised, and this is a fact which we Christians should welcome. We should not go around looking for flaws trying to make someone lose face, as if the only way to satisfy us were to discover that someone else was wrong. We should welcome a social system that shows itself able to raise the level of moral life. But the change of social system can only limit the effectiveness of sin, it cannot solve the problem of sin. Sin can only be healed by forgiveness, salvation, and grace. It is not a matter of social progress.[66]

There is no record of other Christian theologizing comparable to the work done by Bishop Ting. Neither are there later examples in depth of Ting's own work. It may be conjectured that such expressions became less and less frequent after 1958, but at least this much was stated and recorded.

It has been noted that preaching on eschatological themes was forbidden, but Shao Shen-t'ang wrote in *T'ien Feng* that a Chris-

[65] *Ibid.*, p. 158.

[66] *Ibid.*, p. 164. In the course of the address Bishop Ting made several references to both classical Chinese sources and to early Christian literature which added appreciably to the breadth and scope of his remarks.

tian may accept the doctrine of the end of the age without following the world-denying spirit usually associated with that doctrine. One must recognize, he said, that biblical language employs many exaggerations such as "wars and rumors of wars," which phrase does not mean that Jesus approved of war, and therefore does not impede Christians in their work for peace.[67] There is no further development of this idea that eschatology, thus understood, still had a place in Chinese Christian thinking.

China's official ideological journal, *Red Flag*, carried an article in November, 1964, in which current trends in theology in the West were caricatured in the most ludicrous way, all in order to show that theology in Europe and America is intended to serve U. S. imperialism in its effort to enslave the nations of the world.[68] There was a time when church leaders in China encouraged the development of an indigenous theology to replace that inherited from the West. Now, with the Western theological heritage apparently discredited, an indigenous theology, if there is one, is the only type available.

Information on the Orthodox Church in Conmunist China is so negligible that it is scarcely worth mentioning. For the sake of the record, however, its strength was primarily among Russian refugees in Manchuria, in which diocese in 1952 there were an estimated 60 parishes, 200 priests, and 100,000 parishioners. Two monasteries and a theological seminary were also reported. In other parts of China there were said to be 150 parishes and 200,000 parishioners.[69]

Less than a year after the Communist leadership came to power in China, the Rev. Simeon Dou (Du), of mixed Russian and Chinese descent, was consecrated Bishop of the Orthodox Church in Tientsin. At the time Bishop Dou said that this purpose was "to bring about the spiritual rapprochement of the Russian and Chinese peoples." [70] Russian priests left in a steady stream to Japan, Australia, or back to Russia, so that their number in

---

[67] *CHIBUL*, December 1, 1958.
[68] Yang Chen, "How Christian Theology of the West Serves U. S. Imperialism," *Hung Ch'i*, November 21, 1964; *China Notes* III (April, 1965).
[69] *CHIBUL*, May 14, 1952.
[70] *CHIBUL*, April 29, 1952.

Manchuria fell to about 100 in 1953, and to only around 30 in 1955. After their departure, along with most of the Russian laity, the Orthodox Church consisted primarily of those "Chinese who had embraced the Orthodox faith through the Russian mission among the Chinese started in 1858," probably about 20,000 Chinese, who, after 1957, were an autonomous church under the Moscow Patriarchate, with Chinese bishops in Peking and Shanghai.[71] Bishop Basil Shou-an (also transliterated Shuan), who was consecrated in Moscow in June, 1957, resided in Peking; Bishop Dou had moved to Shanghai.

A group of Greek tourists to China in 1956 were apparently surprised to find an Orthodox church in Peking, and said they were "thrilled" to hear a few Greek words in the Mass otherwise conducted in the Slavic language. The curate, Father Leonid, said that there were about 80 Orthodox families in Peking, and a total of 3,000 members in the cities of Peking, Tientsin, and Shanghai. There were 11 priests and deacons in St. Innocent's Church (Peking) who had been "trained in a special seminary." The church was fairly well supported by the congregation, "but the state too has come to the aid of its always-unbalanced budget." The priests also worked in a dairy cooperative operated by members of the Orthodox community.[72]

The New Missionary Review, a news bulletin about the Orthodox Church published in England, reported in 1959 that very few Orthodox churches remained open in China, even in its former strongholds like Harbin. The farewell service in one of them had been rudely interrupted and the church locked at once. Much of Orthodox property was turned over to the Chinese Communist government according to a 1956 Sino-Soviet agreement, which decreed the autonomous status of the Orthodox Church in China as referred to earlier. An exception was the Bei Guan monastery in Peking, which, however, was later deactivated and turned over to the Russian embassy in Peking. A summary of additional information is rather conclusive:

[71] *Catholic Encyclopedia,* Vol. X, p. 794.
[72] Evangelos Papanoutsos, "In an Orthodox Church in Peking," *China Reconstructs* V (December, 1956), 27-28.

Great spiritual and material treasures, monuments of the religious fervor of many tens of thousands of Harbin people, have disappeared, and the cemetery where 70,000 Russian Orthodox people have been buried has been desecrated and turned into a public park. The archdiocese of Harbin, which in 1941 possessed 69 churches, served by 75 priests and 25 deacons, has virtually ceased to exist.[73]

A report of the Easter, 1964, celebration in the Russian cathedral in Shanghai, said that Bishop Dou led the traditional service, but that the congregation was the smallest ever seen in that cathedral for the occasion, about 20 Russians and 20 Chinese.[74] A year later word was received that the Russian community in Shanghai had "dwindled to a mere handful of people," and that Easter was not celebrated at all—the first time since 1905 that Easter had not been celebrated in the Russian church of Shanghai.[75] The church had been closed since February of that year when "the last Orthodox Bishop of Shanghai" had died. Names were not used in the story, but it is assumed that he was Bishop Simeon Dou.

Thus, a Catholic writer who asserted in 1954 that the condition of the Orthodox Church in China was "a little better" than that of the Catholic Church because of Russian protection was distinguishing by an infinitesimal degree.[76] The fact that large numbers of Orthodox Christians were White Russians, or otherwise not highly regarded by even the Russian government, and that relations between Russia and Communist China gradually deteriorated, made Russian "protection" a doubtful blessing. Possible union or cooperation between the Orthodox Church in Russia and the Protestant churches of China, which was rumored shortly after the Communist takeover of China, had it taken place, would have provided only additional headaches for both parties.

[73] The direct quotation is from a summary in *CHIBUL*, November 9, 1959, from which most of the information in the preceding paragraph was drawn. See also *CHIBUL*, February 4, 1957.

[74] "Shanghai Newsletter," *South China Morning Post*, June 1, 1964.

[75] *Ibid.*, May 13, 1965.

[76] *CMBA* VI (January, 1954), 22. Latourette says the Orthodox Church "suffered severely from the Communist regime." *Christianity in a Revolutionary Age, Vol. V: The Twentieth Century Outside Europe* (New York: Harpers, 1962), p. 404.

THE DOGGED CONTINUATION OF A CHURCH UNDER WRAPS

The relative freedom of the Hundred Flowers Period was followed by repressive measures of the antirightist campaign and the wholesale absorption of the entire country in the Great Leap Forward with its commune system. From this time information is increasingly scarce, so that the condition of the church can be ascertained in only the most general way.

For example, reliable estimates from Shanghai on denominations representing the Protestant community in China indicated the following figures for 1957: the Church of Christ in China, which had 176,983 in 1949, had 120,000; the True Jesus Church, 125,000 in 1949, had fallen to 110,000; the Sheng Kung Hui (Anglican) with 76,741 in 1949, had possibly 40,000; and various independent churches which had 11,564 in 1949 had grown to 33,000 in 1957.[77] Commenting on these figures in a 1960 article, Francis Jones suggested that membership in the churches of China dropped radically, as much as 40 percent, in the early years under Communist control, but that gains were made in the mid-50's resulting in something like 75 percent of the 1949 figures.[78] With the consolidation of churches in the cities and the organization of rural people into communes, there is every reason to believe that at least the number of "active members" again went into decline after 1958.

Although there was some superficial information concerning city churches, the sort told to visitors and issued by the New China News Agency, there was even less concerning rural church life. In late 1956, Y. T. Wu and Cora Deng visited churches in Anhwei and noted at several places there was no one to care for "branch churches." Another team visited rural churches in eastern Shantung about the same time. In the area visited there had been about 100 churches before 1937, but after the Japanese war and civil war, the loss of foreign subsidies, the flight of many pastors, the closing of churches during Land Reform (all of which were not reopened), and the general hostility of people in the area to the church, only 24 churches remained open. The team's report stated that an addi-

---

[77] *CHIBUL*, April 7, 1958.
[78] "Church Life in China Today," *Social Action* XXVI (March, 1960), 24.

tional 10 to 15 were ready to reopen, but that there were not enough members in other places to warrant reopening of their churches.[79]

Criticisms made of rural churches at the Second National Christian Conference in 1961 indicate surprisingly vigorous life in the church. Country churches in Chekiang and Shantung are criticized for allowing faith healing and exorcism to interfere with production. In Li-ch'eng county of Shantung, Elder Chang Tao-sheng of the Spiritual Grace Church was criticized for raising too much money for building a church ("ten-room" size) and thus impoverishing the members. But a certain Miss Li Ai-chu (Love-the-Lord Li) was criticized for gathering 150 people to pray for rain when they should have been digging irrigation ditches to bring water to fields parched by drought. Rain did come, but instead of cooperating with the rapid planting that was needed, Miss Li and company gathered for a thanksgiving service.[80]

It is not known how long this kind of nervy noncooperation continued. Practically nothing was heard in the early 60's except for a chance story like that of a country church in Fukien province which sent out a letter asking for funds for the repair of their chapel. The members, farm families and a few small shopkeepers, were led by a bachelor pastor who was left without an assignment when churches were consolidated in the cities. Returning to his native village, he conducted Sunday services, visited among the families, and worked in the fields to supplement his income, which consisted mostly of gifts in kind from his parishioners.[81]

After 1958 most Sunday schools ceased operation. A Sunday school for neighborhood children in Shanghai, operated by Miss Helen Willis, was closed in the spring of 1958, apparently because of pressure on the young man teaching it. The *T'ien Feng* summer issues for 1961 carried numerous attacks on Sunday schools, showing how the materials were full of poisonous ideas, how the move-

---

[79] *CHIBUL*, September 16, 1957. Bishop Ting, however, made a tour of his Chekiang diocese in 1956 to see why there had been an increase in the number of candidates for the ministry from rural churches, and was generally impressed with churches he visited. "Chinese Christians: New Prospects, New Unity," *China Reconstructs* V (June, 1956), 18-20.

[80] *CHIBUL*, November, 1961.

[81] "A Note on the Rural Church," *China Notes* III (July, 1965), 3.

ment was utilized by Chiang Kai-shek's New Life Movement, how the capitalist Robert Raikes founded Sunday schools for capitalist exploitation of children.[82] Refugees from Shanghai churches of the larger denominations in the early 60's said there had been no gathering of Christians for any activity other than morning worship since 1958,[83] but vague reports of a few Sunday schools and even confirmation classes reaching Hong Kong in 1964 and 1965 make sweeping generalizations impossible. It seems safe to say that such Sunday schools as did exist were a fringe activity and no longer a central feature of church life.

There is little evidence that youth fellowships and student conferences were able to continue after 1958. Helen Willis tells of special indoctrination meetings for Christian students in 1958, which indicates that this recognizable category still existed, and which may also point to the end of it.[84] The YMCA and YWCA were still functioning, although Mrs. Kenneth Woodsworth of Toronto, who visited China in the summer of 1960, was told by a Miss Cheng of the YWCA in Peking that there was no YW work being done with teen-agers "because the schools offer a very broad program of activities," and because of Young Pioneer activities. The inevitable exception appears in a contrasting report given Mrs. Woodsworth in Canton, where work with youth was a major emphasis and summer conferences were held every year, sometimes with Catholic and Buddhist youth participating.[85]

Kuang-ming Jih-pao attacked the YMCA in 1962 because it had been used by U. S. imperialism as a "vanguard of spiritual aggression" from the days of President Taft to the time of President Kennedy. The "close cooperation" of the YMCA with the Peace Corps was singled out as an instance of the way in which Kennedy "surpassed his predecessors in using religion to carry out his aggressive and warlike policies." [86]

In the mid-50's, both Miss Ellen Nielsen in Manchuria and Miss Willis in Shanghai reported evangelistic missions being carried on

[82] *Through Encouragement*, p. 75. *CHIBUL*, April, 1962.
[83] *China Notes* I (June, 1963), 2.
[84] *Through Encouragement*, p. 107.
[85] *CHIBUL*, June, 1961.
[86] Reprinted in *T'ien Feng*, nos. 7-8, 1962, 8-10. According to some observers this was the first time the YMCA was attacked in post-1949 Communist China.

with great success.[87] The latter spoke of evangelistic missions among the Miao and Lisu tribes, and of meetings in the Gospel Hall of her own compound in Shanghai, as late as 1957. From *T'ien Feng* and other sources in 1956 and 1957 came reports of baptisms sufficiently numerous to suggest that they were the result of special evangelistic effort. There is no available evidence of any revival or evangelistic meetings after 1958, although Professor Latourette received word from a personal friend that between January, 1959, and June, 1960, 2,900 adults were baptized in the churches of a single denomination in South China, which for Communist China is close to being a mass movement.[88]

Very little literature was published. A striking example was the "Red Sheet Calendar" published by the Foochow Annual Conference of The Methodist Church. It carried Old and New Testament quotations, the Lord's Prayer and Apostles' Creed, and listed five special days on the Christian calendar: Good Friday, Easter, Ascension Day, Pentecost, and Christmas. A special "Chinese Christian Church Three-Self Movement Day" (September 23) was listed among nine national holidays. The calendar encouraged three areas of witness for the church: "(1) Realize the Three-Self Movement. (2) Take part in socialist construction. (3) Uphold world peace." [89]

The Bible, of course, was still available, but there were reports that anyone who purchased a Bible had to register his name with the authorities. This requirement discouraged many people from buying new copies, but the closing of churches in the consolidation program brought many used copies into secondhand bookstores where the requirement did not prevail and where many purchases were made.[90] It is the custom in Chinese churches for Bibles to be

---

[87] *CHIBUL*, March 13, 1961; Willis, *Through Encouragement*, pp. 49-50, 55, 123. The *CHIBUL* account, consisting of a series of excerpts from Miss Nielsen's letters, reveals a dramatic dénoument from "permitted religion," then, periods of revival, to increased control, prohibition of teachers and students from attending worship, to the closing of the church because the pastor did not dare lead services anymore and the people's time was consumed with required work.

[88] Latourette, *Christianity in a Revolutionary Age*, Vol. V, p. 403.

[89] *CHIBUL*, May 9, 1960.

[90] *CHIBUL*, July, 1959. By way of contrast, it was estimated in 1955 that sales of the Bible rose to about 40 percent of the prewar level. *CHIBUL*, April, 1955.

placed in pews along with hymn books so that people may follow the reading; the closing of a church would therefore mean surplus Bibles were available.

When Dr. R. P. Kramers of the Netherlands Bible Society visited Peking in May, 1963, he noticed a Bible Society sign hanging from the roof of the YMCA building. Upon inquiry inside, he was told by a YMCA worker that there was no Bible Society office in Peking, but a pastor in the city was responsible for distribution of the Scriptures. An office was maintained in Shanghai, as for all national Christian organizations.[91]

At about the same time, the Bible was being attacked in a *Jenmin Jih-pao* review of a Chinese translation of a much earlier Russian work, Jaroslavsky's *A Talk on the Bible with Believers and Unbelievers* (Chinese title: *What kind of a Book the Bible Is*).[92] The review makes much of the original author's claim that the Bible has been exposed by science and the experience of the working classes to be religious superstition. The Hebraic-Christian myths, all completely wrong, were collected to deceive the people, which is also the purpose of books by Christian theologians purporting to explain the Bible.

Similar sentiments were expressed by a Canton newspaper editor in reply to a reader's inquiry about the Bible. The editor said that the Bible is a classic by which the pope rules the world, that it is made up of myths and full of contradictions, and is an advertisement for the opiate of the people.[93]

A national conference of the Three-Self Movement from November 12, 1960, to January 14, 1961, brought 319 delegates to Shanghai from all over the country, including 5 representatives of minority tribal groups.[94] Sessions for political study occupied

[91] "Fleeting Impressions," *China Notes* II (April, 1964), 1-2.

[92] *JMJP*, May 9, 1963; *SCMP*, May 27, 1963, pp. 11-12.

[93] Canton *Yang-ch'eng Wan-pao*, November 16, 1963; *URS*, April 3, 1964, pp. 12-14.

[94] The conference was reported in *JMJP* and by *NCNA*, but the most complete reports, along with the substance of twelve of the thirty-four speeches given, are to be found in the January-February, 1961, issues of *T'ien Feng*. These reports are summarized and interpreted in *CHIBUL*, February, April, October, and November, all for 1961, and April, 1962. Miss Wu Yi-fang's report to the conference, the constitution, and the Standing Committee roster are in *Documents*, pp. 194-200.

everyone for the first seven weeks; the conference itself began on January 9 and brought the whole affair to a conclusion.

Apart from reports, speeches on the usual themes, and the expected resolutions against imperialism, two aspects of the conference are worth noting. One was the adoption of a revised constitution for the Committee of the China Christian Three-Self Patriotic Movement. The final authority for the committee was the Chinese Christian National Conference then in session, which had authority to make and revise the constitution, hear and pass upon reports from the committee and elect its members. The committee itself had authority to elect its own officers, who with certain additional members constituted a Standing Committee which was to meet once a year. The Standing Committee also had authority to decide the number of delegates and the method of election to the Chinese Christian National Conference (parent body of the committee), which was to meet every three years. The committee as a whole had authority to establish special committees; the Standing Committee was responsible for raising funds. The statement of purpose, Article 2 of the constitution, reads as follows:

This committee is the anti-imperialistic, patriotic organization of Chinese Christians. Its purposes are: under the leadership of the Chinese Communist Party and the People's Government, to unite the Christians of the country for positive participation in socialist construction and other patriotic activities; to observe all government decrees, and assist the government in implementing its freedom of religious belief policy; to promote in the Chinese Christian Church a complete attainment of self-government, self-support and self-propagation, and root out all imperialist influences; to oppose imperialist aggression, and uphold world peace.[95]

The constitution leaves little doubt that the national committee, especially the Standing Committee, was the actual instrument of power, that the National Conference was primarily a rubber stamp.

The second important element in the conference was the presence there and the inclusion on the national committee of several Chris-

[95] *CHIBUL*, October, 1961. A somewhat simpler version of the Constitution was adopted in 1954. Both versions may be found in *Documents*, p. 97 (for 1954) and pp. 198-99 (1961).

tian leaders who were under attack as rightists following the Hundred Flowers Period—Chia Yü-ming, Marcus Cheng, already mentioned, and H. H. Ts'ui. It is possible that some of the others had not been "rehabilitated" and were undergoing reform by study or by labor. It is also possible that they were no longer active in the church. The point is that condemnation of a man in the antirightist movement did not necessarily mean permanent rejection by the Three-Self Movement.

An editorial in *T'ien Feng* for March 31, 1963, attempts to define the Christian task in terms similar to the Three-Self Constitution, but, in the midst of the anti-imperialist jargon it is stated that study of the freedom-of-religious-belief policy must be intensified "so that everyone understands it completely," religious activities must be held in the church according to law, churches must "beware of admitting reactionary elements," and "must help the government stop all illegal activities using the cover of Christianity." [96] Is it conceivable that people should not understand completely the religious policy after so many years of study and indoctrination sessions? Were *illegal* meetings actually held outside the church? Were people who were in some sense opposed to the government, and therefore reactionary, actually uniting with the church? Although one may regard the editorial as issuing the traditional rallying cry—"We must do better this year than last!"—one may infer that some expression of Christianity apart from the Three-Self approved churches was going on.

The type of activity going on in Three-Self circles was probably one factor in provoking the "illegal" expressions. In 1962, for example, provincial Three-Self committees in Shanghai, Foochow, and Kweilin "celebrated" the shooting-down of an American U-2 plane over Cuba. The Shanghai Three-Self Committee, in addition to sponsoring an evening party with singing, ballet, and a story from *Red Rock* exalting Communist courage, also organized "a

[96] *China Notes* I (September, 1963), 2-3 (actually Vol. II). George Patterson's work, *Christianity in Communist China* (Waco, Texas: Word Books, 1969), was published just as this manuscript was sent to the press, and therefore too late for me to incorporate some of his information about home congregations, pp. 131-34, and about the indigenous churches (True Jesus, Little Flock, Christian Assemblies, and Ling Liang T'ang) which he discusses in chapter V, pp. 69-81.

patriotic hygiene team" and a team for the collection of historical materials about the Three-Self Movement. This latter committee sponsored a meeting to hear from the man who captured Chiang Kai-shek in Sian in December, 1936, but in reporting did not indicate the connection between Chiang's capture and Three-Self history.[97]

The last substantial body of information about Protestantism in China comes from the period 1963-64, from which certain examples have already been cited in the preceding pages. It was during this period that the spate of articles on religion and superstition discussed in chapter I appeared in the Chinese press. One would like to think that these criticisms of religion were prompted by continued devotion to religion, working on the interpretive principle that "you don't call attention to a thing you don't like unless you have to," but such inferences cannot be pressed too far.

On the contrary, much of the evidence points to increasing obstacles. A refugee pastor from Canton, interviewed by a Hong Kong newspaper, said that a pastor, as of mid-1953, had to send the name of any candidate for baptism to the Bureau of Religious Affairs, so that officials might determine whether the candidate was a land owner, counterrevolutionary, or otherwise suspect. In addition the pastor had to guarantee that the candidate would not do anything against the government in the future, which, as the pastor said, was a very daring thing to do.[98]

The Rev. Li Ch'un-wen, pastor of the Community Church in Shanghai, became the general secretary of the Three-Self Movement sometime in the early 60's. In a comment to Mr. and Mrs. Richard Harrington of Canada, in 1965 or 1966, Li said that children under eighteen years of age were not baptized, and added "I baptized several young people two years ago." [99] Although Mr. Li did not refer to the regulation impeding baptism, which is no more surprising than that the Harringtons did not ask, it is rather clear that baptisms were infrequent.

Li Ch'un-wen also confirmed the fact that "all pastors serve outside their churches," giving as the reason that "it doesn't look

[97] All these items were culled from *T'ien Feng* and reported in *China Notes* I (December, 1962).

[98] *China Notes* II (December, 1963), 2.

[99] *The Observer*, June 1, 1966, pp. 18-21.

well for a pastor to spend a week preparing two sermons." Mr. Li
said he and his assistant pastor did do something else beside prepare sermons; they visited in homes and led Bible study and prayer
groups. By outside work he meant not only work to supplement income, but participation in the Chinese People's Political Consultative Conference, the YMCA, and peace committees. He
observed that the closed churches with padlocks on the doors, which
the Harringtons had seen, were in that state because the congregations could no longer maintain them, not because of government
decree.[100] Closed churches, for whatever reason, may have been
one of the reasons why Li Ch'un-wen said in Paris in the summer
of 1964 that individual personal witness was important.[101] It is
significant, moreover, that he was reported at that time to be
dubious about "new forms of lay witness discussed so much in the
West" because of the danger of secularization of the church. Since
evangelism in China at that time had to be carried on within the
congregation and its friends, as Mr. Li confirmed to the Harringtons, it is small wonder that he should be doubtful about lay witness
in the world.

There were contradictory reports during this period concerning
the necessity of including something about Marxism-Leninism in
every sermon. Some people said such references were required;
others said that many pastors would include a Communist quote or
would refer to a current Party campaign in order to be on the safe
side. Dr. Kramers attended a service in Canton in which the pastor
made several references to good things achieved for people by the
new government, but he heard no such references in a church in
Peking. There "the pastor gave an excellent didactic sermon, lucid,
free from emotionalism, speaking on the meaning and work of the
Holy Spirit," which "shone through his words with clarity and confidence." [102]

Since *T'ien Feng,* to the best of my knowledge, was not received
outside mainland China after 1964, and since news items concerning religious affairs in the Chinese press diminished in number and
value until about 1965, when there was nothing, much of the in-

[100] *Ibid.,* p. 19.
[101] Reported in a bulletin from the Far Eastern Office, NCCCUSA, July
13, 1964.
[102] "Fleeting Impressions," *China Notes* II (April, 1964), 1-2.

formation from 1963-1964 is from visitors to China. What they heard and what they were allowed to see generally contributed to a favorable picture, which might be different if other questions had been asked, or if a number of answers were not so oblique, or if sight-seeing had been more extensive.

Miss Gerda Buege of the Berlin Mission felt more confident about the future of the church on the basis of her 1963 visit, in which she had more contacts with Christians, than on a visit in 1960, when she had to look for Christians and churches "with a microscope." [103] At Nanking Seminary, where she was amazed to find even 85 students, she saw an exhibition of documents condemning missionary imperialism,[104] and could thus understand why the number of Christians was so small. She was told there were 700,000 Protestant Christians and notes that this was the same figure given to Professor Freytag six years earlier, but she does not note that it was also the same figure used in 1949. Miss Buege found that most pastors outside the large cities were engaged in farm or industrial work in addition to pastoral duties, and observes that "in Shanghai there are more opportunities for church life than in other places." She was distinctly moved by a Communion service in a small-town church and by the sermon preached there on "being surrounded by so great a cloud of witnesses."

Professor Ralph Lapwood returned to China for a science congress in 1964 and reported several encouraging aspects of the church in *The Christian Century*. He was quite impressed with a team ministry of 15 part-time and full-time pastors in a church in Tientsin. One of the men who had "suffered for his faith in the early days of liberation" was a member of the Tientsin political council in addition to a heavy schedule of pastoral work. Lapwood was

[103] Miss Buege's 1963 visit is described in "Are We Trying to Understand the Christians in China?" *Ecumenical Review* XVII (January, 1965), 54-61. A summary of her observations on the earlier, 1960, visit may be found in *Ecumenical Press Service*, December 16, 1960, p. 3.

[104] Apparently "historical research" was a major activity for Nanking Seminary as well as for many church groups and Christian leaders. Its major focus was how mission institutions and missionaries committed crimes of aggression against China, cheated, or otherwise misused the Chinese people for generation after generation. See *T'ien Feng* for February, March, and April, 1963; *China Notes* II (December, 1963), p. 2.

encouraged by Nanking Seminary, including the leadership of Bishop Ting, the thoroughness of the curriculum, the minimum of attention to Marxism-Leninism, and the fact that students were required to spend twenty days each year in farm work. Observing that the seminary faculty was "attempting to present to its students a religion which is not contradictory to the socialist society," but which accepts with pride what had been achieved in China, Lapwood went on, in the words of the interviewer, to speak of the church in the following vein:

The alliance of church and regime is not a forced or unnatural union but a cooperative relationship emerging out of the particular Chinese situation. [Lapwood] is convinced that the church is alive in China because it has adopted a shrewd, realistic attitude toward the regime, seeing in the China of today an opportunity it should use rather than negatively reject. . . . Dr. Lapwood concludes that [the church] is "holding the ground," providing a shell within which the ferment of China's new life can be contained and perhaps conditioned.[105]

There were only twenty-five regular students in Nanking Seminary, with others coming in for refresher courses, according to sources interviewed by Ross Sherill in the summer of 1964.[106] Dr. Chao Fu-san, of what was then called the Research Institute of Theology in Peking, told Sherill that the four remaining Protestant churches in Peking were doing well. The same encouraging news was recorded for the churches in Canton.

Chao Fu-san described the difference between the pre-1949 church and the church in 1964 as sharply as Y. T. Wu ever did, and with the same generalizations. All was well in 1964: pastors were busy at visitation, they were all treated very well, church union was coming along, but not being pushed. One is surprised to hear, after fifteen years, that "the pastors need time to understand the new situation."

H. Gordon Green, who went to China with a Canadian tour

[105] Cecil Northcott, "China's Living Church" (Editorial correspondence relating interview with Dr. Lapwood), *The Christian Century*, January 13, 1965, pp. 39-40.
[106] "Conversation in Peking," *The Christian Century*, January 15, 1965, 47-50. Essentially the same material is in the same author's "News from China," *Frontier* VIII (Spring, 1965).

group, found eighty-five students at Nanking Seminary, was impressed with Bishop Ting, as everyone else was, and received the usual information about freedom of religion. Ting insisted that no stigma was placed on anyone for his religious beliefs, citing several Christians who held national, provincial, or local office. There was government help in projects such as repair to churches, and churches did not have to pay taxes.[107]

Dean Hewlett Johnson's visit in May and June, 1964, provided no relevant information for the outside world.[108] A Chinese visitor, who was careful to say nothing which might interfere with plans for future visits to the mainland from Hong Kong, reported only that people were too busy for religion.

The Rev. Paul Fernandez Ceballos of Cuba did visit "churches and monasteries of various religions where he saw believers observing their religious rites." This, coupled with the fact that "religious leaders told him that they were satisfied with the facilities the government provided for them," convinced the Cuban visitor that what he had read in the West was all a lie.[109] Probably some of the same leaders told Myra Roper there was "no problem" for Protestant groups, "indeed there could not be by the nature of Communist belief and government policy." [110]

Japanese pastors, from whom deeper insight into the situation might have been gained, reported nothing new in the total picture after their visit in the fall of 1964.[111] Their emphasis on the real conflict between Christianity and Marxism for Christians does serve to correct the rosy glow emanating from Johnson, Fernandez, and Roper.

One might have been encouraged by the favorable impressions rendered by several of these visitors to China in 1963 and 1964, but

[107] "A Canadian Look at the Church in China," *The Christian Century*, August 24, 1966, pp. 1038-40.

[108] *NCNA*, Peking, May 29 and June 22, 1964; *SCMP*, June 3 and June 25, 1964. In addition to these press reports, Dr. Johnson himself wrote an article "To China at Ninety," for the mainland publication, *China Reconstructs* XIII (September, 1964), 16-17.

[109] *NCNA*, Peking, July 16, 1964; *SCMP*, July 27, 1962.

[110] *China: The Surprising Country* (Garden City, N.Y.: Doubleday and Co., 1966), p. 188.

[111] The report of Messrs. Teruji Hirayama, Kenta Takagi, and Kyoji Buma, in *Risoo-sha* (Ideal), December, 1964, was translated by Mr. Buma and published in *RCDA*, March 15, 1965, pp. 34-35.

their impressions were based on remarks by Chinese Christian leaders who were consistently vague and who cited very little concrete supporting evidence. The fact that men and women were being trained for the ministry and that a few churches were open in which they might serve was the most hopeful sign. On the other hand, the fact that Sunday schools, youth fellowships, and memship training classes had all but disappeared meant that the nurture of those who might make up a continuing church was in a precarious state.

In view of these circumstances it was all the more remarkable to hear of young people in attendance at worship services, including youth who were not Christian and did not come from Christian homes. This was due apparently to association with Christian friends, who were able to communicate with fellow Christians and those interested in Christianity through a secret code of words and gestures which only they understood. A still more remarkable phenomenon has been noticed by church leaders in Hong Kong: young people coming from the mainland without church membership or any other evidence of Christian association would immediately seek out a church upon arrival in Hong Kong. Some of these instances can be marked up to a need for relief or welfare services, but there are instances of others who did not seek physical assistance. Many who did seek aid did so only temporarily. This phenomenon was still noted in 1966 and 1967 among refugees from Red Guard terrorism.

AFTER RED GUARD TERROR:
A CHURCH UNDERGROUND

As the tension, which was prelude to the Cultural Revolution, built up in 1965 and 1966, the small fellowship groups which operated quietly and in some cases underground became more and more important. In some cases their existence was known and their life permitted by the government. A Chinese Christian who had visited the mainland in early 1965 said that small congregations not officially organized under the Three-Self Committee in a certain city were allowed if they were entirely self-supporting.[112] From

---

[112] *China Notes* IV (October, 1966), 4.

private sources it has been learned that in late 1965 several "non-Sunday organizations" were still carrying on activities in Peking church circles, including youth groups, women's associations, and Sunday schools, with at least the tacit permission of the authorities, but the evidence is tenuous to say the least. An observer in Hong Kong claimed that small groups which met for prayer were on the increase in that year,[113] but there is no way to be sure that such was the case except scattered reports to the effect that "a new group is meeting in ———'s home."

Dr. Chao Fu-san, referred to in the previous section, neatly parried a question about Sunday schools when he said: "Naturally there are not an unusual number of youths in our church services, but that is the way it has always been. . . . Christian parents are not hindered in bringing their children to the worship service."[114] One should note that bringing children to worship services is not Sunday school and that many observers have remarked about the larger number of young people in Chinese services, even during the Communist period. The author of the article acknowledged that two non-Christians were present in the interview.

A further comment by Dr. Chao to the effect that church attendance was very good, in fact "better among our members than it is in general in the West," is in the same vein as another effort to impress the outside world with how normal everything was. A film produced by Felix Greene, which was showing in the United States in early 1966, had scenes taken at a certain church where the viewer saw people filing out, greeting the pastor at the door, and chatting in the sunshine. It was easy to conclude, as viewers were expected to conclude, that this scene was typical of the idyllic life of the Christian church in China.

Other than the pale announcements of Christmas and Easter services, the news items concerning the church and related matters were all critical. In reply to a letter to the editor of a Canton

[113] George N. Patterson, "Christianity Behind the Bamboo Curtain," *Christianity Today*, July 16, 1965, pp. 1055-57, and July 30, 1965, pp. 1103-4, makes much of these small groups and their role in maintaining a vital Christianity.

[114] From summary in *China Notes* IV (October, 1966), 4-5, of three articles by Arne Eklund, a Swedish journalist, which appeared in *Dagen* (The Day), in February, 1966.

newspaper, an editorial writer explained that there were not only differences of worship and doctrine between Catholic and Protestant churches but also that

the Roman Catholic Church is deeply steeped in feudal tradition while the Protestant churches have discarded some of the decadent things inherited from the Middle Ages and added some "new" things which appeal to the bourgeoisie.[115]

Both the "clamor" for reform and the "movement for religious unity," the writer continued, had been instigated by U. S. imperialism in order to counteract Marxism-Leninism. Another writer asserts that the United States uses nongovernmental agencies such as missions to spread its ideas when official channels are restricted, and "where American religious missions are restricted, it will utilize 'indigenous' missionaries." [116]

A strange kind of "missionary-at-large," a citizen of the Netherlands who managed to get into China and travel through four provinces in 1965 or 1966, visited Nanking Theological Seminary and met the same attitude. The warmth of greetings from two professors disappeared when he said he was a missionary. They replied, "All missionaries are spies." It seems that this Brother Andrew went about trying to give Bibles to people, but found that people declined to accept them on grounds of being too busy. When he tried to leave one in hotel rooms a clerk or maid would always return it as property he had forgotten.[117]

Summing up the pre–Cultural Revolution situation as a whole, Bates observes that in the mid-60's denominational structures still seemed to have limited meaning at the local level, that pressures to unite had not been too successful. He seriously questions the repetition of total membership figures, 700,000 for Protestants and 3,000,000 for Catholics, which were given as reliable estimates in 1949. He also makes the pointed observation that if conditions were as flourishing and glowing as claimed, there would have been many

[115] Canton *Yang-ch'eng Wan-pao*, November 1, 1965; *SCMP*, November 22, 1965, pp. 3-4.
[116] *NCNA*, Peking, November 26, 1965; *SCMP*, December 1, 1965.
[117] "Brother Andrew," with Elizabeth and John Sherrill, *God's Smuggler* (Tappan, N. J.: Fleming H. Revell, 1968), pp. 198-209.

more reports and invitations to Japanese and other delegations to behold the glorious liberty.[118]

First reports of Red Guard frenzy told of the closing of churches and the destruction of furnishings and decorative objects. The correspondent of the *South China Morning Post* in Shanghai said that on August 24, 1966, youths wearing red armbands broke into Protestant churches and into all manner of religious edifices, carried Bibles and other books, religious tracts, and archives out into the street and started bonfires.[119] The Anglican Cathedral on Kiangsi Road, which had been closed for several years, and Moore Memorial Methodist Church on Thibet Road, which had been used as a school, suffered this fate along with the former Shanghai Community Church, which had been functioning as the Shanghai International Church. Literature discovered in offices and store-rooms was also burned. In Mi Shih T'ang, a church in Peking, according to a Reuters dispatch of August 23, the sanctuary was completely rearranged, with a large, white bust of Mao at the center.

The following poster was pasted on the former YMCA building in Peking on August 22, 1966:

There is no God; there is no Spirit; there is no Jesus; there is no Mary; there is no Joseph. How can adults believe in these things? . . . Priests live in luxury and suck the blood of the workers. . . . Like Islam and Catholicism, Protestantism is a reactionary feudal ideology, the opium of the people, with foreign origins and contacts. . . . We are atheists; we believe only in Mao Tse-tung. We call on all people to burn Bibles, destroy images, and disperse religious associations.[120]

Most churches had much simpler signs, such as "Discard the old!" or "This is forbidden!" Crosses and other religious symbols were removed from tombstones in a cemetery for foreigners in Peking.[121]

Later visitors to China found churches closed and locked, with no

[118] Richardson, *China and Christian Responsibility*, p. 76.
[119] *South China Morning Post*, August 30, 1966.
[120] Quoted in "The Handwriting on the Wall" (a study of wall posters), *Current Scene*, May 31, 1967, p. 2.
[121] *South China Morning Post*, September 22, 1966.

sign that they were being used. Professor Maseo Takenaka of Japan, who was able to travel in China in the spring of 1967, could find no churches open and saw only one church, situated next to the Rumanian Embassy in Peking, which still had crosses on its steeples. His many requests to visit churches were never granted, and when he went out on his own to take pictures and found some churches, was never able to go inside.[122]

There are numerous accounts of the suffering of individuals:

Two well-known Christian doctors at a former missionary hospital are reported suicides, one by jumping from the hospital roof after Red Guards had abducted his wife and child. . . . An American-educated Chinese describes the experience of Red Guards, who, in repeated break-ins, burned, ripped or confiscated her American-bought shoes and clothing, textbooks, university diploma, and other college momentos. Confiscation of personal notebooks, two Bibles, and a pocket Testament [was] "a great loss to me." [123]

Since possession of any identifiable Christian objects proved to be so incriminating when Red Guards attacked, many people gathered such objects—Bibles, hymnals, pictures—and destroyed them before Red Guards arrived. In a south China city Red Guards jumped over the wall around a pastor's home and found him burning something. They arrested him and were torturing him when they found that he was burning a Bible.[124]

Tales of the most terrible brutality circulated.

Boiling hot tea was poured on the head of an evangelist's wife while she, her husband, and the minister were made to kneel all night next to a fire fed by Bibles, hymnbooks, and religious materials . . . [by] Red Guard youth estimated to be from eight to twenty years old.

Letters from reliable sources tell of . . . an elder's wife [in South Fukien who] was falsely accused and dragged through the streets of one city;

[122] "Reflections on a Visit to China," *China Notes* (October, 1967), 4. Japanese correspondents confirmed that in the spring of 1967 "all churches, not only those in the great cities but throughout China, have been closed since last August (1966)." V (April, 1967), 4.

[123] *China Notes* IV (October, 1966), 4.

[124] *CNA*, July 19, 1968, p. 6, which quotes the witness of the incident as adding that a Protestant family next door to the pastor had no Bible but continued to say grace at meals, carefully instructing the children to say nothing about it outside.

when she fainted the family were not allowed to carry her to the former English Presbyterian Hospital. After some delay permission was granted to an older son to care for her, but she died shortly after.

Red Guard groups tore down the cross from the church in this same city, broke all the windows, and forced the old pastor to kneel on the broken glass. Then he was shot.[125]

A letter from a former church leader in Central China told of mistreatment of his wife while he was being reformed by labor on a prison farm. She was beaten by Red Guards who then placed her for two hours in a wooden box on which they poured water. She was soon ill with inflammation of the liver, hepatitis, and stomach disorder; her husband was released to care for her, a month before these ailments brought on her death. Savings, winter clothing, and blankets had been seized by Red Guards; medicines were impossible to get. The husband wrote that a funeral was also impossible and asked his relatives in Southeast Asia to hold a service for her.[126]

There were reports of Protestant Christian leaders sent to indoctrination camps—such as the Anglican Bishop Michael Kwanghsu Chang, along with two suffragan bishops and a secretary, and the Methodist leader, Dr. James L. Ding, all of Fukien.[127] Evidently even Bishop K. H. Ting of Nanking finally had to undergo such treatment, for there were reports in 1968 that he had been released after several months of reform by labor, and was said to be quietly working on a writing project.

The experience of several families in Shanghai illustrates a fairly common pattern. In each case there were visits by the Red Guards in which objects such as books, records, jewelry, family letters, and keepsakes were all confiscated. In one case furniture was cut open to search for hidden items. Searches were followed by intensive interrogation to discover any aspect of one's personal background which would reveal overseas relationships, past or present, especially American contacts. One man was questioned for ten days, but he refused to admit that he was an international spy

---

[125] *China Notes* VI (July, 1968), 5.
[126] *Ibid.*
[127] *China Notes* V (April, 1967), 4.

simply because he had received letters from his children overseas. Mention of a missionary friend in one letter caused him finally to admit his "guilt." He was demoted from a "senior specialist" to a coolie, and forced to move from a fairly comfortable house to a small dirty one. A daughter was submitted to "struggle" treatment by Red Guards and finally confessed to being a spy when she heard that her father had confessed. She was ordered to serve as a street cleaner without pay.

Another family had all their furniture taken by Red Guards; the mother was demoted from a teacher to a coolie. They were helped by a married daughter's family for a time, but the daughter's husband, with a degree from a former Christian university, was purged, his salary cut off, and that family's furniture taken.

The head of another family, a teacher, was kept in his school and required to write on his "understanding of Christianity." For a period of several weeks he was allowed to see his wife and children only a few times and then only through the school gate. He was finally released from this regimen of thought reform, but did not think, in the last letter received by his mother in Hong Kong, that he would be allowed to resume teaching.[128]

By the end of 1966 there were few signs of traditional Christian activity. There was at least one Catholic service in an out-of-the-way church in Shanghai, as noted in a parallel chapter, but the only known Protestant Christmas services in 1966 in Shanghai and Peking were those held in British compounds for foreigners. No Chinese dared to attend even these small, inconspicuous celebrations. The report of the Shanghai service said that "all former churches had their interiors stripped of all religious relics and now they stand minus the spires and belfries as well, . . . used mostly as assembly halls of the Red Guards." [129]

Although there was no mention of Protestantism in the Chinese press in 1967, there was one story in *Jen-min Jih-pao* accusing the Soviet revisionists of using religion as an opiate in order to enslave and exploit the people, the case in point being the publication of a volume of Bible stories for children in the Soviet Union. The

---

[128] The experiences of these families in Shanghai are all related in *China Notes* V (July, 1967), 2-3.

[129] Accounts of both Christmas services summarized in *China Notes* V (January, 1967), 3.

Chinese writers said the story of the tower of Babel was included to advertise the Soviet theory of "class reconciliation" and to make people forget about class distinctions and class struggle. They also called the story of Noah and the ark a favorite of Khrushchev's intended "to spread the nonsense about the possible extinction of mankind, to make people stop opposing imperialism and 'throw in their lot' with imperialism on the same 'ark.' " The final paragraph contained a barbed suggestion to the Soviet editors:

You should also include that one about Judas Iscariot. It would be a great help to the Soviet people in recognizing your dirty features as a handful of renegades if you acquaint the Soviet readers with the story of that traitor who betrayed Jesus Christ for thirty pieces of silver.[130]

A letter to a brother in Japan from Loyal Bartel, a Mennonite missionary-farmer who elected Chinese citizenship and thus was able to continue living in China, confirmed that all churches had been closed, that most literature which appeared Western or revisionist (therefore the Bible) to Red Guards was destroyed. He affirmed on the other hand that personal witness continued and that people to whom he could witness continued to come to his house.[131]

An independent Chinese preacher, Moses Yu, who had tried to keep up missionary activity on the mainland under the Communist regime, fled to Macao in September, 1967, and moved on to Taiwan in April, 1968. He also said that churches were closed and stressed that people were being forced to give up their faith.[132] In a private interview he said that this was the difference brought about by the Cultural Revolution, that previously the stress had been on thought reform. It was not until the Red Guards that the attempt was made to force people, through beatings and torture, to give up their faith.

As of early 1968, there was no reliable word of any Protestant church life in China. Bates wrote about the same time: "Much inquiry, reading, and listening, from Hong Kong, Japan, and other

---

[130] *JMJP*, May 5, 1967; *SCMP*, May 9, 1967, pp. 35-36.
[131] Interviewed for *Mennonite Brethren Herald*, cited in *The Christian Leader*, April 11, 1967, then in *China Notes* V (July, 1967), 1.
[132] Taipei *China Post*, April 3, 1968.

posts have failed to discern corporate Christian life or activity, even in the marginal form of the YMCA as operative under the Communists." [133] A non-Christian refugee observed that Christianity does not need external objects or expressions of devotion to survive, in contrast to the traditional ancestral cult.[134] From another perspective, a Christian who regularly heard from friends in China said he was not really afraid for the church in China, indirectly for the same reason:

In a nutshell it is that members of the [church] have sufficient faith to survive as a group, and to give their children all the intangible advantages of a Christian home whether or not they are permitted to attend public worship. I strongly suspect that in terms of belief and practice, if not in outward and visible organization, property, etc., the church is stronger than it was a decade ago.[135]

There were sketchy reports toward the end of 1968 of Christians still in prison, including Wang Ming-tao. The daughter of the famous evangelist John Sung was said to have been arrested during the Cultural Revolution and sentenced to twenty years imprisonment, the charges unspecified. Watchman Ni of the Little Flock, who by 1967 had served out the fifteen years to which he was sentenced in 1952, was still in a Shanghai prison, but allowed to visit his home once or twice a month. He was said to be translating technical works into Chinese, for which he was paid a small salary by prison authorities.[136]

There were still the persistent reports that devoted Christians continued to worship and pray in small groups in their homes. They met infrequently and irregularly to avoid detection, for punishments continued to be severe for anyone who was caught. There was even word of a full-time Christian worker who traveled from one house congregation to another, leading Bible studies and encouraging the people. There were reports of such preachers who were caught by Red Guards and either imprisoned or publicly

[133] Richardson, *China and Christian Responsibility*, p. 77.
[134] *CNA*, July 19, 1968, p. 6.
[135] *China Notes* VI (July, 1968), 5.
[136] *China Post*, December 28, 1968.

disgraced, but the underground church apparently continued.[137] A Western visitor to China, in late 1968 or early 1969, told of attending an "Anglican-type" service in which the Eucharist was celebrated according to the prayer book. A Chinese priest led fourteen people in the upstairs room of a two-story house in a North China provincial city.[138]

In 1968, some Christians on the mainland dared to write letters in response to conservative Christian broadcasts beamed from the Philippines to China. They spoke of the comforts of faith, of joy in their relationship to God. One even asked for a tiny cross to pin to the inside of his jacket. Even though the chaos in some mainland centers made checking of mail an impossibility for government officials, it was still risky to write such letters. A vital faith, in the true sense of the New Testament *pistis*, was still alive.

Thus, for Protestants who had at least some leaders who cooperated with the Communist authorities, as for Catholics who resisted at first but were finally brought into line, the church as an institution was closed. There was a vague possibility that a few churches might be allowed to reopen in time, but after the checkered story related here, one must question whether the opening of a few churches would represent any significant improvement. A church with its door open is better than a church with its door closed in most parts of the world, but even this simple assumption may have to be reconsidered as one examines the amazing situation which prevails in China today.

[137] *Ibid.*, December 21, 1968 and January 18, 1969.
[138] *China Notes* VII (Summer, 1969), 37.

VIII

Islam: Challenge of an Ethnic and Religious Minority

CAREFUL TREATMENT OF A UNIQUE GROUP

The strength of Islam in China is in the northwest regions of the country which are populated by non-Chinese ethnic groups. The languages of these regions as a whole stem from Turkish roots, the way of life is that of pastoral or nomadic people, and Islam is the dominant faith. The Uighurs of Sinkiang, for example, have their own language, engage in agriculture, handicrafts, and commerce, and have adapted Islam to the primitive folk religion of the area. Although a small but recognizable minority of Han Chinese are followers of Islam, Muslims in China must be considered both as members of a religious group and as members of a minority racial group.

Almost any writer on Islam in China comments on the unreliability of statistics on the number of Muslims. Statistics published during the 40's indicated close to fifty million, but this figure is difficult to substantiate. Communist Chinese sources indicate ten million, which has given rise to speculation as to what happened to the missing forty million. John M. H. Lindbeck estimates eight to ten million in the five northwest provinces: three and one half million in Sinkiang, three to four million in Kansu, Ninghsia, and Tsinghai, and over one million in Shensi. Haji Yusuf Chang suggests a total of twenty to thirty million.[1] Communist

---

[1] John M. H. Lindbeck, "Communism, Islam, and Nationalism in China," *Review of Politics* XII (October, 1950), 473-88, is a clear and concise treatment of pre-1949 developments in the Northwest and of the situation at the time of the Communist regime. Haji Yusuf Chang, "Islam in Modern China," *The Voice of Islam* (Karachi) XIV (September, 1966), 683-98, is more up to date.

Chinese sources allow for more in Sinkiang—all minority peoples such as Uighurs, Kazakhs, Kirghiz, Tajiks, Uzbeks, and Tartars—with smaller numbers in the other provinces. There are probably about five million Han Chinese who adhere to the Islamic faith.

Much of the pressure brought to bear upon Christianity by the Communist authorities seems to have been due to its being a "foreign religion." One easily forgets, both inside and outside China, that Islam and Buddhism were originally brought into China from the outside. Buddhism, after a long and thorough process of indigenization, is rarely thought of as foreign, but Islam, because it has taken root primarily among minority peoples, has occupied an in-between status which has made it difficult for Chinese governments, past or present, to categorize and relate to. The Nationalists tended to regard the minorities as a religious group; the Communists have stressed their nationality. Neither is adequate, as Haji Yusuf Chang succinctly points out: "Ethnic solidarity and religious faith are the two fundamental characteristics of the Muslim community in China. The lack of either one of them would mean the dissolution of Chinese Islam." [2]

The challenge for the Communist government is not only that of dealing with a unique, ethnic-religious minority. The challenge has been compounded by the fact that these minority groups are a fiercely independent people, known for their militant, even warlike, spirit. In dealing with Islam, Communist China on a few occasions has had to deal with armed revolt mounted by people who subscribe to the tradition of *jihad*, or holy war. It may be that the resistance of the Hui people (Muslim minorities) has been primarily for economic reasons, but the religious factor has not been lacking. Communist China has had to deal with a people willing to fight, literally, for their faith.

The basic structure for dealing with these peoples has been to give a measure of regional autonomy by establishing autonomous regions, districts, counties, and townships. The exact measure of autonomy can scarcely be measured for several reasons: (1) the

[2] Chang, "Islam in," p. 693. Lindbeck also insists that the majority of Chinese Muslims constitute both a racial and religious group, and points out how difficult it has been for either Nationalists or Communists to recognize this.

Hui council members and government officials are those who have special training from Communist cadres and can be expected to support the central government; (2) it is clearly stated that the " 'unity of all nationalities' must take place within the context of the Communist transformation of agriculture, handicrafts, commerce, and industry." [3] Thus, the granting of "regional autonomy" has proved to be a rather empty gift. The discovery of this by Muslims has provoked resentment, dissent, and even armed revolt.

Communist Chinese authorities moved much more slowly in dealing with these Muslim peoples than with other religious groups. There are two major reasons for this, both of which in some measure apply also to Buddhism. The first is the fact that these minority peoples, many of whom had little love for Han Chinese anyway, lived in border regions far from the seat of power of the central government; from these frontiers they could throw their weight toward neighboring nations and thus threaten Chinese security. The second reason is Communist China's concern, at least in earlier years, to maintain amicable relations with Muslim nations in Africa and the Middle East, as well as with closer neighbors like Pakistan and Indonesia.

The Communists had bitter memories of previous failure to win the support of Muslim minorities. After trifling appeals in the mid-30's to the poor and socially inferior to join them in the class struggle, the Communist armies expected Muslim support against Nationalist forces in Kansu. Quite the opposite happened, however, as Muslim soldiers from Ninghsia, Kansu, and Tsinghai, in January and February, 1937, defeated the Communists soundly and drove them out of Kansu. Lindbeck notes several reasons for the Communist failure in dealing with the Muslims, several of which continued to plague Communist efforts to win them over:

A serious Communist misinterpretation of the nature of Islam contributed in a major way to the organized resistance of the Moslems at this

[3] Hu Chang-tu, et al., *China: Its People, Its Society, Its Culture* (New Haven, Conn.: Human Relations Area Files, 1960), p. 89. The discussion of ethnic minorities in chapter IV of this volume, pp. 64-94, is a clear presentation in brief compass of this subject, and has been extremely helpful in supplying background information.

time. Even after abandoning their antireligious policy, the Communists did not acknowledge that Islam was not merely the collection of religious ideas of a racial group, but a universal religion which transcended not only race but class divisions.[4]

A second reason was the Communist reputation for antireligious measures in Russia as well as China. In the third place, the Muslims did not believe Communist promises of minority group autonomy, and, fourth, resented Communist efforts to divide and conquer by utilizing Islamic sectarian conflicts. A fifth reason was a Muslim-Nationalist alliance which had helped maintain Nationalist influence in the Northwest for a time.[5]

It should be mentioned that during the war with Japan, when Muslims joined in the resistance struggle, the Communists developed a more pragmatic attitude toward the Muslims, tacitly recognized Muslim religious claims as such, and made no effort to impose their control on Muslim areas. Muslims issued a plea for peace to both Communists and Nationalists in 1948. With the collapse of Nationalist forces and a weakening of Muslim morale in 1949, the northwest regions fell to the Communist armies in short order in August and September of that year. Thereupon the Communist government began its cautious, persistent effort to win over the minority peoples.

Some suspicion of the Muslims must have prevailed, however, when the first Chinese People's Political Consultative Conference convened in September, 1949. In contrast to Buddhist and Protestant delegates there was only one Muslim, Ma Chuan, who was classed merely as an alternate delegate. Later, the names of two Muslims, Ma Sung-ting and Ta Pu-shen, appeared on the roster of the Second National Committee of the CPPCC.[6] And there was no early reform movement among Muslims comparable to that already under way in Christian and Buddhist circles.

Striking signs of witness to the Islamic faith in the face of efforts to weaken or undermine it were displayed in northwest China in 1950, both during the month of Ramadan, which fell dur-

[4] "Communism, Islam," *Review of Politics*, p. 478.
[5] *Ibid.*, pp. 479-80.
[6] Yang I-fan, *Islam in China* (Hong Kong: Union Press, 1957), p. 31.

ing June and July, and on the Muslim New Year, which was celebrated on July 16. During the month of fasting "the balconies of all
mosques were crowded with believers singing the Koran. . . . In
the cities, towns, and countryside, the praises were shouted on high,
waking all about, Communists included." Posters displaying
strongly worded imperatives covered walls and telegraph poles:

We must love God above all and our fellow citizens as ourselves. Our chief
is Muhammed, our Law the Koran. Let all the Muslims of the whole world
unite and fight against tyrants. Give yourselves to God and you will never
be perverted. Islam is above all.[7]

An article by one Lu Hung-chi, which appeared in *Kuang-ming
Jih-pao* in January, 1951, was infuriating to Peking Muslims because of the following reference to Muhammed:

You know Muhammed who held a sword in one hand and a book of classics
in another, but you do not know Muhammed who held a gun in one hand
and took money from you with the other. Oh, yes, he had three hands.[8]

Not only had Lu voiced the oft-repeated criticism that Muhammed
converted by the sword; the statement that he "took money" was
made even more derisive by use of the "three hands" figure, which
in China is a way of saying a man is a thief. Whether it was
deliberately written to test what Muslim reaction might be is not
known, but reaction was immediate and intense. As a conciliatory
gesture, Ma Chien, a Muslim leader who cooperated with the
government, was allowed to write a reply which the paper
published. Government officials said that the editors made the
mistake because of lack of study.

This incident was followed by a period during which government
and military officials were extremely cautious in dealing with
Muslims, and in some instances even went out of their way to avoid
offense. Even when the Communist First Field Army proceeded to
the northwest regions against General Ma Hung-kuei, Communist
soldiers were cautioned to respect Muslim customs. They were to
protect mosques, post no notices on mosque walls, were not to in-

[7] *CMBA* III (IV) (February, 1951), 188-89.
[8] Quoted in Yang, *Islam*, p. 25.

terfere with Muslim religious services, and were not to make noise or even watch outside a mosque. The soldiers were ordered not to speak to Muslim women and not to enter rooms used by the women. They were to refrain from eating pork, drinking wine, or smoking in the homes of Muslims, and were not even to say the word "pig" before a Muslim or ask one why he did not eat pork. Further, they were not to take baths at Muslim bathing places and were to wash their hands before drawing water at a Muslim well. Polite terms of address were to be employed, and the Party's policy toward racial minorities was to be carefully explained.[9]

A special hospital for Muslim people was set up in Peking in 1949 with separate kitchens to prepare food for Muslim patients. A similar hospital was opened in Tientsin in late 1953, with several departments and the same careful provision for observing Muslim dietary laws.[10] Father Clifford, in telling of his prison experiences, points out that authorities took care to give Muslims fish on days when pork was served to other prisoners.[11]

Such treatment apparently did not mollify large sectors of the Muslim population. Although the new Communist regime was officially in power in the Muslim regions of the Northwest, there was continuing resistance by the Hui peoples. All through 1951 there were reports of murder, arson, robbery, attacks on officials, and cutting of communication lines. For example, in the Pingliang area along the Ching River in Kansu province, there were sporadic outbreaks all year. Then during Land Reform in 1952, the land belonging to a prominent mosque was confiscated by the government and an armed revolt broke out. Muslims destroyed communication lines, ransacked public granaries, and managed to gain control temporarily of several towns. Finally government troops were brought in to reinforce the local militia and several of the insurgent commanders were put to death.

The Kazakhs of northern Sinkiang revolted in 1950, ranging all over that area until February, 1951, when a prominent leader, Wo-

[9] *Chieh-fang Jih-pao* [Liberation Daily], August 1, 1949; *CMBA* I (II) (November, 1949), 276.
[10] *CMBA* V (VI) (December, 1953), 1000.
[11] Clifford, *In the Presence*, p. 171.

Si-Man, was captured and put to death. The suppression of counter-revolutionaries, along with Land Reform, provoked further opposition. More than two hundred courts were set up, almost a hundred of them "mobile courts," to handle cases of counterrevolutionary activity and election sabotage; these cases totaled some fifteen thousand from 1949 to 1954, at least three fourths of them involving Muslims.[12]

Muslims apparently received special consideration during Land Reform. Although the law provided that all "rural land belonging to ancestral shrines, temples, monasteries, churches, schools, and organizations . . . shall be requisitioned," local government officials were ordered to "devise appropriate measures to solve the financial problems facing such schools, orphanages, homes for the aged, hospitals, etc." that depended on income from the land.[13] There was a special provision for Muslims which provided that "land owned by mosques may be retained according to circumstances, with the consent of the Muslims residing in the places where such mosques are situated." Muslim religious leaders, along with Buddhist and Taoist monks and nuns, were to be given land for production as the peasants were, if they had no other means of support and were willing to work.[14] Thus, Yang I-fan, who is highly critical of the Communist efforts to control Islam, admits that

up to the present time [1957], the provisions affecting the Muslims appear to have been carried out. Land reform in the minority areas has been dealt with in separate and individual decrees or directives, and land owned by the mosques has by and large been left intact. The government has even undertaken in several cases to repair old, deteriorating mosques.[15]

Yang, however, quotes *Jen-min Jih-pao*'s acknowledgment that in several provinces where the Hui and Han people were involved together in Land Reform, such as Kweichow, Kwangsi, Shantung, and Kansu,

[12] *Sinkiang Jih-pao*, September 30, 1954, quoted in Yang, *Islam*, pp. 80-81.
[13] *Agrarian Reform Law of the People's Republic of China* (Peking: FLP, 1953), quoted in Yang, *Islam*, p. 37.
[14] *Ibid.*, p. 38.
[15] *Ibid.*, pp. 38-39.

some of the Han cadres . . . would not treat the national minorities in a spirit of equality. They gave them smaller allotments of farmland in land redistribution, or intentionally gave them a poor grade of farmland or even gave them no land at all.[16]

The same issue of the official government newspaper said that resistance in the Northwest was due to the cadres' "lack of respect for the religious belief of the national minorities, or for their customs, habits, languages, or writings," even to the point of calling Hui people backward because of their refusal to eat pork.[17]

A Muslim leader who worked with the Communist government spoke of this resistance and the propaganda in favor of "Pan-Islamism," or "Great Islamism," as attempts "to divert the attention of the broad masses of workers of national minorities and to sabotage the unity of the Chinese People's Republic and various nationalities within the country." This was followed by a call to unite with the Communist Party to "oppose imperialism." [18]

Ma Chien, who also cooperated with the government, referred to several elements of the pacification program in this address to the third session of the First National Committee of the CPPCC. He claimed that Muslim leaders under arrest or attack were enemies of the Hui peoples as well as the Han. He spoke of how Muslim youth were joining the army, how Muslims had opposed the rearming of Japan by the United States, and how they had joined in the "Oppose America–Aid Korea" drives. Noting the conservative character of the ahungs and the fact that many of them did not know Chinese, he pointed to translations into Arabic of several writings of Mao Tse-tung.[19]

A new translation of the Koran was published by the Commercial Press in Shanghai in 1952, said to be the first translation in the vernacular. According to the preface, "it had been impossible for

[16] *JMJP*, October 10, 1953; quoted in Yang, *Islam*, p. 70.
[17] *Ibid.*
[18] Yang, *Islam*, pp. 35, 40.
[19] Speech entitled "Chinese Muslims Stand by Other Nationalities in Country," *JMJP*, November 2, 1951; *CURBAC*, July 25, 1952. The ahung fulfills more of a teaching role, whereas the imam preaches and presides at ceremonial functions. The lines are not sharp and one man often handles both roles, especially in smaller places.

271

ordinary Muslims in China with no knowledge of Arabic to fully understand the teachings of Islam." Now presumably they could understand, unite together, and give service to the people.[20]

Ma Chien, in his preface to this new edition of the Koran, selected certain passages to show that Islamic teaching and Marxist teaching were not inharmonious. For example, chapter 16, verse 78 of the Koran, reads: "And Allah brought you forth from the wombs of your mothers knowing nothing, and gave you hearing and sight and hearts that haply ye might give thanks." This verse, according to Ma Chien, "admits that mankind's basic knowledge comes from the outside world." [21] The context does speak of the "birds obedient in midair," of houses and cattle and clothing, but all these examples of the "outside world" are gifts of Allah given to man so that man will recognize Allah's favor toward man. The verse expresses Ma's interpretation only with considerable eisegesis.

Another passage cited by Ma Chien is chapter 58, verse 22 of the Koran, which reads:

Thou wilt not find folk who believe in Allah and the Last Day loving those who oppose Allah and His messenger, even though they be their fathers or their sons or their brethren or their clan. As for such, He hath written faith upon their hearts [and will do all kind of good things for them]. . . . Allah is well pleased with them, and they are well pleased with Him.

This passage, Ma Chien says, "makes clear the demarcation between enemies and friends, rejects any compromise measures," and asserts that

universal love has reference to love for all good people. As for those who are hostile to the people, although they may be intimate friends and close relatives, we must sever all connections with them and bring them to censure and justice.[22]

Whereas the Koran envisages a separation between men on the

---

[20] David Lu, *Moslems in China Today* (Hong Kong: International Studies Group, 1964), p. 2. There were, of course, earlier translations of the Koran using the literary or classical style.

[21] Yang, *Islam*, p. 58.

[22] *Ibid.*, p. 59.

basis of faith in Allah, the separation is now based on "love for all good people," which obviously does not include those Muslims who oppose the Communist Party.

The Chinese Islamic Association was organized in Peking, May 8-11, 1953, in a meeting attended by over one hundred "peace partisans" and "democrats" of the Islamic faith representing ten nationalities.[23] A preparatory conference had been held in Peking a year earlier with strong Party representation in the conference and in the preparatory committee which worked until the formal inauguration. The association's purpose was to "assist the People's Government in developing the Muslim people's cultural and education enterprises and strengthening the patriotic ideological education among the Muslim people." [24]

After the preparatory conference, *Jen-min Jih-pao* stated that the purpose would be "to love the Fatherland and to assist the People's Government to implement the religious policy, and to take part in the campaign for safeguarding world peace." [25] More than ten years later, however, a Muslim writer stated that the association's tasks included "running the Chinese Islamic Seminary," and, "among others, study of Islamic teachings, promotion of friendly contacts with Muslims in other countries, and the safeguarding of world peace." [26] Despite the reference to the seminary and to study, the association seems to have had little to do with the strengthening or promotion of Islam. Like the Three-Self Movement among Protestants and the Chinese Patriotic Catholic Association, its prime purpose was that of liaison between the government and a particular religious group. Observers have noted that one of its major functions was indeed the "promotion of friendly contacts with Muslims in other countries."

Burhan Shahidi, Tartar governor of Sinkiang province, was chosen chairman of the new association and, to my knowledge, has never been replaced. A large proportion of the leaders, as well as the members of the organization, seem to have come from the Han

[23] *CURBAC*, March 20, 1955.
[24] *NCNA*, Peking, April 30, 1953; *SCMP*, p. 41.
[25] *JMJP*, August 5, 1952; Yang, *Islam*, 50.
[26] Djamal al-Din Pai Shou-yi (Chairman of History Department at Peking Normal University), "Historical Heritage of Chinese Muslims," *China Reconstructs* XIII (July, 1964), 37-40.

Chinese who are Muslim, since they speak Chinese and are regarded as more trustworthy than minority Muslims by the government. Party leaders were quite obvious in the list of vice-presidents.

A second organization for Muslims was also formed in 1953. The Chinese Association for the Promotion of the Hui People's Culture was formed "to help the People's Government to do research in and to develop the culture and education of the Hui people." [27] The purpose of the research was later stated to be that of understanding the cultural heritage of the various minority nationalities so that Muslims could be mobilized for socialist construction within the country and develop closer relations with Muslims in other countries.

Thus, the aims of both associations proved to be political, rather than Islamic or cultural. The Chinese Islamic Association continued its activities into the mid-60's, but the Chinese Association for the Promotion of the Hui People's Culture was phased out in 1958 during the antirightist campaigns.

There is also evidence of an Association for Muslim Youth which apparently was controlled or "guided" by the Young Communist League. The Young Muslims are reported to have said that they had found in the Communist Party and its leader the ideal savior for whom they had searched so long.[28]

A major thrust in the Communist effort to break down Muslim intellectual resistance was through education. Previously, most Muslims who had any education received it through mosque schools where they studied the Koran, Muslim teaching, and at least enough Arabic to understand the services in the mosque. Intensive efforts were made under the new regime to bring all Muslim children into government schools, where the Chinese language was taught and used as the medium of instruction and where courses in science were emphasized. The story of what happened to the mosque schools is not completely clear, but apparently they were able to continue into the 60's, not only to provide religious instruction, but also to give training in Arabic for men in the diplomatic service who might be assigned to Arabic-speaking areas.

[27] *NCNA*, May 20, 1953; *SCMP*, p. 12.
[28] *CMBA* II (III) (December, 1950), 1059.

A series of special schools or institutes were set up in Peking for Muslims: the Institute for Muslims in 1949, the Central Institute for Nationalities in 1951, with eight branches in cities in the minority areas, and the Islamic Theological Institute in 1955. The first two schools each claimed about 1,500 students the first few years; the Theological Institute went from 109, in 1955, to 130 a year later. Muslim students were encouraged to study in other colleges and universities, especially those specializing in medicine, agriculture, and technical subjects.

Training for religious leaders centered in a four-year course at the Islamic Theological Institute, although a lower grade course was offered at the Institute for Muslims. At all such schools political courses were added to the traditional studies of Arabic language, Muslim history, and theology.

Edgar Faure visited a seminary in Sian which had twenty students, but was told there were fifty students in a "little seminary." There were two teachers, one full-time for Koranic studies, one part-time for Chinese. It was supposedly supported by Muslim families, "but the state gives aid in certain circumstances." [29]

Indoctrination of religious leaders was stressed in Muslim areas because the ahungs and the imams were thought to be particularly conservative. Study classes were introduced, at least by 1951, and supplemented with reform by labor for those who seemed particularly slow. There was also the concerted effort to enlist Muslim religious leaders in regular productive labor, as was also the case with Buddhist monks and nuns.

There was a reference in 1951 to "priests and seminarians" in fifteen mosque schools in the Northwest, who had been "given lessons in political and cultural subjects . . . so that they may come abreast with the times." A visiting team of prominent citizens, including a chief justice of the People's Supreme Court, "encouraged" such courses. As a result of this training, "the priests' political consciousness has increased to the point that they are willing to participate in the various patriotic movements." These movements, in addition to Oppose America–Aid Korea and opposi-

---

[29] Edgar Faure, *The Serpent and the Tortoise; Problems of the New China*, trans. Lovett F. Edwards (New York: St. Martin's Press, 1958). French edition published in Paris by Julliard, 1957.

tion to American rearming of Japan, included the suppression of counterrevolutionaries, which in the Northwest would certainly have meant fellow Muslims.[30]

PEACE AND DISCONTENT IN THE MUSLIM COMMUNITY

There are a few examples of the efforts made to show how life for Muslim minority groups was incomparably better under the new regime than the old. A story on Muslims in Sian contrasted "hand-to-mouth existence," low cultural level, illiteracy, and lack of political consciousness in the past with future opportunities in education, emancipation of women, and "political awakening." [31] No actual evidence was offered to support these claims, except for limited economic relief to the poor, but two examples of uneducated housewives who had become politically active were intended as evidence of what communism could do. The conclusion—that unification of all of China's nationalities can be effected only under a government like the new one—involved a premise that Muslims of the minority nationalities had not by any means accepted, but was weighted in such a way as to leave no alternative but acceptance.

Another example concerns the Muslims of the city of Canton who claimed to have been oppressed under the old order. *Nan-fang Jih-pao* listed about the same reasons for Muslim backwardness in Canton as those which were advanced to account for backwardness in Sian. And the signs of change, focusing primarily on heightened political awareness and activity, were also the same. Special treatment of Muslims by the city government was reciprocated by Muslim services to the community during the Spring Festival, on Women's Day and May Day, and in support of the Oppose America–Aid Korea campaigns. There was a special reference to Muslims operating their own primary school, in which was offered "a special course in Arabic to enable the Muslims to study the language of their religion." [32]

[30] King Chia Cheng, "Mohammedans in New China," *China Monthly Review* CXXI (October, 1951), 182-83.
[31] *Ibid.*
[32] Canton *Nan-fang Jih-pao*, July 9, 1951; *CURBAC*, August 1, 1951, pp. 11-12.

For the Corban festival in Muslim areas in August, 1953, flags of the minority peoples were flying, the sound of drums could be heard everywhere, and services were held in all the mosques. This was according to official government reports through the New China News Agency, which noted that state cooperatives had provided "large quantities of mutton, beef, flour, tea, and sugar." [33]

The same spirit prevailed for the celebration of Muhammed's birthday, according to official reports of that occasion on November 4, 1954. A special ceremony was held at the Tungszu Pailow Mosque in the eastern part of Peking with various Muslim officials in attendance; the officiating ahung "urged the worshipers to do their utmost to preserve peace." [34]

When Y. T. Wu of the Three-Self Committee approached the government in November, 1952, with a request that Christians employed in government offices be allowed a holiday on December 25, on grounds that Muslim government employees were granted a holiday on their festivals, the reply, as quoted in T'ien Feng, May 11, 1953, was: "Christian and Buddhist festivals are purely religious festivals and the decision regarding racial minority festivals does not apply." [35] All of which supports the contention that these distinctive Muslim religious festivals were treated as the holidays of a particular racial or minority group which the government was anxious not to offend.

Another way in which Muslims were favored was through the decree that old monuments offensive to any nationality in China might be torn down. A minority group might apply to have such an offensive monument razed, as was the case when Muslims of Kweilin, Kwangsi, paraded to the grave of former imperial governor Chen Yu-ying, who had suppressed a Muslim revolt during the years 1856-76. Stone tablets erected in honor of his "good work" by the Manchu emperor were torn down in a very festive spirit.[36]

Two articles appearing in the Chinese press in the summer of 1952, following almost the same outline and using the same

[33] NCNA, August 24, 1953; China Bulletin (British), New Series XIII, September, 1953, p. 4.
[34] NCNA, Peking, November 4, 1954; CMBA VII (February, 1955), 164-65.
[35] Reported in China Bulletin (British), New Series XIII, September, 1953, p. 4.
[36] China Reconstructs II (July-August, 1953), 6.

language at many points, confirmed certain dominant themes in government efforts to win the support of Muslims and the minority groups in which Islam played such an important role.[37] After different introductions, both writers launched into gory recitals of the way in which Muslim peoples suffered under the Kuomintang, followed by a glowing contrast with happy Muslims who had become "masters of the state in New China," with emphasis on the large number of Hui people who held office in the new regime. Various instances of economic improvement were cited: Muslims got better prices for the goods they produced, Land Reform had brought small plots to people who never had any, and they did not have to pay taxes or fees to Muslim "bandits." Cultural and educational betterment was heralded: in new schools established by the government the minority peoples were able to study their own languages and develop their own culture. Benefits for religion under the new freedom-of-religious-belief policy were proclaimed, such as discounts on many items at Muslim festival times and time off at such festivals for Muslim workers.

Although there has been tension between Han and non-Han peoples through the centuries, including the Nationalist period, it is rather ironic that the Pan-Hanism attributed to Chiang Kai-shek should be lampooned when the Communist leaders were pouring Han Chinese into the minority areas in a much more active assimilation policy. It is difficult to assess the accuracy of the claims for economic improvement, but it is not difficult to see that economic gain involved greater political control. It is fairly clear that the study of minority languages was minimized and the study of Chinese accelerated. And minimal benefits granted at festival times hardly balanced mounting atheist propaganda.

In the midst of all the favorable reports by the people who made the standard tours, the observations made by the Indonesian journalist Asa Bafagih, who went to China several times in the mid-50's, proved to be rather startling. During his first visit in 1954, which was described in a series of articles later published in book form, so many of his questions were sidestepped and so much of

---

[37] P. C. Yu, "Moslems in New China," *People's China*, August, 1952; *CMBA* IV (V) (October, 1952), 666-69; Han Tao-jen, "The Emancipation of Islamic Nationals of China," *JMJP*, June 6, 1952; *CURBAC*, July 25, pp. 6-10.

what he was told was propagandistic that he decided the leaders of the Islamic Association to whom he spoke had sold out to the Communists. He saw signs of activity but not of vitality, and was particularly disturbed by remarks from Muslim leaders that communism presented no problem to them. From what he saw of other religions, however, Muslims were "happy by comparison." [38]

Asa Bafagih's second trip was made in company with Indonesian Prime Minister Ali Sastroamidjojo and other Indonesian officials. His request to visit Sinkiang was again not granted, although he was promised a trip the next time he came. He was allowed to meet with Ma Chien, who, to Asa Bafagih's surprise, expressed agreement with the Islamic Association line that Muslim life had advanced under the Communists. Willard A. Hanna concludes with Asa Bafagih's comment that he had not changed his views.

This later visit, if anything, reinforced him in his conviction that the Muslim population of the People's China faces a grim future, unless, as he says, something altogether unforeseen should occur.[39]

Hikmah, an Indonesian newspaper, questioned whether conditions for Muslims in China were as pleasant as reports would have one believe. The newspaper took exception particularly to a book, published in the Arabic language and circulated in Indonesia, which pictured the condition of Muslims in China as being a happy one. The newspaper cited the situation in East Turkestan where there were arrests and trials of religious leaders after the area was occupied by Chinese Communists in 1949. When the area was divided between China and Russia in 1950, further oppressive measures were introduced.[40]

On the other hand, an Egyptian Minister of Religious Foundations made a visit to China and found that Chinese Muslims were a

[38] Willard A. Hanna, *The Case of the Forty Million Missing Muslims* (New York: American Universities Field Staff, 1956). Another Indonesian Muslim, Mochtar Gazali, of the Muslim Labor Federation, who had visited China in 1952, was shocked that a Muslim woman in high office had offered him an alcoholic beverage. She explained that drinking alcoholic beverages was expected of Communist Chinese officials. *Padoman* (Djakarta), March 6, 1953; *CMBA* V (VI) (November, 1953), 895.

[39] Hanna, *The Case*, p. 10. I have no record of the proposed third visit.

[40] Reported in *CMBA* VIII (January, 1958), 82.

"model group," that Communists had interfered only to abolish polygamy. He noted new rights for women—for example, that they might dance with men in public. The Egyptian proceeded later to press Saudi Arabian officials to grant entry visas for Chinese pilgrims to Mecca.[41]

Ma Chien continued this approach in his article in early 1953, but added to the pattern of argument which had been previously used the fact that Chinese Muslims had been permitted to leave China to make the pilgrimage to Mecca in 1952. He adds that these pilgrims were unable to reach their destination "as a result of external hindrances," but met with fellow Muslims in Singapore and Pakistan. The point is that their being allowed to leave China "made it clear to all Islam that Chinese Muslims have not only freedom of belief, but also freedom of contact with their brothers elsewhere in the world." [42]

A group of Pakistani Muslims who toured China in the spring of 1956 were not favorably impressed. Speaking for the entire group, Maulana Ehtishamul Ruq said that Chinese Muslims were allowed only "to embrace their faith passively as long as it does not interfere with the state's ideology and policies." The full statement in the *Times* of Karachi went on to say that there was freedom for an individual to choose a religion but that efforts were being made to wipe it out.

Maulana pointed out teaching of religion was banned in the schools. He said the next generation in Red China would know nothing about religion because children were being deprived of all religious training. He said it was true a few girls and boys were being taught Arabic, Urdu, and other foreign languages, but this was not done to teach them the Holy Koran or Holy Bible, but to prepare them for diplomatic assignments in the future.

Maulana said in Red China people did not enjoy freedom of speech or assembly. There are no free newspapers, and the library contained books which mainly talk about communism. He was surprised to find that all ra-

---

[41] L. Constantine, "Hands Across the Curtain," *New Republic*, September 5, 1955, p. 7. The Egyptian official was also said to have been somewhat embarrassed when he recalled that the only dance done by Egyptian women was the belly dance.

[42] "How Muslims Live in China," *China Reconstructs* II (March-April, 1953), 13-15.

dio sets were tuned only to Peking. He tried to listen to other stations but every time his radio set was connected to Radio Peking.[43]

Faure was also puzzled by the ease with which Muslim leaders adapted to a Communist state. He conversed with Ta Pu-sheng, who held high office both in the Islamic community and in the government, who saw no contradiction between communism and Islam. He admitted that "communism is atheist, but the practice of religion is free." [44] Faure noticed that several Muslims, when asked about a man being a practicing Muslim and Communist at the same time, replied vaguely, with embarrassment, and according to Faure's judgment, in error. He felt "they were not really convinced of the spiritual incompatibility between Marxism and religion."

They know very well that the Communist Party is atheist and they admit it when the conversation turns that way, but does that atheism seem to them anything more than a sort of laicism? They know that the Communists are atheists, but they do not know exactly *why* they are and *why* they cannot be otherwise. [This proves that] communism has penetrated their spirits more as a regime than as a doctrine, but it also proves that it has penetrated deeply, that the cogs of political thought and religious thought interlock easily in a single brain, and that even Moslems whose religious constance is sure do not find any real difficulty in "ideological coexistence." [45]

Faure heard of no Muslim protest during the struggle or thought reform sessions, and came to the conclusion that resistance probably came from the older members of the Muslim communities. He went so far as to suggest that the Muslims, particularly the younger ones, appreciated in the Communists

the spirit of control, the personal discipline, the faith that seems analogous to his own . . . , [and may be] grateful to the Communist

[43] Story in *CMBA* VIII (September, 1956), 527, based on *USIS* report datelined Karachi, June 26, 1956.
[44] Faure, *The Serpent*, pp. 145-48.
[45] *Ibid.*, p. 148.

regime for having freed them from certain feudal survivals which have been falsely regarded as religious traditions.[46]

There was continuing resistance, however. More than twenty thousand Muslims in Kansu staged an insurrection between April and July, 1952, in which, according to Communist figures, three thousand cadres were killed and three districts seized before the People's Liberation Army put down the revolt. It was not reported until October, 1952, when dissatisfaction with Land Reform provoked such widespread criticism that there was no avoiding it.[47]

The term "adventurist tendencies," which had previously been used to apply to those who had revolted, was now used in the Chinese press to apply to the cadres who had gone too far in suppressing religion. *Jen-min Jih-pao* admitted that it was common practice for the minorities not to be consulted, and that they were often ignored. Members of the Party's Central Committee found that minority group officials had empty titles and no power. The newspaper warned nevertheless against "narrow nationalism" and "small cliques" as being against patriotism and internationalism.[48]

Muslims in Sinkiang and the Kansu-Ninghsia area were charged in 1956 with "local nationalism," evidently meaning that they had opposed Communist control, collectivization, and the immigration of Chinese into the area which had followed. Some of the officials were purged. Two years later a Muslim leader, Ma Chen-wu, was arrested for organizing popular revolts in Ninghsia.[49]

Outright attacks were made on imams, along with Buddhist lamas, in 1958. Communists accused them of "charlatanism, fraud, and crimes against the state," then went on to tell the people that "there are no such things as spirits and gods. All this religious nonsense was designed to deceive the people. The reactionary imams and lamas speak good but do evil." [50]

In the midst of the Hundred Flowers Period everything seemed

[46] *Ibid.*, pp. 149-50.
[47] Richard L. Walker, *China Under Communism: The First Five Years* (New Haven: Yale University Press, 1955), p. 187.
[48] *Ibid.*, p. 186.
[49] Harold C. Hinton, "Religion in China since 1949," ed. S. Chandrasekhar, *A Decade of Mao's China* (Bombay: Perennial Press, 1960), p. 47.
[50] *Ibid.*

to be blissful for Muslims. One of the Huis employed in the Hui People's Hospital in Peking wrote an article describing an idyllic life among his people on Ox Street in that city.[51] The mosques were proceeding as usual, schools were flourishing, a seminary had been established, homes were neat and clean. The Muslims were good citizens in every respect and they had a high proportion of deputies in the various councils of state. This was pictured, of course, as a great contrast to the situation under the Nationalists, who had not recognized them as a separate nationality but as "persons with peculiar habits."

At the same time, however, Muslim imams were complaining about the anomaly of receiving Communist cadres into the Muslim faith because they were marrying Muslim girls.[52] To be both a Communist and a Muslim was generally conceived to be an impossible contradiction. For a Communist to become a Muslim in order to fulfill a requirement for marrying a Muslim girl was regarded, therefore, as a mockery, especially since his marrying the girl was motivated in part at least by the Party's desire to blend with the Muslim community.

As the Hundred Flowers began to blossom, Muslims began to criticize more openly the Party's policy on nationalities and to advocate a separate state. They contended that there were more poor people under the socialist "system of starvation." The Hui who had become cadres were called "traitors," progressive imams were called "men without a religion." It must be acknowledged that most of these charges, and the others which follow, are known through accounts of the antirightist campaigns which followed the blooming and contending.

One "rightist" who was attacked, Liu Sheng-ming, had challenged the government's religious policy, claiming that freedom of religious belief was not provided in actual practice. "The Communist Party is not so good as the Kuomintang. The Communist Party wants to exterminate all religion." [53] At least this is

[51] Liu Sheng-lin, "Muslims in Peking," *People's China*, March 1, 1957, pp. 36-39.

[52] Macfarquhar, *The Hundred Flowers*, p. 249.

[53] Hsin Tsung-chen, "True Freedom of Religious Belief Is Possible Only Under Communist Party Leadership," *Hopei Jih-pao*, January 11, 1958; *CUR-BAC*, June 15, 1958, pp. 8-10.

what Liu was quoted as saying by Hsin Tsung-chen, who proceeded to reply by pointing to the number of imams who had become people's deputies, the establishment of the Chinese Islamic Association and of an institute for the study of the Koran (Theological Institute?), concessions from the government in such matters as taxes, the supply of special foods, and financial assistance to imams.

Hsin's reply was marred by the way in which he stressed the necessity for the Hui to cooperate with the Han:

> History and innumerable facts in our life have shown that the Hui and Han people can never be separated. The clothing, food, housing, and transport of the Hui people, and even the building of mosques and management of Islamic affairs, are inseparable from the direct or indirect aid of the Han people.[54]

What Liu was saying to the Muslims could hardly be missed: unity is not only desirable—without it there are no benefits. The note of freedom as protection, the suggestion of a "kept religion," continually creeps in.

The relationship of the Hui people to the Han people was by far the major issue in these antirightist struggles of 1958. An editorial writer for a monthly periodical for minority peoples, *Min-tsu T'uan-chieh*, was shocked at the way in which the Hui people of Shantung and Honan had spoken and acted:

> These rightists advocated that "all Hui people under heaven belong to the same family" and "the Hui people should fight for their religion but not for their country," in order to blur the Hui people's class viewpoint and their attitude to state authority; they propagated such absurd theories as "the Hui people stand for the Hui religion," "religious interests are the same thing as nationality interests," and "the leader of the Hui people is the Ahung." . . . They scolded Party members of Hui nationality and Hui cadres supporting the Party and enthusiastically serving the people as "dissenters and traitors of the Hui people" . . . and they denounced the autonomous policy of nationality regions in a vain attempt to set up independent kingdoms. Some of them even plotted to organize counter-revolutionary cliques to stir up the people to cause trouble and distur-

---

[54] *Ibid.*, p. 10.

bances, so as to directly sabotage law and order of the state and our socialist enterprises.[55]

The same editorial indicated that there were "wicked elements" which had said, "Our religious code forbids the people to participate in cooperatives," and that according to the Muslim religion it was not proper for Hui women to roll up their trousers and work in the fields. The "cooperatives" to which the writer refers are undoubtedly the communes in which it was extremely difficult to openly practice any religion, and in which people who required special food would find even more obstacles. For many Muslims this would be a concrete manifestation of the impossibility of Hui and Han people living in such close unity.

The seriousness of this unity question for Party authorities may be seen in the fact that the slogan promoted in the Hui areas in 1957 was "Eliminate Greater Han Chauvinism." This would indicate that the last thing in the world the Party wanted was to absorb the minority peoples into the "Great Han race," and was therefore appropriate for the Hundred Flowers Period when everyone seemed to have more freedom. By 1958, however, the "in slogan" was "Do Away with Local Nationalism." Obviously there had been too much assertion of local feelings and goals, both in what Muslims were saying and in the revolts which concretely challenged central government authority.

Numerous Muslim leaders were accused of stirring up revolts, trying to set up independent kingdoms, and of oppostion to the younger ahungs who cooperated with the Party. From August 17 to September 6, at a forum in Yinch'uan, Ninghsia, Ma Chen-wu was "thoroughly exposed and criticized" for instigating revolts in Ninghsia in 1950 and 1958 and for just about every crime imaginable. He lost all his property and leadership posts (he was a vice-president of the Chinese Islamic Association), and was condemned in extravagant language wherever Muslims could read or hear about the demise of their leader.[56]

Also charged as rightists were those who criticized the Party's

---

[55] *Min-tsu T'uan-chieh,* June 14, 1958; *URS,* August 12, 1958, pp. 187-88.
[56] "Crimes of Ultra-Rightist Ma Chen-wu Exposed at Forum of Hui People," *NCNA,* Yinch'uan, October 17, 1958; *CURBAC,* November 7, 1958.

effort to win over younger ahungs. These rightists were quoted as having

called the Party's nationality policy a policy "to fool the people," saying that the Party's cultivating Hui cadres and young ahungs was "to rule the Hui people by the Hui people" and "destroy the foundation of Islam," and heartlessly calumniating the Party's care about ahungs as "buying over" the ahungs.[57]

An ahung by the name of Ting Wen-hao was brought to trial as a counterrevolutionary because he had "spread reactionary theories among the masses and conduct[ed] reactionary activities." The latter included inciting a conflict between Hui and Han peoples in Shantung and sabotaging labor production.

Hung En-ch'ing, an imam in another place, had been "hostile" toward a progressive ahung and had made all kinds of derisive remarks in the mosque, such as "nowadays it is the turtle that prospers, not the dragon," and "now is the time when the tortoises, turtles, prawns, and crabs are ruling." [58] Others were accused of trying to return to feudalism by working with landlords and even hiding them in the mosques. And still others were accused of injecting an apocalyptic note.

The discontent which expressed itself in these verbal attacks and occasionally armed revolt during the late 50's was eventually put down. There is evidence that it sprang up again in the early 60's. There was an allusion to revolt in an article by Wang Feng, vice-president of the Commission for National Minorities and First Party Secretary for Kansu province.[59] He admitted that "reforms" introduced by the Party had provoked revolts by people who, in the name of "nationalism," were unwilling to accept such reformation. Consequently there had been an extensive program of socialist education and criticism of local nationalism.

Discontent reached such a peak in Sinkiang in the early 60's that

[57] *Anhwei Jih-pao*, June 29, 1958; *URS*, August 12, 1958, p. 196.

[58] Both examples cited by Chin Kuang, "The Struggle Against Reactionaries in Religious Circles Has Brought a New Atmosphere to the Hui People in Shantung" (same issues of Chinese periodical and *URS* in note 57), pp. 190-91.

[59] Article in *Min-tsu Tuan-chieh*, 10 and 11, 1961; *Fides*, March 21, 1962, pp. 160-61.

thousands of Uighur, Kirghiz, and Tajiks fled across the western borders into the Soviet Union to live among the same ethnic groups on the Soviet side. Chinese efforts to stamp out their culture were cited as one of the reasons for so many refugees—100,000 according to one count—but reports of the incident are clouded by the fact that Russian-Chinese relations were deteriorating, and either country would use the incident to embarrass the other.[60]

Liu Chen-huan, writing in the same magazine a year later, also referred obliquely to revolts as well as efforts by Muslims to return to their former ways. Writing from a "We Communists" stance, and without any corresponding "We Muslims" orientation, Liu goes through the usual line of thought on freedom of religious belief which has been seen many times. The most revealing section follows:

Although great successes were scored in 1958, yet like the other reactionary ruling classes which have been overthrown, the feudal reactionary forces of religion will not bow to their fall and will vainly try to restore themselves. The appearance of some undesirable phenomena in the religious field in the past year or two is a clear proof of this. Among the elements of the upper strata in religious circles, a few people utilized the religious belief of the masses of the Hui people to levy money and grain from the masses by coercion in the course of conducting religious activities. They exploited the masses in a big way, practiced extravagance and waste, and seriously affected the production activities of the Hui masses. Some disguised themselves as gods and ghosts to cheat people for money. A very few of them even attempted to restore the religious feudal prerogatives and feudal oppression and exploitation which had been abolished. This is a concentrated reflection of the class struggle in Islam, and must arouse our vigilance.[61]

It is not easy to determine just what Liu has reference to at every point, but it is clear that the government was still having trouble in handling Islam. And, like all theoreticians, Wang and Liu insisted that the government's aim in handling such rightist activity was

[60] *South China Morning Post*, December 22, 1963, and April 8, 1964.
[61] Liu Chen-huan, "Further Implement the Party's Policy of Freedom of Religious Belief among the Islamites in Ninghsia Hui Autonomous Region," *Min-tsu T'uan-chieh*, May, 1963; *SCMM*, July 8, 1963, pp. 12-13.

not to suppress religion, but rather to "gather" the masses around the Party.

GOOD FOREIGN RELATIONS AT ALL COST

It was during the mid-50's that travel abroad for Chinese Muslims and entertainment of foreign Muslims in China became such an effective instrument for building good foreign relations. Delegations of pilgrims to Mecca were sent from China from 1952 through 1966, but it was not until 1955 that the delegation was actually able to enter Mecca. In the summer of that year, nineteen Chinese Muslims made the pilgrimage to Mecca, and in the process toured various parts of Asia and North Africa telling anyone who would listen that there was no religious persecution in China. The 1956 delegation was the largest, reputed to include about one hundred pilgrims.[62]

Thirty-nine Muslim pilgrims, both men and women, who went to Mecca from Lhasa in 1957 received great publicity, and on their return were welcomed at a forum which included Buddhist leaders. It was pointed out that the government supplies passports and foreign exchange, that the Chinese Consulate in Bombay rendered aid. The pilgrims gave banners, prayer rugs, and photographs to the Religious Affairs Commission in Lhasa upon their return, and were said to have extolled the new China and its freedom of religion wherever they went.[63]

By the early 60's, the number of pilgrims going to Mecca and visiting countries in the Middle East had dwindled to less than ten as coolness in Chinese diplomatic relations with such countries became apparent. At this juncture, contacts with Pakistan and Indonesia were stressed with the result that it is very clear how Islamic leaders in China were used to promote better relations between Communist China and predominately Muslim countries. Ma Yu-huai of the Chinese Islamic Association, for example, led a

[62] *JMJP*, May 6, 1955, and other newspaper reports, summarized in *CNA*, January 20, 1956, p. 5. We have heard there were "several hundred pilgrims" from China in 1948.

[63] *Tibet Jih-pao*, December 27, 1957; *CURBAC*, May 6, 1958, pp. 6-9.

delegation of Muslims to Indonesia in late December, 1962, at which time they greeted several Indonesian officials.[64]

In the spring of 1964, several Chinese Muslims visited Syria and "reiterated China's stand in supporting the Arab people in their struggle against imperialism and the Palestinian Arab people in their struggle to return to their homeland." The group visited a refugee camp of Palestinian Arabs on the outskirts of Damascus.[65] The same group of pilgrims later visited Karachi in West Pakistan and Dacca in East Pakistan but, according to reports, limited themselves to the usual expressions of hope for continued friendship and solidarity between Chinese and Pakistanis who would unite with other people to "support, encourage, and learn from each other in safeguarding national independence, building their countries, and preserving peace." [66]

Chinese Muslim leaders also entertained a stream of visitors from Muslim countries. Sheik El-Hadj Ibrahim Niass of Senegal was feted at a banquet during which Burhan Shahidi said:

We hope that by our continued efforts we shall consolidate and develop the friendship and cooperation between the Muslims of the two countries and the friendship and solidarity between the peoples of China and Senegal and the rest of Africa.[67]

The visitor responded by saying that the imperialists' lie that there was no freedom of religious belief in China had been proved wrong:

We have personally seen that Chinese Muslims enjoy full freedom of religious belief and that they are working with the rest of the Chinese people to safeguard and build up their motherland." [68]

There are similar accounts of religious leaders from Pakistan and the Sudan, and undoubtedly there were many others about which there are no reports available. Many times the Chinese

[64] *NCNA*, Djakarta, January 7, 1963; *SCMP*, January 11, 1963, p. 30.
[65] *NCNA*, Damascus, May 5, 1964; *SCMP*, May 11, 1964, 25.
[66] *NCNA*, Karachi, May 17 and May 20, 1964; *SCMP*, May 22, 1964, pp. 35-36, and May 26, 1964, p. 35.
[67] *NCNA*, Peking, October 29, 1963; *SCMP*, November 1, 1963, pp. 30-31.
[68] *Ibid.*

Islamic Association and the various friendship associations, such as the China-Pakistan Friendship Association, would co-sponsor such visits. On some occasions the visitors were hailed as a "friendship delegation," such as the Syrian friendship delegation which was entertained at a dinner by Vice-Premier Ch'en Yi. In his speech Ch'en said, "At the bidding of U. S. imperialism, Israel every once in a while creates provocations against you and the entire Arab people, posing a constant threat to your security." He referred to the discovery of "a spy ring of the U. S. Embassy" in Damascus and to "expelled U. S. espionage diplomats." [69]

Special attention was devoted to Indonesia in 1965. When Indonesia withdrew from the United Nations, the Chinese Islamic Association sent a message of support for that action and for "the Indonesian people in their just struggle against the colonialist created 'Malaysia.' " [70] When an Asian-African Islamic Conference opened in Indonesia in March, Chou En-lai sent a message of greeting which included the following sentence:

I sincerely hope that the Asian-African Islamic Conference will promote the Bandung spirit, strengthen the unity of Muslims, and make positive contributions to the cause of opposing imperialism, colonialism, and neo-colonialism, supporting national independence movements and defending world peace.[71]

The Chinese delegation to the conference was headed by Yusuf Ma Yu-huai, who echoed Chou En-lai's words in a speech. Ma went on to speak specifically of U. S. imperialism and of the way in which it controlled the United Nations, then linked the Indonesian withdrawal from the UN, the Indonesian struggle against Malaysia, the struggles by the Vietnamese and Congolese peoples, and the struggle of Palestinian Muslims against Zionism as part of one anti-imperialist effort.[72] A few days before the Asian-African Islamic Conference, there was a meeting of the Indonesian Muslim Trade Union (Sarbumusi), to which the All-China Federation of Trade

[69] NCNA, Peking, March 15, 1965; SCMP, March 18, 1965, pp. 34-35.
[70] NCNA, Peking, January 11, 1965; SCMP, January 15, 1965, p. 25.
[71] NCNA, Peking, March 5, 1965; SCMP, March 10, 1965, p. 30.
[72] NCNA, Djakarta, March 8, 1965; SCMP, March 15, 1965, pp. 29-30.

Unions sent a delegation, some of which presumably were Muslim.[73]

On the surface at least, the normal patterns of Muslim life continued after the antirightist campaigns had stripped several Muslim leaders of power. Each year there have been reports from Peking and minority centers in the northwest of the celebration of Bairam, marking the end of Ramadan, the month of fasting. Muslims received a day off, and were reported to be wandering about in a gay and happy mood. Special services were held in the mosques, attracting diplomatic personnel and students from Muslim nations.[74]

The Corban festival, two months or so later, which marks the end of the pilgrimage to Mecca and is celebrated by Muslims throughout the world, has also been observed in Communist China. News reports mention religious services only in passing, but usually play up a reception held in the capital attended by Muslim leaders from China and diplomatic envoys from Muslim countries. Officers of the Chinese Islamic Association, such as President Burhan Shahidi, in 1963 and 1964, and Vice-President Hadji Muhammed Ali Chang Chieh, in 1965, made speeches extolling friendship between China and Muslims throughout the world, attacking U. S. imperialism, and praising the life of Muslims in People's China.[75]

There were occasional news releases in the early 60's intended to indicate what a pleasant life Muslims were leading in China.[76] There were further accounts of the marvelous changes in the Muslim community living in and around Ox Street in Peking, following the same general outline of a previous article in *People's China* which has already been referred to.

Ma Yu-huai, who represented Chinese Muslims abroad on several occasions, wrote an article about progress in the Ninghsia Hui Autonomous Region of which he was vice-president.[77] He pointed par-

---

[73] *NCNA*, Djakarta, February 26, 1965; *SCMP*, March 3, 1965, p. 27.
[74] Miscellaneous *NCNA* reports in *SCMP*, March 1, 1963, p. 17; February 19, 1964, p. 22; February 9, 1965, p. 23.
[75] *NCNA* reports in *SCMP*, May 9, 1963, pp. 6-7; April 28, 1964, pp. 15-17; April 15, 1965, pp. 24-25.
[76] *NCNA*, Peking, March 16, 1964; *SCMP*, April 2, 1964, pp. 19-20.
[77] *NCNA*, Peking, March 16, 1964; *SCMP*, March 6, 1964, pp. 18-19.

ticularly to the number of officials from the Hui people in government and the number of delegates to the regional People's Congress, and put great stress on the economic growth of the region. He also spoke of the "emancipation of Hui women," which was the point behind a special feature story concerning a twenty-nine-year-old woman who had been sold as a child bride in the old China, but in 1964 was a deputy magistrate at the People's Congress of Haiyuan county in the Ninghsia Hui Autonomous Region.[78] The listing of numerous benefits to women under the new government —special schools, opportunities for work and service outside the home, special benefits, such as eight-week maternity leave with full pay and free medical care—was undoubtedly a major point in the Party's ideological struggle with Muslims who were sensitive to the criticism that the status of women had been negligible in traditional Islam.

The official view of the state of Islam in Communist China may be seen in the report to the Third National Conference of the Chinese Islamic Association by its president, Burhan Shahidi. Burhan referred with pride to participation of Muslims in socialist construction and in political, economic, and cultural activities in the regions where they lived, and to Muslim aid to the government in carrying out the policy of freedom of religious belief. He spoke of Islamic theological study, exchange of visits with Muslims of other countries, of government aid at times of festivals and in repair of mosques. Burhan did not give figures, according to the New China News Agency report, but said that the Islamic Thological Institute in Peking "had trained many imams and Islamic scholars" of various nationalities since 1955. There were the usual pledges of support to the government within and to people involved in various anti-imperialist struggles without.[79] One of the "tasks" to be undertaken in the future was "to make a determined effort to strike blows at counterrevolutionary and bad elements operating from among the Islamic circles under the cloak of religion," which points to the same problem that the two writers, Liu and Wang, were nervous about.

[78] *NCNA*, Yinch'uan, March 3, 1964; *SCMP*, March 6, 1964, pp. 13-14.
[79] *NCNA*, Peking, November 8, 1963; *SCMP*, November 14, 1963, pp. 13-16.

Writing in 1966, on the eve of the Cultural Revolution, Haji Yusuf Chang said that mosques had been maintained in good condition and that Muslims had a disproportionately high representation in the First National People's Congress. He noted that these statements were based on a publication by the China Islamic Association. Chang goes on to say, however, that

available information suggests that the situation of Islam in Communist China is not uniformly bright. Since 1949, many mosques in rural areas have been used for other purposes, such as slaughterhouses; the use of old textbooks on Islam has not been allowed in all Muslim schools; all the ahungs now have to participate in the Agrarian Reform Work Corps, assisting Muslim peasants in their struggle against the landlord class, or otherwise be replaced by Communist-trained Muslim cadres. All the ahungs also have been forced to interpret the Koran from the Marxist-Leninist point of view, and numerous Muslim youths working in producing centres have been compelled to take the same meals as non-Muslims.[80]

This statement is probably a rather conclusive summary of the situation which prevailed before the Cultural Revolution which, as Chang says, provided a greater degree of tolerance in the cities than in the rural places.

In the spring of 1966, the Corban celebrations went off as usual, with the affirmations of "complete freedom of religious belief" and condemnations of the United States in Vietnam and of U. S. and British imperialism in the Middle East. There is a brief human-interest story of a farmhand who set out a feast in Urumchi and said, "I lived in abject poverty and was head over ears in debt in those days [before Liberation]. It is the Communist Party and Chairman Mao Tse-tung that have led me on the road to happiness." [81]

A few days later a Chinese Islamic Friendship delegation left on a visit to Iraq, Kuwait, Sudan, and Pakistan. There were notes on their arrival at several of these places where they received a warm

[80] Chang, "Islam in Modern China," *The Voice of Islam* (Karachi), XIV (September, 1966), 693.
[81] *NCNA*, Urumchi, April 1 and 2, 1966; *SCMP*, April 6, 1966, pp. 16-17.

welcome and exchanged pledges of friendship. At Muzaffarabad, the chairman of the delegation, Hadji Muhammed Ali Chang Chieh, attributed all of Azad Kashmir's troubles to U. S. imperialism and Soviet revisionism.[82]

One of the first Muslim victims of Red Guard terror was Ya Dzechou, an elderly imam in Peking, who was beaten, forced to confess extortion, arrested, and led away.[83] The Red Guards formed a new organization called "The Revolutionary Struggle Group for the Abolition of Islam," and put up wall posters calling for mosques to be closed and for the abolishment of Koran study, marriage within the Islamic faith, and circumcision.[84] Two Moroccan newspapers published the text of one such Red Guard poster attacking Islam:

From now on you will no longer be permitted to hide behind your religious mask—we shall destroy you. You will not be allowed to waste your time in prayers, because all you mutter there in Arabic is anti-Chinese. You will be forbidden to read your so-called Koran." [85]

Other posters called for abolition of all Islamic organizations and Muslim feasts and holidays, and demanded that all imams must go to work in work camps and that traditional burial practices be replaced by cremations.[86]

The Chinese Embassy in Morocco, a few days later, called this report in the Moroccan press "entirely a tissue of lies and calumnies." Ch'en Yi, Deputy Premier and Foreign Minister of China, took a different tack and fell back on the reasons given years earlier for the expulsion of Christian missionaries. He said to a Muslim reporter from Pakistan that the action of Red Guards against Catholic priests, Buddhists, and imams "was necessary because under the cloak of religion these religious leaders had been

[82] *NCNA*, Peking, April 12, 1966; *SCMP*, April 12, 1966, p. 28. For speech see *NCNA*, Muzzaffarabad, June 25, 1966; *SCMP*, June 30, 1966, pp. 42-43.
[83] Japanese news agency report in *Wisconsin State Journal*, August 27, 1966.
[84] *Ceylon Daily News*, November 12, 1966; recorded in publication called *China Notes* (not to be confused with the NCCUSA publication), January 5, 1967.
[85] *Rabat L'Opinion*, December 17, 1966 and *Le Petit Marocain*, December 16, 1966; both stories from Morocco reported in above mentioned *China Notes*.
[86] *China Notes* (NCCCUSA) V (April, 1967), 4-5.

spying for the imperialists, but that not a single Muslim had been attacked because of his religion." [87]

Out in Sinkiang, Uighurs, Kazakhs, Uzbeks, and Tartars were told by Urumchi Radio on March 19, 1967, that Corban had been canceled because the Cultural Revolution had entered a "new stage," and spring plowing had reached a crucial period. A former officer in the Sinkiang Liberation Army said only 3 out of a former 150 mosques were open in the Kuldja district of that province. Red Guards had attacked mosques while Friday noon prayers were being said, and bloody clashes followed.[88] Russians joined the chorus of those who called attention to persecution of Muslims in those areas bordering Russia and China, particularly the Uighur and Kirghiz peoples. TASS International in an English broadcast from Moscow on January 24, 1967, announced that Red Guards "tore down ancient mosques and splashed the Muslim clergymen with paint and paraded them through the streets." [89] *The Kommunist*, a Moscow publication, said that in addition to tearing down mosques, Uighurs and Kazakhs had been forced to eat pork and cremate their dead, thus going against both dietary laws and traditional funeral rites.[90]

There were disturbances in a Muslim middle school in Shanghai (Hui Min Chung-hsueh) and an anti-Mao organization started. Pro-Mao teachers had a difficult time until the school studied "three great disciplines" and "eight points to attend to," then everything was all right. The organization, called Pao Tsu Hao, was said to have been a resurrected secret society.[91]

On two counts Muslims managed to weather the Cultural Revolution better than members of other religious groups: a few festivals continued and a few places of worship remained open. Bairam was celebrated at the Tung Szu Mosque in Peking on January 2, 1967, but the report says "diplomats, experts, and students from Pakistan, Guinea, the United Arab Republic, Iraq, Yemen, and Nepal" attended. There is no reference to Chinese par-

[87] *Pakistan Times* (Lahore), October 2, 1966; *China Notes* V (April, 1967).

[88] *Communism and Religion*, March-April, 1967.

[89] *RCDA*, February 28, 1967, p. 34.

[90] *RCDA*, September 15 and 30, 1967, p. 149.

[91] Reported from Shanghai press in *CNA*, May 19, 1967, p. 6.

ticipating.[92] The Corban festival was celebrated in the same mosque on March 22 (but not in Sinkiang), and only foreigners (embassy officials) are indicated as being present.[93] On December 26, 1968, Bairam was celebrated in Peking, and there is specific mention of Chinese as well as foreigners being present for the Corban celebrations on February 28, 1969, in Peking.[94]

The other difference is that whereas there was no word of any Christian church or Buddhist temple being open for any kind of public worship at the beginning of 1968, there were two Muslim mosques open, one in Peking and the other in Shanghai. The evidence is that of visitors to China who saw the two mosques open and reported this fact in Hong Kong. And a year later there were reports that Muslims in the Hui areas carried out their religious practices openly, and that a school operated by mullahs for training clergy was still in operation.[95]

The fact that accounts of festival celebrations specifically mention foreigners, and the fact that mosques were open in two cities which have had a high percentage of foreigners, would seem to indicate that the importance of good relations with governments of Muslim nations overrides the driving passion to eradicate the Muslim version of old culture, old thinking, old habits, old customs. Buddhism, as we shall see, has also been used to improve China's foreign relations, but by the time of the Cultural Revolution there was little hope for better relations with Ceylon or Burma. Hope had also died for Indonesia in the Communist mind, but Pakistan and certain states in Africa and the Middle East could not be written off. To allow Muslims a limited range of activity—their chief festivals, some open mosques, and a training school—was a small price to pay for the few friends that remained.

[92] *Eastern Horizon* VII (January-February, 1968), 69.
[93] *Ibid.* VI (May, 1967), 72.
[94] *Ta Kung Pao*, December 26, 1968; *SCMP*, December 30, 1968. *NCNA*, Peking, February 28, 1969; *SCMP*, March 6, 1969.
[95] *China Notes* VII (Summer, 1969), 37.

IX

Buddhism: Altered, Utilized, and Buried

MONKS AND NUNS DISPERSED—AN ASSOCIATION LAUNCHED

Although a number of outstanding Chinese Buddhist leaders made considerable progress in their efforts to reform Buddhist life, thought, and organization in the first part of this century, Buddhism was in very poor condition as the advent of communism drew near. Many temples and monasteries were in need of major repair; some had been confiscated or had reverted to local ownership. Twentieth-century intellectuals regarded the common practices of Buddhism with disdain, even though they might enjoy a stimulating discussion of Buddhist philosophy. It was common talk that the monks were poorly trained, without discipline, and interested only in performing Masses for the dead and other rites so as to get enough money to keep body and soul together. Such was the generally accepted picture, despite remarkable exceptions.[1] Each monastery and temple was autonomous; there was no central organization around which resistance might be focused.

In view of this generally uninspiring background one cannot but be impressed by the character of Buddhist activity in 1949. The Buddhist Youth Association of Shanghai held its third annual convention on February 20 of that year; the proceedings were broadcast by a local radio station. The theme was "the greater good of the neighbor," which led to consideration of "works beneficial to so-

---

[1] Hu Chang-tu, *China: Its People*, p. 121.

297

ciety," as well as the "restoration of right morals in men's hearts." [2]

The Buddhist Benevolent Association in Shanghai was engaged in significant relief and welfare work; there was word of repair and refurbishing of monasteries and temples in various parts of the country (contradicting what was said above). The following advertisement was placed in the Shanghai *Ta Kung Pao*: "When calamities, sufferings and misfortune come, . . . have confidence in Buddha, adore Buddha, and pray to him. He can alleviate your sorrows." An editorial in the Shanghai *Shen Pao* made the point that the Buddhist precept against taking life applied to killing on the battlefield as well as to the slaughter of animals. The editorial advocated acts of compassion toward the suffering and Masses for the dead, including the war dead, in order to assist them "in crossing the infernal river." All of this would be a Buddhist contribution to peace.[3]

Out in Kunming, on the occasion of a visit by the Grand Lama of Kung Ko, Tibet, in late 1948, eight Buddhist groups asked the visiting dignitary to reestablish a "Buddhist Society for Averting the Calamaties Afflicting the Country." A preparatory committee was appointed and plans were made, but there is no record of any significant results.[4]

From Lhasa the twelve-year-old Dalai Lama proclaimed a "religious war against communism." More than one hundred "living Buddhas" serving under him had consulted their horoscopes and had read the warning that Tibet's isolation would be violated by unbelievers, so the Dalai Lama called on them to pray for deliverance. In the meantime, with great pomp and ceremony, the tenth Panchen Lama was installed in Sining, capital of Tsinghai, under sponsorship by the Chinese government but opposed by Tibetan religious authorities in Lhasa.[5]

Whereas it has been noted that the new Communist government moved slowly in dealing with Catholics, Protestants, and Muslims, whether because policies had not yet been defined or because the

[2] *CMBA* II (April, 1949), 426-27.
[3] *Ibid.*, pp. 427, 432-35.
[4] *Chung-yang Jih-pao*, December 21, 1948; *CMBA* II (May, 1949), 553.
[5] *South China Morning Post*, August 12, 1949; *CMBA* I (II) (October, 1949), 168-69.

new government's position had not been firmly secured, there was no such hesitation in dealing with Buddhists. By February, 1950, one could read an extensive account of the changes which already had taken place in Buddhist temples and monasteries in Shanghai. The author Alfred Kiang was particularly interested in the change in the monks from parasites to workers in the new society.[6] One sign of liberation was that five hundred of the two thousand monks and nuns in Shanghai's three hundred temples left those establishments and went back to their home places to labor, or to join the South Expedition Corps, or the East China Military and Political Academy. Those who remained went under the tutelage of the newly organized (January 20, 1950) "Association of Shanghai Buddhist Youth," which had as its purpose "to unite all the progressive elements among the Buddhist monks to study the New Democracy and to become useful members of society." It was the younger monks who went into this study program; the older monks still tried "to cling to the idea of getting easy money from the Buddhist Mass services performed for clients," even though "business was poor." Mr. Kiang's contrast of the older and younger monks undoubtedly suggests a growing cleavage between them.

The monks were directed to all kinds of new enterprises: they set up vegetarian mess halls at eighteen temples in the city and small factories for knitting hosiery at ten others. At the Bubbling Well Temple two study groups on the new ideas replaced a school formerly devoted exclusively to Buddhist teaching. Monks from two other temples started a farm outside the city, while another temple was set up for preparing oats for market. Nuns specialized in sewing classes, the knitting of hosiery, and the making of cotton quilted shoes.

Kiang quotes one young monk, Shao Chung, as saying:

Buddhism does not mean turning away from the people or creating a superman living in a nonexistent world of escapism. The ultimate goal of the great Sakyamuni's untiring effort during his lifetime was the emancipation of the whole of mankind.[7]

And there was another young monk, named Tao Yuan, who reinter-

[6] "A New Life Begins in the Temples," *China Weekly Review*, February 11, 1950, pp. 173-74.
[7] *Ibid.* Yves Raguin, "Nouvelle attitude des jeunes Bouddhistes," *CMBA* II (III) (December, 1950), 996-98, tells of a focus on action among the young

preted the old saying—"To ferry across all the living souls"—to mean "actively serving the people with a view to bringing about a cosmopolitan world." Tao Yuan was the chairman of a Committee for Production and Austerity.

A brief article in a Communist paper tells of how a Buddhist nunnery was infiltrated. No one ever paid any attention to these nuns in their solitude until cadres from the Canton Women's Democratic Federation came in to give the nuns "a helping hand." The older nuns tried to keep the younger ones away, but the patient cadres finally succeeded

in revealing to the nuns the true meaning of life and liberation. Many nuns were awakened as if from a long dream, and since then have taken part in study classes and groups sponsored by the Women's Democratic Federation. They now attend political classes, hear reports from cadres, and hold group meetings to voice their tragic experiences. Their eyes have been opened. Some of them have already renounced their vows of nunhood and returned to the laity, going into factories as workers.[8]

Others asked for training, many took part in Oppose America–Aid Korea parades, some helped in exposing counterrevolutionaries. The author carefully stated that there was freedom of religion, that "nuns in Canton are free to chant liturgies, tell beads, desist from taking meat, and otherwise practice Buddhism. Their life and belief are never interfered with." It is simply that "the emancipation of women is having its effect on them." Nuns in a small nunnery in Kiangsu were reported in a Tientsin newspaper to have "cast away their shackles and started a new life. Some of them married; others turned to productive work. Only one old nun now remains looking after the deserted nunnery." [9]

It must be questioned, however, whether monks and nuns were free to "otherwise practice Buddhism." The former Religious Affairs Bureau official, who was quoted in connection with the treatment of Christianity, said that the freedom not to believe and the

---

Buddhists of Shanghai, who in the new order felt the struggle against three evil powers—a feudal spirit, imperialism, and superstition—was the "revolutionary spirit" of Buddhism.

[8] Sun Yu, "Nuns in Study Movement," *Ta Kung Pao*, August 8, 1951; *CMBA* III (IV) (November, 1951), 782.

[9] Tientsin *Ta Kung Pao*, May 31, 1951; quoted in William Hsu, *Buddhism in China* (Hong Kong: Dragonfly Books, 1964), p. 2.

freedom to be against religion meant that religious activities had to be confined to a designated place of worship. Consequently, "Buddhists could not 'liberate living creatures' out of doors, and Buddhist or Taoist priests could not be engaged to conduct a ritual for the dead in a private home." [10] This former official tells the story of a Buddhist abbott who married twice, the second wife being a nun who became an interesting example of the working wife. She was allowed to let her hair grow, but continued to wear a nun's habit as she performed her daily tasks at the nunnery and as secretary of the Kuangchow Buddhist Association. Each evening she changed to the clothes of the common people and returned home to her household tasks. The official implies that such cases were typical: strict discipline was neglected, monks and nuns let their hair grow, ate meat, and got married.

There are, of course, no reliable statistics on how many monks and nuns actually left the order or quietly relaxed their discipline. Figures running into several hundred thousand are undoubtedly exaggerations, but so are the figures given to André Migot, who was told that the number of monks in a monastery had increased from 1,000 when he had visited it in 1947, to 3,500 when he was there in 1957.[11] Such an increase is rather strange since Chinese Buddhist

[10] Statement in quotation is from *China Notes* I [actually II] (September, 1963), 4. Material about monks and nuns is from unpublished sections of manuscript.

[11] Chan Wing-tsit, *Religious Trends in Modern China* (New York: Columbia University Press, 1953), p. 90-91, cites what he calls a "gross exaggeration" in the following figures from Hong Kong and New York Chinese newspapers: "Four hundred thousand out of a total of seven hundred thousand monks and nuns have been forced by the government to return to lay life, and two hundred thousand younger monks have been drafted to 'fight for the New Democracy.' "

Ernst Benz, *Buddhism or Communism: Which Holds the Future of Asia?* (Garden City: Doubleday and Co., 1965), p. 178, quotes the Japanese Buddhist magazine *Young East* which had reported Chinese, presumably Nationalist, figures that only 2,500 monks and nuns remained alive in Communist China and all but one hundred temples had been destroyed. The remark by Migot is from his article "Le Bouddhisme en Chine," in *Presence du Bouddhisme* (Saigon: France-Asie, 1959), p. 712, with which we may contrast the Catholic report that in Anhwei province in 1950 Catholic priests were still tolerated but that Buddhist monks had been "greatly molested, expelled from monasteries and put to work." *CMBA* II (III) (March, 1950), 303. It is rather unfortunate that Trevor Ling, *Buddha, Marx, and God* (New York: St. Martin's Press, 1966), p. 109, should conclude on the basis of Migot's figures that the Buddhist community has been "strengthened" and "may even have benefitted from the change and experienced something of a revival."

leaders and various reporters all acknowledge that the number of monks has decreased radically and make no claims for the type of increase that Migot cites. One possible explanation may be that there was a return to the monasteries in certain places during the Hundred Flowers Period when pressures were relaxed and when foreign visitors like Migot made their way into China in comparatively larger numbers.

Levenson's judgment that "the monastic life . . . has been laid in ruins" is more likely to be accurate.

The ban was the Communist Party's, denouncing monks as parasites who should be turned out to work, not left to exploit the land and live on others. But the voice of rationalization was the Buddhist Association's, which approved the attack on monasticism—as a vindication of the Buddhist ideal of mercy.[12]

The confiscation of lands belonging to Buddhist temples and monasteries was a serious blow. Many were converted for other uses. The San Mei Temple in Shanghai was converted to a military barracks, Chungking's Chu Ling Temple and Sang Kuo Temple to army hospitals for wounded Chinese soldiers from Korea, and the back portion of the Pao Ling Temple in Ta Leong, Kwangtung province, into a prison.[13] In all fairness it should be noted that Buddhist temples have been used for such purposes many times in Chinese history, especially for the quartering of soldiers. The new element was the consistency with which Buddhist properties were converted all over the country, in contrast to the use of several temples in a particular area during the period that the area might have been occupied by an army.

Buddhist properties, especially landholdings, were largely broken up through the Land Reform Law of 1950. Land was confiscated from the monasteries (the abbotts of monasteries were classed as landlords) and redistributed to the people, which could mean that monks and nuns might also qualify for a small plot of land just as an ordinary farmer would. For example, the monks in

[12] Joseph R. Levenson, "The Communist Attitude toward Religion," ed. Werner Klatt, *The China Model* (Hong Kong: Hong Kong University Press, 1965), p. 26.

[13] Yang I-fan, *Buddhism in China* (Hong Kong: Union Press, 1956), pp. 60-61.

a particular monastery, greatly reduced in number during the first year of the new regime, each received a *mou* (about a sixth of a U. S. acre). Some chose to cultivate that small plot alone; most of them who continued in the monasteries formed mutual aid teams in 1954, were drawn into cooperatives in 1956, and into communes in 1958.[14] Very few monks had previously worked in the fields; in one group of 103 monks only one had any agricultural experience.

In spite of the confusion and disarray brought about by the return of monks and nuns to lay life and by the loss of property, there were a few encouraging aspects to the new situation. Much was made of the fact that two Buddhists were in the first session of the Chinese People's Political Consultative Conference and at succeeding sessions. Chao P'u-ch'u, Secretary-general of the Chinese Buddhist Association, claimed that Buddhist monks and laymen helped in the framing of Article 88 of the constitution providing for freedom of religious belief.[15]

The Chinese Buddhist Association was organized in the course of a meeting which lasted from May 19 to June 3, 1953. The first ten days were preparatory in nature, beginning with a celebration of the Buddha's birthday and consisting largely of the discussion of questions such as:

the improvement of the cultural and religious education of the monks; the provision of special training for those with talent for preaching and spreading the Buddhist doctrine; the imparting of the Vinaya Rules to disciples; the preservation and study of Buddhist antiquities and the translation of Buddhist classics. We also discussed how to help the People's Government get rid of charlatans who practice exorcism, sorcery, and other harmful superstitions under the guise of religion.[16]

It is noteworthy that the Dharma Master who wrote this summary placed distinctly Buddhist matters first and cooperation with the government second, even though the training and discipline of the

[14] This information is from Holmes Welch, "Buddhism Under the Communists," *The China Quarterly*, 6 (April-June, 1961), 2. As an example of the reduction of numbers in temples, Welch says that in one monastery the number dropped from 800 to 200.

[15] "New Ties Among Buddhists," *China Reconstructs*, V (April, 1956), 14.

[16] Chü Tsan, "A Buddhist Monk's Life," *China Reconstructs* III (January-February, 1954), 42-44.

monks and the preservation of Buddhist sacred objects were activities through which the government "aided," "protected," and eventually controlled Buddhism.

The stated objectives of the association were

1. To unite the Buddhists of China so that they might participate under the leadership of the People's Government in the movement to love the fatherland and defend peace;

2. to help the People's Government thoroughly carry out the policy of freedom of religious belief;

3. to link up with Buddhists in various places in order to develop the excellent traditions of Buddhism.[17]

The above points were amplified and made more than concrete when Chang Kuo-hua, deputy secretary of the Party's Tibetan Work Committee, said in 1957 that the Tibetan Buddhist Association was "duty-bound to transmit regularly and propagate to the Buddhists, the policies, laws, and decrees of the Party and the government," and to organize the various study courses and patriotic campaigns. The association was also to report to the Dalai Lama and Panchen Erdeni, as well as various authoritative committees, "on the proper opinions and lawful demands of the broad masses of the monks," so the authorities could better understand and promote Buddhism in Tibet.[18] The Chinese Buddhist Association and its various branches were in a most strategic position.

The top-heaviness of the organizational structure was astounding, even though most of the officers were figureheads. Of the four honorary presidents, two were young men, the Dalai Lama and Panchen Erdeni from Tibet, and two were far to the other end of the age scale, the Venerable Chagangogun, Grand Lama of Inner Mongolia, and the 117-year-old patriarch of the Ch'an school, the Venerable Hsu-yun. The first president, the Venerable Yuan Ying,

[17] *NCNA*, Peking, June 8, 1963. Quoted by Welch, "Buddhism Under," p. 5, where one may also note the association resolved "to continue distinguishing friend from foe in thought and action, to eliminate the spies and special agents sent by the imperialists and Chiang Kai-shek's bandit clique, and to eliminate the reactionary secret society elements that try to take cover under the cloak of Buddhism."

[18] *Tibet 1950-1967* (Hong Kong: Union Research Institute, 1968), p. 240. A valuable collection of documents.

was also advanced in years and died four months later. According to Chao P'u-ch'u, there were 11 vice-presidents, a Standing Committee of 48 members, and a Board of Directors of 220.[19] The real power rested in the hands of Chao P'u-ch'u, who was chosen secretary-general, and, to a lesser degree, Shirob Jaltso (sometimes written Hsijaochiatso), one of the original vice-presidents chosen to succeed Yuan Ying.

The Buddhist Association claimed to represent 500,000 monks and 100 million lay followers.[20] This figure for monks was the same in 1960 as in 1950, in spite of large numbers who withdrew or were expelled. The number of monks is difficult to determine; the number of laymen is impossible to even estimate. The extent to which the association represented any of them is also a matter of conjecture.

Chao P'u-ch'u, a businessman who served with the International Red Cross before 1949 and afterward in various posts with the Communist government, said in retrospect that there were four areas of work for the association in its first three years. The first was the perennial "to assist the government in carrying out the policy guaranteeing freedom of religious faith." The second was the education of Buddhists, with special reference to the Buddhist Academy, established in 1956. The third area, promotion of Buddhist cultural work, included the repair and renovation of sacred sites and buildings, publication of Buddhist texts and other materials, and the publication of the magazine *Modern Buddhism*. As a fourth type of activity, Chao listed the one in which he himself played such a prominent role, the development of "Buddhist international intercourse," and mentioned practically every visit made by Chinese Buddhists abroad and every foreign Buddhist entertained in China before 1957.[21]

Holmes Welch maintains that "the Chinese Buddhist Association has been used primarily as an instrument for remolding Buddhism

[19] Chao P'u-ch'u, *Buddhism in China* (Peking: Chinese Buddhist Association, 1957), p. 40. Welch, who uses the terms "chairman" and "vicechairman," instead of "president" and "vice-president," gives different figures: seven vice-chairmen, eighteen for the Standing Committee, and ninety-three for the Board of Directors.

[20] Kenneth K. S. Ch'en, *Buddhism in China: A Historical Survey* (Princeton: Princeton University Press, 1964), pp. 464-65.

[21] Chao, *Buddhism in China*, pp. 41-52.

to suit the needs of the government," [22] which is another way of saying what Chao suggested implicitly in his first two areas of Buddhist work. One of the instances of "remolding" is what Welch calls the "socialization of monasteries," which has been discussed in another connection. The other areas he has in mind are "limiting religious activities, revising Buddhist doctrine, purging anti-Party elements and mobilizing Buddhists to participate in national campaigns."

Having condemned "the superstitious belief in spirits and the heterodox belief in or practice of divination and healing," the association went on to condemn and discourage burning paper money, the celebration of festivals, sacrifice to gods and spirits, and accepting money for conducting ceremonies (regarded as "cheating the masses"). The reasons given are the great expenditure of money and the loss of time from production.[23] The Tientsin *Ta Kung Pao,* for example, carried an article by Chü Tsan, an officer of the Buddhist Association, in which the view was expressed that "religious ceremonies hinder production and hold up the execution of governmental orders." Therefore, to allow them "might stiffen this backward attitude in the religious world and increase the separation of religious believers from the masses." [24]

Protection from "bad people" is another area which the association stressed. One aspect was to prevent monks from "indiscriminate recruitment of disciples," thus impeding the recruitment of younger monks and limiting the opportunities of an older, "unreformed," monk to spread the teaching which might not be correct according to current Communist standards. Another phase of protecting Buddhism from "bad people" was requiring a pledge from heads of monasteries not to provide hospitality for traveling monks. Chinese Buddhist monks have long had the practice of going on a kind of pilgrimage from monastery to monastery at various times and seasons, at each place receiving hospitality for a few days. But, as Welch says,

such monks are evidently objectionable to the government, both because they are parasites, not engaged in production, and because they accept

[22] Welch, "Buddhism Under," p. 7.
[23] *Ibid.,* pp. 7-8.
[24] Quoted in *CNA,* July 23, 1954.

306

alms from devout believers. They are also independent individuals who, like fortune tellers, disturb the atmosphere of regimentation.[25]

It is also possible that someone from that motley collection of "landlords, counterrevolutionaries, persons under surveillance, members of heterodox Taoist sects or societies, and all those who are anti-Socialist," might masquerade as a traveling monk, or even ask to be a disciple of a senior monk.

BRINGING TIBET UNDER
EXPANDING COMMUNIST "PROTECTION"

A most important segment of the Buddhist community in China is to be found in Tibet. Since the Tibetans are one of the non-Han minority nationalities, the way of handling Tibetan Buddhism or Lamaism bears certain similarities to the way in which Islam was handled. But, whereas the strength of Islam is to be found in ethnic minority groups, the strength of Buddhism is among the Han people, compared to which Tibetan Buddhists are a small minority. The high proportion of Tibetan honorary leaders among the officers of the Chinese Buddhist Association bears no relation to the actual size of the Tibetan Buddhist community.

When Chinese Communist armies marched on Tibet in 1950, Tibetan leaders, with some support from India, tried to make the case that Tibet should be regarded as an independent country or at least a region with genuine autonomy. The Chinese Communists, like the Nationalists before them, remained adamant that Tibet was a part of China. Tibet appealed to the United Nations, but to no avail. The Dalai Lama fled to Yatung in the Chumbi valley, between Sikkim and Bhutan near the Indian border. A delegation of Tibetans then went to Peking and on May 23, 1951, signed an "Agreement of the Central People's Government and the Local Government of Tibet on Measures for the Peaceful Liberation of Tibet." [26] Tibetan nationality was affirmed, but as one of many nationalities in China, and the preamble added that unspecified imperialist forces had entered Tibet, unopposed by its local govern-

[25] Welch, "Buddhism Under," p. 8.
[26] *Tibet, 1950-1967*, pp. 19-23.

ment which had "adopted an unpatriotic attitude toward the great motherland." Since the People's Liberation Army had achieved a victory, all nationalities would be incorporated on an equal basis in "one big family of fraternity and cooperation." It was further specified that "all nationalities are to have freedom to develop their spoken and written language and to preserve or reform their customs, habits, and religious beliefs," assisted by the Central People's Government. "The policy of freedom of religious belief" would be protected, and "the central authorities will not effect any change in the income of the monasteries."

As provided in the agreement, additional Communist troops marched into Tibet in the fall of 1951 to see that the agreement was followed. In December, the Panchen Lama returned to Lhasa from Tsinghai after having been under Communist "protection" and indoctrination, and the Dalai Lama returned from Yatung. The Dalai received a six-month observation and education tour to Peking, and apparently was impressed. In October, 1952, Mao Tse-tung received a delegation of Tibetans in Peking. The head of the delegation, Leosha Thubmentarpa, made a radio address to Tibetan leaders the following month, in which he reported that Chairman Mao had said the "policy of protecting religion" would be followed, that it was for the Tibetans to decide whether or not land would be divided, that comrades working on military and administrative committees in Tibet had been cautioned to go slowly, and that the central government only wanted to help the Tibetans develop in numbers, economy, and culture.[27]

Actually the pace was rapid and the pressures intense until 1954. Efforts to bring about Land Reform and to control the monasteries, involving attacks on landlords and monks, brought such resistance from the people that efforts were concentrated on road building, establishment of schools, and assignment of large numbers of Han cadres to Tibet. Both the Dalai Lama and the Panchen Lama, often designated Panchen Erdeni, attended the first meeting of the First National People's Congress in 1954. They attended again in 1955, along with Shirob Jaltso, and made speeches which expressed interesting contrasts. The Dalai Lama, whose speeches were models

[27] *Ibid.*, pp. 44-45.

of adroit diplomacy, took pains to say (in March, 1955) that government personnel had "consulted with Tibetan ecclesiastical and lay officials and the Tibetan people on all measures, major or minor," and had implemented these measures "step by step according to local desires." The Dalai Lama also mentioned extensive repairs to monasteries and that "legal protection" had been given to all religious people.[28]

Shirob Jaltso, on the other hand, spoke of the counterrevolutionaries who were "exploiting religion for sabotage purposes." In Tsinghai, for example, "heavenly edicts" were circulating which predicted that the world would soon be destroyed, that people would meet calamities and suffering. This was the work of the devil, he said, "ferocious and bloodthirsty, disguising himself under the cloak of Buddhism." People were thus beguiled into spending their time in chanting prayers, an insult to Buddhism. The masses must be saved from deception, so these saboteurs had to be smashed.

If they are not purged or if they are believed and allowed to influence the people, then freedom of belief will be lost. Only by fully purging these elements can we obtain real freedom of belief.[29]

The same Shirob Jaltso expressed a strikingly different attitude in a report at the third session of the same First National People's Congress on June 2, 1956.[30] Perhaps stimulated by the Hundred Flowers call to bloom and contend, he urged the delegates, and through them the government and its functionaries, to "Pay Attention to Special Characteristics of Minority Nationalities." Officials should (1) go slow in putting to work Tibetan lamas who follow the "Buddhist rule and custom whereby they cannot take part in farm work"; (2) find ways to cover expenses of religious activities, since the organization of former benefactors into cooperatives had severely limited funds; (3) allow cooperatives to sponsor religious activities previously sponsored by groups and not interfere with individually sponsored religious activities; (4) not force those who,

[28] JMJP, March 13, 1955; CURBAC, May 31, 1955, p. 10.
[29] Tibet, 1950-1967, pp. 39-40. In spite of all the time spent on this concept, I must confess that the logic entirely escapes me.
[30] NCNA, June 27, 1956; CURBAC, September 21, 1956, pp. 18-19.

accustomed to private ownership and individual operation, are "unwilling to join the cooperatives at present. They should be given sincere assistance instead of being discriminated against." Shirob Jaltso concludes with a strong appeal for patience with people devoted to local customs who have been so gripped by conservatism that they are reluctant to accept new ways.

Thus the same phenomenon may be observed among Buddhists which has been discerned many times in the context of Protestant Christianity. Those leaders who were won to cooperation with the government found themselves in the position of trying to carry out government directives in the religious community to which they belonged, but also in the position of having to caution the authorities who were oppressive, pushing too fast, and insensitive to local feelings. It is also quite clear that resistance to Communist control was so determined that it could not be ignored.

Shirob Jaltso may have had good reason to talk out of both sides of his mouth. By 1955, and certainly by 1956, more oppressive measures were adopted. Taxes were increased and large estates confiscated and redistributed, following the same pattern of public humiliation and occasional executions as had happened in China proper.

... Attacks on religion became more violent. Lamas were assaulted and humiliated; some were put to death. The ordinary people who refused Chinese orders to give up the practice of religion were beaten and had their goods confiscated. Attacks on their religion, property, and social system inflamed the people to furious resistance....[31]

The people carried on sabotage and guerrilla warfare; the Communist occupation army responded by shelling and bombarding monasteries.

Possibly because of a nudge from Pandit Nehru, whom the Dalai Lama had seen while in India, or possibly because it fit the pressure-relaxation pattern which characterized so much of Communist China's approach to cultural problems, a Preparatory Committee for the Tibetan Autonomous Region was formed in April,

[31] H. E. Richardson, *A Short History of Tibet* (New York: E. P. Dutton, 1962 [English edition entitled *Tibet and Its History*]), p. 201. A clear rapid survey of the period.

1956, with the pledge: "No reform for six years." At the same time the Tibetan Committee for Religious Affairs was established; this committee undoubtedly was responsible for setting up in October of that year a Tibetan branch of the Chinese Buddhist Association, three years after the national association was formed.[32]

In a speech delivered on the first anniversary of the founding of of the Tibetan branch,[33] Chang Kuo-hua, deputy secretary of the Party's Tibetan Work Committee, singled out those who did not want to wait six years to make reforms, and praised them as true patriots who must be supported. A second group wanted to move ahead but they were filled with doubts, due to "imperialist and reactionary rumors," so "we must explain the reasons to them and relieve them of their anxieties." Then there was a group who were using "no reform for six years" as an excuse to delay doing anything. It was Chang's way of saying that the problem was still there and that action was still necessary.

The resistance continued, so much so that Communist officials in Tibet had as much of a "rightist" movement to put down there as in the rest of China in 1958. An intense anti-Buddhist propaganda campaign was in effect, at least by that year, as evidenced by this astounding interpretation of the Buddha Sakyamuni (Gotama) which appeared in the Tibetan newspaper *Karzey Nyinrey Sargyur* (Eastern Tibet) on November 19, 1958, four months before the uprising in Lhasa.

To believe in religion is fruitless. Religion is the instrument of autocratic feudal lords, and religious works have no benefits whatsoever for the people. To explain this we trace the historical background of the origin of Buddhism. The founder of Buddhism was Sakyamuni—son of the King Sudhodana of India. His kingdom was very aggressive among all the Indian kingdoms of his time. It always used to invade the small kingdoms. It was during the reign of Sakyamuni that his subjects revolted against him and later other small kingdoms also rose against him spontaneously. As they attacked Sakyamuni, he accepted defeat but escaped amidst the fighting. Since there was no other way out for him, he wandered into the forests. Having founded Buddhism, he brought about a pessimism and idleness in the minds of the people, weakening their

[32] *Tibet, 1950-1967*, p. 237.
[33] *Ibid.*, pp. 237-39.

311

courage, and thus reached his goal of redomination over them. This fact was clearly recorded in history.[34]

The same interpretation of the Buddha appeared later in a pamphlet circulated by the Chinese, in which lamas or monks were said to be "more ferocious than wild animals." Everyone of them was accused of having violated a woman or of having violated the young monks, an obvious reference to homosexuality. The writer of the pamphlet was supposed to be a Tibetan calling to his people to throw off such "potentates." He said the god he believed in was communism.[35]

Monks objected to indoctrination lessons in Marxism, and Tibetans in general complained about high prices and the influx of Hans. Khamba tribesmen from a neighboring territory continued to carry on guerrilla warfare against Communist Chinese troops. When Communist officials suggested that the Dalai Lama might use his influence to quiet things down, he issued statements which appeared to carry out Communist demands but which between the lines encouraged the people. Finally, he received an order to appear before Communist officials in March of 1959. The Tibetans, fearing that he would be taken prisoner, revolted, during which confusion the Dalai Lama was slipped out of Tibet, arriving in India at the end of March.

The revolt was put down in three days. Communist officials claimed that the Dalai Lama had been kidnapped and was being held in India against his will. The Dalai Lama replied that he and his people "welcome change and progress consistent with the genius of our people and the rich traditions of our country," but insisted that the Chinese had contravened several points in the May, 1951, agreement. He said that a report filed with the International Commission of Jurists was

correct in stating that, until 1958, over 1,000 monasteries were destroyed, countless lamas and monks killed and imprisoned, and the extermination of religion actively attempted. From 1959 onward, a full-scale campaign was attempted in the provinces of U and Tsang for the extermination of religion. We have documentary proof of these actions and also of actions

[34] *CMBA* XII (March, 1960), 275.
[35] *CMBA* XII (May, 1960), 494-95.

against the Buddha himself, who has been named as a reactionary element.[36]

The Communists charged that the statement was a forgery and that the whole affair was "under the direction and instigation of foreign imperialists and Indian expansionists," [37] but few outside the Communist world gave such charges credence.

After the revolt was crushed even more severe repression and recrimination was the order of the day. A refugee monk, who came out to India several years later, said that ancient art objects in the monasteries were confiscated. Those with rare alloys were melted down; clay objects were thrown away. Scriptures were burned, except for those thick manuscripts which could be used as inner soles for shoes. Monks suspected of taking part in the revolt were shot; others sent to unknown destinations and never heard from again—some to work on the railroad between China and Lhasa, many forced to marry. The monk said that only three hundred of the former twenty thousand monks in three big monasteries in Lhasa were retained for visitors to see, and these did manual labor. At Tashi Lhunpo monastery in Shigatse only two hundred out of four thousand remained.[38]

After the uprising, the monk said, a Chinese officer told the monks at Tashi Lhunpo that the government of Tibet had been destroyed because that government had said they were going to destroy Tashi Lhunpo, which the Chinese had prevented their doing many times. The officer promised that no changes would be made, but at the end of December, 1960, the monastery was surrounded by soldiers who arrested many monks and accused them of complicity in the revolt and of secretly supporting the Tibetan government, the latter a crime supposedly worse than open revolt. In

[36] *Tibet, 1950-1967*, pp. 375-78; see also *CMBA* XII (March, 1960), 275.
[37] Shirob Jaltso in *Modern Buddhism*, October 30, 1959; *URS*, December 29, 1959, p. 392. In "For the Unity of Our Country," *China Reconstructs* VIII (June, 1599), 2-5, Shirob Jaltso said of the Dalai Lama's statement, "the style is not at all Tibetan" and the content differed from previous statements." It is quite true that the content differed; while under Communist supervision the Dalai Lama's statements were marvels which seemed to support the authorities but actually gave only routine deference.
[38] The story was released by *Tibetan News Agency*, release no. 10, London, March 30, 1965, distributed by *Free Central European News Agency*, reprinted in *RCDA*, May 31, 1965, pp. 74-75. I would dismiss the story as an exaggeration were it not corroborated by other reports.

March of the following year, the people of Shigatse were summoned to a meeting at which ten prisoners were brought forth, one of whom, a monk, was shot. The people were warned of the same fate. Seeing no way out, a number of the monks committed suicide.

An appeal to the United Nations resulted in passage, forty-five to nine with twenty-six abstentions, of a resolution which called for respect for human rights. Its only effect was to provide an open forum for presentation of the Tibetan plight.

The International Commission of Jurists in their June 19, 1960, report from Geneva brought out four points related to allegations of genocide against the Chinese Communists:

a. That the Chinese would not permit adherence to and practice of Buddhism in Tibet.

b. That they had systematically set out to eradicate this religious belief in Tibet.

c. That in pursuit of this design they had killed religious figures because their religious belief and practice were encouragement and example to others.

d. That they had forcibly transferred large numbers of Tibetan children to a Chinese materialistic environment in order to prevent them from having a religious upbringing.[39]

Such statements raised questions concerning Communist China in the minds of world leaders who had been impressed by China's openness from 1955 to 1957 and had been wooed by China's diplomatic efforts during the same period. But Communist control on Tibet was not affected, and, with the exception of sporadic guerrilla warfare, became increasingly secure.

SMOOTH DIPLOMACY ABROAD—RENEWED SUPPRESSION AT HOME

The People's Republic achieved notable success in using Buddhism for diplomatic purposes during the mid 50's. A Chinese delegation went to Burma in April, 1955, in response to an invitation from Premier U Nu. Chou En-lai invited Burmese Buddhists to

[39] *CMBA* XII (November, 1960), 978.

reciprocate, which they did in September of that year when they were allowed to take back a tooth of the Buddha for Burmese Buddhists to worship. The tooth was later loaned to Ceylon for the same purpose and carried to that place in a Chinese government plane. When it was returned by the Ceylonese, it was housed in a new temple in the Western Hills of Peking, built with government funds.[40]

Buddhist-centered relations with Japan did not fare so well. On November 5, 1955, Chao P'u-ch'u asked Japanese Buddhists for the skull of a famous Chinese monk, Hsuan Chuang. The skull had been taken to Japan in World War II. Chao made it very clear that any attempt to remove it to "another place" would meet with failure. He sent a second appeal on November 19, saying the Chinese had no objection if the Japanese retained the relic, but that sending it to Taiwan (the "other place") "is absolutely intolerable to us." On November 25, the skull was transferred to Taiwan. There was an official protest from Peking, then all press comment ceased.[41]

Chao P'u-ch'u attended a conference in India, in March, 1956, at the invitation of the Indian state of Bihar. A delegation headed by the Dalai Lama and Panchen Erdeni was invited by the Indian government to participate in a symposium on "Buddhism's Contribution to Art, Letters, and Philosophy" in November, 1956, commemorating the 2,500th anniversary of the Buddha's Nirvana. Chinese Buddhists also took part in similar commemorative ceremonies in Nepal and Cambodia. The fourth conference of the World Fellowship of Buddhists was held in Katmandu (Nepal), in which Chao P'u-ch'u and others took part. Chao then visited Ceylon where, on behalf of Chou En-lai, he presented a wooden Buddha image to Ceylon's Minister of Cultural Affairs. The Chinese Buddhist Association also presented a relic bone of Hsuan Tsang and a set of his works to the Nalanda Institute, where the famous Chinese monk had studied on his pilgrimage to India in the seventh century.[42]

One must remember that the Sixth World Buddhist Congress

[40] Benz, *Buddhism or Communism*, pp. 201-9, gives an extensive survey of these diplomatic efforts with Buddhist countries from the beginning in 1950.
[41] *CURBAC*, February 17, 1956, p. 14.
[42] Chao chronicles these and other visitations in his booklet, *Buddhism in China*, pp. 46-52.

(*not* to be confused with the fourth meeting of the World Fellowship of Buddhists) was held in Rangoon from 1954 to 1956. Also, 1955 to 1957 was a period when China was most open to the outside world and its emissaries were quite popular in South and Southeast Asia. Prime Minister Nehru of India and Premier Chou En-lai had, for example, in 1954 jointly affirmed the Pancha-sila (Mutual respect for each other's territorial integrity and sovereignty; nonaggression; noninterference in each other's internal affairs; equality and mutual benefit; and peaceful coexistence). The governments of India, Ceylon, Burma, and Indonesia were most friendly to the mainland Chinese government, which took advantage of this situation with remarkable skill, particularly in utilizing past Buddhist traditions and outstanding contemporary Buddhist personalities in its diplomatic efforts. The point was often made, as Chinese Buddhists became rhapsodic over the opportunities for fellowship with other Asian Buddhists, that such contacts were not possible in the colonial era dominated by Western imperialists. Although perhaps not impossible, contacts were at least difficult and the point was well worth making. All in all, these years constituted a golden opportunity to be used to the full. Only on this basis can one explain the phenomenon of doctrinaire Marxists maintaining straight faces in ceremonies honoring a tooth of the Buddha, the kind of relic which under any other circumstances would be labeled the height of superstition.

Many of the visitors to China were impressed by the beautifully repaired Buddhist temples and by the statements affirming religious freedom; but a Western visitor to China, Edgar Faure, was again surprised at the way in which Buddhists answered the question which he had asked followers of just about every religious group in China: Are Marxism and religion compatible? The answer from Buddhists was: no incompatibility. Faure asked at a certain temple if there were any Buddhists who were members of the Communist Party. A layman answered that there were none in that place but there were in the south. A cleric said there were, but they practiced their religion at home—they were not to be seen in the temple.[43]

[43] Faure, *The Serpent*, p. 154.

A Burmese Buddhist, upon reading a reprint of "New Life in Chinese Temples," asked why Chinese Buddhists, if everything was going so well, were not allowed outside. (Actually, a few were allowed to travel.) U Ohn Ghine went on to comment on the Communist charge that Buddhist monks in the past had taken money for prayers and preaching:

From the purely Buddhist viewpoint there is not much to choose between the wearer of the Yellow Robe who takes money for preaching, and the wearer of the Yellow Robe who takes money for making towels. Neither is Buddhist, and the propagandist had no idea of Buddhism and was evidently a pure materialist. . . . I am entitled to wonder whether it is towel-making or Buddhism, or whether it is just another attempt to use Buddhism for political propaganda purposes.[44]

Nonetheless, Chao P'u-ch'u was proud of those Buddhists who had won the awards of "meritorious worker" or "model worker" for their salvage work in flooded areas, in the afforestation movement, and in the prevention of disasters. He issued a striking piece of Buddhist apologetic:

We should also acknowledge that owing to the universal spirit of serving the people and the large-scale growth of our national construction, the Buddhist ideal of "benefitting all sentient beings and glorifying the country" has also obtained opportunities for its realization in many fields, thus strengthening the confidence and courage of Buddhists. . . .

We are living in an environment in which all speech and action which is beneficial to the people is praised and supported, while all speech and action which is not beneficial to the people is criticized and stopped. We have discovered that our teaching of "committing no evil, doing all that is good and purifying the mind" is in harmony with the whole social movement today. We have discovered that we can work together with the people of the whole country with an easy mind, not only according to our duties, but also according to our religious faith, for the sublime task of the peace, happiness, morality, and wisdom of mankind."[45]

The full Chinese Buddhist Association held a second national conference in March, 1957, and amended the constitution to allow

[44] Quoted from the *Burma Star* in *CMBA* VII (February, 1955), 165.
[45] Chao P'u-ch'u, *Buddhism in China*, pp. 38-39.

317

for branches in provinces and major cities. There was no provision for this in the 1953 constitution, according to *Modern Buddhism,* "because a certain confusion still existed among Buddhists in various places, and the level of Buddhist consciousness had to be raised." [46] By 1957, however, there was sufficient confidence on the part of those leading the national association to proceed on the provincial level. It was also the peak of the Hundred Flowers Period when criticism, which might be expected in various Buddhist centers, was supposedly welcome. Some Buddhists obviously were still suspicious, for 52 of the 265 invited delegates did not attend.[47]

A whole series of branches were established. At least in the case of the Shansi branch, established in September, 1957, the inauguration was carried out in the spirit of the antirightist movement which had just begun. Seventy monks, lamas, and nuns received twenty-one days of indoctrination preceding the actual establishment of the Shansi association, at which time they heard the head of the provincial Bureau of Religious Affairs say that the struggle against rightists was "a violent struggle in which the Buddhists must also take part." [48]

A few examples will suffice to show the character of Buddhist discontent voiced during the Hundred Flowers Period and the manner in which those who expressed themselves were criticized and brought into line during the antirightist campaigns. One of the most vocal was Liu Ah-hsiu, a member of the Chinese Buddhist Association and director of propaganda of the Provincial Committee of Szechwan, who was reported to have said that the repair of temples at government expense was merely for the purpose of "suppressing the independence of the Buddhist temples." He went further to say:

The Communist Party is the only true force of oppression that we have known since the Manchu invasion. To aid the Party is to aid this power of oppression. . . . We are far from the freedom of religion that is proclaimed by the constitution and by Communist propaganda.[49]

[46] *Modern Buddhism,* April, 1957; quoted in William Hsu, *Buddhism in China,* p. 34.
[47] *CNA,* 221, March 21, 1958, p. 5.
[48] *Modern Buddhism,* 10, 1957, p. 23; *CNA,* March 21, 1958, p. 7.
[49] *CMBA* X (January, 1958), 5.

Liu's self-examination and confession, as published in *Modern Buddhism*, made no reference to such remarks, but concentrated on his relations with Ch'en Ming-shu (1) to promote the KMT Revolutionary Committee, (2) to manipulate the Chinese Buddhist Association, and, through these two avenues (3) to gain his own personal advantage instead of working for the Party and the people.[50] He asked the people to "punish me," but there is no record of the results.

Ch'en Ming-shu, referred to above, was an old general who claimed that government leaders had picked him to lead the Chinese Buddhist Association as early as 1950. Ch'en, a lay Buddhist of some repute, in that year had published a pamphlet entitled *The New Meaning of Buddhism*, in which he proposed "a new dialectical, materialist Buddhism." He said the monks were "rich exploiters, . . . a caste despised by the world," and that "the temples are nests of gangsters." He also charged that the monks were "backward, miserable, and weak," generally regarded as "weak parasites, not worthy of mercy," and claimed that he had come to Shanghai to train them to do manual work. The monks who claimed that Ch'en had not studied Buddhism had a certain degree of satisfaction in 1957 when Ch'en was purged from government favor because of anti-Communist declarations, and Shanghai's *Wen Hui Pao* said that his words about the monks were "an insult to the Buddhists, to the government, and to the Communist Party." [51]

Chü Tsan, an outstanding monk and a vice-president of the Chinese Buddhist Association, gave the most extensive criticism of Ch'en Ming-shu at a conference called by the Central Committee of the KMT Revolutionary Committee. The main point of the criticism was that Ch'en was an ambitious man who tried to use Buddhism as a cloak to cover his own power grabs. Chü Tsan reported Ch'en's confession of guilt, in stereotyped phrases, and that Ch'en wanted to "repent and start a new life." [52]

[50] *Modern Buddhism*, December, 1957; *CURBAC*, June 15, 1958, pp. 3-4.

[51] Much of this gleaned from an article by the monk Chü Tsan in *Modern Buddhism*, 12, December, 1957, and discussed in *CNA*, March 21, 1958, pp. 5-6. There are quotations from and a short summary of Ch'en Ming-shu's "Buddhist Tasks and Future Outlook" in Yang I-fan, *Buddhism in China*, pp. 47-52.

[52] *Modern Buddhism*, December, 1957; *CURBAC*, June 15, 1958.

The most famous of those attacked as antirightist was the monk Pen Huan, who was arrested at the Nan Hua Temple near Chüchang in the north of Kwangtung province in 1958. What he said, or might have said, is known only through the charges against him; if he actually said half of what was attributed to him, however, he was a most courageous monk. He was said to have announced, during a period of registration in 1954, that there was no religious freedom for Buddhists. He had been given a government allowance, but had spread the story that monks lived in misery. At the time of Land Reform he had said, "One will never forget so much wickedness and so much hatred," and had added that things were better under the Kuomintang when the monks did not have to work. He had charged the Communists with being cruel, and had "frightened the Buddhists by saying that nobody can be a monk who reads the selected works of Mao Tse-tung." He was also charged with other misdemeanors—the usual things like consorting with reactionaries and landlords—and was finally imprisoned and not heard from since.[53]

As a means of implementing the antirightist campaign among Buddhists, a series of regional forums were convened in different parts of the country, followed by local meetings where resolutions were passed, pledges taken, and indoctrination courses set up. Such themes as "Follow the Leadership of the Party," and "Draw the Line Between Enemy and Self," were followed through a process of ideological remolding and labor.[54]

All the heavy-handedness of the antirightist temper was expressed when Ulanfu, chairman of the Inner Mongolia Autonomous Region and first secretary of the Communist Party in that region, made a speech to a forum of lamas in which he told them flatly "No work, no eat." There was no middle ground between socialist and nonsocialist thinking. Taking the socialist path meant joining a cooperative, as the vast majority of lamas had done, or engaging in some other kind of physical labor. The chanting of prayers did not qualify—one could say prayers after the day's work was done.[55]

[53] *Modern Buddhism*, 8, 1958, pp. 30-31; *CNA*, February 19, 1960, pp. 6-7. See also Hong Kong *Wen Hui Pao*, June 13, 1958; *CURBAC*, June 15, 1958. Welch adds additional information in "Buddhism under," p. 9.

[54] Hsu, *Buddhism in China*, p. 35.

[55] *KMJP*, August 14, 1958; *URS*, October 21, 1958, pp. 72-75.

Certain newspapers printed specific details of what lamas in various temples had done, such as planting trees, donating empty rooms for use by factories, and taking part in various construction projects. Most impressive was the pledge taken by the monks of Liaoning to support the Party and government, to walk the socialist path with the people, and to draw a line between themselves and Taoist elements, landlords, and the like. The summing up:

In accordance with our conditions, we, members of the religious circle, shall actively participate in physical labor to temper ourselves, so that we may become laborers both in name and in fact. We shall exert our efforts in agricultural and supplementary pursuits; we shall love our country, religion, labor, and co-op as much as we love our own home.[56]

It is fairly certain that the antirightist campaigns strengthened the hand of the Chinese Buddhist Association as a means of government control. Already at the beginning of the antirightist campaign there is evidence of the association's control over monks and nuns. A French monk claims he was told the following regulation prevailed for anyone who wanted to become a monk or nun and for one's continuing life in monastery or nunnery. Association control is explicit at some points, implicit in others. The claim, at any rate, is that the following prevailed in mid-1957:

1. First there was the formation of the CBA to be the representative organization of Buddhist monks and nuns, and to be the examining body on knowledge and practice of the disciplines. All monks and nuns had to be examined this way. If they could not pass they would be expelled.

2. All monks and nuns had to be registered by the CBA. Anyone whose name was not in CBA registration books was not allowed to wear the special robe (chia sha).

3. The CBA would estabilsh schools, colleges, and universities for training of monks and nuns. Only graduates of these schools could become clergy. Before permission is granted applicants must join a publicly recognized monastery for at least one year of monastic practice.

4. After one year of practice in the monastery one must get the recommendation of ten monks who have had at least a decade of experience as monks. This recommendation is necessary to start the first stage of monkhood.

[56] Modern Buddhism, July 13, 1958; see note 55 for URS data, p. 81.

5. For the next two years the initiate studies under monks with a deep understanding of Buddhism. Then he can be raised one degree, to become an official clergyman (third degree).

6. The position of a third degree clergyman in the past was not awarded to ordinary monks and nuns but only to those of superior intellect, knowledge and moral attitude and character, and who are respected by everyone.[57]

Such regulations would guarantee that only those monks and nuns willing to support the prevailing order would be admitted. The type of criticism which erupted during the Hundred Flowers Period would hardly be possible in the future.

Although the government appeared to win all the battles in the antirightist campaigns, the common people had a way of handling things occasionally. An incident illustrative of the power of the masses occurred in Chunghsiang county of Hupei province and was important enough to be reported in *Jen-min Jih-pao*. It seems that a cadre entered a temple and removed a Buddha image before which many people made their offerings. Such a large crowd gathered in protest before the gates of the county headquarters building the following day that the county government committee agreed that the image should be restored.[58]

Shirob Jaltso's article for *Modern Buddhism*, in 1959, and his speech to the second session of the third Chinese People's Political Consultative Conference in April, 1960, were essentially identical. Everything was settled, including Tibet. For him it was important that Buddhists had been involved in study that had raised their political consciousness. They had left behind the old, negative, pessimistic mentality and were now involved in labor. Monks in particular had given up their former parasitic lives and were at work to support themselves and to build up society. The famous Buddhist mountains still had their attraction, especially because the government had done wonders in restoring these and other Buddhist shrines. Many of the traditional religious activities were still going on: monks preached the dharma, people held vegetarian

[57] Hong Kong *Ta Kung Pao* (a Communist newspaper), July 14, 1957; included in *Sourcebook on Buddhism in Mainland China, 1949-1967* (Hong Kong: Union Research Center, 1968), pp. 153-54.

[58] *JMJP*, May 8, 1957; *CNA*, July 19, 1957, p. 6.

feasts, gave alms, lived in retreat, made pilgrimages—all proof that the freedom of religion was fully maintained.[59] One wonders, in view of all the acts condemned from the early days of the Communist regime—such as burning paper money, festivals, sacrifices—just what meaning the continuing activities had.

STUDY PROMOTED, CULTURE PRESERVED, TEACHING REVISED

When the board of directors of the Chinese Buddhist Association met in Peking, August 16-31, 1955, the main decision was to set up a training center for Buddhist priests. The decision was quickly implemented, for only a year later, on September 28, 1956, the Chinese Buddhist Academy opened in Peking with leaders from all over China and from other countries present. There were 110 students in 1957, some in a two-year course which would qualify them to be a "Buddhist Religious Worker," others in a four-year course leading to the title "Buddhist Scholar and Preacher." Plans were made at that point to later introduce Pali, Sanskrit, and other languages "so as to prepare a better foundation for the promotion of cultural exchange and religious cooperation between China and other countries." [60] There were also plans to open branches in other places for the study of Pali and Tibetan Buddhism, and a branch for nuns as well.

The Buddhist Academy added a research department in September, 1961. The great influence of Buddhism on Chinese philosophy and the need for thoroughly trained research scholars in Buddhism were cited as reasons for establishing the research department, which was subdivided into sections on history and teaching. A reporter found one group of students working on the Pali language "for propagation southward," although better relations with southern Buddhists probably was the meaning intended. He found another group working on Hetuvidya logic, originally a school of logic in India but later quite important in Tibet.[61]

[59] Shirob Jaltso, "Buddhists of the Socialistic New China," *Modern Buddhism*, October 30, 1959; *URS*, December 29, 1959, pp. 390-402; "New Appearance of Buddhism in China," *JMJP*, April 15, 1960; *CURBAC*, July 18, 1960, pp. 26-30.
[60] *NCNA* reports in *CURBAC*, October 5, 1955, p. 28; December 23, 1955, p. 4; *CMBA* VIII (January, 1956), 81; Chao, *Buddhism in China*, pp. 41-42.
[61] *KMJP*, August 28, 1962; *SCMP*, September 24, 1962, pp. 13-15.

A year later a department of Tibetan Buddhism was inaugurated at the Buddhist Academy. In a ceremony held at Yung Ho Kung, largest lamaist temple in Peking, Shirob Jaltso said that "the new term and the inauguration of the new department at the institute show the prosperity of Chinese Buddhism." [62]

Chao P'u-ch'u, in his report to the February, 1962, conference of the Buddhist Association, said that two hundred students had graduated since 1958 from the Buddhist Academy in Peking. The academy's aim was "to bring up Buddhist intellectuals possessing a certain degree of Buddhist knowledge who are willing to take the socialist path," which task had been facilitated by the establishment of the research department. [63]

Chao also referred in the same report to the San Shih Buddhist Institute in Peking which compiled three books: *Outline of Buddhist History in Asian Countries*, *Historical Material on Buddhist Relations Between China and the Asian Countries*, and *Historical Material on Economics in Chinese Buddhism*. The institute had translated four books into English and three into Chinese, published a Chinese-Tibetan Buddhist dictionary, and had a Sanskrit-Chinese and Pali-Chinese dictionary in preparation. The Nanking branch of the Chinese Buddhist Association prepared articles for an *Encyclopedia of Buddhism* published in Ceylon, the first volume of which was presented by Madame Bandaranaike to Chou En-lai.

Chao praised as well the socialist study movement (which might be better classed as political indoctrination), saying that from January to May, 1958, more than 1,100 Buddhists (Han specifically, not from minority groups), in Peking, Shanghai, Wuhan, Sian, and Chengtu learned that the "whole country must take the socialist path resolutely and unswervingly under the leadership of the Communist Party," and then passed the word along to other groups. There were those, however, who did not go along:

There are still some problems in our midst. For instance, some Buddhists still lack a clear understanding of the development of the situation; some are still unable to unite properly the individual and the collective interests, the immediate and the long-term interests; some still have doubts

[62] *NCNA*, Peking, September 25, 1962; *SCMP*, October 1, 1962, p. 16.
[63] *Modern Buddhism*, May 15, 1962; *CNA*, August 17, 1962, p. 6.

about the religious policy; and a very small number of them are doing illegal things in violation of social order.[64]

It is quite significant that Chao P'u-ch'u, in this context of Buddhist studies, also praised the way in which monks had devoted themselves to agricultural production, with the result that many had been elected to groups called model or advanced workers. He commended further those who had worked in industrial, public educational, and sanitation enterprises.

By contrast, a Tibetan Buddhist research class in Lhasa was publicized in the press because lamas who had previously had to work in the monastery or on corvee labor were now free from labor to study and attain a coveted degree. Thus, study involves labor in one place, frees one from labor in another. The Tibetan class was formed in 1961 and reportedly enrolled 140 lamas in 1962, some of whom were studying for the degree of "Geshe" (something like Doctor of Literature and Philosophy), which had been instituted by the famous Tsongkhapa. Others apparently had the degree already. One young lama said that he had long wanted to study for the degree but had no social position or money and had to work in the monastery instead of studying the scriptures.[65] Several stories like the following are cited:

Twenty-one years ago, Tselho Tarchen came to Lhasa from Kangting, some two thousand kilometers away, to work in Sera Monastery in the hope of becoming a Geshe. But heavy corvee labor made it quite impossible for him to study.

He was admitted to a research course in 1961 and has now finished four of the five volumes of essential scriptures of the Yellow Sect. He is preparing himself for the Geshe examinations next year.

The living expenses of the lamas studying in these research courses are covered by the state, with a monthly issue of Tzampa (barley meal), butter, and other necessities.[66]

In a broadcast from Peking in September, 1965, it was claimed that in a period of five years thirty-three lamas had qualified for the Geshe degree and eleven sent to the Chinese Buddhist Academy in Peking. It was noted that "seventeen research courses in Buddhist

[64] *Ibid.*, p. 7.
[65] *NCNA*, Lhasa, November 20, 1962; *SCMP*, November 26, 1962, p. 17.
[66] *NCNA*, Lhasa, November 23, 1964; *SCMP*, November 27, 1964, p. 19.

theology had been set up in the big monasteries," enrolling two thousand lamas.[67]

The preservation of various expressions of Buddhist culture at state expense was highly touted as a sign of the government's benevolence toward Buddhism. Welch said in 1961 that "at least twenty sets of buildings and five caves, all of outstanding historical or artistic importance" had been repaired since such repairs were called for in a Party directive in June, 1950.[68] A new pagoda outside Peking was also constructed at government expense, a thirteen-story affair to house the Buddha tooth relic. Shirob Jaltso, at the time acting chairman of the Chinese Buddhist Association, made a public statement thanking the government for the repairs made to Yung Ho Kung, the large lamasery in Peking.[69]

The government's handling of Buddhist buildings was not all benevolence, however, at least not toward Buddhism. William Hsu lists several examples of the destruction of famous Buddhist structures, recounted in the *New China Monthly:*

The Hua Pagoda of Kwong-wei Temple, Chengting, Hopei province, was demolished; this was a structure of the Chin Dynasty (A.D. 265–316) which occupied an important place in China's ancient architecture. The Three-Ministers' Hall of Kwong-chi Temple, Paotin, Hopei, which was built in the year A.D. 1205 was demolished and its timber used to build a bridge. Hai-wei Hall of Hsia-yen Temple, Taitung, Charhar province, which was built during the Liao Dynasty (13th century A.D.) was torn down by the local authorities. The timber was used to build a house and the colored tiles taken down piece by piece to make dustpans.[70]

The justification for such destruction was undoubtedly to make various materials available to the people.

Just before the Buddha tooth was enshrined in the new pagoda, a beautifully illustrated pamphlet was published by the Buddhist

[67] Reported in *RCDA*, October 31, 1965, p. 140.
[68] Welch, "Buddhism under," p. 10.
[69] *NCNA*, Peking, September 29, 1954; *CMBA* VI (December, 1954), 992. As a further example, Shirob Jaltso in a 1959 article on "Buddhism in Socialist China" said that up until 1958 the government had appropriated 477,740 *yuan* from Shansi province to restore Buddhist statues and buildings, and that a further 100,000 *yuan* was appropriated in 1959 for repairing and building monasteries and temples. At that time one *yuan* was equal to 42.6 U.S. cents.
[70] Hsu, *Buddhism in China*, p. 49. Benz, again quoting Nationalist figures, said only one hundred temples had survived.

Association. Entitled *The Buddha's Tooth Relic in China*, it contained a hymn to the relic written by Shirob Jaltso, which hymn for the most part expresses Buddhist ideas. One verse, however, has a direct contemporary reference:

> In spite of the malicious attempts made by devils and foes
> To perpetrate every kind of vandalism,
> The light of the Relic has never been extinguished,
> And now in China it shines again in radiant splendor.[71]

A beautiful collection of photographs of Buddhist works of art, many presumably restored by the Communist government, was published in Peking and sold in Hong Kong at a very reasonable price. In a brief introduction to the collection it was observed that the Nationalists had done all in their power to destroy Chinese culture, but that the People's Republic and the Communist Party had stepped into the breach and saved these cultural treasures of Buddhism.

The "saving Buddhist culture" aspect of the Communist government's "protection of Buddhism" had its problems. In trying to collect folk songs in Yunnan, for example, it was discovered that many of the songs ridiculed Buddhist monks, which was all right since this revealed the "unconscious opposition" to Buddhism on the part of Buddhist believers. On the other hand, when those who were recording folk songs went to a temple to observe a religious dance, they were told that spirits would appear during the dance, so three pigs and three hundred chickens had to be sacrificed for them. The monks would get half after it was over, so the collectors were rather disturbed that people were taking advantage of the situation in order "to propagate superstition and to get something." [72]

Drama groups in Kwangtung and Kansu were criticized for putting on plays in which monks appeared or which were based on Buddhist stories. Plays should be more realistic, the critics said, rather than spreading "terror, lust, and antirevolutionary sentiments in the weak-minded masses." [73]

[71] (Peking: Chinese Buddhist Association, 1961), p. 2.
[72] *Folklore Literature*, November, 1959; related in *CNA*, December 16, 1960, pp. 4-5.
[73] *Theater Journal*, related in *CNA*, November 14, 1958, p. 7.

On the other hand, there is a little classic of this genre from *Jen-min Jih-pao* in which one comrade tells another that he has heard of famous pagodas from the tenth century being demolished and the bricks used for constructing roads. The other comrade admits that this is possible since some cadres do not have a very high cultural standard and can hardly be expected to distinguish what is of value and what is not. The first comrade asks, "But is it not the duty of the kanbu [cadre] to implement instructions from above?" (which instructions evidently are to preserve objects of cultural value). The second comrade tosses it off by asking in return "What is the value of culture?" Production and food and building roads are important. "It is no harm to remove some ancient relics and to use some old Buddhas as scrap." But *Jen-min Jih-pao* concludes the article with a defense of old cultural monuments, remembering eight Communist soldiers who risked their lives in Shensi twenty years earlier to save some precious old Buddhist books.[74]

Apparently the refurbished monasteries and temples more than made up for those closed, used for other purposes, or destroyed. A Nepalese monk, Bhikkhu Amritananda, a vice-president of the World Fellowship of Buddhists, told in a booklet about extensive travels in China, of the beautiful monasteries and temples, what he ate in each place, and the people he talked to. All this convinced him that religious freedom existed in China.[75]

At least until the Cultural Revolution of the mid-60's, there was continuous attention to the Buddhist artistic expressions of Chinese culture. I think Joseph R. Levenson's interpretation of the restoration of Buddhist temples and historic sites is correct: "It was historical restoration, an invitation to see it as it was, and to leave it, then, in the past tense." [76] Just as Marxist history reads the story of Buddhism and other religious cults as an alternative to the classic Confucian tradition, and therefore in a sense ennobles such movements, they are nevertheless

stranded in history, put out of their modern misery by being consigned to the past. As a Communist, the Chinese Communist is ready enough to bid

---

[74] *JMJP*, March 17, 1957; *CNA*, March 21, 1958. It must be noted that the story appeared at the peak of the Hundred Flowers Period.

[75] *Buddhism in Socialist Countries* (Peking: New World Press, 1961).

[76] Joseph R. Levenson, "The Communist Attitude," in *The China Model*, p. 25.

farewell to religion. As a Chinese, for the Chinese specimens, he may stretch to hail and farewell, but still, farewell.[77]

We do not have numerous examples of changes in Buddhist thought or doctrine as Buddhist thinkers adjusted to communism, but those available are striking indeed. On a somewhat popular level is an address by Shirob Jaltso in 1959, in which he claimed that before 1949 Buddhists had misinterpreted their doctrine of detachment, thinking that it meant leaving the family to study Buddhism and transcending material existence, which were negative attitudes at best. With the Communist victory came

the great enlightenment . . . that there is no such thing as "transcending matter," that a Buddhist must march in union with the whole population and under the guidance of the Communist Party, in the way of socialism. A Buddhist must throw himself into real life, and must strive to build up a richer and stronger country: that is the future of Buddhism.[78]

This could be accomplished, according to Shirob Jaltso, by thorough indoctrination and monks and nuns engaging in labor, which was probably a matter of course by that time anyway. He added that productive labor did not impede religious faith, that labor is service to people, the best way of practicing virtue, and an aid to monks who want to attain concentration of mind.

Parenthetically we may note that at the organizational meeting of the Chinese Buddhist Association in 1953 some monks attempted "to abolish the rules of ordination and discipline, so that monks could marry, eat meat, and drink spirits as they pleased." [79] This proposal, combined with the deployment of monks in labor projects, would have meant the complete secularization of the clergy according to traditional Buddhist standards, but it was defeated, possibly because the government at that point did not want to stir up opposition among older Buddhists.[80]

Moving from the level of the discipline and role of the monk to a theoretical level, there is an extensive treatment of "A Brief

[77] *Ibid.*, p. 30.
[78] *Modern Buddhism*, 10, 1959, pp. 10-15 and 32-33; *CNA*, February 19, 1960, p. 3.
[79] Ch'en, *Buddhism in China*, pp. 463-64.
[80] In unpublished manuscript of former Religious Affairs Bureau official.

Treatise on Thoughts of the Hua-Yen School," written by Jen Chi-yü in 1961. After a lengthy and scholarly introduction to the history of this school in Chinese Mahayana Buddhism and its primary sutra, the Avatamsaka, Jen says that the aristocracy of the southern and northern dynasties

> needed theoretical pretexts with which to legalize their privileges, . . . to stamp out the people's resistance against the ruling classes, and . . . to propagate slavery and gentle character. . . . The common object of Buddhism was to propagate happiness in the spiritual Buddha realm of lives to come, so the people were told not to concern themselves too much about their sufferings in the present world.[81]

This use of Buddhism to keep the masses in subjection, according to Jen, continued into the T'ang dynasty. Far more serious for him is the Hua-Yen denial of any objective existence to matter, and the assertion that matter was only the "manifestation of mind" and in turn the "contributing cause of mind." The *"dharma-dhatu* [or dharma-realm] of the one reality" is purely spiritual, and therefore unacceptable to a Marxist, as is the catalog of opposites which ignores the relationship of the particular to the general. The result flies in the face of a commonsense, scientific recognition of the objective world which the Communist espouses. Jen then moves from the earlier thought of Fa-Tsang, his interpretation of which has just been summarized, to the T'ang dynasty thinker Tsung Mi, who stressed even more the idealistic nature of Hua-Yen. Tsung Mi even rejected certain materialist strands in previous Chinese thought. Jen also claimed that the ultimate experience of Hua-Yen was an instantaneous thing and ignored the need to reform the world about him, which to him was also unforgiveable.[82]

Jen Chi-yü continued this line of thought in a volume of essays on Buddhist thought in the Han and T'ang dynasties. Although I have not been able to secure a copy, an extensive review was published in *Red Flag* which indicates that the same essential criticisms of Buddhism are made.[83] Both writer and reviewer

[81] *Che-hsüeh Yen-chiu,* 1, 1961, pp. 13-31; *URS,* July 18, 1961, pp. 59-79, quote on p. 64.
[82] *URS,* July 21, 1961, pp. 81-91.
[83] The title of the book is *Han T'ang Chung-kuo Fo-chiao Ssu-hsiang Lun-chi* [A Collection of Works on Chinese Buddhist Thinking in Han and T'ang

insist that the "principles of historical materialism" are the essential key to the analysis of Buddhist or any other type of thought.

One of Communist China's most outstanding historians, Fen Wen-lan, also has written on Buddhism in the T'ang dynasty. An article in *Jen-min Jih-pao* purports to set forth his view of three great evils of Buddhism during that period:

First, innumerable monasteries and temples were established with a view to propagating superstition. . . .

Second, many sects were founded to spread poison . . . [all in favor of the ruling classes].

Third, peasants were benumbed and uprisings obstructed. . . . Buddhism was preached precisely for the purpose of preventing the peasants from rising to oppose oppression.[84]

Professor Kenneth Ch'en, in an article on the attitudes of scholars and intellectuals in Communist China toward Buddhism, says that Jen's treatment of Hua-Yen "is the most important full-length article against Buddhism to appear on the mainland." [85] Ch'en also describes the attitude toward the Ch'an (Zen) school on the part of Chinese scholars, who say that it was used by the Empress Wu Tse-t'ien at the end of the seventh and beginning of the eighth centuries as an aid to elevating a new aristocracy from ranks of commoners. The Ch'an school

did not insist on intellectual efforts and prolonged periods of study of the scriptures, which only the upper classes could afford; it insisted that the Buddha-nature was in every one of us, regardless of station, position, or learning. It was, therefore, egalitarian and progressive.[86]

Later, however, Ch'an "became identified with the ruling class, and

---

Times]. It was reviewed by K'ung Fan in *Hung Ch'i*, August 31, 1964; *SCMP*, October 12, 1964, pp. 28-31.

[84] Originally two chapters in Professor Fan's *Simplified History* scheduled for publication by the People's Publishing House, Peking, but presented as popular article in *Hsin Chien-she* (*New Construction*), October, 1965; *SCMP*, December 16, 1965, pp. 16-17.

[85] Kenneth Ch'en, "Chinese Communist Attitudes Towards Buddhism in Chinese History," *The China Quarterly*, 22 (April-June, 1965), 14-30, quote from p. 19.

[86] *Ibid.*, p. 18.

as supporters of the rulers, it ceased to be egalitarian but became oppressive." Or so the Communist interpreters argue.

Buddhist contributions to Chinese culture are not denied, Ch'en says, perhaps because Buddhist influence on Chinese culture is too well established to be denied. Its influence on neo-Confucian philosophy, on literature and phonology, art and architecture, science, medicine, even on the magic tales which entertained the common people, is acknowledged.[87] One may see an example of this when a writer, Ch'u Chung, points to Buddhist contributions to almost every area of life, carefully crediting Buddhist sculpture with having "expressed the wisdom and toil of our laboring people in ancient times." [88]

One of the lectures given to the Peking Association of Philosophers stressed that Chinese philosophy cannot be understood apart from Buddhist philosophy. The lecturer gave passing deference to his Marxist comrades when he said (as summarized in a secondhand account) that the

study of Buddhism widens our field of knowledge and enables us to understand better historical materialism, for it is an excellent example of a cultural superstructure with a definite relation to the economic foundation in society.[89]

Lu Cheng, in an article comparing Chinese Buddhism with the original Indian schools, notes the difference between the notion in Pali Buddhism of a "pure heart" and "personal deliverance from suffering" apart from the social environment and the idealistic conception of the Buddha nature in later movements.[90]

One must note, however, that Buddhist influence on or contributions to Chinese culture have been in the historic past, which leads to the inevitable conclusion that Buddhism as a contemporary force or influence is impossible. Levenson's phrase—"stranded in history"—is pertinent in this connection, as it was in reference to the preservation of old temples. The lack of contemporary influence

---

[87] *Ibid.*, pp. 23-30.

[88] *KMJP*, June 12, 1962; *CNA*, August 17, 1962, p. 2.

[89] *KMJP*, April 16, 1962, reprinted in *Modern Buddhism*, 2, 1962, p. 43; *CNA*, August 17, 1962, pp. 3-4.

[90] *KMJP*, June 6, 1962; *CNA*, August 17, 1962, pp. 3-4.

or power is illustrated by the fact that there is no record of any reply by Buddhists to criticisms like those of Jen Chi-yü, which can only mean that it is inadvisable to enter into dialogue, that there is no alternative but to accept criticism, confess past and present sins, and thus hope to survive.

Several new trends of thought and practice which are visible in Chinese Buddhism as it adjusted to Communist control are outlined by Holmes Welch.[91] In the first place, all religious practice must be related to the here and now, not isolated from daily life, just as "the highest form of the Bodhisattva conduct is to benefit all living creatures." Secondly, as monks and nuns are to lead a collective life, so all Buddhists should take no thought for the self, for one's own ego, but be involved in socialist construction. For a third point, one may speak with Chao P'u-ch'u of building the Western Paradise on earth: "The first Five-Year Plan is the initial blueprint for the Western Paradise here on earth."

There is even more radical change in the fourth area. The ancient Buddhist ideal of compassion is to be directed only toward "good people":

Not only is it wrong to be compassionate to bad people, but it is also wrong for bad people to be compassionate to anybody at all, because that might make them appear less bad.[92]

The suggestion that landlords should give land and tools to the people was rejected, for this would "blur class consciousness in the class struggle," struggle being the only way to deal with landlords.

It is important to note with Welch that these shifts in Buddhist thinking, from its traditional lack of concern for this-worldly realities to a complete espousal of man's task in society as the true Buddhist way, is the work of "progressives" who wanted to be identified as Buddhists, but were dissatisfied with Buddhism's social and political ideals.

They wanted to change it as much as might be necessary to make it respectable in the world they lived in, even if this meant changing it to

[91] "The Reinterpretation of Chinese Buddhism," *The China Quarterly*, 22 (April-June, 1965), 143-53.
[92] *Ibid.*, p. 149.

the point where it was no longer Buddhism: no matter, they thought, it could still be *called* Buddhism.[93]

The parallel with Protestant Christians like Wu Yao-tsung, at least in motivation, is rather striking.

MAINTAINING APPEARANCES UNTIL THE CATASTROPHE

In the early 60's the Chinese Buddhist Association began to have its problems with the World Fellowship of Buddhists. At the fifth conference of the WFB in Bangkok, in 1958, when there was no delegation from Communist China present, a resolution was passed making Taiwan one of several regional centers of the WFB. Chao P'u-ch'u claimed that the Chinese Buddhist Association was not informed of this action until 1961, when the WFB met in Cambodia, whereupon the delegation from Communist China which was present demanded that the resolution be canceled. The motion failed, according to a Communist account, because of the unscrupulous methods of the imperialists.[94]

The Chinese Buddhist Association was further angered by the transfer of WFB headquarters from Rangoon to Bangkok in 1964. U Chan Htoon, president of the WFB was detained by the Burmese government, so leaders in the WFB decided to transfer the headquarters to Bangkok, and Princess P. Diskul of Thailand was made the acting president. The regional center in Peking lodged a protest, claiming that the General Council had not been consulted, which of course meant that Chao P'u-ch'u, a member of the council, also had not been consulted. There was a sharp edge to the statement:

We have reasons to believe that the demand on the part of Thailand for the removal of the headquarters of the WFB to Bangkok has been inspired by U. S. imperialism. The object is to control this world Buddhist organization more conveniently, so as to make use of it to deceive

[93] *Ibid.*, p. 152.
[94] I have followed the account in the *Far Eastern Economic Review*, March 8, 1962, and in *CNA*, August 17, 1962, p. 5.

the Buddhists and people of Asia, and to serve the U. S. reactionary policy of aggression and enslave the people of different countries.[95]

The protest was ignored, and Chao claimed that he received only an "informal notification" in July of a meeting of the General Council in Bangkok in November, 1964. The seventh conference of the WFB was held in Benares, India, from November 29 to December 4 the same year. The Chinese Buddhist Association objected to the invitation to a delegation from Taiwan ("the Chiang Kai-shek clique") and was incensed that the invitation received in Peking was addressed to the Chinese Buddhist Association in "mainland China." The whole business "all originated with the political plot of U. S. imperialism to create 'two Chinas' or 'one China, one Taiwan.'" The Communist Chinese called on the WFB to withdraw the invitation to Taiwan and convene the General Council to discuss the site, or Peking "absolutely will not send delegates to the conference." The conference went on as planned and the Communist Chinese delegations stayed home.[96]

In spite of these defeats in the World Fellowship of Buddhists, or perhaps because of them, an almost endless stream of Buddhist visitors were invited to China—Japanese, Vietnamese, Cambodians, Laotians, Indonesians, Ceylonese, Pakistanis, Nepalese, Koreans, Thais, and Burmese. They traveled to a few Buddhist sites and talked with leaders of the Buddhist Association, issued statements saying they were convinced that religious freedom prevailed in China, expressed support of world peace, and quite often condemned the U. S. venture in Vietnam. A number of the Japanese Buddhist visitors came in association with peace groups or organizations promoting cultural activities.

A high point in bringing foreign Buddhists to China was the Buddhist Conference of Eleven Asian Countries and Regions, October 17-19, 1963. In addition to the host country, monks and laymen came from Cambodia, Indonesia, Japan, Korea, Laos, Nepal, Pakistan, South Vietnam, Thailand, and the Vietnamese Democratic Republic. The purpose was to focus on the "crimes and atrocities" of the U. S.–Ngo Dinh Diem clique and to express sup-

[95] *NCNA*, Peking, January 8, 1964; *SCMP*, January 13, 1964, p. 35.
[96] *NCNA*, Peking, October 23, 1964; *SCMP*, October 28, 1964, p. 31.

port for the Buddhists of South Vietnam who were suffering under that tyranny.[97]

Conspicuous for their absence were India, Ceylon, and Burma. Although not one of several accounts distributed by the New China News Agency gave the actual number of delegates present, a Hong Kong magazine ran a picture of the delegates posing with Chou En-lai, which shows just less than fifty. The same magazine suggests that delegates from Nepal, Cambodia, and Japan were responsible for getting the final statement changed from the political piece presented and promoted by the Chinese to a more religious expression of genuine agony at the horrors of the conflict.[98]

The ceremonies related to the transfer of the Buddha tooth relic from Kwangchi Monastery to a new pagoda in Peking's western suburbs and the official opening of the latter, alluded to above, also attracted numerous foreign guests. It was carefully pointed out that the new pagoda stood only one hundred meters from a pagoda where the tooth had been "kept for more than eight hundred years before it was destroyed by gunfire in 1900 when the armed forces of eight imperialist countries invaded Peking." [99]

"Support for the just, anti-U. S. imperialist struggle of the South Vietnamese people" was a constant refrain. In June, 1963, a service was held in the Yung Ho Lamasery in Peking "in memory of the Buddhists persecuted and killed by the U. S.–Ngo Dinh Diem gang," with special mention of Thich Quang Duc, the monk whose fiery suicide was a "protest against the persecution." [100] At other occasions in 1963 and succeeding years, visiting Vietnamese Buddhists were guests of honor, occasionally joined by fellow Buddhists from Laos, Cambodia, and Japan. Muslims, Protestants, Catholics, and Taoists joined in a protest meeting in January, 1965, expressed their support for the South Vietnamese Buddhists, and demanded release of arrested monks, nuns, and laymen. *Modern Buddhism*

[97] There are several *NCNA* reports on this conference dated October 19, 1963; *SCMP*, October 24, 1963, pp. 28-31. See also *China Notes* II (December, 1963), 4-5.

[98] "Buddhists in Peking," *Far Eastern Economic Review*, November 21, 1963, pp. 381-82.

[99] *NCNA*, Peking, June 24 and 25, 1964; *SCMP*, June 29, 1964, p. 15, and June 30, 1964, pp. 17-18. Madame Bandaranaike, Premier of Ceylon at the time, sent a sapling from the Bo tree of Ceylon, under which, according to Ceylonese Buddhist tradition, the Buddha attained Nirvana.

[100] *NCNA*, Peking, June 21, 1963; *SCMP*, June 26, 1963, pp. 38-39.

was usually full of accounts of protest meetings, as well as its own editorial contributions on Vietnam. A film, "Undaunted Buddhists of South Vietnam," was also circulating.[101]

Considerable publicity in 1964 was given to ceremonies commemorating famous Chinese Buddhist monks. Throughout the spring of that year special services and meetings were held commemorating the thirteen hundredth anniversary of the death of Hsuan Tsang, the pilgrim monk of the T'ang dynasty who went to India in search of Buddhist scriptures and translated quite a few of them. Buddhists from several Asian countries attended these ceremonies, in which the theme of friendship among Asians was stressed. The climax was a rally in Peking on June 27, 1964, sponsored by the Chinese Buddhist Association and six cultural organizations, attended by Buddhists from all over Asia. Speeches emphasizing the cultural contribution of Hsuan Tsang were made. Chao P'u-ch'u said that Hsuan Tsang had sown seeds of friendship among the peoples of Asia who were now demanding

equality, mutual help, friendliness, and solidarity among themselves. Although evil forces are using every means to provoke trouble, sabotage things, cheat us, and estrange us from each other, our fate is in our own hands now, and the days when the peoples of Asia were subjected to enslavement and division is definitely gone forever.[102]

In May and June, as well as in October, 1964, there were celebrations of the twelve hundredth anniversary of the death of Chien Chen, another T'ang dynasty monk, who is credited with having taken Buddhism to Japan. Japanese Buddhists were usually present at ceremonies in China; a Chinese representative was also to be found at the ceremonies in Japan.[103]

Some traditional Buddhist practices continued. The Buddha's

[101] *NCNA*, Peking, January 31, 1965; *SCMP*, February 8, 1965, p. 44. See also *NCNA* reports in *RCDA*, November 4, 1963, p. 22.

[102] *NCNA*, Peking, June 27, 1964; *SCMP*, July 2, 1964, p. 21. The list of the sponsoring organizations is impressive: China Peace Committee, People's Association for Cultural Relations with Foreign Countries, Federation of Literary and Art Circles of China, Union of Chinese Artists, Chinese Historians' Society, Chinese Historical Museum, and the Chinese Buddhist Association.

[103] *NCNA*, Peking, October 4, 1963; *SCMP*, October 9, 1963, pp. 9-11.

birthday was celebrated, at least in Shanghai and Peking, where the faithful sprinkled water on a Buddha image, burned incense, made offerings, and chanted hymns. The Shanghai reports tell of a fair for several days, during which handicrafts, food items, and various daily necessities were sold.[104]

There are a few accounts of pilgrims visiting Buddhist sacred places, such as Wut'ai Mountain in Shansi, which was said to have attracted fifteen hundred pilgrims in the summer of 1962. The New China News Agency said that this was the largest number of pilgrims in recent years, which indicated considerable decline since many thousands formerly made the trek each summer.[105]

Tibetans, as well as Nepalese Buddhists, made a pilgrimage to sacred places in the Ari area of western Tibet in the summer of 1962. Peasants, herdsmen, and handicraft workers circled the peak of the Kailas range and Manasarowar Lake, praying and chanting sutras, picking up blades of grass, gravel, and lake water to take home. The point was made that all their needs were supplied, although it was not specified by whom.[106]

There were reports each year of the Monlam festival being celebrated in Tibet by followers of the Yellow Sect, with the note that the government made certain foods available. There is a reference in the report for 1964 that General Chang Ching-wu gave alms to the monks attending the Monlam festival in Lhasa, that a monk who was the ninety-sixth successor to Tsongkhapa, founder of the Yellow Sect, gave a lecture on the Buddhist scriptures before the almsgiving.[107] There are equally pleasant accounts of the celebration of the Tibetan New Year and other festivals.

Some repairs and improvements were made on temple buildings, as on the Gumbun Monastery, largest lama temple in Tsinghai province, where there was not only extensive redecoration, but also the installation of lightning rods to protect the metal roof and objects on it.[108] Rare Buddhist scriptures belonging to the people of the Pai nationality in Yunnan province were carefully preserved, as

[104] For example, NCNA, Shanghai, May 1, 1963; SCMP, May 7, 1963, p. 14.

[105] NCNA, Taiyuan, August 17, 1962; SCMP, August 23, 1962, p. 18.

[106] NCNA, Lhasa, August 21, 1962; SCMP, August 27, 1962, p. 14.

[107] NCNA, Lhasa, February 24, 1964; SCMP, February 27, 1964, p. 21.

[108] NCNA, Sining, December 2, 1964; SCMP, December 7, 1964, p. 14.

they "provide valuable data for the study of the history of the Pai nationality and the economic and cultural conditions of Yunnan province at that time." [109]

There are obscure allusions to changes at the organizational level in Tibet. The involvement of many sects in the Buddhist Association and in what was called "democratic management" of the monasteries was lauded in a third conference of the Tibetan branch of the Chinese Buddhist Association, which was held from September 20 to October 4, 1963. It is obvious that minimal control remained in the hands of monks, and they were the younger men who supported the Party. It also seems likely that the several sects in Tibet, among which there had been considerable rivalry in the past, no longer had any controlling power over monasteries previously under their jurisdiction. Chienpai-Tzuli, vice-chairman of the Tibetan branch, said that it was impossible before "democratic reform" in 1959 for all sects "to discuss religious questions on equal footing and with unity," which statement contains the veiled suggestion that divisions or rivalry had been suspended.[110]

At any rate, Panchen Erdeni, who became acting chairman of the Preparatory Committee for the Tibet Autonomous Region after 1959, along with others present, expressed his "warm support" of "democratic management," whatever it meant. These men evidently pledged their cooperation in its implementation, for they affirmed that "the enforcement of the democratic management system in monasteries would be conducive to better implementation of the Party's policy on religion." [111]

There was a hint that all was not well in Tibet if one may go by the report of the Seventh Enlarged Session of the Preparatory Committee for the Tibet Autonomous Region, which met in Lhasa in December, 1964. Political and economic matters were stressed, intending to detail the advances made from serfdom; but in a final sentence a speaker "condemned the acts of sabotage and schemes for restoration by a tiny handful of the reactionary serf owners under the cover of religion." [112] Such a reference to a "tiny handful"

[109] NCNA, Kunming, August 3, 1963; SCMP, August 8, 1963, p. 14.
[110] NCNA, Lhasa, October 6, 1963; SCMP, October 10, 1963, p. 15.
[111] NCNA, Lhasa, October 15, 1963; SCMP, November 7, 1963, p. 18.
[112] NCNA, Lhasa, December 13, 1964; SCMP, December 17, 1964, p. 3.

usually means there were quite a few, and the fact that such a reference was even made meant that the problem was serious.

The Panchen Lama, generally considered loyal to Peking, or at least willing to cooperate with the Communist authorities during the first fifteen years of their rule, in all likelihood was linked with "restoration," if not a restoration of the Tibetan government, at least of the authentic practice of Tibetan Buddhism (Lamaism). With the flight of the Dalai Lama, the Panchen Lama assumed the highest religious authority in Tibet, as well as a semblance of temporal or political authority, as noted above. During this time there were many attacks on the Dalai Lama and on those who supported him, prayed for him and his return, or even kept his picture in their homes.[113] He was denounced for having "staged a traitorous armed counterrevolutionary rebellion," and having plotted against his country while in India. He had "long cut himself off completely from the motherland and the people and [was] an incorrigible traitor, . . . a running dog of imperialism and foreign reactionaries." [114] But in all of this the Panchen Lama, who obligingly joined in attacks on the Dalai Lama, seemed above reproach from the Communist point of view.

By the middle 60's, however, it became clear that the Panchen Lama had used his position to impede the secularization of the lamas in 1960 and 1961, interceding with high officials in the Peking government.[115] At least the Chinese authorities became suspicious and, in 1964, again brought him to Peking; this was confirmed in an interview that Edgar Snow had with Mao Tse-tung, during which Mao said that the Panchen Lama was in Peking and being given a last chance to turn over a new leaf.[116] The Panchen

---

[113] In 1962, one of five crimes of which monks at Tashi Lhunpo monastery were accused was "Keeping the portrait of the Dalai Lama and praying for his long life." *Tibetan New Agency* (distributed by *Free Central European News Agency*), London, March 30, 1965; *RCDA*, May 31, 1965, pp. 74-75.

[114] *Peking Review*, December 25, 1964; *RCDA*, January 31, 1965, pp. 13-14.

[115] *CNA*, April 28, 1967, p. 3.

[116] Interview reported in *Le Nouveau Candide*, February 11, 1965, and then in *Informations Catholiques Internationales*, March 1, 1965, p. 16. Mao said incidentally that the truly faithful in the lamaist religion were not limited, the temples were open and the services carried out. The only concern was that "the living Buddhas do not practice all that they preach and are completely indifferent to the affairs of this world."

Lama was said to have been publicly humiliated in 1965, and then denounced in the most extravagant terms by Red Guards in 1968.[117] And there were rumors that he escaped in 1969.

Once again the stereotypes were drawn: those wanting a restoration of the former regime in Tibet were the "bad people," whereas the "good people" (those praised in news accounts and feature stories) were those who had risen out of serfdom to a new life of service to state and people and to happiness. The old serfdom was associated with fatalism, superstition, and Buddhism; the new was associated with the "democratic reform" brought by the Party. This was expressed most vividly at the end of one of the many stereotyped stories of change from abject serfdom to glorious freedom:

Asked if it was the Lord Heaven that had brought her the new life, Drolma Tsering shook her head and, pointing at a portrait of Chairman Mao Tse-tung hung on the wall, she said, "I owe my good life today to the Communist Party and I will follow the Party to build a still better life." [118]

A newspaper correspondent played up the same idea when he reported from his visit to Tibet that extermination of rats and insects was progressing nicely because Tibetans had been dispelled of their belief that rats are "resurrected lamas" and insects are "lice on the body of the Buddha," and that either could be exterminated by the prayers of lamas. The new word was "Dalai said his prayers for the serfowners, while Chairman Mao speaks for us. . . . Chairman Mao's works are a gold key to all locks." Since peasants and herdsmen "believe in science and materialism" and "have raised their consciousness, . . . the power of gods and ghosts is declining." [119]

By the mid-60's, there were few stories in the Chinese press about Buddhist advance under Communism. They had been replaced by stories which depicted people who had left superstitions to follow new ways, who had forsaken gods and Buddhas for Chairman Mao. *Modern Buddhism* carried the testimony of a monk enti-

[117] *China Reporting Service*, August 18, 1969.
[118] *NCNA*, Lhasa, August 31, 1965; *SCMP*, September 7, 1965, pp. 19-20.
[119] *NCNA*, Lhasa, June 20, 1966; *SCMP*, July 6, 1966, pp. 20-22.

tled "The Party Causes a Monk [to Move] from Great Death to New Life." It was the story of a monk who was "sick unto death," but was sent by the Party to a hospital where he received careful treatment by Party members working in the hospital. He now understood Buddha's teaching—"Look at all living things as one's son"—for he could feel the whole nation as a big family and had dedicated himself to follow resolutely the leadership of the Party, take the road of socialism, work, and study.[120]

A Tibetan monk went even further. After a miserable life under the lamas in former times, which he claimed would have reached a climax in his burial alive, he found with the new order such a "happy life, . . . personal freedom, . . . and democratic rights" that he left the monastic life, became an evening school teacher at the age of nineteen, and was elected a model teacher and a member of the Security Commission.[121]

There was evidently considerable encouragement to return to life in the world. A New China News Agency broadcast pointed out that monks and nuns who returned to their families were "given financial help and allotted a share of land, housing, and various means of production," whereas those who stayed in the monastery or novices who wished to enter were merely "respected and protected." It was implied that only aged and disabled monks and nuns were provided with allowances and free medical attention.[122]

In the summer of 1966, one has the impression, gained largely from Tibetan Buddhism (since word about Buddhism in China proper is almost nonexistent), that Buddhism was grinding to a meaningless halt. Some semblance of the facade remained, of course. Two groups of Japanese Buddhists came to China, the first to help the Chinese Buddhist Association observe the June anniversary of the death of the Venerable Yi Hsuan, founder of the Linchi Sect of Ch'an Buddhism, the second to visit the Chinglung Temple in Sian where their Shingon school of Buddhism originated.[123] And Neale Hunter says he spoke with Buddhist monks

[120] *Modern Buddhism*, 2, 1964, pp. 36-37.
[121] *NCNA*, Lhasa, December 24, 1965; *SCMP*, December 30, 1965, pp. 22-23.
[122] *NCNA*, English broadcast from Peking, 0854 GMT, September 3, 1965; *RCDA* October 31, 1965, p. 140.
[123] *NCNA*, Peking, June 16, 1966; *SCMP*, June 21, 1966, p. 20. Also *NCNA*, Peking, August 3, 1966; *SCMP*, August 9, 1966, pp. 31-32.

in half a dozen monasteries, along with other religious leaders, only to conclude that all of it was "religion at its worst." Though it could be called religion, anyone who followed through on his freedom to worship "knew that by so doing he was isolating himself from the main current of China's development." [124]

The story of what happened to Buddhism under the Cultural Revolution and the Red Guards reads very much like what can be read of Christianity and Islam under the same movement. Buddhism, however, with its magnificent temples and brooding images inside, provided a most vulnerable target to youth out to destroy the "four olds." Hunter says he saw a truckload of Buddha images roaring down the street, to what fate one could only guess.[125] Cecile Nicholls, a Canadian writer for the Associated Press, arrived at the Lin Yin Temple in Hangchow just before

a detachment of teen-agers had defiled the images of Buddha and pasted on the two large temples crude signs scrawled on sheets of old newspapers.

By the time I reached the main temple paper notices already were pasted on the face and body of the main Buddha while two boys, one armed with a paste bucket and brush, slapped notices on other Buddhas in the upper temples.

On being questioned through my interpreter, the head monk was reported to have said that "this is probably a very good thing."

As Lin Yin Temple is a national monument, the vandals made only the symbolic gesture of breaking one bench and throwing a small Buddha to the ground.[126]

Not all the destruction was "symbolic," nor was it only foreign correspondents who noted such destruction. A New China News Agency bulletin of August 25, 1966, said that "revolutionary students and teachers" of the Central Institute of Arts had the day before set "a revolutionary fire" to such "old world" sculptures as "images of the Buddha and niches for Buddhist sculptures." They

[124] Colin Mackerras and Neale Hunter, *China Observed* (New York: Frederick A. Praeger, 1968), pp. 81-91.

[125] *Ibid.*, p. 84

[126] No dateline on story itself, but seen in *Wisconsin State Journal*, August 28, 1966.

had also "carried axes, picks, and iron spikes to crush the sculptures to pieces." Government radio broadcasts from Nanning said that revolutionary youth had "burnt the images of Buddha and many other superstitious objects, replacing them with Chairman Mao's portraits and Mao Tse-tung's quotations." [127]

I have seen an example of this in a photograph of a temple in Peking with new sayings replacing the older Buddhist sayings. Across the top was "Erect the New—Destroy the Old." The left panel reading downward said "A Thousand Years of Buddhism Harms People." On the right the matching line said "Today We Wipe Out with One Stroke." The whole thing now bore the heading "Reform Gate" with banners saying "Change the Universe—Reform the World."

It is noted in several publications that the famous Temple of the Bubbling Well in Shanghai was razed.[128] A reporter of the Japanese Press Agency Asahi Shimbun said that the Lung Fu Sz monastery in Peking had become a storage place for the people's market. He stated, however, as of late 1967, that the Temple of the Sleeping Buddha and eight other monasteries in Peking suburbs still stood, that the Sleeping Buddha image was preserved under lock and key, and that all other images had been destroyed.[129]

World Buddhism and other publications reported the posters plastered on the Lung Yung Temple in Canton, demanding that it be closed, proposing that it should be used as a kindergarten or be reassigned to a box manufacturing company where the monks might be employed, and declaring that "the revolutionary action of the Red Guards in pulling down those dead wooden idols is most pleasing." [130]

It was the same in Tibet. The famous Jhokang and Ramoche monasteries in Lhasa were ransacked and their relics and images dragged through the streets. At Ramoche the Red Guards beat and maimed an old priest who had bolted the door against them. Other temples and shrines were desecrated or destroyed. There were reports of increased numbers of refugees fleeing to India, and of

[127] Quoted in *China Notes* V (April, 1967), p. 4.
[128] *E.g. Église Vivante* XIX (May-August, 1967), 185.
[129] *Hong Kong Times*, December 7, 1967.
[130] *China Notes* V (October, 1967), 7.

numerous suicides by people under pressure who could not leave. The Panchen Lama, who had been out of favor for two years, was imprisoned. Lamas were openly ridiculed, large numbers forced to marry, others sent to labor camps. *Jen-min Jih-pao* made it official that Red Guards in Lhasa

went against the former serf-masters, went into palaces and temples, gave rough treatment to those lamas who were still there. They turned against places which for hundreds of years were the hotbeds of the opium of religion.[131]

And Chou En-lai himself, according to Yomiuri Shimbun, said that 90 percent of the lamas had been secularized in order "to take part in production." [132] The Chinese press praised the Tibetan people who "have smashed the clay idols and dragged out some lamas on parade," and one man in particular, Ngapo Ngawang Jigme, who "has gained merits by exposing the treacherous activities of the Dalai Lama and the Panchen Lama." [133]

The lamas were compared to mice, whose inroads on the crops make them the worst enemy of the Tibetan people. The comparison also suggested that the monks were a corrupting influence, using old thoughts to destroy the people.[134]

Toward the end of 1968, a Buddhist temple at Lokang near Canton was devoted to a Class Education Struggle exhibition, which consisted largely of old "symbols of superstition" such as Buddha images.[135] And in early 1969, the call was still to do away with the four olds, including "burning incense to Buddha." The call was to study and work.

Why did the steady suppression of Buddhism come to such a violent climax? Why were temples and images, including at least

[131] Summarized from *JMJP*, August 29, 1966; *CNA*, April 28, 1957, p. 3. Preceding paragraph based on *RCDA*, February 28, 1967, pp. 35-36; *Communism and Religion*, January-February, 1967; *China Notes* V (April, 1967), p. 4.

[132] Cited in *CNA*, April 28, 1967, p. 3, from Japanese news agency report.

[133] *Fighting Canton News*, September 30, 1967; *URS*, October 6, 1967, p. 22.

[134] *Tibet, 1950-1967*, pp. 536-40, which also has some of the information cited above.

[135] *Hong Kong Chou Mo Pao* [Weekend News], November 2, 1968.

some which had been repaired at government expense, destroyed in such wanton manner? Marlene Tuininga, a French writer, asked why the temples were attacked and was told by her interpreter: "We are not against religion, but we have no need." [136] Ian Thomson, commenting on the stillness and beauty of an old Buddhist monastery near Tsinan, was told by his guide-interpreter: "It is a monastery no more. It belongs to the people." Thomson notes that indeed hundreds were enjoying it. [137] But such soft answers hardly explain the enormity of the change.

Not only did Buddhism suffer as a symbol of the old culture of China; there was the blow struck at China's relationships with other Asian countries—Ceylon, Burma, Japan. One may argue that these relations had become so negligible by the mid-60's that they were hardly worth maintaining, particularly if by the Cultural Revolution Mao and the top echelon of loyal leaders were able to maintain their hold on a nation which seemed to be slipping away. Good foreign relations are hardly as important as remaining in power at home, whatever the cost. It still seems a waste, however, to trample what had been so painstakingly cultivated.

One may hope that some of the priceless art treasures and magnificent temples escaped destruction. And one may hope that the Buddhist community of monks, nuns, and lay followers, having disappeared in name and form, may possess enough of that resilient spirit which it has exhibited in past ages in China to discover new avenues by which to express the profound insights of the Middle Path.

New avenues may not be necessary. Since meditation has been the heart of Buddhist practice and its primary discipline through the centuries, Buddhism is perhaps best equipped of all the religious movements in China to survive a period when all external, institutional expressions of religion are impossible. The question is whether or not the meditation masters have been able to transmit

[136] *Informations Catholiques Internationales*, September 16, 1966. Immediately before the Cultural Revolution Miss Tuininga visited the White Horse Temple at Loyang and was told there were fourteen monks in the temple, the only active one in Loyang, to which about a hundred people came from as far as fifteen kilometers.

[137] *China Notes* VI (January, 1968), 4.

to younger Buddhists the discipline which cannot be learned from books, which must be learned or "caught" by a student from his teacher. If this transmission has continued, an authentic Buddhist cultivation continues, and that is one factor in the survival of Buddhism in China.

X

Confucius and His Changing Fortunes

Many will find it strange to have a chapter on Confucianism and related philosophical currents in a book on religion in China. China's scholarly class, her intellectuals and students, will contend sharply that Confucianism is not a religion—and then proceed to discuss it, Buddhism, and Taoism as the "three religions of China." Chinese Communists do not consider Confucianism a religion, which means that all I have said about Communist policy does not apply, except inferentially.

Nonetheless, I am convinced that the Confucian tradition with all its stress on "this world," man, and society, is essentially a religious tradition which elicits from those involved in it that "ultimate concern" which Tillich called religion. Particularly when one considers or participates in that ceremonial tradition blessed and encouraged by Confucius is one aware of this, but ultimate concern in Confucianism goes far beyond its rites and ceremonies. One may make the distinction that Confucianism is a way of interpreting or "handling" indigenous Chinese religious tradition, as is Taoism or Chinese Buddhism, and not specifically that religion itself, but this does not mean that Confucianism can be excluded from a consideration of religious movements in China. Nor does the Confucian focus on man and society and its avoidance of metaphysical questions mean that it is not a religion. The same phenomenon can be found in the history of several religions, as well as the desire among their adherents not to be called a religion.

Therefore, the way in which the Confucian tradition is regarded in Communist China will be considered. Major attention must be devoted to modern China's ranking scholar in the field of philosophy, Professor Fung Yu-lan, whose work is perhaps the outstanding example of the effort made to keep Confucianism alive. There is a sense in which in China any philosopher, any teacher or student of philosophy, even any intellectual in the broadest sense of the word, must express himself with respect to Confucius, and this has clearly been the case with discussions among philosophers at two periods under the Communist regime. Thus, we may not at every point be dealing with the Confucian tradition as such, but will be dealing with movements or thinkers at the fringe of that tradition whose work is in some way relevant to or helpful to the understanding of that tradition.

RAPID DEMISE OF CULT—SLOW EMERGENCE OF THOUGHT

The last expressions of Confucian ceremonial in the closing days of the Nationalists sound almost unreal as one glances at them now. On Confucius' birthday anniversary, which fell on August 27 in 1948, there were fairly elaborate ceremonies in Shanghai conducted by the Mayor, Mr. K. C. Wu, a Protestant Christian. The hall was decorated in traditional manner, incense was burning before the altar, and after a presentation everyone bowed before the Confucian Tablet.[1] Essentially the same ceremony was performed in Canton in 1949, even though the Communist armies were about to enter the province of Kwangtung. There were lectures on Confucianism in many cultural and educational organizations, and a commemorative bulletin in honor of the 2,500th birthday of Confucius.[2]

All public ceremonial in honor of Confucius disappeared after 1949. Many of the shrines of the Confucian cult did not disappear under communism; they merely took on the aspect of museum pieces. The Confucian temple at Sian was restored and made into a historical museum. The new government in time repainted and refurbished the Confucian temple, tomb, and related buildings at Ch'ü-fu. Levenson, whose work includes this data, also points out that those who came to nearby graves to perform the Ch'ing Ming rites (for the dead) in April, 1962, found themselves "guided," as

---

[1] Shanghai *Ta Kung Pao*, August 28, 1948; *CMBA* I (October, 1948), 610.
[2] *CMBA* I (II) (October, 1949), 154-55.

it were, along a route that led by the Confucian grove to the temple. But Levenson also cites a reporter who, in a story about a cooperative at Ch'ü-fu which improved the economic and cultural life of the people in Confucius' native village, implied that socialism was superior to the Confucian classics.[3]

Although there might have been vague traces of an institutional or cultic expression in the general direction of Confucius, Hu Chang-tu's observation is basically correct—that as a cult (Hu says religion) Confucianism has disappeared.

All local Confucian temples or shrines that remained were converted into schools, cultural centers, or storage depots. This was made easy by the fact that there were generally no priests or caretakers about the premises, and the local people were sympathetic to the idea that these temples should be put to practical use. Thus all the external appurtenances of the Confucian cult have disappeared. At the same time Confucianism as a system of philosophy finds it increasingly difficult to withstand the attack of modern ideologies.[4]

These modern ideologies were not long in finding comrades ready to proclaim them. "Attack" on Confucian philosophy is not mentioned, but a new Philosophy Research Institute, organized in Peking in July, 1949, before the Communist government had actually established itself throughout the country, left no questions as to its objective:

It was unanimously approved that the principal mission of the institute was to unite all workers of philosophy to study and disseminate Marxist-Leninist philosophy as well as the philosophical thought of Mao Tse-tung.[5]

That admirers and devotees of Confucius and his philosophy should be somewhat apprehensive with the rise of the new regime

[3] *Confucian China and Its Modern Fate.* Vol. III, *The Problem of Historical Significance* (Berkeley: University of California Press, 1965), pp. 79-80.

[4] Hu, *China: Its People*, pp. 131-32. Ch'ing Ming, a spring festival when the ancestral graves are swept and offerings made to the ancestors, as well as other festivals and rites, may be considered a part of the Confucian tradition, but we shall deal with them in the following chapter on folk religion.

[5] *North China Daily News*, July 15, 1949; *CMBA* I (II) (November, 1949), 276.

is hardly surprising. Mao Tse-tung's essay "On New Democracy," which first appeared in January, 1940, called for a new culture to completely supplant two types of old culture. One was the "imperialist culture" associated with institutions run by imperialists or those Chinese "who have lost all sense of shame." The other was a semifeudal culture

whose exponents include all those who advocate the worship of Confucius, the study of the Confucian canon, the old ethical code and the old ideas in opposition to the new culture and new ideas. . . . This kind of reactionary culture [semifeudal and imperialist combined] serves the imperialists and the feudal class and must be swept away. Unless it is swept away, no new culture of any kind can be built up. There is no construction without destruction, no flowing without damming and no motion without rest; the two are locked in a life-and-death struggle.[6]

This must be what M. Etiemble has in mind when he says that Mao announced a "struggle to the death" against Confucius and Confucianism as soon as he had taken over, and that honoring Master K'ung and reading the classics "became, in the space of a day, a 'feudal' crime." [7]

On the other hand, Mao advised his followers to learn from Confucius and Sun Yat-sen, as well as from Marx and Lenin. They "should sum up everything from Confucius to Sun Yat-sen and inherit this valuable legacy," but without "lauding what is old, disparaging what is new, or commending any feudal poisonous element." Furthermore, Kuo Mo-jo, for years a party spokesman on almost any matter having to do with cultural affairs, had pictured Confucius as one who defended the common people and who had even supported armed rebellion. And Liu Shao-ch'i, until 1965-66, the chief theoretician next to Mao, drew heavily on the Confucian tradition, particularly the sayings of Mencius, in his booklet *How To Be a Good Communist*.[8]

Perhaps it was due to the ambiguities in the new situation, the

[6] *Selected Works of Mao Tse-tung*, Vol. II (Peking: FLP, 1965), p. 369.
[7] "New China and Chinese Philosophies," *Diogenes*, 11 (1955), p. 103.
[8] David S. Nivison, "Communist Ethics and Chinese Tradition," *Journal of Asian Studies* XVI (November 1956), 51-74, shows substantial use of Confucian, neo-Confucian, and even Buddhist ideas in Liu's *How To Be A Good Communist*. See especially pp. 59-61 of the Nivison article.

uncertainty as to just which line should be taken, that very little was said along philosophical lines during the first six years of the Communist regime. Ch'an Wing-tsit says that only seventeen books and about twenty-five articles on traditional Chinese philosophy appeared during those six years, whereas more than two hundred books and around eight hundred articles were produced between 1955 and 1963, the period on which we shall concentrate.

Fung Yu-lan, of course, was far from silent during that early period. Undoubtedly the most famous philosopher and teacher of philosophy in contemporary China, he has been the key figure in the effort to find an acceptable way of treating Confucius so that the teachings of China's great sage might in some way be tenable, acceptable, or at least tolerated in the new day. He received a doctorate in philosophy at Columbia University in the 20's, taught at several universities in China, was at Tsinghua University in Peking when the Communists came to power, and, after a period without a post, was brought to the faculty of Peking University in 1952.

In an article written shortly after the Communist takeover, Fung Yu-lan engaged in a kind of mild confession. He had thought of himself as enlightened and even a little leftist, but he was really backward and "pro-landlord." He recognized that his books (some of them quite famous) had served as a refuge for people unwilling to change, precisely because he was himself emotionally unwilling to change. Contrary to his former understanding, he now saw that philosophy has a relation to politics and society, that "the principal task of philosophy is to remold humanity and the world." He expressed the belief that the moral standards of Chinese society had been raised, that what were previously considered to be high standards were now the bare minimum.[9]

Fung also had occasion to pay his respects to Mao Tse-tung on the occasion, in 1950, of a reissue of Mao's famous essay, *On Practice*. In a short review, Fung hailed its reappearance because it was such a valuable treatment of the relation of knowledge and action. Fung claimed that there was interest in action on the part of

[9] Lynn and Amos Landmann, *Profile of Red China* (New York: Simon and Schuster, 1951), pp. 120-21, have included excerpts from Fung's article which appeared in *People's China*.

Chinese thinkers from Confucius to Sun Yat-sen, but that most of them missed the point because they worked from a metaphysical base. Mao, in showing that knowledge depends on practice, had made the conclusive statement. Fung was at his most learned and diplomatic best, whether he believed what he said or not.[10]

Two years later, when invited to give a lecture to a group of scholars in Italy, Professor Fung compared the new philosophy with the old, making three points: (1) the new philosophy is connected with actuality because it is the philosophy of the laboring people; (2) in the new philosophy theory has grasped and his been grasped by the masses, who "will realize it with their personal experience and practical activity"; (3) growing out of the belief in the new philosophy that "the world is created by human labor," its correctness is "verified in the practice of reconstructing the world." He distinguished between the old mechanistic materialism and the new dialectic materialism, found traces of materialism in the Confucian doctrine of man and of dialectical thinking in the Book of Changes, and rudimentary aspects of both materialist and dialectic thought in Taoism.[11]

During the mid-50's Fung walked a rather tight rope. He was trying to say a good word for Confucius and to lift up materialist elements in the history of Chinese thought wherever possible in order to satisfy the Marxists around him. In September and October of 1956, he attended conferences in Geneva and Venice, and reported that speakers at both conferences had referred to the harmonious development and coordination of science and Christianity in European culture, that some had spoken of the "saving role of Christianity, which is neither old nor new, but eternal." He pointed out very carefully that people in the West were interested in Chinese culture and hoped that it would not perish, and added that it was wonderful that Marxists, religious believers, and agnostics could courteously exchange their views.[12]

Fung's short article, done in late 1956 and entitled "Problems in

[10] This brief summary is based on a French translation (Mao Tse-toung et la Philosophie chinoise," *La Pensée*, New Series 55 (May-June, 1955), pp. 79-87.

[11] "Philosophy in the New China according to Fung Yu-lan," *East and West* III (July, 1952), 105-7.

[12] *JMJP*, November 27, 1965; *CNA*, August 15, 1958, pp. 4-5.

the Study of Confucius," raises in brief fashion many of the problems Fung discussed in greater detail in "On Confucius" several years later. In this earlier article, however, Fung had already indicated the last stand for "saving Confucius." In spite of differences men might have on Confucius' philosophical, social, and political views,

no one will deny his achievement in the propagation of ancient Chinese culture. That is sufficient to ensure him a high place in Chinese history. The feudal system which appropriated his name as a symbol has gone for good; but the name of Confucius himself is, and will always be, respected and cherished by the Chinese people.[13]

Although ten years later men were to "deny" his achievement, or to condemn him as the symbol of "the old," Fung's 1956 effort was admirable, for it sought to distinguish between what others had done with the sage's admittedly out-of-date teachings and what one might respect in the man himself.

By 1955, the lines of thought which were to be repeated over and over again in following years were beginning to emerge. An editorial in *Jen-min Jih-pao* "deplored the prevalence of idealistic philosophy in China," and especially the fact that "many Party members and intellectuals are unable to distinguish what is materialist thought and what is idealist thought." Acknowledging that many in these two groups were still infected with idealist thought, the editor expressed what was to be the guideline for any discussion: "Academic criticism and discussions should, in general, be subordinate to the basic principle of preaching materialism and Marxist thought among the intellectuals and the people." [14]

Idealism was one of the charges brought against Hu Shih, well known in intellectual and philosophical circles as a disciple of John Dewey and Bertrand Russell (and therefore hardly an idealist). He was condemned further because he did not see history as a conflict between materialism and idealism and failed to see the importance of materialism in Chinese philosophy.[15] A criticism of Hu Shih as

[13] *People's China*, January 1, 1957, p. 31.
[14] *JMJP*, April 11, 1955; *CHIBUL* V (July, 1955).
[15] Helmut Wilhelm, "The Reappraisal of Neo-Confucianism," *The China Quarterly*, July-September, 1965, pp. 122-139.

a literary man charged him with separating theory from practice and science from politics, for his subjective attitude in his "purely literary point of view," and for a research method based on both (!) formalism and subjectivism.[16]

What can be seen developing, according to Wilhelm, is a "tug of war" between two groups:

Those who worked entirely along doctrinaire lines attempting as best they could to apply to the Chinese intellectual tradition the meager assortment of concepts provided by Marxist and Soviet theory, and those who wanted to retain room for traditional values.[17]

The first group had its strength in the Institute of History (of the Academy of Sciences in Peking) and included such men as Hou Wai-lu, whereas the second group was to be found in the Academy's Institute of Philosophy with people like Fung Yu-lan. The orthodox usually were in control, in spite of brief periods when Fung and his disciples asserted themselves.

Wilhelm says that it was Yang Yung-chih who turned the discussion in a new direction, in 1956, with an "emotional plea for the loving preservation of the cultural heritage of the father-land." [18] Backed by quotations from Mao and the Communist fathers he proposed the absorption and transformation of all that was valuable. The problem was how to determine what was valuable, and indeed if anything out of the feudal past could have any value, tainted, as it inevitably had to be, with idealism.

This effort to "lovingly preserve" what is valuable from the past can be seen in a booklet entitled *The Chung Yung on Human Nature* by Liu Tse-ju, which is an effort to show how the Chung Yung (Doctrine of the Mean), one of the Confucian four books, might

[16] Léon Trivière, "Les Intellectuels en Chine Populaire," *CMBA* VII (October, 1955), quoting from *JMJP*, November 5, 1954. I have not been able to include in this chapter insights which might be gained from a study of Communist Chinese treatment of intellectuals, but the reader may refer to several excellent works, among them Theodore H. E. Ch'en, *Thought Reform of the Chinese Intellectuals* (Hong Kong: Hong Kong University Press, 1960) and Merle Goldman, *Literary Dissent in Communist China* (Cambridge: Harvard University Press, 1967).
[17] Wilhelm, "The Reappraisal," p. 127.
[18] *Ibid.*, p. 128.

have contemporary meaning.[19] Mr. Liu said that the idea in this ancient book that human nature is "what heaven ordains," that the patterns of feudal society were "founded in the heavenly order," must of course be rejected, or turned around. If we "explain human nature from the Way, and the will of heaven from human nature, . . . then we can arrive at a scientific understanding of human nature." It is actually a way of saying that existence determines consciousness. According to the Chung Yung, the training which leads to the realization of human nature was based on the five relationships, and the goal represented "the complete fusion of one's own feelings with the feudal pattern of the five relationships." But, says Mr. Liu, this can be put into modern language: the goal "is to make one's own thoughts and feelings represent and embody the proper human relationships of objective society."

The main problem is that the writer of the Chung Yung did not recognize that the notion of a heaven-bestowed human nature and the five relationships by which it was cultivated actually arose from ancient society. These relationships served the ruling class, therefore an understanding of human nature was developed which was consistent with it. Though this was not recognized and an idealist view of nature constructed, the Chung Yung's "method of morality and self-cultivation is good."

Think of it: if we could take the practice of moral cultivation as advocated by the Chung Yung and apply it to our modern society; if we could, with the help of this system of self-cultivation, analyze reality and find out how to be in accord with the common welfare of the broad masses of the working people under the leadership of the workers' class, and constantly guard against too much "left" or "right," against bypassing and not reaching up to (the Golden Mean); if we could, after seeing this clearly, apply ourselves with energy to its practice, so that our thoughts and feelings would completely reflect the people's common welfare and be in harmony with it, thus becoming representatives, incarnations of this common welfare—is this not the highest Communist morality?

[19] Published by Shensi People's Press, 1957; translated and summarized by R. P. Kramers in a bulletin, "Chinese Tradition and Communist Ethics," prepared for an East Asia Christian Conference–World Council of Churches Consultation at the Christian Study Centre, Hong Kong, November, 1960. This mimeographed bulletin also included a summary of a criticism of Liu Tse-ju's work by Mr. Ch'en Ming-lin. The long quotation is from page 6.

A critic replied that it certainly is not. Mr. Liu had suggested that the Chung Yung contained the idea that existence determines consciousness. The critic, a Mr. Ch'en Meng-lin, says that the way a historic materialist understands "existence determines consciousness" has nothing to do with what the ancient writers were talking about. The goal of fusing one's own feelings with the feudal pattern of five relationships is mystical and completely unacceptable. And for anyone to advocate something so closely related to feudal morality must clearly indicate that he has feudal concepts in his own mind.

The first real plunge into philosophical waters under the aegis of communism came in a conference on the history of Chinese philosophy in Peking in January, 1957. The critical spirit which was then being manifested in the Hundred Flowers Period was expressed in one instance by Jen Chi-yü, who opposed the practice of deciding whether or not Confucius was an atheist by counting the number of times he used the term for heaven. Jen also criticized the use of the Russian philosopher Zdanov's definition of the history of philosophy—a struggle between materialism and idealism—as a basis for the study of that discipline in China. Jen asserted that philosophy had a somewhat wider scope than such a limited definition would imply. Other men present added the point that some philosophers were idealist in some respects and materialist in others, but the orthodox Party representatives upheld the Zdanov definition. Fung Yu-lan proposed that Confucian emphases—on study, on eternal human values, inner knowledge (from the neo-Confucian Wang Yang-ming), and morality from the depth of the heart—could be used in new ways, with sincere and honest words, and full acceptance of criticism (which the new era demanded). The Party faithful were critical of Fung, especially of the bit about eternal human values, which seemed a harbinger of a return to metaphysics.[20]

Fung later said that no achievement had been made at the conferences, but that he understood better the relation between the

[20] My account of the conference is based on CNA, March 7, 1958, pp. 1-6. Jen Chi-yü's paper, "An Essay on the Object and Range of the History of Chinese Philosophy," was published in KMJP, January 11, 1957, and Fung's address appeared in the same newspaper, January 8, 1957.

general and the particular, especially the importance of the latter. Ch'an Wing-tsit, in his account of the conference, agrees that there was "no really final conclusion," that the history of philosophy as "nothing but the history of the struggle between materialism and idealism" was not a resolution adopted, but "a major opinion [which] emerged in clear outline." [21] Professor Ch'an adds that opinions favorable to idealism were expressed, and Wilhelm says that the dogmatic use of such terms as materialism and idealism was attacked. Even though what Wilhelm call the "doctrinaires" counterattacked,

they do not seem to have won the day, . . . for the yearning for the preservation of the heritage seems to have been too general. Again it is abundantly clear that what was to be preserved was not just the reinterpreted record but the values contained in the record.[22]

It was only after the conference when the dread charge of "revisionist" was hurled at the "preservationists" that the call for preservation was hushed, not to be raised again until the discussions concerning Confucius arose in the early 60's.

Papers from the 1957 discussions, collected in a 526-page book, revealed to the doctrinaire group that many scholars had revisionist tendencies and were opposed to Marxist-Leninist party principles. The book, entitled *A Collection of Discussions on Questions in the History of Chinese Philosophy*,[23] became a standard source for determining who said what in the recriminatory antirightist campaigns which followed.

During 1958, Fung Yu-lan made several confessions, some undoubtedly in response to the antirightist campaign. At one point he said he had made 135 self-examinations over a period of several years and added that even that many were not enough. Among the things he confessed were his approval of the rightists' desire for power, his claim that "in technical questions not even Chairman Mao can be a guide," his reluctance to learn from Russia, his being

[21] "Chinese Philosophy in Mainland China," *Philosophy East and West* XIV (December, 1964), 27.

[22] Wilhelm, "The Reappraisal," p. 129.

[23] Published by Science Publishing House in Peking, 1957; see *CNA*, October 31, 1958, p. 2.

continually inspired by idealist philosophy, and that even in intending to develop Marxism he had actually been destroying Marxism.[24]

Right at the time of one of these confessions it was proclaimed that "leaders of party committees at every grade are the real philosophers." [25] Fung took pen in hand and carefully distinguished between "philosophy workers" and "philosophers," lifting up the need for genuine theoreticians in every field if there was to be genuine unity of theory and practice. He was undoubtedly criticized for this, since it was the era of philosophers going to the villages to work. A few months later Fung confessed that one source of evil for him was his past theory of talent (*t'ien ts'ai*), which led him and his colleagues at Tsinghua in the old days to engage in empty-headed analyzing. He exclaimed: "Heavy is the burden of my feudalist and bourgeois philosophy, but I am not yet anxious to go to meet God with a mind hard like granite." [26]

In still another confession[27] that he was obliged to make the following year (1959), Fung Yu-lan said to the first session of the third National Committee of the Chinese People's Political Consultative Conference that he had had antagonistic feelings toward the Party, that he resented taking leadership from Party members whom he thought knew nothing of philosophy ("people outside the trade cannot lead those inside it"), but now he recognized that "the Party is the soul of all undertakings" and the motivation of all that is dynamic and active. He had thought being "expert" was more important than being "red," that being "red" was easier. This was wrong: "To change one's stand, one must genuinely change his entire self, body, and soul." And looking back over his forty years in philosophy, Fung recognized that he had been much too intimately associated with bourgeois philosophy, that he had tried "to protect old, conservative, and reactionary things," but that after making a "preliminary criticism" of himself,

[24] *CNA*, 244, September 12, 1958, p. 4.
[25] *KMJP*, July 1, 1958.
[26] Fung's article appeared in *KMJP* Philosophy Supplement, August 3, 1958; *CNA*, September 12, and July 4, 1958. Mao Tse-tung had referred to people who resisted the collective in the following words, to which Fung was alluding: "There are certainly people who would rather die than change, and hard-minded like granite, they prefer to go to meet God."
[27] "I Feel Young Again as soon as I Understand My Past Mistakes," *JMJP*, April 25, 1959; *CURBAC*, June 3, 1959, pp. 9-11.

I have elevated slightly my ideological and theoretical level, . . . restored my confidence and enhanced my courage; I not only do not have the feeling of emptiness, but even feel the zeal of striving to improve my position and march forward in this era of great development.[28]

In late 1958, Fung wrote an article in which he maintained that there had been no bourgeois class philosophy in the history of Chinese philosophy. Kuan Feng challenged him on this point, to which Fung replied with thanks for the criticism and an acknowledgment of mistakes. He asserted, however, that Chinese philosophy as such was not bourgeois, but that bourgeois class philosophy had come in from without.[29]

Fung got into another argument, in 1961, by charging that Marxist ethics are utilitarian ethics. Lo Ko answered that this was not the case, that they were for the good of the people, that ethical theory was valuable since it might raise moral standards.[30] I do not have Fung's reply, if any, but the point is lost anyway since a utilitarian ethic can have all the characteristics Lo Ko advances and still be utilitarian.

Thus the first phase of philosophical discussion in Communist China came to its gossipy close with distinguished philosophy professors dealing in clichés and stereotypes. The use of stereotypes had prevailed from the beginning and we shall meet them again in the next phase. For example, in 1961 we can read an article summarizing the "probing" of certain problems in the history of Chinese philosophy at Peking University. With respect to Chang Tsai and Chu Hsi, the discussion is based almost entirely on whether a man was idealist or materialist, progressive or conservative. About all a free mind could introduce in the discussion would be an observation to the effect that "although a man's views were conservative, he was ahead of his time," or "there was at least this one materialist element in an overall idealist view." [31]

In spite of the deadening character of such an approach to

---

[28] *Ibid.*, p. 11.

[29] *CNA*, August 19, 1960, p. 6.

[30] Fung's article appeared in *New Construction*, 4, 1961, Lo Ko's in *KMJP*, December 6, 1961. Both were briefly summarized in *CNA*, June 1, 1962, pp. 3-5.

[31] Reported by Lu Yü-san in *KMJP*, January 25, 1961; *URS*, June 23, 1961.

philosophy, some men kept at it. They were like the professor during the Hundred Flowers Period who said to his class that the real Confucianists "were not afraid to die for the cause of justice." A commentator, in 1958, said that such teaching had a "deplorable effect" on youth, so the professor undoubtedly suffered for expressing his convictions.[32] Men were not only committed to philosophy as a way of life. For them the questions they were discussing—the relation of Heaven to man, the nature of man, love or human-heartedness, rites or propriety—were part of a way of life, an expression of ultimate concern. These men kept trying to find a way, even in the morass of stereotypes, to work out the problems of philosophy in the new era in China in which by choice or circumstance they found themselves.

Wilhelm puts it quite cogently when he reminds us that the intellectual, like anybody else in Communist China, is made to feel a high degree of social as well as intellectual responsibility. The philosopher in the new China, as well as the man writing about him outside China, must work

in the knowledge that the intellectual processes of analysis and reassessment will reach far beyond the strictly intellectual scene; he forges the sword that is then applied in battle, possibly against himself.[33]

In spite of the resulting attitude of diffidence, one finds according to Wilhelm, "an almost uncanny sense of the politically possible," so that at certain moments a voice dares to speak out for the extension of boundaries or the preservation of traditional values.

THE CONCENTRATION ON CONFUCIUS IN THE EARLY SIXTIES

Whether the government thought the antirightist campaigns had taken care of the real troublemakers and duly scared all the rest, or whether officialdom relaxed ideological controls in a period of great physical want and suffering (Wilhelm), or whether it was

[32] *CNA*, 233, June 20, 1958, p. 1.
[33] Wilhelm, "The Reappraisal," p. 125.

the determination of philosophical minds to say their piece, discussion got going again in 1960. This time it was discussion in earnest about Confucius, with a few asides on other figures in the Chinese philosophical heritage.

There is in Fung Yu-lan's article "On Confucius," [34] written in 1960, an admirable example of the attempt by a keen mind to select all those points in the Confucian teaching which might make the sage palatable to Communist China. Confucius, in addition to being the first to create a school of learning, also created a "private school of learning" to be distinguished from the aristocrats' "official learning." The master insisted on the absolute distinction of upper and lower classes, identifying his "superior man" with the aristocracy and the "small man" with the common people. He also approved the plan of the slave-owning aristocrats who were in a state of transition to the new landlord class "to elevate the status of laboring producers and improve their livelihood." "Although he did not want to do away entirely with 'the principle of favoring the relatives' of the aristocrat system . . . he also advocated the 'principle of respecting the virtuous.' " His approval of the practices of "inviting men from far away places" and of "selecting men of virtue," is evidence of his espousal of "benevolence."

Confucius' principle of the "rectification of names," by which reality was "rectified" or brought into correspondence with abstract "names" or terms, was clearly an example of idealistic thinking. He wanted men to follow the traditional ceremonies (which Fung calls "ceremonies of religion"), and he wanted men to respect and fear the decree of heaven, which some of the time at least he used as a term for God. One can say, therefore, that Confucius was an advocate of religion, and thus of various ideas and practices by which the ruling classes keep the common people in submission. Thus far, Fung is the doctrinaire Marxist.

Confucius, however, according to Fung, said that even though man's deeds were decided by heaven's decree,

man could do his utmost and do anything which he himself thought he ought to do, despite its success or failure. . . . Whether a man was "vir-

[34] *KMJP*, July 22 and 29, 1960; *URS*, October 25, 1960, pp. 92-111.

tuous or base" was not decided by heaven's decree, . . . [but instead] mainly depended on one's effort.[35]

And benevolence meant not only filial piety and love for those in a man's clan; for Confucius it

demands . . . that he should extend this love to the people outside his clan. . . . "A benevolent man" should "not do to others what he does not want done to himself," . . . and should "seek to establish others when wishing to be established himself; seek to enlighten others when wishing to be enlightened himself." [36]

Fung cites several further examples to show that Confucius was a child of his time, then launches into a discussion of Confucius' way of thinking which "laid stress on reality and particularly on objective reality; this was very advanced at that time." Moreover, in addition to study of the ancient classics, Confucius held that one's individual experience and the experience of others were sources of knowledge. The sage "was also of the opinion that one must make investigation into the experiences of one's self and others before one could believe them." And only if study accompanied thinking would thinking be of any value.[37] In all of these areas—stress on objective reality, experience, investigation, and study—Fung was feeding back to the Communist theoreticians their own pet words.

Professor Fung's presentation did not go unanswered. Li Ch'i-ch'ien first criticized Fung's statement that the "private schools" were started by individuals in order to make a living.[38] According to Marxist theory they had their "class foundations" and "political mission." Anyone ought to know that individuals don't do things. Secondly, Li criticized Fung because he attributed the rise of benevolence to the kindness of the rulers, inviting men from far places and extending love beyond the clan, whereas according to Marxist theory it was due to class struggle by the masses which forced the ruling classes to do this. Finally, Mr. Li jumps Mr. Fung

[35] *Ibid.*, p. 100.
[36] *Ibid.*, p. 101. The Confucian quotations are from the Analects.
[37] *Ibid.*, pp. 106-8.
[38] "A Few Comments on Mr. Fung Yu-lan's Article 'On Confucius,'" *KMJP*, August 5, 1960; *URS*, October 28, 1960, pp. 113-23.

because the latter referred to a couple of abstract problems or principles, including the principle of benevolence or "loving the people" which according to Mr. Li is dead wrong because

we love those people who strengthen proletarian dictatorship and who positively take part in socialist construction; to those people who oppose [these two] we not only do not love them, but we should also ruthlessly oppose and suppress them.[39]

Thus, according to his critics, Fung did not fully understand the meaning of class struggle and therefore missed fire in his rather remarkable article.

Fung Yu-lan tried again. He put out a revised edition of his famous *History of Chinese Philosophy,* of which many sections were completely new, written, Fung said, with Marxism-Leninism and the thoughts of Mao Tse-tung as a guide. Ch'an Wing-tsit in a review[40] says that the Party had two people working with Fung, each of whom revised his draft, which was then printed and discussed by a committee on textbooks in the history of Chinese philosophy. It was finally adopted as a reference work and 12,500 copies printed, but all were registered and prohibited from export. Professor Ch'an was able to get a copy of volume one, published in 1962, but had not been able to get a copy of the second volume published in 1964.

Comparing Fung's earlier and later treatments of Chinese philosophy in the seventh and sixth centuries B.C., to which period Confucius belongs, Professor Ch'an finds in the earlier version that "a great emphasis is laid on spiritual beings, on divination, and on the various interpretations of heaven," whereas in the later version "instead of presenting the 'ruling heaven' whom 'the masses obeyed,' the stress is on the opposition between the ruling heaven and the materialistic viewpoint." Opposition to China's first published law code in the sixth century is treated in the earlier version as an example of humanism—the main theme of that version—whereas the later version takes it "as a new instrument of the newly arising landlord class to restrict the declining slave-owning feudal class." "In the *History* [earlier version] religious

[39] *Ibid.,* p. 122.
[40] *Journal of Asian Studies* XXIV (May, 1965), 495-97.

sacrifices are expressions of man's gratitude to ancestors and are therefore humanistic, but in the new version they are evidence of an atheistic viewpoint."

In his earlier work Fung portrayed Confucius as "the first one to have made learning available to the masses," but in the later work the master is "a representative of the slave-owning class in transition to the newly arising landlord class." The Confucian rules of ceremony (*li*) become "the tools of the land-owning rulers," and the statement about understanding the mandate of heaven at fifty meant that Confucius had acquired an understanding of nature.

In fact, Fung goes as far as to say that inasmuch as Confucius attempted to do the impossible, it shows that in the moral sphere, at least, Confucius was "denying the mandate of heaven" and thus laid the foundation for atheism in late Confucianism.[41]

Jen (love, human-heartedness, benevolence) no longer is the conscientiousness and altruism present in all people; it has "acquired a class nature," and each person should practice these virtues "in his particular position as a ruler or a minister." Ch'an Wing-tsit shows that Fung, in spite of his apparent conversion to Marxism and Maoism, had not given up the idea that *jen* had a universal form in spite of bitter attacks on him for advocating a class-transcending concept.

One cannot but be startled by the different tenor of Fung's article "On Confucius" and that of the revised *History*. The article reveals a man thrusting out of the mental confines, aware of what Marxism requires but using to the full every opening his keen mind can find to state what Confucius said or an approximation of it. The revised *History* is the work of a man who toes the line.

We should not limit ourselves to Fung but examine work of his critics. In what purports to be an exhaustive appraisal of Confucius in order to highlight certain progressive elements, Kuan Feng and Lin Yü-shih appear to be setting official limits to the "what-do-we-do-with-Confucius" debate.[42] Because Confucius tried to restore

[41] *Ibid.*, p. 497.
[42] "On Confucius," *Che-hsüeh Yen-chiu*, July 25, 1961; *URS*, October 24, 1961, pp. 90-116; October 27, 1961, pp. 166-84; October 31, 1961, pp. 185-205.

Chou *li* by reviving it with *jen*, he "meant to meet the tide of the time and did not go beyond it, which was, of course, conservative. He was also conservative in that his teaching of *jen* and *li* was to make the people submissive, uncomplaining, and thus to harmonize class contradiction. Although he stood for harmony, he also "stood against the struggles of the poor and those holding low stations rising up to struggle." [43] Kuan and Lin may be striking at Fung when they stress that "loving men" is an abstract saying and that they cannot find "love for people" in the Analects. They point out the contradiction between "love for one's relatives" and "exaltation of men of worth," but resolve the contradiction by saying that Confucius' mission was to restore West Chou culture, which was based on "love for one's relatives," so he had to advocate this principle if he was to proceed on to introduce "exaltation of men of worth," in which he also believed and which represented the progressive side of his political philosophy. [44]

In their discussion on Confucius' philosophical ideas, Kuan and Lin are most confusing and hardly true to the data. At one point they have the master skeptical over gods and spirits, later he is opposed to Heaven as a purposeful reality, then they have him believing in fate as a mechanical inevitability, and finally say he

did not cherish any materialist conception of Nature but believed in the mystic "Decree of Heaven" which, he thought, controlled everything of mankind. Thus Confucius' "Decree of Heaven" differs little in principle from the personified supernatural being—the decree of the supreme being. [45]

It is in the discussion of the Decree of Heaven that Kuan and Lin express most clearly their opposition to what Fung Yu-lan had earlier said, although without mentioning his name. They say that for Confucius the Decree of Heaven

in essence is the will of the "great man" (the owner of slaves) and the teaching of the "sage." To infringe the will of the "great man" and the words of "sages" means a transgression of the "Decree of Heaven." And

[43] *Ibid.*, pp. 100-101.
[44] *Ibid.*, pp. 107-8
[45] *Ibid.*, p. 171.

the so-called "Decree of Heaven" is nothing more than mystifying and objectifying the will of the "great man" and the words of "sages" into an absolutely spiritual thing.[46]

Confucius' "Decree of Heaven" excludes human effort, say the two writers; but they follow this rather dogmatic statement with the same thing Fung had said—there are passages in which Confucius "acknowledged human efforts."

For Kuan and Lin the "Doctrine of the Mean" in Confucius means a kind of eclecticism, compromise, or mixture of opposite or contradicting thoughts, for which they give eight examples. Perhaps the most glaring "mixture of opposites" is their own judgment that in Confucius' philosophical thought fatalism and idealism are blended, and that his idealism was both objective and subjective!

Confucius the educator is deserving of praise according to these men. He was the first great teacher, even though his teaching served his reactionary political views and he seemed to forget his humble origin among ordinary men. They acknowledge that he taught in order to make a living, that he accepted students from all classes, and that he combined learning and practice.[47]

Finally Kuan and Lin examine Confucius' involvement in the history of his period in tortuous detail, all to prove that he was not on the side of rebellious landlords but that he supported the fading slave-owner class.[48]

In Fung's revised *History* and in the Kuan-Lin treatment of Confucius just examined, one can see foreshadowed the fate of Confucius in Communist China. He was a great teacher, but he has nothing of value to teach men whose values are those of Marx, Lenin, and Mao.

A flurry of conferences was called to discuss philosophical questions in 1961-62. The Peking Philosophical Association sponsored four lectures in the latter half of 1961, including appearances by Fung Yu-lan and one of his chief critics, Kuan Feng. The Peking Teachers' University invited scholars in the field of education to

[46] *Ibid.*, p. 172.
[47] *Ibid.*, pp. 178-84.
[48] *Ibid.*, pp. 186-205.

discuss problems of the history of that field in China, which meant a discussion of Confucius the educator. In early 1962, Kirin University held two conferences with Professor Kin Chin-fang's "On the Evaluation of Confucius" as the basis for discussion. Several conferences were held in Kwangtung province, the first a joint meeting of the Philosophical, Economic, Historical, Educational, and Archaeological Associations, just as the new year dawned, with several topics on Confucius. The Historical Association of Kwangtung itself held three discussions on Confucian thought. All in all, four discussion meetings on Confucian thought were held in Kwangtung in the first half of 1962.[49]

Scholars related to the Society of History and the Institute of History of Shantung province presented a joint statement published in *Kuang-ming Jih-pao*, entitled "An Appraisal of Confucius."[50] Selecting *jen*, benevolence, as over against *li*, propriety, or *chung-yung*, the golden mean, as the core of Confucianism, these scholars proceeded to trade views on the true meeting of benevolence. A wide range of virtues were cited to invest this general term with meaning, including propriety and the golden mean, but the desire to "enlarge others," the practice of reciprocity, even of "love for the people," loomed large. A further question—was Confucius conservative or progressive?—could be answered, the scholars affirmed, only when one defined what "people" were to be loved, which the scholars finally agreed, meant "all the people."

As to the political stand of Confucius, there was considerable disagreement. The papers submitted show that a number of scholars thought that Confucius called for strict following of the "rites of Chou" (the dynasty) and that he stood with the declining slave-owner class against the rising landlords, and therefore was conservative. Another group read Confucius as one who revised or even did not follow at all the traditional rites and maintained that

---

[49] Yee Ming provides this list in his article, "Confucius and His Thought as Seen by China Mainland Scholars," *Quarterly Notes* VI (December, 1962), 20-21. He also provides a convenient summary under such topics as *jen, li, t'ien,* showing how various scholars fell into groups in their discussion.

[50] Reported in *KMJP*, November 12, 1962; *SCMP*, November 30, 1962, pp. 3-8.

he really supported the rising landlord class, and thus for his time at any rate, was a progressive. On one thing they were agreed: that it was necessary to continue the study of Confucius under the guidance of Mao Tse-tung's thought.

Much of the 1962 debate centered on *jen* and *li,* with the old divisions on whether Confucius meant that love should be extended to all (Fung Yu-lan) or only to slave owners (Kuan Feng), and whether *li* was the continuation of feudal rites and, if so, was it applied to all or just the aristocrats. Fung got in trouble particularly because of his claim that love had a universal character. He later conditioned this remark by saying that in a class society there is no *jen* that could transcend class; it would still have class character if it were possible. It still pressed toward equality in its application and this was the spirit in which Confucius treated the peasant. Strangely enough,

even Kuan Feng conceded that the Confucian doctrine of *jen* performed a constructive function in the feudal society, since it contributed to the decline of feudalism. The debaters agreed also that Confucius represented the new landlord class instead of the declining slave-owner class.[51]

How Confucius thought of Heaven, or the Mandate of Heaven, received emphasis in discussions at Kirin in the spring of 1962, again with the company divided on whether heaven was a physical force or a spiritual being, whether the way of heaven meant natural laws or not, and thus divided on whether Confucius was a materialist or idealist, or what kind of idealist.[52]

The climax to all the discussion meetings and proliferation of articles in newspapers and magazines was a "Forum on Confucius" held in Tsinan, capital of Confucius' home province of Shantung, November 6-12, 1962. More than 150 philosophers and historians converged on the place for the presentation of 110 papers and for debates on Confucius' teaching vis-à-vis "politics, ideology, philosophy, education, literature, philology, music, history, psychology, physical culture and military science."[53] The forum

[51] Ch'an, "Chinese Philosophy," p. 33. We have been following Ch'an's description of the 1962 debate in this paragraph.
[52] *Ibid.,* p. 32.
[53] Yee Ming, "Confucius and," p. 28.

was sponsored by the Shantung Historical Association and the Shantung Institute of History and included an excursion to the Confucian ancestral temple and cemetery in Chü-fu. The papers were published in two volumes in early 1963.

The same wide variety of views which had prevailed in the discussions for the preceding two or three years were advanced at the conference: Confucius is progressive for his time if he supported the landlord class, but then maybe he sided with the slave-owners; *jen* does perhaps extend to the common people, but it is after all an abstract class-oriented concept; he did welcome new talent to officialdom, but he was still an aristocrat; possibly he wanted to make some changes in the Chou *li*, but it was all to keep the masses in subjection. One tends to conclude that it was just this continual exchange of views without ever reaching unanimity—and how could philosophers agree on every point—which resulted in a loss of patience on the part of the government and the issuance soon after of an authoritative line which inevitably was accepted.

After all the debate on Confucius, there was general agreement, according to Ch'an Wing-tsit that "there is a progressive element in Confucius . . . , that Confucius represented the new landlord class instead of the declining slave-owner class," and that he had made a great contribution to China, particularly in education.[54]

There are a few other thinkers either within, on the fringe of, or outside the Confucian tradition whose fate in Communist China we must examine. We would expect materialists or even those who had materialistic tendencies to come off fairly well, but what is most surprising is the favorable attitude toward Mo Tzu (fifth century B.C.) whose teaching on universal love, rather than love limited to the five relationships, put his work outside the canon of orthodox Confucian philosophy.

Hou Wai-lu, who has opposed the preservationists on many an occasion in Communist China, was pleased to find that Mo Tzu came from the lower classes and that he was scientific in his outlook and a materialist in epistemology—"sense experience as the basis of

[54] Ch'an, "Chinese Philosophy," p. 33.

knowledge and human experience as an important test of truth." [55] Yang Jung-kuo, another contemporary in the field, pointed out that Mo Tzu wanted to correct social evils through social change and development, that his "universal love" undercut the power of the aristocracy, and that he advocated advancing common people who had arisen from slavery to higher positions in the government. He opposed ceremonial extravagance and rejected the idea of the heavenly mandate.[56] Although other contemporary Communist intellectual leaders are quite critical of Mo Tzu, among them Kuo Mo-jo, it is most interesting to find that a few are attracted to Mo Tzu's universal love. It is a bit ironic that missionaries and Chinese Christians, looking for parallels in Chinese thought to their own doctrines, were also attracted to Mo Tzu in past years.

Mencius' subjective idealism, including his belief in man's innate capacity to know the good as well as his religious and political conservatism, evokes little praise from these present-day philosophers.[57] He is credited with some concern for the world and belief in the value of people, but this is hardly enough to redeem him, particularly since Liu Shao-ch'i, whose demise was beginning in the early 60's, made such liberal use of Mencius' ideas.

Hsun Tzu, to whom is attributed a naturalistic view of heaven and a materialistic view of man, obviously finds favor in the present day. His advocacy of law, which shows his concern to protect the rights of the common man, is a score in his favor. In spite of a residue of idealism in his thought, "most mainland scholars conclude that Hsun Tzu was the major materialistic and atheistic thinker of the One Hundred Schools period." [58] I am also inclined to think that the rejection of Hsun Tzu and of Mo Tzu by the orthodox Confucians through the centuries is one of the reasons why these two extremely different thinkers find such favor today.

The handling of one other group of thinkers in Communist China is a source of considerable insight. This is the neo-Confucian school

[55] Donald J. Munro, "Chinese Communist Treatment of the Thinkers of the Hundred Schools Period," *The China Quarterly*, 24 (October-December, 1965), p. 127.
[56] *Ibid.*, p. 128.
[57] *Ibid.*, p. 129.
[58] *Ibid.*, p. 130.

which came on the scene during the Sung dynasty. The Ch'eng brothers, Chu Hsi, Chang Tsai, and, much later, Wang Yang-ming, were the great names in this renewal of the Confucian spirit; Chu Hsi is generally regarded as the greatest.

Chu Hsi came under fire during the May Fourth Movement (1919) as China's greatest enemy, and intellectuals of a modern, scientific temper had little use for him in later years.[59] In Communist China, as Wilhelm points out, Chu Hsi was attacked not only on philosophical grounds but because his thought was imperially sanctioned and because later conservatives and reactionaries, such as Fung Yu-lan, have been identified with his school.[60] Critics such as Hou Wai-lu try "to show that the social contradictions of the time of its [neo-Confucianism's] development were reflected in an intellectual struggle," Ssu-ma Kuang representing the old party, Wang An-shih the new party of small clans and developing petty capitalists. It is difficult for critic Hou to label Ssu-ma Kuang as "old party," however, for neo-Confucianist that he was, Ssu-ma's ideal was the materialist Yang Hsiung and his "enemy" the idealist Mencius.[61]

Among the neo-Confucians, Chang Tsai with his strong materialist and dialectic tendencies comes off best of all. Chang interpreted the notion of ch'i (usually translated "vital force") as being much closer to material existence than other neo-Confucians, which Hou appreciates; but he has difficulty in explaining ch'i's closeness to li (meaning principle, not rites or propriety), and to the Great Void of Buddhism. He also has to find a reason for Chang Tsai's nonprogressive politics, and comes up with the idea that Chang failed to understand the relationship of mind over matter, and thus defended the ruling class against peasant rebellions.[62]

Both the Ch'eng brothers and Chu Hsi, whose philosophical positions are based on li, a basic principle which is to be found in every individual object, are condemned for propounding an absolute

[59] Harold Kahn and Albert Feuerwerker, "The Ideology of Scholarship: China's New Historiography," The China Quarterly, 22 (April-June, 1965), 12.
[60] Wilhelm, "The Reappraisal," p. 131.
[61] Ibid., p. 133.
[62] Ibid., p. 135-36.

idealism. Since this is related to and influenced by Hua-Yen Buddhism and Taoism, Hou thus has further grounds for objection because it represents for him a "religious clericalism." Furthermore, Chu Hsi's alleged scientific method is not scientific at all; his interest in things is only for the purpose of adorning an idealistic system.[63]

Wilhelm's conclusion to his admirable survey of the debate with respect to neo-Confucianism is that although a point here and there can be defended—such as saying that the Ch'eng brothers and Chu Hsi provided support for the imperial system—the case against them and the neo-Confucians in general is based on distortions of what they said. Wilhelm sees this not just as an intellectual or political exercise, but as a matter of value choices by orthodox Communist philosophers, "a strange, if largely unconscious, fear of archetypal values and an eager, if undiscriminating hope enticed by utopian values." [64]

In addition to Fung Yu-lan and his efforts to find in the Confucian tradition those elements which might at least coexist with Marxism, there is another thinker who has been far less accomodating in his defense of Confucian ideas, much more independent of outlook and manner. Liu Chieh, a member of the history department of Chungshan (Sun Yat-sen) University, was strongly influenced by the teachings of Mencius and by the Ch'eng-Chu school of neo-Confucianism. He clearly rejected both the theory of class struggle as a key to understanding ancient Chinese history, and the polarization between idealism and materialism as a category into which all philosophers had to fit. He saw philosophy as the study of the nature of the union between heaven and man, accepted Mencius' definition of human nature as heaven's endowment to all men, and treated *jen* as an abstract concept having universal validity beyond time and class.[65] At all these points Liu was flying in the face of the standard Marxist interpretation of the Confucian tradition; in the attacks which fell on him I am reminded of the criticisms of thinkers like Fung Yu-lan and am

[63] *Ibid.*, pp. 137-38.
[64] *Ibid.*, p. 139.
[65] Munro, "Chinese Communist Treatment," p. 121.

ready to conclude that they would be applied to any thinker regardless of the individual drift of his thought.

Liu was criticized in particular for papers on the Confucian doctrine of *jen* and the neo-Confucian doctrine of the unity of heaven and man; these papers were presented to two Shantung scholarly gatherings and later published.[66] Li K'an, his critic, asserted that Liu had used certain Marxist phrases and terms which had nothing to do with the idea of *jen*, that Liu had presented *jen* as an abstract idea transcending time and class which would lead to perfection if everyone would follow it. He had presented Confucius as one who spoke for the people, who hoped to raise their standard of education and culture and to bring "peace and stability" to them. This, the critic Li K'an says, means that Liu Chieh sees no need for Marxism-Leninism, that instead he wants people to "foster great affection for mankind through *jen*, and, in a word, to venerate Confucius." Even though Liu Chieh recognized that *jen* "inclined toward idealism," and admitted that it was the feudal class which welcomed Confucian thought, it means nothing to Li K'an but a glorification of idealism and feudalism. Thus Li K'an identifies Liu with K'ang Yu-wei and Yüan Shih-k'ai, who in the closing years of the Ch'ing dynasty and the early years of the Republic, respectively, advocated a return to Confucian teachings and the veneration of Confucius along religious lines.

Li K'an's criticism was based on Mao's dictum that "we should sum up everything from Confucius to Sun Yat-sen and inherit this valuable legacy," but without "laudation of what is old and disparagement of what is new, or commendation of any feudal poisonous element." One could say that Liu Chieh was "summing up" and doing it critically, but Li K'an finds only "laudation and commendation" of what is old, and is particularly resentful of Liu for finding antecedents to Marxism-Leninism before it appeared full-blown upon the scene. In the final analysis Li seems to be saying that Liu has not understood or appreciated the role of class struggle and class analysis; had he done so he would have realized

[66] Li K'an, "In Refutation of the New 'Venerate Confucius' Doctrine," *KMJP*, August 17-18, 1963. In answer to Liu Chieh, "The Confucian Doctrine of *Jen*," *Hsüeh-shu Yen-chiu*, 3, 1962. Li's criticism was translated in *SCMP*, September 30, 1963, pp. 1-9. *See* Ch'an, "Chinese Philosophy in," p. 36.

the necessity of struggling against, or relegating to a museum, such remnants of feudalism as love, propriety, and music.

By 1963 the axe began to fall. In the first issue of *Che-hsüeh Yen-chiu* (Philosophical Studies) for 1963, Tung Fang-ming discussed "An Extremely Harmful Method in the Work of the History of Philosophy." [67] Highly critical of those who say that Confucius taught the theory that knowledge comes from experience, he states conclusively:

We may see clearly [from such examples] that it is wrong to say that ancient thought did not differ from Marxism. To say this is unhistorical for it is at variance with the fact that it was Marxism which discovered the law of development of human knowledge. These people do nothing but tag the terms of Marxist philosophy on to ancient thought. . . . The gravest error is that this magnifies ancient people, a thing which may lead to trouble.[68]

Following the same tenor of thought, but even more sharply expressed, was a statement by the editorial department of *Hsin Chien-she* (New Construction). Particularly disturbed by the way in which people were quoting Confucian epigrams and reading Marxist ideas into them, as if to say that Confucius thought of Marxist ideas before Marx, the editors said:

Confucius was, after all, a thinker of the exploiting class, living more than 2,400 years ago. There is no doubt that he did not, and could not, advance scientific principles of epistemology which could only evolve from Marxism. His advice on "learning with constant perseverance and application" and "cherishing old knowledge to acquire the new," his great attention to learning and his affirmation of the process of self-cultivation are of positive significance to the history of the cognitional development of mankind and should be accorded a definite place in science. However, they cannot be spoken of on equal terms with the epistemological principles of dialectic materialism. We cannot grasp the meaning by glancing at a text. Neither can we hang the label of Marxist principles under the name of Confucius or any other ancient figure. The reason is that this approach is unscientific. It will not, in the least, benefit the scientific study of

[67] Summarized in *CNA*, April 19, 1963, p. 2. Note that it is philosophical *workers*, history of philosophy *work*.

[68] *Ibid.*, p. 3.

ideological history or the inheritance of ideological legacy. Moreover, it is likely to lead people to the road of worshipping ancients blindly.[69]

The editors went on to voice criticism that others had voiced: that Confucian thought was not something eternal, transcending class and time, that his most profound teachings had a feudal class character. Again, only when his teachings are approached from the viewpoint of class analysis and class struggle can they be understood.

It should now be quite clear that the efforts to make Confucius or certain elements in his teaching acceptable or tolerated in Communist China were beyond any hope of fulfillment. If pointing out that Confucius hoped to raise standards of education and culture and bring peace and stability in the fifth century B.C. is interpreted as meaning "no need for Marxism-Leninism," then it is clear that Confucius is finished.

In 1962, it was possible for Yee Ming to say that the Communists had not decided what to do about Confucius, that there was a possibility that certain aspects of his teaching might be useful.[70] Fred Parrish, who wrote a most intriguing article, "The Persistence of Confucianism in Communist China," about the time the discussions were going on, may have had some reason to hope that

The "new culture" . . . seemed destined to be a revision and an elaboration and enrichment of China's traditional culture, with its Confucianism, and not a culture which was to be identified as the culture of modern science.[71]

But Parrish went a little too far in stating how "Confucian" Mao was and he overstated the way in which "the 'new culture' in the early stages of its emergence retained the dominant ideas and practices of Confucianism." Whether Mao or any of the doctrinaire Chinese Marxists ever thought seriously about retaining "the dom-

[69] "Problem of Inheritance of Ideological Legacy in Light of Discussions on Confucius," *Hsin Chien-she* editorial department statement in *KMJP*, January 23, 1963; *SCMP*, February 21, 1963, p. 2.
[70] Yee Ming, "Confucius and," p. 29.
[71] *Midwest Quarterly* IV (January, 1963), 161-62.

inant ideas and practices of Confucianism" is open to question, but one can hardly question that by 1963 or 1964, in Communist China the official death knell had been sounded for Confucius.

From that time on any serious discussion of Confucius or his teaching is difficult to find. Presumably still respected as a teacher and educator, the content of his teaching had been left behind. The papers and magazines were full of a new morality: Going to the countryside to labor, politics not family considerations or love as the criterion for selecting a mate, the necessity of a revolutionary art, stress on being "red" instead of "expert," the training of red successors. None of these were particularly new, but the stress was intensified. The meaning of these various aspects of the new ethic, which may even be called the new religion, is another story. Suffice it to say here that the older moral and religious patterns were completely crowded out.

It was at certain points—the "training of red successors" and the importance of "red" over "expert"—that one could see in the mid-60's a nervousness, a fear that some people were looking backward to the feudal past with its ideals of harmony and human-heartedness. This was but one of the many lingering "olds" which called forth the turmoil of 1966.

The Cultural Revolution with its Red Guards moved against Confucius several months after the blows struck against religions as such, but, by late 1966, the Red Guards were engaged in a campaign to condemn and destroy the writings of the "number one criminal of feudal thinking." Travelers say portraits of Confucius were carried through the streets of Canton, the pictures labeled "I am an ox, a demon, a snake, and a devil." [72]

The Red Guards also raided the birthplace of Confucius at Chü-fu in Shantung province and destroyed a temple built many centuries earlier in honor of the sage. The incident was reported in *Jen-min Jih-pao* as due to Confucius' teachings being feudalistic and out of step with Mao's Communist doctrines.[73] The editors com-

---

[72] *China Notes* V (January, 1967), 3.

[73] Reported in Hong Kong *Sing Tao Daily*, then in *China Post*, January 18, 1967. I have noted a box in connection with one of Fung Yu-lan's articles in *People's China*, January 1, 1957, a brief sketch of Confucius and then this item: "There are to this day in Chü-fu [Confucius' birthplace] many relics of

mented that "Confucianism should be eradicated and put to death immediately. . . . Red Guards have buried Confucianism, once and for all."

A violent and bitter article appeared in *Jen-min Jih-pao*, January 10, 1967, written by a group (or written for them) called the Chingkangshan Combat Group of Red Guards in the Study of the Thoughts of Mao Tse-tung at Peking Normal University. There is reference in the article to their determination to "set out for Chü-fu, Shantung, to rebel against the old feudal den of Confucianism."

The major part of Red Guard venom was directed against the "Forum on Confucius," held in Shantung in November, 1962, and the "monsters and demons" who assembled there to talk about "benevolent government" and "rule by moral virtues," which the incensed youth claimed was an attack on socialism and dictatorship of the proletariat, as well as an attempt to provoke a counterrevolutionary restoration.[74] The "monsters and demons," though not named specifically, undoubtedly had reference to Fung Yu-lan and Chou Yang, the latter having gone out of favor after being a leader in the Propaganda Department of the Party's Central Committee.

Statements made by the scholars who had attended the conferences are quoted, then a "Red Guard Comment." For example, a statement that Confucius' greatness as a philosopher, statesman, and educator, even though some of his theories are out of date, has been a source of unity for the Chinese nation, brings the retort that anyone who tries "to establish the absolute authority of Confucius in the vain hope of using Confucian ideas and concepts to unify the thought, language, feelings and habits of 700 million people" is employing "every conceivable means of disparaging and attacking Mao Tse-tung's thought, hoping thereby, to induce a counterrevolutionary restoration."

A quotation from the scholars on benevolence, "Do as you would

---

Confucius, among them the Confucius memorial arch, the Chinese juniper tree planted by Confucius himself, the place where Confucius taught his pupils in his later years, his tomb, and the famous ancient K'ung Miao or Temple of Confucius [presumably the one destroyed]. All these places and objects are now cared for by the Institute for the Protection and Management of Cultural Objects in Chü-fu."

[74] *China Notes* V (July, 1967), 4.

be done by," a plea for the lessening of hostility, is followed by a Red Guard reminder that it is reactionaries who "denounce us for not being 'benevolent,'" and who want a benevolent government by "doing away with proletarian dictatorship." Someone in the 1962 group at Shantung had spoken of "doing things blindly and recklessly," and of "those who are so conceited that they claim they know half the things in heaven and everything on earth." The Red Guards claim that "under the wise leadership of Chairman Mao and guided by the three red banners our people have won brilliant victories." The scholars had referred to benevolence, living in harmony, loving people, to which the Red Guards respond that there is a "life and death struggle"—totally devoid of the idea of "loving one another," an idea propagated by "monsters and demons" only "to blur the class boundary line and to repudiate class struggle." [75]

Another source states that some of these scholars had noticed in Liu Shao-chi's writing the use of certain ideas from Confucius and Mencius, "remolded and absorbed as important components to be cultivated in the character of Party members." This, according to the Red Guards, was "to distort and confuse the truth, in an attempt to disguise the idealist world outlook of Confucius as a dialectical-materialist one, and to oppose Mao Tse-Tung's thought." [76]

After all the effort to make Confucius acceptable in Communist China, and after a conference of respectable scholars had set forth the ways in which he was, even this residue was wiped aside. Only the most extremist of the Red Guards would say that the master has been permanently swept aside, but for the moment at least, Confucius is a dirty word.

The attacks continued. Confucius himself, historians such as Szu-Ma Ch'ien and Szu-Ma Kuang, and modern thinkers like Liang Ch'i-ch'ao, Hu Shih, and Ch'ien Mu, were all lumped together as those who support the exploiting classes:

Do not all of them, without exception, exert their utmost in glossing over and distorting the history of class and class struggle, in covering up the

[75] *Ibid.*, pp. 5-6.
[76] *China News Summary*, 154, January 19, 1967.

cannibal tyranny with a rose veneer, and in drawing on such fallacies as "Providence dictates one's fate; wealth and fame are predestined" to paralyze the will of struggle of the exploited and the oppressed? Don't they draw on the fallacy that "neither Heaven nor the Way changes," exhaust their wits in apologizing for "it is justified to oppress and to exploit but not justified to rebel . . ." [77]

One of the reasons why T'ao Chu, a writer in disfavor during the Cultural Revolution, was severely criticized was his showing respect for Confucius and Mencius in his 1960 book, *Ideals, Integrity and Spiritual Life.*[78] And as late as May, 1969, Liu Shao-Ch'i was attacked in a joint editorial written by editors of several journals and newspapers for trying to revive the teachings of Confucius and Mencius. "The renegade, hidden traitor, and scab Liu Shao-ch'i wildly preached the ways of Confucius and Mencius to poison the minds of Party members and young people." [79] Once again Confucius is identified with the declining slave-owner class of the Chou dynasty, his teachings "upheld by the feudal exploiting class as an inevitable law."

After all the debate, whether in periodicals or at conferences of philosophers, the thought of Confucius proves to have no significance for the present day. After all the care lavished on certain treasured monuments and shrines, they are defaced or destroyed because they are old and have no place in the new day.

Confucianism has passed through many periods of trial since its inception, and Ch'an Wing-tsit reminds us that it has passed several crises in the past fifty years.[80] Almost anyone who speaks about Chinese history observes that Chinese tradition, culture, philosophy, or Confucianism, in spite of invasions by barbarians, Manchus, Japanese, or the West, always manages to reassert itself. That which is distinctively Chinese (and what is more Chinese than Confucius?), though out of favor, suppressed, corrupted for a century or two, will inevitably rise again like the sun. The fulfillment of such a hope, which is very much a part of the

[77] Shih Hung-ping in *KMJP*, May 30, 1967, p. 5; *URS*, June 9, 1967, p. 282.
[78] In review by Hsiao Chueh and T'ou Ch'ang in *Chieh-fang-chun Wen-i*, 15, September 25, 1967; *SCMM*, December 4, 1967, pp. 10-12.
[79] *AP* release from Tokyo; *China Post*, May 5, 1969.
[80] *Religious Trends in Modern China*, p. 53.

Chinese, Confucian way, depends in part at least on what happens to China as a whole, particularly to that new ideology, new teaching, new way which seems bent on supplanting all the old ways. Only when we are able to see more clearly what is in store for China as a whole can we say realistically that Confucianism "will be alive."

With the temple and tomb at Confucius' birthplace restored, as Levenson says, the authorities have "retired Confucius honorably into the silence of the museum." [81] Now with temple and tomb defaced, there is no honor, only the silence.

---

[81] *Confucian China*, Vol. III, p. 79.

XI

Taoism and Folk Religion: Elusive as Always

SEVERE PRESSURES FROM THE BEGINNING

It has been customary to approach Taoism as a bifurcated phenomenon: the quietistic philosophy which issues from books bearing the names of Lao Tzu and Chuang Tzu on the one hand, and a tremendous assortment of popular or folk religious practice, which may or may not be derived from the earlier philosophers on the other. I have chosen to approach this vast amalgam of indigenous Chinese religion under the rubric of "Taoism and folk religion," which includes devotion to many gods, powers, and deified heroes, only some of which are Taoist, and such disparate elements as the ancient and honorable veneration of ancestors, which also undergirds the Confucian tradition, as well as such practices as magic, sorcery, and fortune-telling.

Emperors of the past, leaders of Republican China, as well as the Communist leaders of today, have been wary of that which goes under the name of Taoism, especially the so-called "Taoist" secret societies. These societies, with membership rosters and activities known only to initiates, have been suspected of harboring men dangerous to the government and of being centers of dissenting thought. These suspicions are not unjustified: the societies have sheltered unsavory characters and at certain times in history have provoked or staged revolts.

On another level, government and civic leaders of this century, many of them stemming from the intellectual or educated classes, have deplored the way in which common people have been milked by various practitioners known as "Taoist," men who have preyed on the popular imagination with promises of prosperity, healing, and a glimpse into future delights or torments.

Even the Nationalist government was prepared to suppress the "superstitious worship of spirits" practiced by fortune-tellers, astrologers, witches, wizards, geomancers, sorcerers, and magicians attempting to heal the sick, as well as the producers and distributors of literature supporting or promulgating the above. The prohibitions, announced in a Ministry of Interior decree on September 7, 1948, also were to fall on such vaguely stated categories as

Those who operate unorthodox religious houses to delude the people; those who contribute to spirits of impurity to obtain riches; . . . those who build shrines for the spirits and fabulous birds to come in to rest; . . . all who initiate or participate in those processions in which idols are carried to thank the gods; all who invoke superstition in their actions; other illegal movements and secret societies.[1]

Some who fell under the above prohibitions might be admonished and released, but most of those in the list were to be suppressed or brought to trial. Since Nationalist days were numbered, the decree undoubtedly was never enforced.

When we turn to the Communists we find, as Bertuccioli says, that Taoism was put on an even lower level than religion. It was regarded as a superstition without ethical foundation, a barrier to raising the cultural level of the masses, and a political danger because the secret societies associated with it had been the source of past revolts. Taoists had no fellow believers outside of China whose cultivation might prove helpful in diplomatic relations, as was the case with Buddhists and Muslims. For these reasons Bertuccioli says the attitude of the Peking government toward Taoism was one of clear opposition.[2]   The Administrative Council of the new People's Government announced on August 4, 1950, its "Decisions Concerning Differentiation of Class Status in the Countryside," one paragraph of which read:

[1] *CMBA* II (January, 1949), 183-84.
[2] Guiliano Bertuccioli, "Il Taoismo nella Cina Contemporanea," *Cina II* (Rome: Italian Institute for the Middle and Far East, 1957), p. 69.

All those people who for three years immediately prior to liberation derived the main part of their income from such religious and superstitious professions as those of clergymen, priests, monks, Taoists, lay Taoists, geomancers, fortune-tellers, and diviners, are to be classified as religious or superstitious practicioners.[3]

The last five in the list fall into the general category of Taoism and folk religion. It is also interesting to note that "religious" and "superstitious" seem to be synonymous.

Even before this classification was announced, Taoist priests and their establishments, already in a moribund state after the upheavals of twentieth-century China, had felt the impact of the new regime and the new temper of the times. The situation for Taoist priests in Shanghai deteriorated rapidly in the first year under the Communists, according to Alfred Kiang. Compared to Buddhist temples, there were very few belonging to the Taoists in Shanghai and only one of them in Nantao still followed the old tradition of providing hospitality to Taoist priests passing through. Although some of the old fanciful banners and tablets still were visible "an uneasy atmosphere of desolation and depression reigns in the temples. The Taoist priests are facing a complete collapse of their fabricated kingdom of fantastic superstition in the face of changing developments." [4] Kiang went on to say that the Yü-huang Shan Temple on Wuting Road had not received a single order for a Taoist Mass since liberation, that most of the young priests had gone back to their homes. Women Taoists were making hosiery in another temple in Nantao.

A similar report, later in 1950, stressed the political reorientation and efforts to establish communal living for Taoist priests in Peking. "They are no longer social parasites; they are active producers now." [5] Much the same word came from the South: "all temples and shrines in Canton have been requisitioned by Communist authorities for use in public meetings." Priests, monks, and nuns were sent to the suburbs for training as carpenters and

[3] Quoted in Yang I-fan, *Buddhism in China*, p. 38.
[4] "A New Life," p. 174.
[5] *CMBA* II (III) (December, 1950), 1050.

seamstresses, and for Marxist-Leninist studies.[6] Also on Hainan island temples were taken over by the government and male and female clergy sent to an orientation center for training in manual work.[7] In both places Buddhists as well as Taoists were involved.

A few months later in Canton the authorities began to demolish ancestral shrines and temples, which because of feudal influences were obstructing the progress of Marxist-Leninist studies. Shrines to local deities along the streets were particularly objectionable because large numbers of women worshiped there.[8]

Out in Kansu, however, Catholics reported that the authorities in Pingliang allowed folk religious practices, such as burning incense and paper money, in spite of the fact that such practices had been strongly condemned by Communist officialdom. This exception was probably due to the fact that the folk rituals were being carried out before the body of a woman who had died after an injection in a Catholic dispensary.[9]

In the village of Nanching, where C. K. Yang directed studies upon which his *A Chinese Village in Early Communist Transition* was based, there was an indiscriminate smashing of temples and much antireligious violence by ardent supporters of the new regime at first, but as social-political order was established emphasis fell on organized religious activities.[10] This meant that Christianity was the focal point, but since there were so few Christians in Nanching, the total effect on the community was not great when these were caught in the purges by which the government sought to divorce the Christian church from its foreign connections.

The most popular religious center in Nanching, the Taoist-type Temple of the God of Fire, was not molested, but its ten *mou* of land were redistributed to the peasants, with a share to the Taoist priest who was required to cultivate it like anyone else. A seeress who had an altar in her home was pressured to give up her practices, but she continued and was not put on public trial or subjected to mob violence. An officer found out that she had gone to a medical

[6] *South China Morning Post*, August 24, 1951. See also *CMBA* IV (V) (March, 1952), 206.
[7] *China Mail*, September 4, 1951.
[8] *CMBA* IV (V) (February, 1952), 153.
[9] *CMBA* IV (V) (March, 1952), 228.
[10] (Cambridge: Technology Press, 1959), see pp. 194-96.

doctor instead of using her own magic and thus called her a fraud. Whether for this reason or other reasons, her practice declined. Ancestor worship could still be carried on in private homes, but clan celebrations were curtailed because income from the land was cut off. Birthday festivals for various gods were discouraged strongly and virtually disappeared after 1950. Yang sums up by saying:

Without violence, but by the impoverishment of the rich families and the clans, religion was, so to speak, driven from public view back into the homes, where the unchangeable older generation of peasants could cherish their traditional customs and beliefs undisturbed. But the power of religion to strengthen community spirit and to evoke a sense of community sharing was already nearly destroyed. Most important of all, the Communists had embarked on a long-term program . . . aimed at the eradication of traditional influence in Chinese life. At the heart of that program was the education of the younger generation. It was not on the compulsive remaking of the minds of those who were beyond the age of thirty that the Communists pinned their main hope for the final triumph of atheism, but on the youth who were so universally subjected to Communist education.[11]

In another work Yang tells of the special tax imposed on "superstitious commodities"; this tax served as a deterrent to the purchase of such items as joss sticks, candles, and paper articles to be burned for the dead. And in Kwangtung province, where people had long believed that the dikes would collapse if women worked on them, officials simply hired some women for dike repair, the dikes stayed firm, and thus the fallacy of ancient beliefs was demonstrated.[12]

At the other end of the spectrum from these indirect methods for dealing with folk religion were rampaging, antireligious mobs acting on the freedom to oppose religion, which was later written into the Constitution. Yang says that, in 1951, he

visited an ancestral temple in a village in Kwangtung province and saw only an empty building left after a Peasants' Association mob had com-

---

[11] Ibid., pp. 195-96.
[12] Religion in Chinese Society (Berkeley: University of California Press, 1961), p. 389.

pletely stripped it of honorific and religious objects and burned them in order to "sever the present generation from the roots of feudalism." [13]

Most temples, as was the case in Buddhism, were transformed for the use of public organizations and group activities. The buildings thus became headquarters for the Peasants' Association, village and town cooperative stores, jails, and barracks for soldiers. There is mention of the famous Tin Hau Temple at Chik Wan Bay, twenty-five miles northwest of Hong Kong, being torn down and the materials used for military fortifications in 1954, but I have heard of very few such extreme cases.[14]

We have observed already that the Communist government is not the first Chinese government to be troubled by "Taoist" secret societies. These widely scattered, independent, amorphous societies have no central organization; when dispersed by police or military they have seemed to disappear, only to regroup and start up again. Communist authorities tackled the problem in their first year in power with a census in which Taoists had to register as "belonging to reactionary associations and [following] Taoist superstitions." Measures by which such associations were declared illegal were enacted about the same time, the first temples were confiscated for use as military barracks or schools, and small shrines along the roadside were demolished. Several chiefs of secret societies were arrested and charged with having organized armed counter-revolutionary bands in Manchuria and Kaifeng.[15] As a result of pressures put upon them, Bertuccioli says that "by the end of June, 1951, more than a hundred thousand members of the I Kuan Tao [Way of Pervading Unity (Society)] had apostasized in Peking alone, taking advantage of the amnesty granted by the government." [16]

These religious societies were accused by the Communists of sheltering a large variety of counterrevolutionary organizations. Such societies as Pai-yang Chiao (the White Sun Religion), Lung-

---

[13] *Ibid.*, p. 391.

[14] *CHIBUL*, February 1, 1954.

[15] Bertuccioli, "Il Taoismo," p. 70. Based on *JMJP*, December 20, 1950; and *Chieh-fang Jih-pao* [Liberation Daily], Shanghai, December 29, 1950.

[16] *Ibid.*, p. 70. Based on Hong Kong *Ta Kung Pao*, January 20, 1951.

hua Hui (Dragon Flower Association), Chiu-kung Tao (Nine Mansions Sect), and Sheng Hsien Tao (Unity Sect) were recognized to be in some sense centers of resistance to the new government, as they and other organizations had been to previous governments since the eighteenth century. The crimes for which they were charged, of course, were new: carrying on underground activities for Chiang Kai-shek and the Nationalists, and supporting American imperialism.[17] C. K. Yang notes the claim of Lo Jui-ch'ing, chief of the security police, that the liquidation of leaders of many religious societies in the autumn of 1952 was a great achievement, but he goes on to point out that in spite of such liquidations these societies were still judged by the authorities to be carrying out their counterrevolutionary role in 1954.[18]

The fact that such groups had not by any means disappeared but were still a problem is attested by the severity of measures adopted by the authorities in Shanghai. The Shanghai Municipal Military Government on May 30, 1953, outlawed Taoist cults and ordered their leaders to register with the government. The deputy mayor said in a radio statement on June 7 that these cults "had harbored criminals, spies, and saboteurs who had worked for the Manchus, Japanese, Nationalists, and Americans, and had swindled people mercilessly," and went on to charge the cults with sexual immorality.[19] An anti-Taoist exhibition of what purported to be secret messages distributed in the form of holy pictures, along with flags and weapons allegedly used by members of the societies and photographs of their leaders, was staged at the same time. Numerous sect leaders were arrested and brought before one of seven military tribunals which met in extraordinary session on June 11, at which time the leaders were accused by people from "educational, cultural, industrial, and commercial circles."[20]

Chang Yin-yu, head of I Kuan Tao, was accused of being in contact with "Chiang Kai-shek bandits and foreign imperialists,"

---

[17] Yang, *Religion in*, pp. 400-401.

[18] *Ibid.*, p. 399, based on *JMJP*, September 29, 1952.

[19] Summary from Chinese press in *CURBAC*, March 20, 1955, p. 6.

[20] Bertuccioli, "Il Taoismo," pp. 71-72, based on *Chieh-fang Jih-pao*, June 13, 1953.

and one of his lieutenants of robbing the people, driving even some to suicide. Chao Yu-yu, head of another sect, was charged with having promoted a revolt and leading an armed band of four hundred bandits in 1948. Shen I-ching, head of Chiu-kung Tao, was accused "of having tricked his parents by inducing them to use the ashes of incense sticks as medicine," thus causing continued illness. Following the pattern of similar trials in Christian circles, the crowd, said to be 91,000 strong, called on the judges to pronounce the gravest of penalties and shouted indignantly: "Suppress the Taoists!" Some received the death penalty; others were to work for two years during which time their labor would be observed and judged.[21]

In the face of such repressive measures, leaders and members of the secret societies either dropped all traces of their special allegiance or, literally, went underground. I Kuan Tao, for example, took the name of Chung Tao (Middle Sect) in some places and many of its members traveled about as itinerant merchants. Most remarkable was the construction, reported at various points from Shensi to Hopei, of underground chambers with a network of connecting tunnels.

Some of the subterranean chambers are large enough to accommodate over thirty people, and the tunnels long enough to connect strategic places throughout entire villages. In 1955, the Communist police uncovered 102 subterranean hiding places in Shensi alone, arresting 434 sectarian leaders. In Tungkuang county of Hopei province, several long-hunted sectarian leaders were found to have taken refuge in tunnels for over four years.[22]

Emerging from their hideouts, often posing as tradesmen, members of the sects penetrated mutual-aid teams and agricultural producers' cooperatives. They encouraged people "to store up grain as an act of religious piety," thus impeding the achievement of quotas set by the government. They attracted many people with their "claim of age-old miracles, such as the potency of a new magical formula or the healing power of a magical water." These

[21] *Ibid.*
[22] Yang, *Religion in*, p. 400, based on *JMJP*, July 2 and July 29, 1955.

societies were able to survive as long as they did, Yang maintains, because of

the popular belief in the gods and their magic to bring deliverance from suffering, and in the popular tradition of organizing religious groups to offer resistance to an oppressive ruling power against which the individual seems helpless.[23]

I have noted in several sources that a Chinese Taoist Association was founded in 1953, along with Muslim and Buddhist Associations; but Bertuccioli maintains that the Taoist organization did not actually come into existence until November 26, 1956, when a New China News Agency release announced the formation of a promotion committee which would establish a Chinese Taoist Association.[24] It is possible that plans for the establishment of such an association were made in 1953, but not really implemented until 1956. Bertuccioli, at any rate, makes the point that the first mention of Taoism which was not "Anti-Taoist" was at the close of 1954, and that it was not really until Li Wei-han, vice-president of the Standing Committee of the National People's Congress, in a speech on September 25, 1956, referred to Taoism as one of several religions that enjoyed freedom of worship in China, that there was indication of a change.[25]

At the organizational meeting a manifesto was issued in language which parallels statements made by the other associations:

In order to unite all the Taoists of China in the protection of the fatherland, in the participation in socialist reconstruction, in the defense of peace; in order to cooperate with the government in its policy of religious liberty; in order to further promote the good teachings of Taoism, we feel the need of a national Taoist organization, and therefore propose the establishment of a Chinese Taoist Association.[26]

Ho Chen-hsiang, Director of the Bureau of Religious Affairs, was

[23] *Ibid.*, p. 401.
[24] Bertuccioli, "Il Taoismo," p. 67. *CNA* agrees, placing formation of the preparatory committee in November, 1956, and the actual formation of the Chinese Taoist Association in April, 1957.
[25] Bertuccioli, p. 76.
[26] *Ibid.*, p. 67.

present at the meeting, and assured members of the support of the government. An aged Taoist priest, Yueh Tsung-tai (or Ch'un-tai), was elected president, and Ch'en Ying-ming and Meng Yün-hui vice-presidents.

The new president made a speech to the Chinese People's Political Consultative Conference, in which he claimed that Taoism was the only truly Chinese religion with origins going back to primitive society, to the veneration of thunder and rain, rivers and trees, all of which was still being carried out. He stressed an ancient Taoist saying—"The Tao consists of teaching"—but without saying whether he meant this as a criticism of the current military discipline, or whether he was complimenting the Communist ideological training program. The saying has traditionally meant that the wise teacher or sage uses persuasion and not law and punishment. He was trying to point out, apparently, that Taoism could be of use to the ruling class, and went on to say that Taoists no longer tried to live for themselves away from troubles and struggles and politics, but had, after Liberation, gone through indoctrination and were participating in politics.[27]

Although the new association was heralded as the first national Taoist organization in Chinese history, there is very little information about its activities. One may note an occasional reference to a representative of the Chinese Taoist Association being present at a public gathering along with representatives of other religious associations in order to condemn American activity in Vietnam.[28] The little information available does not in any way suggest that the association was intended to build up followers of the Taoist faith. As C. K. Yang says:

The aim [was] to build an organizational apparatus for more effective national control of the religious population and for making them accept the "guidance of the Party and the government," abide by Communist law and policies, and participate in the "socialist construction and various patriotic movements of the motherland." [29]

[27] *JMJP*, March 14, 1957; summarized in *CNA*, March 21, 1958, p. 4.
[28] For example *NCNA*, February 11, 1965; *SCMP*, February 16, 1965, p. 25.
[29] Yang, *Religion in*, p. 394, quoting from *CURBAC*, February 13, 1959, p. 8, and January 15, 1960, p. 4; *SCMP*, March 29, 1957, p. 11.

The Chinese Taoist Association, intended to control Taoism and folk religious practices associated with Taoism, is clearly the weakest of the various associations. There is nothing to which the association could relate at the local level. There were Taoist monasteries, which could be taken over, and groups of Taoist priests, who could be reeducated or dispersed, but how does such an organization control folk religion which, when forbidden in one place, pops up again in another? How does a government control a priesthood which can take off its robes for a few years, seemingly forget about the rituals which priests are forbidden to exercise, and thus to all intents and purposes comply with regulations? At any time, whenever it is convenient, such a priest may start up again. Other religious movements have adopted such techniques of survival; Taoism and the folk religious movements have had them all along.

OVERT SUPPRESSION AND PRACTICAL EXPLANATION

By whatever combination of courage, cleverness, and natural resilience the common people were able to muster, their folk religious practices still continued in the mid-50's, although the government does not seem to have allowed even the limited freedom which other religious movements enjoyed during the Hundred Flowers Period. On the contrary, there are several reports from the mainland Chinese press which make it clear that there was no let up in efforts to control and suppress the religion of the masses. *Kuang-ming Jih-pao,* for example, picked up the news in the spring of 1956 that people were praying to the gods to heal the sick, and summarily approved the suppression of such activities:

The measures taken by the local militia, under the direction of the local Party and government organization and under the unified guidance of higher police authority, are justifiable. Such practices are being stopped.[30]

The authorities also followed drastic measures in Hupeh province, but found it advisable to temper their approach. People had the

[30] *KMJP*, January 9, 1958; *CNA*, March 21, 1958, p. 2.

custom of visiting the tomb of Goddess Ma (Ma Hsien Ku), which stood by a temple erected in her honor, in order to burn joss sticks and seek holy water with which to heal the sick. The shrine had not been too popular during the early years of the Communist regime, but in 1957, when rumors spread that "the other world is drafting new recruits for its armed forces and those on the call-up list will not survive," people crowded around the tomb in large numbers, usually about three to four hundred a day with as many as six hundred a day. On grounds that agricultural production would be affected by such absenteeism, local Party leaders dispersed the crowds and began to dig up the tombstone. The people were incensed and threatened to attack the Party men, whereupon the latter called the police, who were in turn ridiculed by the people. Wiser heads finally prevailed and conducted an investigation which showed that the public health department had done a poor job in dealing with measles, meningitis, and influenza, which had attacked the area, leaving the old people no recourse (their "superstitious ideology was not completely removed") but to ask the goddess for the holy water. The authorities therefore arranged for scientific explanation of the cause of diseases and made the necessary medicines available to the people. Upon the arrival of the medical team the number of devotees dropped to one hundred, and in three more days declined from sixty to thirteen, and finally to zero.[31]

In Lingshan County of Kwangtung province people venerated a sacred stone "to the detriment of production." One cadre got the bright idea that if the stone were destroyed the superstition would cease. The stone was destroyed, "but this not only did not eradicate the superstition of the masses but provoked great discontent among the masses." Mob rioting broke out in one place where a Buddha image was removed, and in another place when it was heard that a small temple was to be destroyed.[32]

A Yen Kung temple in a town called Tienpai on the coast of Kwangtung province was a place where Lady Hsit'ai was venerated. After Liberation the temple was destroyed, by whom it was not clear. When an epidemic of influenza broke out in that

[31] Yang, Religion in, p. 390, from SCMP, May 23, 1957, p. 21.
[32] JMJP, April 19 and May 8, 1957; both in CNA, March 21, 1958, p. 3.

region in April and May, 1957, people flocked to the place where the temple had been in response to the news that Lady Hsit'ai had come back to save the people. Some eighty thousand people came to the place during the two months to say prayers, give donations, and burn incense. The word was spread: "Lady Hsit'ai has come to save the country from the Communists, the leaders of the collective will be killed; the Kuomintang is coming back in August." Government houses were beseiged, cadres were beaten up. Finally the police came, destroyed a temporary shrine, and burned the picture of Lady Hsit'ai.[33]

The stories just examined indicate that folk religious traditions had great staying power in the countryside. From the cadres' point of view, the rural people had received insufficient "scientific education" to counter their age-old, feudal beliefs, so the cadres could not afford to get too tough with them. As reformers in any culture know, the obdurate will of the masses, especially when aroused emotionally and excited to fever pitch, is not an enviable thing to face. And the cadres could hardly use their customary measures on peasant masses, the heroes of Marxism-Leninism.

In the city it was another story if we look at the desultory scene in the Temple of the Dignitary in Shanghai as described by Faure. Five monks, only two of whom belonged to the temple, were seated around a table in prayer, undisturbed by visitors or by the children who were attracted by the visitors. Faure says the chief monk took off his robes and received him in the clothes of a worker. In response to questions, the monk gave only "banal replies" to the effect that Taoists were "satisfied with the solicitude of the authorities," that although they received no regular state subsidy there was occasional aid, such as that recently received for repairs to the temple. Faure later heard that the temple had been closed for quite a period and not merely because it had been in bad repair.[34]

Taoist temples, like their Buddhist counterparts, were dressed up with government funds, but there are fewer examples. The most outstanding was the restoration of the Temple of T'aishan on the mountain of the same name in Shantung province. The work was

---

[33] *JMJP*, August 9, 1957; *CNA*, March 21, 1958, p. 3.
[34] *The Serpent*, p. 156.

begun in 1956, during the period under discussion, but it was not finished until 1964. Whether the work was so extensive that eight years was required to finish it, or whether it was pursued intermittently is not known, but huge murals with mythical themes were restored, and wax and paint were used to protect more than a hundred stone tablets. It attracted many visitors from 1962 to 1964.[35] Another example is the Hsüan-wu temple near Canton which received major repairs and redecoration in 1956, involving a complete renovation of the main hall.[36]

On the other hand, Wutang Shan, the historic central holy place of Taoism, with eight palaces, thirty-two temples, twelve shrines, and countless bronze images, was invaded by county officials in 1955 and 1956. C. K. Yang says these officials

broke up hundreds of "scattered, damaged, or duplicate" bronze images and sold them as scrap metal to help provide funds for the county budget. Over 50,000 catties (about 65,000 pounds) of bronze were collected. In the 1956 campaign it took forty-eight days to destroy the images, one of which weighed over three thousand catties or nearly two tons, and a large number of which had been preserved in good condition. Leading Taoist priests, some even with limited political status, could only watch the heartrending destruction helplessly.[37]

The case was widely publicized and the officials were finally given demerits (!), but Yang thinks there were undoubtedly many other such incidents on a smaller scale and in remote places which were never reported.

Evidently the Taoists were still circulating some of their literature, for a *Jen-min Jih-pao* editorial in 1955 referred to the bad influence of "all feudalistic, superstitious stories of gods and devils," as well as of books with sexual themes. These "Taoist-inspired stories," many of which told of mountain hermits who taught people occult practices by which to gain superhuman power,

[35] *NCNA*, Tsinan, September 9, 1964; *SCMP*, September 16, 1964, pp. 21-22. An earlier *NCNA* story for August 16, 1962, told of tourists from many parts of China climbing the seven thousand steps to the top of T'aishan, and claimed that the largest temple attracted over one thousand visitors daily.
[36] Yang, *Religion in*, p. 398.
[37] *Ibid.*, p. 391, based on report in *SCMP*, April 26, 1957, p. 10.

were said to mislead youth into running away from home to find such hermits in the mountains.[38]

They were a "bad influence" in another sense, according to reports in the Chinese press in 1954 and 1955 announcing the arrest and condemnation of Taoists guilty of sabotage of agricultural and industrial production. There was also reference to discoveries of food and arms deposits, and of radio transmitters. In Anhwei province government forces caught and arrested several leaders of a "Chinese National Expedition for the Suppression of [Communist] Rebels" and brought them to trial in May, 1955.[39]

The former Bureau of Religious Affairs official says that a secret document circulated to officials like himself in 1955 classified Buddhism and Taoism as having no relationship to the imperialists, but as having association with the Nationalists. The organization discussed in the immediately preceding paragraph would appear to give some substance to the classification. Officials of the Bureau of Religious Affairs were to push the prohibition of secret societies and reactionary organizations in Buddhist and Taoist circles in order to discover hidden Nationalist spies. Patriotic learning sessions for Taoist priests, along with those for other religious leaders, were to be established. Taoists were to be helped to organize handcrafts. Since Taoists were weak in organization and systematic thought and had little social foundation according to Communist judgment, they were more difficult to pinpoint and control, but in our informant's opinion this was no major problem. During the early 60's when he made these statements, he was of the opinion that both Buddhism and Taoism were nothing but names and as living realities had essentially disappeared.[40] I question his judgment, but the identification of Taoists with the Nationalists is essential to understanding the Communist crackdown on sects in 1958.

In that year, attempts to revive a Taoist sect called the "Divine Healers of Tzu Chu Hall" were nipped in the bud, because "the masses" informed the Public Security Bureau of Shanghai whose men arrested the sect leaders. The sect had been "smashed by the

[38] *JMJP*, March 28, 1955; *CNA*, March 9, 1956.
[39] Bertuccioli, "Il Taoismo," p. 75, based on *KMJP*, June 22, 1955.
[40] From previously cited unpublished manuscript.

authorities" in 1951, but one of the female leaders had escaped to Canton. She (Ts'ai Kuei-ying) returned to Shanghai in 1958, made contact with a dealer in coffins (Li Wen-ying, also female), and was trying to revive the sect. Miss Ts'ai claimed to be the *avatar* (incarnation or "descent") of a living Buddha, and was said to have gained forty-one "Taoist disciples." The writer of the story emphasizes that it was not religious activities which were suppressed in 1951 or 1958. It was because the sect was founded by a "counterrevolutionary bully" whose "activities included extortion of money, murder, concealment of firearms, and plotting to restore the Kuomintang regime." And Miss Ts'ai, the story goes on,

often indulged in prostrations before her idols and other mystic rites, which were only a screen for her rumor mongering, slanderous attacks on the government, and protestations of the innocence of some of the convicted counterrevolutionaries.[41]

The arrests in Shanghai were probably part of the antirightist campaigns, as were the arrest of Taoist "reactionary leaders" for stirring up a revolt in Kirin in March, 1958, and the arrest of a Taoist vegetarian group in Tsinan in April of that year. The Tsinan group was called a "reactionary armed organization," and the press report said that death sentences were handed out.[42]

At no point in the year is folk religion more evident than in celebrations for the birthdays of the gods, with processions, feasts, dramas, and colorful, special shows. The celebrations were ended, according to a proud announcement from Nan-an County in Fukien, but further reading of the story indicates only drastic "reform." [43] The practice in that place was to have such celebrations as often as twice a month in each household, where joss sticks and candles were burned and rice offered to the gods. Then there were the community celebrations which called for a feast, processions, and a tremendous outlay of funds which, the authorities decided, caused real hardship for many families, a great deal of indebtedness, and a loss of time from work. So in Nan-an County in November, 1957, there were mass debates in the course of

[41] Shanghai *Wen Hui Pao*, December 28, 1957; *CURBAC*, June 15, 1958, p. 6.

[42] Both newspaper reports summarized in *CHIBUL*, August, 1958.

[43] *KMJP*, January 9, 1958; *CURBAC*, June 15, 1958, p. 7.

which "many peasants were made to realize that they could not have good crops and felicity for themselves and their domestic animals by merely praying to the gods of heaven and earth." Peasants from another county testified that birthdays of the gods were "days of burden" for them and demanded that the custom be done away with.

The People's Congress of the whole area met and decided to celebrate all the birthdays of the gods on one day of the year, the sixteenth day of the twelfth lunar month, although "it was also agreed that individuals who did not want the change might continue to celebrate. . . ." The masses "universally approved," however, and as word spread the decision was "warmly applauded by the masses." One should note that the story was written so as to show that the masses themselves rose up to deplore the ancient practices, that the peasants who came over from the neighboring place were more than likely sent, and that a decision by the Poeple's Congress could hardly have been opposed.

By 1958, as was the case with other religious groups, government authorities were hardening the line for folk religious practices. In the summer of that year popular religious practices and the ancentral cult were suppressed in the villages, often provoking deep resentment by the people. *Jen-min Jih-pao* made the following rejoinder:

There are some people who have the most astonishing ways of thinking. In the places which had a bumper harvest they attributed this to Lao T'ien Yeh [the "old man in heaven," a popular deity] and they say that "there was provided good rain and favorable wind." In places where owing to natural disasters the harvest suffered, they imputed it to the people's communes, saying that "the communes spoiled it." . . . The root of such a way of thinking lies deep in a reactionary soil."

In a village of three hundred families near Peking, there were said to be seven places for popular worship and all kinds of superstition. Mao's picture replaced that of the God of Wealth in some homes and in others the old saying—"The source of wealth is in heaven; the

" *JMJP*, October 15, 1959; *CNA*, January 15, 1960, p. 2.

spirit of happiness is among men"—was changed to: "Thrift and more production; saving is more glorious."

When Communist authorities tried to deal with the veneration or worship of ancestors, the main stream of the folk religion, they faced their greatest test. Once again the methods and approaches to a problem are varied. The statement by Lo T'ien, first secretary of the Communist Party Committee for Waton, Kwangtung, is said to be an illustration of Mao Tse-tung's principle, "If religion does not interfere with the People's Republic, the People's Republic will not interfere with it." Lo T'ien said:

Ancestral tombs long regarded as sacred have been removed by the masses themselves. In many localities, family altars, gods of the city, gods of thunder, local gods, and the Queen of Heaven have been eliminated. . . . Grave stones, coffins, etc., are used by collective farms for building irrigation works, pig sties, latrines, carts, manure buckets, sheds, small water gates. . . . Many temples which formerly housed images have been turned into pig sties or processing plants, thus saving large amounts of expenditure for the collectives.[45]

The point would seem to be, if ancestral tombs, family altars, grave stones, and coffins are devoted to the collective or eliminated, then the religious practice in which these objects play a part will be left alone. The statement is also an illustration of the oft-quoted dictum about the peasants rising up to destroy their idols themselves.

In a village near Sian in Shensi province, however, there was an unequivocal Party directive in 1958 to level the graves. The ideological journal *Red Flag* noted that the peasants approved this only externally, that when the leveling actually began they offered prayers to the spirits: "Spirits, spirits! I am not the one who wants to move you. It is the cadres who want to do so." There were also public meetings in which the geomancers and divination experts were discredited. The second part of the *Red Flag* article, in attacking the idea of spirits and ghosts, said that Mao Tse-tung had long ago disproved such theories, and maintained

[45] Quoted from *JMJP*, May 12, 1958, by M. M. Thomas and M. Abel, "Religion, State, and Ideologies in China," *Religion, State, and Ideologies in East Asia* (Bangalore, 1965), pp. 15-30, quote on p. 21.

that the revival of such ideas was the work of counterrevolutionaries.[46]

It is a bit difficult, in the face of reports in *Red Flag* of Party directives to level graves, to accept what Felix Greene was told and apparently accepted, that burial mounds taking up land that could be used for agriculture could be removed only with the permission of the family. The government knew better than to interfere, he says, and also was content in the knowledge that "the younger, less superstitious generation will give the necessary permission." [47] As we have seen in countless instances, it is rather hard to discern whether a group of people really give up their church building "voluntarily" or "permit" graves of their ancestors to be dug up. One suspects that the "permission" to do so is the only alternative when presented with a directive.

Hu Chang-tu asserts that one of the reasons the family system in general was attacked, and the ancestral cult repudiated and ridiculed as superstitious, antisocial, unscientific, and wasteful of time and money, was that the Chinese family with its ancestral cult competed with Communist social control. This was why study groups in the early years of the Communist regime, in connection with Land Reform programs or to occupy free time in the winter, spent a part of their time "ridiculing ancestor worship and folk religion," depicting them as "ignorant superstitions, psychological crutches for a weak and cowardly people." [48] Graves were leveled and tombs removed so as to free land for production in the late 50's as we have just seen. Still more drastic measures were employed in the Cultural Revolution.

In contrast to the more extreme measures just considered, a "practical, common-sense" article appeared in *Jen-min Jih-pao* in June, 1958, outlining in some detail the government's policy toward funeral rites and burial customs.[49] Chao Chien-min, secretary of

---

[46] *Hung Ch'i*, August 16, 1958, pp. 18-20; *CNA*, January 15, 1960, pp. 3-4.
[47] Felix Greene, *The Wall Has Two Sides* (London: Jonathan Cape, 1962), p. 109.
[48] *China: Its People*, p. 131.
[49] "Reform Funeral Customs, Encourage Thrifty Burials without Coffins and Graves without Sepulchral Mounds," *JMJP*, June 17, 1958; *CURBAC*, June 15, 1958, pp. 24-30.

the Shantung Provincial Committee, presented the standard Marxist view that such rites and customs were part of an old social superstructure which was built on an old economic base. A new superstructure had not yet fully emerged from the new economy, thus many peasants were still following the old customs:

The masses in the rural areas . . . still "announce the death in the ancestral temple," have a priest "lead the soul of the deceased," provide a wooden coffin and a lavish funeral, give dinners to relatives and friends who have come to mourn, and make frequent sacrificial offerings to the dead.[50]

Mr. Chao then went into great detail showing the cost of funerals, the amount of land consumed by graves and therefore not available for production, the tremendous amount of wood which went into a traditional Chinese coffin. He claimed that peasants were becoming aware of these problems, but that they were "perplexed by the absence of new rites that will replace the old." They call on the government, he said, to reform the old feudal rites and customs. Agricultural cooperatives had adopted slogans like the following: "Let us compete with heaven; let us save land from graves and tombs; let us fight against nature; let us rely not on the gods and heaven, but on our own hands, for more production!"

Mr. Chao's recommendations are interesting. He proposed the abolition of wooden coffins, to be replaced by coffins constructed with a wooden frame and filled in with a mixture of grass stalks and mud or cement. He recommended deep burials so that the land above the grave could be cultivated, and that any gravestones be placed at the side of the field in which the graves were located. Tombs not claimed or that date back more than five generations should be leveled; more recent tombs which interfere with production and construction should be leveled or removed. Cremation should be "introduced gradually." [51]

The most striking proposals, from my point of view, are those for new, thrifty, and simple funeral rites, different from the old.

[50] *Ibid.*, p. 25.
[51] *Ibid.*, p. 29.

The old funeral rites and customs were created to serve the exploiting classes, to fool the people, and to instill such feudal and superstitious ideas into their minds as "a man has a soul, which lives on after he is dead" and "filial piety is the supreme virtue." Our new funeral rites and customs, on the other hand, are designed to serve socialist production and construction, to commemorate the dead and encourage the living, and to educate the people with Communist ethical standards.[52]

Mr. Chao assured his readers that Communists were not giving up filial piety or respect for the aged, and quoted Mao Tse-tung in support of holding a memorial service for one who has died: "Whether he was only a cook or a soldier, we should attend his funeral and hold a memorial service for him, if in his lifetime he has rendered some meritorious service." But Chao adds that both the mourners and the mourned should be in their working clothes with possibly a simple arm band or a border sewed on the hem to indicate a mourner. People should bow to the dead, then stand in silence; the elaborate kowtowing of the past should be abolished. Commemorating the deceased with a likeness of him, some of his relics and a compilation of his achievements, is in order. Such "experiments" should be made cautiously, but after experience in the

adoption of the new rites and customs in the Han areas, the broad masses will be able to shed the heavy spiritual and material burden imposed on them by the old funeral rites and customs, and their thinking will be reformed.[53]

The fact that clear-cut examples of new forms to replace the old are advanced, reminiscent of the wise missionary who does not criticize the old without suggesting something to take its place, makes of this piece one of the most constructive statements of its type. It is quite an exception to the usual denunciations of superstition and feudal customs.

Since we have just considered one of the more thoughtful statements in the treatment of Taoism and folk religion, this is perhaps the most appropriate point at which to make a brief comment on

[52] *Ibid.*, p. 28.
[53] *Ibid.*, p. 30.

treatments of Taoist thought. The exceedingly brief material available is drawn from the late 50's and early 60's, and thus follows chronologically the data we have just examined.

Ch'an Wing-tsit tells us that Lao Tzu was discussed at a meeting at Peking University in May, 1959. Opinions were about equally divided on the date of the Taoist classic, the *Tao Te Ching* (or simply the *Lao Tzu*), and on whether Lao Tzu was an idealist or a materialist. Professor Chan's summary statement reminds us of the results of the discussion of a similar question concerning Confucius:

> Some interpreted the concept of *Tao* in materialistic terms on the ground that *Tao* is the basic substance of all things, their necessary nature, the law of change, the condition of existence, and the sum total of things. Others, on the contrary, argued that the concept of *Tao* is idealistic because *Tao* is indescribable, transcends time and space, comes from nonbeing, is the One and Absolute, and an absolute spirit.[54]

There is an even more astounding interpretation of Lao Tzu as a materialist in the work of Yang Hsing-shun and Jen Chi-yü, who, according to Donald Munro, define Lao Tzu's *Tao* "as a primal mass of chaotic matter from which all things derive their substance (something like the Unlimited of early Ionian philosophy) and their laws of change."[55] These two commentators say that Lao Tzu's "Heavenly Way" includes no heaven, only *wu-wei* (nonaction), and since Lao Tzu regarded *Tao* as prior to Shang-ti (the Lord on High), there is in Lao Tzu an antireligious view as well as an overall materialism.

Chuang Tzu, a fourth century B.C. Taoist thinker who continued and developed the thought of Lao Tzu, is generally dismissed as a subjective idealist by Communist interpreters, because "he views *Tao* as emptiness and his total focus is introspective with no concern for the external world at all. . . ." This view of Chuang Tzu as a victim of the "negativism" of the "sunken slave-owner class" to which he belonged was challenged by others who cited "his

[54] Ch'an, "Chinese Philosophy," pp. 30-31.
[55] Munro, "Chinese Communist Treatment," pp. 130-31.

criticisms of exploitation and oppression and his opposition to religious superstition." [56]

The men who have expressed themselves on these questions, regardless of the side they uphold, all agree that "rudimentary dialectical thought" may be found in the two early Taoist thinkers. What saves Lao Tzu and Chuang Tzu is their "discovery of pairs of opposites (Being-Not Being, wealth-poverty, heavy-light, etc.) and . . . the doctrine that things transform into their opposites and that such is the nature of change." [57] Even so, this primitive dialectic in Lao Tzu and Chuang Tzu did not involve an understanding of struggle, so there is only limited value even in those elements which do have some appeal to a Marxist.[58]

Undoubtedly more was said, but there seems to be no record of it or of how it ended. We may assume, however, that the discussion ground to a halt in the early 60's just as the more extensive debates on Confucius did.

FESTIVALS TRANSFORMED—OLD RITUALS AND SYMBOLS DISCREDITED

From the late 50's to the middle 60's there is almost no information upon which to base any kind of a continuous story. Practically the only item of any substance tells of an advanced study class for Taoists sponsored by the Chinese Taoist Association. The opening ceremonies were held in the White Cloud Temple in Peking, at which occasion addresses were made by Ch'en Ying-ning, who had moved from vice-president to president of the association, by a vice-president, and by Hsiao Hsien-fa, director of the Religious Affairs Bureau. There was no indication in the press report of how long the class would last, but it was intended "to foster intellectuals and teaching personnel among Taoists," and students were "picked from famous Taoist monasteries and houses of worship and devotion in various parts of the country." [59]

By 1964 and 1965, however, one may find numerous references to ways in which vital areas of the popular religious tradition were

[56] *Ibid.*, p. 131.
[57] *Ibid.*
[58] *Ibid.*, p. 135.
[59] *KMJP*, October 12, 1962; *SCMP*, October 29, 1962, p. 6.

being transformed, usually told in the form of "human interest stories" which compose a very human and personal picture. The first of these areas in the folk tradition to be discussed are the festivals, with almost exclusive attention to the Chinese New Year and Ch'ing Ming.

The New Year Festival, or Chinese New Year as Westerners call it, ordinarily is not considered a religious festival, but there are many elements in the celebration of it which belong to the Chinese folk religious tradition. At a deeper level, the attitude toward time and the changing seasons is a profound expression of the Chinese world view, of the Chinese understanding of themselves in relation to reality. On the eve of the lunar New Year, when the family is supposed to gather at the old home, send the Kitchen God up to heaven with his report, and make offerings to the ancestors, there is the familial setting so basic to Chinese religion. The joy of welcoming the new year, expressed in poetic couplets at the door or in the purchase of new garments for every member of the family, is part and parcel of that sense of happiness or felicity which is the *summum bonum* of the Chinese common life. And in the visits to homes of relatives and neighbors with respectful bows and good wishes for the adults and small red packets of money for the children, one becomes unmistakably aware of good will for humanity.

In Communist China the celebration of Chinese New Year is designated the Spring Festival. Most, if not all, of the practices referred to above were first discouraged, then condemned as inappropriate for citizens in the new society, and finally replaced by a whole new framework of attitudes, groupings, and practices.

Obviously such practices as offerings to the ancestors or any attention to a deity would be the first to draw fire. Workers returning from the city to their homes were urged not to carry such articles as joss sticks and not to wear fine clothes in order to impress the folks back home. Here is a letter to the editor ridiculing a worker who,

besides giving his family and his relatives and friends a number of superstitious articles, . . . also personally worshiped the gods and his

405

ancestors by burning joss sticks. He pasted on the door of his house a motto: "When you step out of this house, peace be with you." By doing so he exerted a very bad influence on the masses around him.[60]

Other workers were criticized for taking back "joss sticks, clay images of the 'Door God,' red paper, and other superstitious stuff," because they might otherwise disappoint their families, and for continuing to give red packets of money to children just because others might do so. There was a call from a commune member to other workers to do away with sacrifices to the Kitchen God, since, he said, under the old order there were different days for different classes to perform these sacrifices with the common people always last; so the whole business was an insult to the laboring people.[61]

Some workers' groups made positive suggestions of ways in which the Spring Festival might be invested with new meaning. A group in the Shanghai Kiangnan Dockyard made several proposals, the first of which paralleled those above: do away with superstitious practices such a burning joss sticks and paper money. But they urged as a new practice the installation, as one woman worker had tried out, of a portrait of Chairman Mao with banners reading "Long Live the People's Government! Long Live the Great Leap Forward!" The second proposal was to pass the holiday in an industrious, thrifty, and simple way, which meant no exchange of gifts, no heavy eating or drinking, no purchase of new clothes, etc. The third proposal was quite penetrating: as the family gathered on New Year's Eve, the younger generation would be told "family histories," stories of how they had suffered before Liberation and how they had made "ideological progress" in the new era. Each worker would take one of Mao's essays to read; the whole group would gather to discuss their experiences in study when they returned. In conclusion the writer adds that "Of course . . . we should have proper rest and amusement . . . , go to the theater, see movies, organize ball games, and take part in recreational activities.[62]

[60] Canton *Nan-fang Jih-pao*, January 15, 1965; *SCMP*, February 10, 1965, p. 13.
[61] *Ibid.*, p. 14. For other instances see *Nan-fang Jih-pao*, January 25, 1965; *SCMP*, February 15, 1965, pp. 13-14.
[62] Peking *Kung-jen Jih-pao*, February 7, 1964; *SCMP*, April 8, 1964, pp. 7-9.

In a similar vein, the Young Communist League branch in a Shantung compound recommended telling revolutionary stories and producing revolutionary dramas which would aid the collective economy and help to eliminate the older superstitions. Teachers were invited to tell youth the origin of the Kitchen God: "entirely an instrument used by the feudal rulers to exploit and oppress the poor people and a superstition to fool the people." At this the youth resolved to go to their homes and mobilize their families against the practice. The economies of not using joss sticks and of not serving large dinners were also emphasized. And as for acts of piety toward the elders:

To prostrate oneself before the elders in greeting during the Spring Festival is also an old custom. Therefore, our league branch advised the young people that this year they should adopt the form of enquiring after the health of one another as a way of greeting during the Spring Festival.[63]

One practice which could readily be invested with new meaning was that of writing couplets, usually gold lettering on red strips of paper, one line of which is placed on either side of the door. So a vigorous campaign was initiated to replace mythological allusions or expressions of the old culture, which often expressed religious sentiments, with new couplets like the following:

Take a firm stand in face of heavy storms and rough seas;
Follow the path of the Party with one heart and one will.

Keep a proletarian family record, hold the family seal tight;
Be faithful children of the Party, revolutionaries to the end.

The East Wind whistles the tune of a Leap Forward;
The spring thunder heralds a bumper harvest.

The revolutionary cause will last a thousand years;
The country will remain red for ten thousand generations.[64]

The same process may be observed in the replacement of calendar pictures which appear at the time of the Western New

[63] *Chung-kuo Ch'ing-nien Pao*, February 8, 1964; *SCMP*, April 8, 1964, pp. 9-10.
[64] *Chung-kuo Ch'ing-nien Pao*, January 14, 1965; *SCMP*, January 29, 1965, pp. 10-14.

Year. People were encouraged to buy pictures such as "We and Chairman Mao Tse-tung Are of One Heart," "Successors to Communism," "The Great Sinkiang Hydro-electric Power Station," and "Our Good Bookkeeper," rather than older types like "Sweet Dew Monastery," "Dragon and Phoenix Bring Prosperity," "Moon Worshipper," and "The King Says Goodbye to His Concubine." The story of an old peasant was told in order to encourage purchase of the new pictures. The old gentleman found only two new pictures in a store, both of which he already had, but he bought the duplicates of those rather than buy the old ones.[65] The wonder is that the old style pictures were still available.

Other new features of the Spring Festival in Communist China were visits by "greeting teams" to dependents of martyrs and servicemen and to veterans of the Red Army. This extended from New Year's Day throughout the Spring Festival period, and later became a part of "Support-the-Army-Month." [66] This undoubtedly served to extend one's loyalty and devotion beyond the family group to a larger grouping and sense of belonging.

It should be acknowledged that the constantly recurring advice to avoid expensive outlays of food and drink, to stop giving expensive gifts and showering children with red packets of money, and to pass up expensive new clothing was all to the good. For centuries the tendency of many families to go into debt while "passing the year" has been accepted as a fixture of Chinese society which could not be changed. The counsels of thrift and industry, if followed, would have a salutary effect.

Obviously it is impossible to estimate how much of a change has been effected in China's chief festival. The following New China News Agency report may be propaganda, and there is no way of telling how typical it is if it is true, but I suspect that it could be repeated across the country:

The Spring Festival this year saw a big drop in the number of idol worshippers among the residents of Shanghai. The number of visitors

---

[65] *JMJP*, December 7, 1964; *SCMP*, December 23, 1964, p. 12. See also *NCNA*, Shanghai, December 30, 1964; *SCMP*, January 5, 1965, p. 28.

[66] *Nan-fang Jih-pao*, December 20, 1962, and February 4, 1965; *SCMP*, January 10, 1963, p. 6, and March 2, 1965, pp. 17-20.

offering sacrifices at the local Ch'enghuang Temple on the first day of the first moon of the Chinese calendar was over two thirds less than that of last year. Candle and incense shops dealing in "superstitious things" throughout the city generally returned poor sales. Their total sales dropped by nearly 50 percent, compared with last year. A large number of customers sent back their "superstitious purchases" to such shops.[67]

As was the case with calendar pictures, it is amazing to find that shops were still selling incense, although candles would have other uses and their sale was not forbidden.

The decline in traditional practices at the Chinese New Year was confirmed by the Shanghai correspondent of the *South China Morning Post*, who visited several temples at the time of the Spring Festival in 1965. At the Hung Miao, or Red Temple, a Buddhist temple dedicated to Kuan Yin, the shop selling joss sticks was surrounded by young people who gave lectures against superstition and would not allow members of their peer group to enter. Only older people were allowed to buy joss sticks and enter the temple. It was much the same at the temple for the City God. The correspondent visited the temple twice, at which times in former years it would have been crowded, only to find it closed and to be told to "come back in the morning." At both of these times there were crowds of people in the streets. The correspondent could see that the temple had been cleaned of its former dust and soot, and noted that its access areas had been cleaned of the soothsayers, fortune-tellers, and geomancers who had once been stationed there.[68]

Much the same process of change can be seen in the Ch'ing Ming festival which for centuries has brought people each spring to the cemeteries to sweep the graves and made offerings to the ancestors. The new attitudes toward the ancestral cult and related activities have had their effect, for the ceremonial aspects of the festival were much less noticeable in 1964. People did sweep the graves, which is as much a ritual as an actual cleansing, but the kowtowing, lighting of joss sticks and paper objects, and the family meal at the graves were much less noticeable. The Shanghai cor-

[67] *NCNA*, Shanghai, February 27, 1964; *SCMP*, March 17, 1964, pp. 10-11.
[68] *South China Morning Post*, February 16, 1965.

respondent reported public announcements that the public urn depositories were "not conducive to holding old-time rites," and commented that cremation was increasingly used.[69]

In 1965, the same correspondent reported a banner reading "Abolish 'old superstitions,' replace the old harmful customs with new" stretched across the closed central gates of the Hungjao Road cemetery in Shanghai.

At the entrance were displayed posters on the subject of the correct understanding of the existence of man and the life "beyond," as proved by science, and repudiating old beliefs based on superstitions. There were also recommendations for cremations, . . . reminding the people that land required for national reconstruction may be ordered to be cleared of the graves.[70]

To counteract those who did go to the cemetery, for which tickets were required, there were delegations of wreath-carrying youths and workers who marched to the graves of revolutionary martyrs and those who had died in the Liberation of Shanghai. There was no sign, the correspondent said, of traditional rites such as the burning of joss sticks.

Jen-min Jih-pao condemned the burning of paper money and other paper objects, but its editors maintained that such practices should be combated by educating the masses rather than by suppression, and suggested instead of the old practices the paying of tribute to revolutionary martyrs on that day. The editors specifically stated: "We are not against the broad masses 'sweeping' the tombs of their deceased close relatives." [71]

By 1966, this temperate attitude coupled with the approach of investing an old tradition with new meaning had changed. Ch'ing Ming had become National Memorial Day (I am not aware of the date when the name was changed officially), commemorating heroes who had died in the Revolution of 1911 and during the Liberation period. Some individuals and families did visit graves, but a correspondent reported that burning of paper money and joss sticks, ceremonial bowing and offerings had largely ceased in the

[69] *Ibid.*, May 4, 1964.
[70] *Ibid.*, April 19, 1965.
[71] *JMJP*, March 31, 1965; *SCMP*, April 8, 1965, pp. 4-5.

cities, that most people who visited graves made simple bows and left fresh flowers. Posters were to be seen denouncing superstition and advocating economic and other advantages of cremation.[72]

The Mid-Autumn or Moon Festival and the Dragon Boat Festival fall in a different category than the New Year or Ch'ing Ming festivals. The Mid-Autumn Festival was still being celebrated in 1965, when people ate great quantities of the traditional moon cakes, but I have seen no reference to people gathering to look at the moon. The day was not an official holiday, but it received attention, especially since coming at harvest time it can be regarded as a peasants' festival.[73]

The Dragon Boat Festival, celebrated in the fifth lunar month in honor of a poet who drowned himself because the emperor would not utilize his services (so one story goes), was also celebrated in 1965. According to the Communist version, the poet Chu Yuan, committed suicide "in protest against the corrupt regime of his day," so the festival has great patriotic significance.[74]

Thus, those festivals which had distinctly religious elements were transformed by abolishing some of the customs associated with each festival, or by investing other old practices with new meaning. The festival in modern dress would undoubtedly have greater meaning for youth, whereas the older generation would be reminded of the customs of former days, even while going through motions required by the new. A new couplet would remind one of the older type; extolling revolutionary martyrs could not help but bring to mind family members who had died, revolutionary or not. As we shall see, a year or two after the initial thrust of the Red Guards, some of the traditional New Year practices were observed again in the villages and in private homes, but it is still premature to predict the future of these festivals in Communist China.

The reform of temple fairs was another way in which folk religious practices were supplanted by new patterns. In the old days, so the advocates of change said, people went to the temple to receive a blessing on themselves and their children, and to see plays or operas with a religious or mythological theme, which was

[72] *South China Morning Post*, April 15, 1966.
[73] *Ibid.*, September 15, 1965.
[74] *NCNA*, Peking, June 4, 1965; *SCMP*, June 10, 1965, p. 12.

the way in which "landlords and reactionary rulers . . . spread the feudal ideology, culture, and moral ideas by which they fooled and ruled the people." [75]

The primary method for handling this objectionable custom was to present plays, operas, and concerts with revolutionary significance. The masses were thus provided with a

socialist ideological education, in the course of which extensive explanations were given to such questions as "Are there gods and ghosts?" "How were children born?" "Oppose commercialism in marriage!" and "Promote planned childbirth. . . ." [76]

One opera, "The Story of Conquering a Devil," was adapted from a story about the elimination of superstition in a rural county. After presenting a number of such plays it was hoped that no one would believe in gods and ghosts.

As an illustration of how the program worked, there is the story of an older couple who finally had a son, their first baby. The baby became ill, so, to seek the help of a god, they took him to a temple where a fair was going on. They were met by a propagandist who persuaded them to take the child to a doctor. The doctor gave the boy some medicine, he improved, so the fifty-seven-year-old husband said to his wife that from that time on they must see the doctor early and not bother to seek the help of a god.[77]

There is a kind of folk opera which is a delightful example of the plays intended to ridicule religion.[78] Entitled "Meeting of the Three Clowns," the play begins with Mother Chao lighting incense before a Kuan Yin image because her grandson has a fever. The boy's mother, Hsiu-yu, blows out the match, berates her mother for

[75] *JMJP*, August 25, 1964, *SCMP*, September 16, 1964, pp. 18-19.
[76] *Ibid.*, p. 17.
[77] *Ibid.*, p. 18.
[78] One of two translations by Miss Jocelyn Milner which appeared under the title, "Expressions of a New Tradition," in *Ching Feng* VIII (Winter, 1964), 15-20. The play, "Meeting of the Three Clowns," appeared in *Chung-kuo Ch'ing-nien Pao*, December 14, 1963. Simone de Beauvoir tells a similar type of story from a collection entitled *Scenes from Village Life*, in which an old grandmother is devoted to the Kitchen God but actually chuckles under her breath about it and finally laughs out loud about it. See *The Long March*, trans. Austryn Wainhouse (New York: World Publishing Co., 1958), pp. 240-241. French edition published in Paris by Librairie Gallimard.

such superstitious conduct, especially since Hsiu-yu herself is a cadre, and proceeds to take the baby off to the doctor.

During Hsiu-yu's absence Mother Chao is visited by a stream of three practicioners who offer their services, for pay of course. They fear Hsiu-yu, but recognize in the old grandmother easy prey. The first is a fortune-teller, Ironmouth Sun, who has a preposterous story of what must be done for the child, for which he demands first money, and then rice. While Mother Chao goes to get the rice, Sun hears someone coming and hides under the table. It is not Hsiu-yu, whom he fears, but Third Auntie Chien who is, or pretends to be, a spirit medium. When Mother Chao returns, Auntie Chien goes into a trance, welcoming a spirit who supposedly tells her more astounding things that must be done. Auntie Chien demands rice and money also, which Mother Chao begins to gather as Sun, still under the table, curses away. At this point a geomancer named Hu Yin-yang enters, whereupon Auntie Chien dives under the table where she and Sun have to tolerate each other's company. (The *yin* and the *yang* are the negative and positive, female and male forces in nature which, when used as this rascal's name, are clearly intended to ridicule both the geomancer and the ancient concept.) Hu has noticed a new barn and has decided that the baby's illness is due to the building being in the wrong position; he recommends to Mother Chao that the barn be pulled down and offers to read from his geomancy book for five dollars. At this point the dear old grandmother is becoming rather confused, which changes to complete befuddlement as Sun and Auntie Chien emerge from beneath the table and the "three clowns" proceed to denounce each other. A happy ending comes when Hsiu-yu returns with the baby whose fever has abated after a dose of penicillin. Hsiu-yu joins with Mother Chao in singing a song about doing away with the old beliefs and superstitions under the guidance of Chairman Mao, and then Hsiu-yu leads the three clowns off to the production brigade for punishment.

Economic changes affected religious practice, as in the case of the annual fair at the famous Bubbling Well Temple in Shanghai. It was the practice in former years for rural people to bring in their products, sell them for the best possible price, and then buy at the fair or at other places in town those articles needed back on the farm. Most of the people would stop at the temple and make offerings to the gods. In 1963, we are told, the fair was held, occupying an even larger area of land around the temple than before, but the rise of the state cooperatives had made unnecessary the economic function formerly fulfilled by the temple fair. We may assume, though the writer does not say, that religious devotion would decline with the temple's declining economic role.[79]

Economic pressures were used to break down old customs, including popular religious practices. Certain articles used in religious devotion simply disappeared from the market. The Wen-fang Supply and Marketing Cooperative in Kiangsi province, for example, which dealt in paper products had a debate on whether or not it should continue to sell paper money, joss paper, and the like. In spite of those who said "business is business—sell what the people want!" the true socialist attitude prevailed: "A supply and marketing cooperative is a socialist commercial organ and must not deal in feudal things. It should not sell superstitious goods." Paper money, tinfoil, yellow joss paper, and colored paper which were in stock were "appropriately disposed of," and households which had been making these articles were "assisted . . . in switching to the production of toilet paper and packing paper." [80]

It was not enough, however, simply to refrain from selling or distributing "superstitious products." Customers who came asking for such things were to be "gently persuaded . . . to believe in science, not in superstition," and if it was a case of illness the doctor in the health clinic should be called.

In some places these cooperatives which had made paper religious objects switched to making plastics, but the ones which are extolled are those who changed to making toilet paper, which, if of good quality, enjoyed good sales and thereby increased the income of collective and individual members.[81]

Pilgrims stopped coming to the mountain temples and shrines around Chün-hsien, Honan, because the supply and purchasing cooperatives were forbidden to sell objects used in worship.

---

[79] *South China Morning Post*, May 18, 1963.
[80] Peking *Ta Kung Pao*, January 17, 1965; *SCMP*, February 1, 1965, p. 10.
[81] *Ibid.*, p. 12.

Whenever these objects were found for sale in the coops there was a tremendous furor, although they had been sold for years during the Communist period.[82]

One must still marvel at the resistance of the common people. In spite of the concerted pressures in the mid-60's to end their adherence to old ways, and the clear advantages to health and life which would follow a break with old ways, there were still references to villagers who called in a sorceress to heal a sick child, to the practice of geomancy, and to a cult built around the historic figure of Kuan Yü. One could still find private cemeteries in spite of the campaigns for public cemeteries to save land.[83]

To indicate just how deeply rooted the old ways were, a commune health clinic director in Tingan county (presumably Kwangtung province), and therefore a public figure in his own right, installed an image of the God of Wealth in his home. Director Lin's elder son had hurt his leg while playing, but the father attributed the accident to something unfortunate in the family and thus made offerings to the deity. The previous summer, when a third son lost weight, Director Lin had called in Taoist priests to chant a litany, just as he had done when a dog appeared on the roof (an evil omen). The masses as well as the editors of the newspaper to which the incident was reported, were incensed: how the director of a health clinic, who had some medical knowledge, and therefore could hardly have been ignorant of scientific truth, could have done such a thing was inconceivable. The editors wrote that some cadres who still carried around "ideological vestiges of capitalism and feudalism" needed to exorcise a few ghosts.[84]

The continuation of folk religious life was responsible for a shift in government policy and procedure during 1964 and 1965, the period from which most of the illustrations in this section have been drawn. Instead of patiently educating the peasants who had

[82] Peking *Ta Kung Pao*, January 20, 1965; *CNA*, February 25, 1966, p. 5.

[83] *Kung-jen Jih-pao*, November 25, 1964; *Chung-kuo Ch'ing-nien Pao*, July 21, 1964 and August 5, 1964; all summarized in *CNA*, February 25, 1966, pp. 3-4.

[84] *Nan-fang Jih-pao*, January 15, 1965; *SCMP*, February 10, 1965. It is quite possible that the tales about Director Lin were manufactured and used to discredit him because people had it in for him for other reasons.

long been the victims of feudalism, the authorities began to take a harder line. The absolute elimination of old features of the festivals, whether replaced by something new or not, is a case in point. In order to put more bite into the implementation of the harder line, the Party turned to its youth section, the Young Communist League, and to young people in general to be the primary agents.

The Young Communist League of Luching Commune in Shensi province, discovering in the summer of 1964 that customs and habits of the past still had a great influence on youth, asked and discussed the question, "Should the YCL chapters actually interfere with or obstruct outmoded customs and habits?" There were those who hesitated to interfere and therefore hesitated to face the question until a YCL secretary gave a "personal experience."

People said that the idol of a god in a temple in our village could answer prayers and woe betide him who would blaspheme it. When turning this temple into a granary for the use of our production team a few years ago, I threw this earthen image into a stream, and nothing has happened to me. Those who learned what I had done said: "The god is no longer effective. Are there still gods and demons?" [85]

I would like to speculate on how typical the story is, but the point is that what one YCL secretary did a few years earlier was presented as a model in 1964.

In reply to a reader (not necessarily a YCL member) whose mother "worships gods and Buddha," Nan-fang Jih-pao of Canton spoke sharply, because the youth in order to avoid his mother's disfavor went so far as to kneel and bow his head. Such compromise, the editors said, propagates feudal and superstitious ideas.

As an educated youth you certainly have some scientific knowledge. As such, you should get rid of the bondage of feudal and superstitious ideas. You should be a promoter in the movement to break down the old and establish the new. You should constantly talk to your relatives and people around you about atheism and science. As for your mother, you must

[85] Chung-kuo Ch'ing-nien Pao, May 16, 1964; SCMP, June 12, 1964, p. 17.

tirelessly work on her, making her see the harm done by old ideas and old customs and rid her mind of the concepts of "gods and spirits." [86]

In the Wukang People's Commune of Ch'angko county, Honan province, young intellectuals "armed with the thought of Mao Tse-tung," and therefore ready to "grapple with heaven and earth" and "wage an irreconcilable struggle against the theocracy holding sway over the peasants for several thousand years," returned to the countryside where they "enabled atheism to topple clay idols," and a lot of other things. They quoted Mao's statement that the peasants must be left to destroy their idols themselves, but the young intellectuals seemed to have gone just a bit beyond this.

With such methods as setting out facts and reasons, they patiently worked at convincing the peasants. After two or three years of tireless efforts, they at last caused the witches and sorcerers themselves to smash up the altars and throw the clay idols onto the field as fertilizer. They also caused the ancestral tablets and shrines under various names in the commune members' homes to give way to new couplets and New Year pictures in rapid succession. They enabled the brides to prefer walking to being carried in a bridal sedan chair. A change of these customs reflected a great liberation of the people's spiritual world. [87]

The meaning of "enable" may be found in the story of a returning female student who wanted to get married sans sedan chair. The Party branch supported her, but her grandfather, though a Party member, disapproved. After several meetings the members convinced him, he withdrew his objection, and the girl was thus "enabled" to have the kind of wedding she wanted. "Leaving it to the peasants themselves" apparently left room for a great deal of pressuring and persuading.

Thus the idols are smashed and sedan chairs left behind. What about death if the usual ceremonies are not fitting in a revolutionary age? When a young soldier returned home for his father's funeral, his elder sister told him the old man should be "well-buried," that the commune would cover expenses since he (the son) was a soldier. But how could a revolutionary soldier and Youth Corps

[86] *Nan-fang Jih-pao*, February 8, 1965; *SCMP*, March 24, 1965, p. 18.
[87] Editorial and article in *KMJP*, April 12, 1966; *SCMP*, May 23, 1966, pp. 9-15.

member practice superstition? With the support of the Party branch secretary, the young soldier's view—"Our life is guided by the Party and Chairman Mao"—finally prevailed and the father was buried by thirty peasants who marched but made no offerings or kowtows, burned no incense, and missed no work.[88]

In the above instance it was a case of youth dealing with youth, but there are also instances of the aged who demand the new ways and are hailed widely for "breaking the force of the habits of the old society." In his last will or testament an old peasant who was a Party member

(1) requested that no monks, Taoists, and nuns should be engaged to perform any ritual after his death; (2) asked his sons and grandchildren not to wear any white mourning clothes as symbol of their filial piety, but asked them to remember more of the class sufferings and forever follow the Communist Party and Chairman Mao; and (3) asked his relatives and friends not to waste money by worshiping him with rice and other food, but to use the money for production instead.[89]

A peasant from Lunghai commune in Yunnan province left a similar testament which contains slightly different "requests" concerning the folk religious practices at his funeral. He urged

his relatives not to believe in spirits and gods after his death, not to invite Taoist priests to perform rites for delivering a soul from purgatory, not to ask a geomancer to find a site for his grave, and not to waste money on his funeral.[90]

This last old man had kept a hat which he had worn at the age of eighteen when working for a landlord as a reminder of the hard times.

[88] *Chung-kuo Ch'ing-nien Pao*, December 12, 1964; *CNA*, February 25, 1966, p. 5.

[89] *NCNA*, Hangchow, reported to *JMJP*, May 28, 1964; *SCMP*, June 22, 1964, pp. 10-13, quote on p. 10.

[90] *NCNA*, Kunming, reported to *JMJP*, August 21, 1964; *SCMP*, September 9, 1964, p. 15. There were reports in 1964 of several discussions in Party branches of what makes a suitable funeral for a Party member. The consensus is always away from traditional rites and in favor of a simple memorial service in which the man's sacrificial revolutionary deeds are extolled. *See JMJP*, April 25, 1964; *SCMP*, May 12, 1964, pp. 7-10.

ENTER THE CULTURAL REVOLUTION; FOR FOLK RELIGION—NO EXIT

We have seen that all the efforts to discredit, explain away, and suppress the folk religion of China did not actually remove it from the scene by 1965. At the end of that year there was an estimate that "rural people had cut 'ceremonial expenses' for weddings, burials, and religious services to a negligible sum." Such expenses were reported to have taken 20 percent of the average farmer's income in former years. The estimates are recorded in the report of "a staff correspondent recently in China," who does not indicate the source of either estimate.[91] Although government or Party sources would rejoice in having this kind of victory to report, it is probably true that the expenses of religious devotion had been cut to a minimum. People had very little money and shops no longer handled the articles used in religious exercises. The big occasions such as feasts and processions in honor of ancestors or gods almost certainly had disappeared.

Information about specific incidents related to Taoism and/or folk religion during the Cultural Revolution is scanty. A Hong Kong newspaper quoted "arrivals" from the mainland as saying, "Religious shrines in every farmer's house were destroyed and superceded by Mao Tse-tung's pictures." [92] Whereas several thousand people usually went from Hong Kong to cities in south China for an autumn ancestral festival, very few even attempted it in the fall of 1966. At the same time there were reports "that all ancestral tablets in Canton have been removed . . . " and that ancestral tablets, altars, and relics, had been destroyed in mainland villages north of Macao.[93]

Street names which were drawn from the folk tradition, such as "Filial Piety Road," "Fortune and Longevity Road," and "Virtue and Chastity Road," were all dropped. This process was initiated as early as 1964-65, however, and included changing the names of

[91] "China Seeks to End 'Reliance on Heaven,'" *South China Morning Post*, February 17, 1966.

[92] *Sing Tao Daily*, January 5, 1967; *China News Items from the Press*, January 12, 1967.

[93] *South China Morning Post*, October 22, 1966; also that paper's Sunday edition [*Post Herald*] for August 28, 1966.

streets, shops, and even people from names associated with the old culture to names with revolutionary significance. The name of a drug, "Universal Remedy Helping All," ignored class consciousness and therefore had to be changed.[94]

At the time of the Spring Festival or Chinese New Year in the winter of 1967, even though the changes discussed above would surely have been followed, "revolutionary organizations" in Peking denounced the coming celebrations as the work of "capitalist power holders and stubborn bourgeois reactionaries." Class enemies, the revolutionary groups said, were allowing workers to go home to family reunions because of "concern" for them, thus tying up trains needed for returning Red Guards to their home localities. Some saw in this suggestion—that Red Guards should be given first place on the trains—a subtle hint that the Red Guards should be shipped out of the capitol.[95] Despite this byplay between groups, a festive atmosphere prevailed in Peking where workers were given four days off, which was regarded as a challenge by "power holders" to the rebels.

It was different in Shanghai where a reported fifty-seven "mass organizations" proposed abolition of the Spring Festival. The State Council responded by canceling the holiday and the home leave of workers.[96]

In Canton Red Guards arrested a sixty-one-year-old man and his wife because they had been celebrating the New Year festival and marched them through the streets. Fifty workmen who outnumbered the Red Guards demanded and achieved the couple's release.[97]

China News Analysis later reported that some religious devotion continued in the villages at the time of the 1967 Spring Festival.[98] After the Red Guard campaign of late 1966, "serious unrest was visible in the villages" which found "expression in revival of

---

[94] From a Hunan radio broadcast, August 26, 1966, reported in *URS*, September 6, 1966, p. 308.

[95] *JMJP*, January 29, 30, and 31, 1967; *China News Items from the Press*, February 16, 1967.

[96] *Ibid.*

[97] *Ibid.*

[98] *CNA*, July 19, 1968, is replete with material on folk religion during the Cultural Revolution. Father Ladany, drawing upon C. K. Yang, points out that at various times in Chinese history religious devotion has increased, even to the extent of inspiring revolution as during the T'aip'ing rebellion.

traditional religious practices." The Chinese press continually referred to the need to suppress "evil deeds," which included "feudal superstitious practices" (usually mentioned along with gambling). A broadcast from Anhwei province, announcing that there would be no holiday during the Spring Festival of 1967, referred to the "veneration of spirits, New Year wishes, sending presents, having a good meal" as "dirty feudal customs," but the order proved ineffective. Reports from Chekiang condemned trouble-makers, such as leaders of Tao Hui Men and professional Taoists, as well as the superstitious activities widely practiced at weddings and funerals. People in Honan were criticized because "the four olds are revived, paper offerings at graves have reappeared and so have prayers to the gods and to Buddha, and performance of bad old plays." [99]

Hong Kong residents, who were able to visit relatives in Kwangtung during the Spring Festival of 1968, said that there were no outward signs of any revival of traditional religious practices, no Buddhist or Taoist priests around, no sale of incense and candles, but the paper to be burned in ceremonies was made at home, food was offered to gods and spirits, and guests invited in as usual. [100]

Soldiers who visited T'ai Shan in May, 1968, discovered that there were people who still venerated the gods and who supported themselves by selling water and objects of superstition. There were inscriptions in the homes dedicated to the Old Mother of T'ai Shan, before which incense was burned on the first and fifteenth days of the lunar month. The soldiers were told that the Red Guards "destroyed the four olds and established the four new," which apparently did not mean that the ancient temple of T'ai Shan was destroyed, but rather that it was turned into a "Hall for the Study of the Thought of Mao Tse-tung." [101] It is noted earlier in this chapter that an extensive process of redecoration at government expense was carried out at T'ai Shan from 1956 to 1964.

[99] *JMJP*, February 1, 1967; *Chekiang Jih-pao*, March 27, 1968; Kiangsi People's Broadcasting Station broadcasts in the spring of 1968; Honan People's Broadcasting Station broadcast of April 24, summarized in *CNA*, p. 5.

[100] *Ibid.*

[101] *KMJP*, May 1, 1968; *CNA*, July 19, 1968, p. 7.

Some of our most helpful and picturesque information comes from a man who sojourned in a south China fishing village while trying to escape from the mainland. In that village he found the people "superstitious," with many gods of which he could remember only the Heavenly Mother and the Heavenly Elder Brother. He lived next door to a fifty-year-old woman who worshipped the gods at home all day long and would go twenty or thirty miles to see some miraculous event which people were talking about. There were stories constantly circulating about visions in the sky, about graves moving. People went to "grave-moving places" to get hold of the "divine earth."

The sojourner maintained that, in spite of such religious feeling, "there is no statue of any god left in the town, no ancestral tablets, no religious objects whatever; they had all been destroyed by the Red Guards in 1966." [102] He said that during the Spring Festival of 1967, old inscriptions on the town gates were replaced by "Hail Chairman Mao" at the top and "Do not forget class hardship" and "Remember blood, tears, and hatred" on the sides. Pictures of Mao replaced the ancestral tablets in the homes. But during the Spring Festival of 1968, an invocation to the Heavenly Elder Brother was pasted over "Hail Chairman Mao" and the invocations to the gods of wealth and prosperity were put back on the side columns. Mao's picture remained in the homes, but an inscription—"Seat of Father and Mother of Heaven and Earth"—was placed above it and candles and an incense urn beneath. An old lady who was asked about the incongruity of it smiled and said:

Last year was the lucky year of Chairman Mao, and the Old Man in Heaven and the God of Wealth were chased away. This year Chairman Mao is declining, so the God of Wealth came back to its proper place. [103]

Fishermen in the village told the sojourner about a fishing center more than a hundred miles away, where fishermen do not go out to sea on the seventh day of the lunar month and do not come back home on the eighth day. Bad luck is supposed to befall the first boat which puts out to sea after the Spring Festival; lots have to be cast

[102] *CNA*, July 19, 1968, p. 3.
[103] *Ibid.*, p. 4.

each year so someone will start. In 1967, the Red Guards would not allow this and forced one group to take their boat out first. The boat had an accident in June and caught few fish all year. In 1968, the people managed to cast lots according to the old custom and the commune allocated three hundred *yuan* (about $70) to the brigade whose boat had to go out first. The brigade used the money to buy incense, firecrackers, and other objects which were used for several days to make sacrifices to the spirits of the sea. The boat on which the lots fell made only a round near the shore as a symbolic "first outing." [104]

Such is the ubiquitous folk religion which has yet to be ushered out.

In the Communist handling of Taoism and folk religion we have seen the crux of the problem for the Communist government. That amorphous, phoenix-like phenomenon, so difficult to identify or classify, so unorganized and yet possessing such a firm hold on the lives of the people, has been the most difficult to control, and apparently impossible to stamp out completely.

Although I avoid the use of "superstition" as a loaded term, and I have used it largely in quoting or stating the views of others, there are many practices in the Taoist-folk religious framework which with good reason may be called "superstitious." If one were in the position to give praise or blame, one should praise the Communists for their efforts to root out genuinely superstitious practices which are wasteful and a burden on people. But the striking fact remains: with all the onus placed on anything and anybody who can possibly be labeled superstitious, "superstition" continues.

One may say that Taoism and folk religion continue, not just because of the few examples cited, but because of the nature of this religious phenomenon, namely that it is impossible to say with any real accuracy what its present state really is. Temples and shrines have been destroyed or converted to secular uses. Artifacts and literature have been hidden by their owners or seized by the Red Guards. But there is recurring evidence that the folk cult goes on, although with less influence than in old China. It is impossible to say that it has been suppressed, just as it is impossible to say precisely what remains.

[104] *Ibid.*

It is in this area of Taoism and folk religion that we have our most provocative questions concerning Chinese communism and religion, or, to go even further, the religious nature of Chinese communism. Is it coincidence or is there some overall method or plan in the use of various motifs from Chinese folk religion in the appeals made to the people by the Party, or in the structure of the Chinese Communist movement?

Ways in which the New Year and Ch'ing Ming festivals have been invested with revolutionary significance have been mentioned. Both in the new style festivals and at other times ancestors are venerated, though to be sure for their revolutionary zeal and sacrifice rather than their family relationships. There are the deified heroes (actually several in addition to and lower of course than Mao), who as spotless, glowing images are glorified because of their awesome deeds. Because of their deeds the heroes are more than respected—they are to be trusted with a faith that is reputed to be more profound than that ever given to any god of earth or heaven. Liturgies composed of didactic songs and sayings are full of overtones of meaning and enthusiasm which evoke feelings of group belonging quite similar to those which resulted from old temple rituals.

Therefore in Taoism and the religion of the masses we discover a transition from our study of religious movements in Communist China to a study of the "new religion" which has been developing over the past half century. This next topic—Chinese communism as a religion—must be left for another volume. Suffice it to say here that one does not grasp the significance of communism, particularly in China, if one does not recognize its religious character. I for one am prepared to go beyond talk of religious "character," "analogy," or "aspects," to drop the quotation marks when speaking of communism as a religion, to delete such prefixes as "pseudo-" or "quasi-" and say that Chinese communism *is* a religion.

Chinese communism is, of course, many other things: a political ideology, an economic system, a method of social organization and control. But the fact that it is all of these things does not prevent its being a religion too. I look forward with great anticipation to further study of this whole question of Communism as a religion, recognizing that conclusions quite different from these opinions may result.

As far as this study is concerned I must add that it is communism as a religion which has raised the greatest difficulty for followers of any faith in China. As long as Communist officialdom acted on the policy that religion would wither away, with occasional blows to accelerate the withering, people like Y. T. Wu and Chao P'u-ch'u could play for time, keep their people in line, and ride out the winter of their lives. But when the Red Guards were unleashed to destroy everything old, everything which conflicted with the new life lived according to the teachings of Chairman Mao, it was something else again. When the revival to frighten those who are backsliding reaches its peak, there is no recourse for the nonestablishment groups but to meditate in silence with the Buddhists or become a will o' the wisp with the Taoists.

The revival seems now to be fading. Its key figure is near the end of a long life. In other religions one expects a period of relaxation to follow, whereupon other cults and movements are free once again to raise their heads. If the "religious analogy" holds, churches and temples may again be open, but Chinese communism is no ordinary religion and I hesitate to speculate on the basis of religions as we have known them. In a Taoist-like state of flux, we must wait until various elements find their own level. At this point, the nature of things, which we may call Tao, is uncertain; the Tao which can be named is not the Tao.

INDEX